African American Politics

In loving memory of our Auntie Kate:

Your willingness to stand alone, your persistence to be you, and your very special utterance of "I have faith" is forever etched in my heart. I pray that I remain a conduit of the unconditional love you gave to me.

African American Politics

KENDRA A. KING

polity

First published in 2010 by Polity Press

Polity Press
65 Bridge Street
Cambridge CB2 1UR, UK

Polity Press
350 Main Street
Malden, MA 02148, USA

ISBN-13: 978-0-7456-3280-3
ISBN-13: 978-0-7456-3281-0(pb)

A catalogue record for this book is available from the British Library.

Typeset in 9.5 on 13 pt Swift Light
by Servis Filmsetting Ltd, Stockport, Cheshire
Printed and bound by MPG Books Group, UK

For further information on Polity, visit our website: www.politybooks.com

Contents

Illustrations

Figure

Boxes

Acknowledgments

African American Politics has been a labor of love that has taken me on my own personal journey of doubt and faith. I am grateful that faith has prevailed and that I have been blessed with such an awesome opportunity to share my perspectives on the political development, evolution, and empowerment of African Americans. I'd like to thank my editor Louise Knight of Polity Press. From our initial conversation, it seemed as if Louise and I knew each other as we found a synergistic like-mindedness, perspective, schoolgirl friendship and comradeship in things both political and personal. I'd also like to thank Emma Hutchinson of Polity Press for all of her editorial assistance, direction, and genuine goodwill, encouragement, and commitment to this project. I also want to thank Dr William E. Nelson, Jr, my major professor in the Department of Political Science at the Ohio State University. Dr Nelson taught me to think beyond the surface, ask the question behind the question, and most importantly, view the political landscape from an analytical mindset that begs to raise the question of who will/is caring for the powerless. The professor I am today has undoubtedly been impacted by his stern yet sensible, direct yet charismatic, and formidable yet friendly disposition both inside and outside of the academic arena.

I'd also like to thank my students at the University of Georgia and Oglethorpe University. So many of you have been a source of inspiration, encouragement, reconsideration, and rejuvenation as every day I am blessed to "go to life." I'd be remiss if I did not acknowledge several students who have been extremely instrumental on this collective journey – T. Ruth, C. "Alonna" Davis, J. Rand (UGA), T. Lawhead (UGA), C. Green, J. Cross, J. McDaniel (UGA), A. Niland, R. King, and C. Huff – *thank you*! Finally, I remain thankful to the President of Oglethorpe University – Lawrence M. Schall – whose visionary leadership led to the creation of a Junior Faculty Sabbatical program which provided me with the time needed to complete *African American Politics*.

On a more personal note, I'd like to thank my family for their love, support, encouragement, and *prayers* throughout this entire process. To my immediate family, Jacquelyn, Benjamin, and Olufunmilayo, and BMK, Jr. (aka Markosysis), I love you very much! Mom, thank you for making me respect the value of hard work, independent thinking, and finding a way or making a way. Bejay – my twin in heart – "you know!" Funmi, always remember that a heart of love may come in a broken vessel, *still* the spirit of Christ remains strong. Nana Logan

– the first writer in the family – thank you for your unconditional agape love, support, and listening ear! Dad, I am grateful for reconnection as it provides a foundational window of understanding as I *now* know "I be stunnin' like my daddy."

I'd also like to thank Bernice A. King for your spiritual deposit, mentorship, and genuine commitment to my holistic growth and development. I appreciate the investment and know that I am better as a result of having been entrusted to receive the deposit of your anointing. To Bishop Eddie L. Long, I will forever be grateful for "Welcome to the Age of Possibilities." Thank you for boldly declaring what thus says the Lord. I am also extremely appreciative of Dina Marto of Def Jam and Six Degree Relations. Thank you for believing in this project and connecting me with Too $hort, The YoungBloodZ, Killer Mike, and Bryan-Michael Cox, all of whom provided rich analytical depth for the chapter on the politics of hip-hop. To my friends, close associates, and homeys, you know – thanks for being in my life and adding value to this side of the journey.

Finally, I want to thank my Lord and Savior, Jesus Christ; you have shown me unequivocally that "in you I live, move, and have my being."

1

Introduction

For the past eight years I have had the wonderful opportunity to teach African American politics on the college and university level at both a large research institution – The University of Georgia – and most recently at a small, private, liberal arts university – Oglethorpe University. In both of my professional academic experiences, I've noticed some interesting commonalities as it relates to the study, analysis, and discussion of racial politics in the United States of America. First, a large portion of students in both environments have been misinformed and seemingly misguided as Carter G. Woodson (1933) contended in *The MIS-Education of the Negro* as it relates to the political ambitions, desires, setbacks, obstacles, and accomplishments of African Americans in the United States. One seemingly never-ending example is affirmative action. In both of my academic environments it has not been uncommon for students to believe that affirmative action is a government-mandated and enforced quota system that hires and promotes unqualified African Americans at the expense and detriment of qualified Whites. Rarely have my students been aware of the history of the presidential executive order, the changes that occurred as a result of Bakke vs. University of California Regents (1978), or the data which solidify the fact that the greatest beneficiaries of affirmative action policies in the United States have been White women.

Another commonality I've experienced in both environments is that students tend to have pre-established opinions about the economic, political, and educational failures and successes of the African American community. For example, many students believe that African Americans are not doing as well as other groups because they do not work hard enough. Interestingly, the "not working hard enough" beliefs are in alignment with national survey data trends that reflect the same beliefs related to African Americans. A final commonality I've experienced in both environments is the tendency of African American students to engage in fight or flight as they either become overly defensive of the African American liberation struggle in America – sometimes to the point of intimidating all other voices (fight) – or, as in other instances I've witnessed, African American students completely shut down to the point that they have become clock watchers who leap from their seats as soon as our 75 minutes have expired (flight).

In spite of these occasionally awkward yet always interesting scenarios, over the course of my academic journey I've personally witnessed students in both environments engage in a change of heart concerning their initial thoughts and predispositions. It is my sincere belief that the change of heart is the result of the creation of a learning environment which sheds light on the complicated mix of pain, promise, triumph, testing, shame, and success that has all been a part of the African American political, economic, and sociocultural experience in America. In this regard, the classroom environment becomes a laboratory of genuine dialogue, exchange, exposure, and uplift as I seek to take my students on a journey of intellectual empowerment and emancipation that allows them to be both the judge and jury as it relates to the African American experience. I have sought to do the same thing in *African American Politics* in that I hope to take you – my readers – on a journey of the political successes, failures, and persistent challenges of the African American collective community in America.

A ground rule about our journey

Both my personal and professional academic experiences have led me to believe that discussions of race, similar to discussions of politics and religion, produce some of the most severe "knee-jerk" reactions since everyone has an opinion about racial topics and issues. As such, similar to the discussion etiquette I establish in my courses on African American Politics and the Politics of Hip-Hop, I'd like to establish a ground rule at the beginning of our journey.

To be clear, our ground rule is actually a disclaimer. In particular, it is important to share with you – the reader – that *African American Politics* is not another in a long list of "so-called" victimization books that blames the infamous (White) "man" for all of the ills and misfortunes of African Americans. As *African American Politics* is designed to provide analytical insight into arguably one of the most complex political cadres in America, it is important for the reader to approach the book from the vantage point of it being an exploratory analysis of how Black people have navigated the thicket of political institutions, structures, policies, and leaders that shape and guide American political, economic, and sociocultural life.

In this regard, *African American Politics* is designed to shed light on both the problems and promises of Black politics predominantly in the post-civil rights era. Using both historic and present-day political phenomena as its backdrop, *African American Politics* incorporates US Census data, a variety of election survey data, landmark Supreme Court rulings, speeches, personal interviews, and political commentary as a means of capturing the compass of the collective interests and sometimes contrasting ideologies of the Black community in the United States.

One of the underlying themes expressed in this book is the importance of recognizing and understanding the difference between symbolic and substantive political acts/policies. Nearly four decades after Dr Martin Luther King, Jr delivered his "Give Us the Ballot" speech, and despite the election of a Black

man to the highest office in the land, African American political incorporation and empowerment in America remains highly symbolic and relatively
limited in terms of "actual" political power. There are a variety of examples
of the limitations of African American political power we will examine
throughout the book. However, one glaringly disappointing example of the
limited power of African Americans occurred during the 2000 presidential
election fiasco. Although there were documented cases around the nation of
African Americans being denied the right to vote, African American members of the House of Representatives could not get even one member of the
United States Senate to support their election recall proposal. The failure of a
member of the US Senate to align with African American members of the US
House of Representatives denied these members the ability to exercise power
and protect the political interests of their constituencies. The film *Fahrenheit
911* provides an excellent portrayal of the pain and frustration of the African
American representatives as one by one they spoke on the floor of the House,
presided over by former Vice-President Al Gore, to no avail.

Keeping this example in mind, the reader is challenged to look beyond the
surface level of seemingly positive political gains, i.e., the post-civil rights era
election of African American members of Congress, and explore what, if any,
substantive (tangible) political gains have been accomplished as a result of an
increase in the number of Black elected officials in the United States. Moreover,
the book hopes to provide a compass for and road map of African American
political success as well as of areas of growth in the midst of the election of the
nation's first African American president – Barack Hussein Obama.

Terminology

I will use both the term African American and Black interchangeably throughout the text. I have opted to use both terms as each has its own historical and
political significance and potency. For example, it is virtually unthinkable to
discuss the more radical political ideologies of Huey Newton absent the use of
the term "Black" in relation to his party's mission and Ten Point Plan. Similarly,
it is rather unthinkable, given all of the political correctness of the 1990s,
to discuss the positive gains of Blacks absent the introduction of the term
"African American." As such, this text will incorporate both terms, using one as
opposed to the other when and where the author deems such use necessary.

African American Politics also uses biblical references to characterize some of
the historical experiences and journeys of Blacks in America. These references
are purposive in that one of the most distinguishable characteristics of the
African American experience in America has been the reliance on "faith in God"
and the implementation of spirituality as a means of overcoming racial, political, economic, and sociocultural oppression. Further, the Black Church has been
the most viable and long-standing African American institution in the United
States. The Black Church, especially during the movement from slavery through

civil rights, served as an intra-community producer of both economic, leadership, and demographic resources. Today, the Black Church, specifically Black Mega-ministries, have become multi-million dollar corporations that use their spiritual influence in a variety of political, economic, and social capital arenas.

Finally, I use the term "hip-hop" to reflect a holistic lifestyle of music, dance, language, clothing, and artwork. In *African American Politics*, "hip-hop" connotes the interchangeable relationship between the five elements of the genre as well as the political influence and acts of some of its key voices including Jay-Z, Outkast, P. Diddy, Kanye West, and Nas.

Overview of chapters

African American Politics is divided into four thematic areas. Part I sets the foundation and framework of our journey as it details a variety of factors that impact African American political behavior and participation both historically and in the post-civil rights era. As such, chapter 2 provides an overview of democracy in America, examines both traditional (pluralism and elitism) and non-traditional (colonialism and coalition politics) models of governance as a means of accessing the political inroads, incorporation, and empowerment of African Americans, and explores the differences between, as well as significance of, symbolic and substantive policies on African American political outcomes. In an effort to illuminate the theoretical frameworks introduced in the preceding chapter, chapter 3 details the inability of "political acts" to produce substantive social and economic gains for African Americans. In particular, chapter 3 employs socio-economic data from the US Census in an attempt to shed light on the ways in which historical legislative acts including The Civil Rights Act of 1964, The Voting Rights Act of 1965, The Fair Housing Act of 1968, and the Community Reinvestment Act of 1991 impact the racial divide in key areas such as home ownership, college education, and income in America. We conclude Part I by providing an examination of African American voting behavior and participation and the ways in which group consciousness, linked fate, and the Black utility heuristic play a deterministic role in the political agenda of African Americans. Chapter 4 also examines the impact of the hip-hop community on African American voting behavior, the impact of the 2000 and 2004 presidential elections on African American voting behavior, and the future of African American voting behavior and participation.

African Americans and American political institutions

The second theme of *African American Politics* deals with the nature of the relationship between African Americans and American political institutions. Chapter 5 begins with a basic introduction of the purposes and functions of the United States Congress as well as the constitutional requirements of office for members of the United States House Representatives and the Senate.

Additionally, the chapter explores some of the inroads and challenges faced by African American members of Congress from the Black Reconstruction Period to the present, the creation, development, and leadership of the Congressional Black Caucus, and the political activity and power of Black elected officials at the local, state, and national level.

From the insidious comments of former Supreme Court justice Roger Taney to what some contend was the hyperactivity of the Warren Court, in chapter 6 we explore the seemingly schizophrenic, on-again/off-again nature of the American judiciary as it relates to African American political incorporation and empowerment. Additionally, chapter 6 explores the ways in which African American liberty and justice remain subject to the political currents of US Supreme Court justices, public opinion, and larger institutional and structural tides. In chapter 7, we explore the executive branch and the ways in which this long-standing institutional structure has both assisted and denied African Americans in their quest for political incorporation and empowerment. Dating back to the mixed political bag of Abraham Lincoln to the largely symbolic acts of former President Bill Clinton to the political charades and contradictions of the Bush II administration, chapter 7 also examines the political leadership of presidential administrations on African American politics.

Chapter 8 begins with an overview of the purpose, objectives, and political scope of political parties. Chapter 8 also examines the relationship between African Americans and the two major political parties and the ways in which the Democratic and Republican Party have evolved over time in relation to the political inclusion and empowerment of Blacks in America. Chapter 8 also discusses the role of the Congressional Black Caucus (CBC), the nature of Black conservatism in America, and the rise of Black Elected Officials (BEOs) in the post-civil rights era. Finally, chapter 9 begins with a discussion of the role and nature of interest groups as well as the resources and incentives of interest groups. Chapter 9 concludes with a discussion of African American interest groups, recent African American interest group activity, and the rise of alternative voices of African American interest articulation including the Black Church and the hip-hop community.

Behind the veil of African American political activism and leadership

The third part of *African American Politics* delves into the non-traditional political activity and activism of African Americans in the post-civil rights era. Chapter 10 predominantly focuses on the civil rights/Black Power movement of the 1950s and 1960s and the ways in which non-traditional political activism and leadership served to reshape and realign the political landscape of America. Additionally, chapter 10 examines the leadership styles and strategies of African American leaders and organizations including Dr Martin L.

King, Jr, Malcolm X, Huey Newton, Fannie Lou Hamer, the NAACP, SCLC, the Black Panther Party, and the Student Nonviolent Coordinating Committee (SNCC). Chapter 10 concludes with a discussion of the viability of protest politics as a means of African American political activism, leadership, and service delivery in the post-civil rights era. In chapter 11, we explore the role of the Black Church and the ways in which it has served as a long-standing leader of African American political voice, leverage, and incorporation.

Chapter 11 also details the rise of Black Mega-churches and the ways in which they have been able to utilize their spiritual capital to advance political, economic, and sociocultural agendas of transformative change. Additionally, chapter 11 highlights several African American Mega-ministries, explores the controversial "Stop the Silence" march of 2004, and examines the apparent divide between the traditional civil rights vanguard and the Mega-church leadership elect.

Part III concludes with one of the most innovative approach to the study of African American political activism and leadership as we explore the impact of the hip-hop community on African American politics. Chapter 12 also explores the ways in which hip-hop has provided a voice to those impacted by political and economic events as well as the ways in which the culture has been impacted by political invitations and access granted as a result of its global and economic veracity over the past 30 years. Finally, chapter 12 examines whether the social and economic capital of hip-hop can be transformed into a powerful political engine of change in the post-civil rights era.

Where do we go from here?

The final chapter of *African American Politics* also encapsulates our final theme in that it seeks to provide some concluding thoughts about the future of African American politics in the new millennium and beyond. Utilizing Dr Martin L. King, Jr's landmark 1967 SCLC 10th Anniversary keynote address – "Where Do We Go from Here?" – chapter 13 looks at the ways in which the African American community can align together to engage in the politics of growth as well as utilize pre-established access, influence, and power to impact the economic, political, and sociocultural life of African Americans in the United States.

Author's hope

It is my hope that *African American Politics* piques the reader's interest to raise questions and engage in discussion about the political participation, behavior, and incorporation of Blacks in America. I also hope that students, scholars, activists, and everyone reading this book obtain a better understanding and appreciation of the economic, political, and sociocultural strides and setbacks of African Americans from slavery through freedom and into the new millennium. Moreover, similar to the experiences of many of my students, I also hope that you will gain new perspective on and depth of knowledge of Black political life in America. Finally, I hope that this book becomes an instrument for discussion, debate, and healing as it relates to the peculiar phenomenon of "race" in America.

Part I

2

African Americans and Democracy

> We hold these Truths to be self-evident, that all Men are created equal, that they are endowed by their Creator with certain unalienable Rights, that among these are Life, Liberty, and the Pursuit of Happiness. – That to secure these Rights, Governments are instituted among Men, deriving their just Powers from the Consent of the Governed, that whenever any Form of Government becomes destructive of these Ends, it is the Right of the People to alter or to abolish it, and to institute new Government, laying its Foundation on such Principles, and organizing its Powers in such Form, as to them shall seem most likely to effect their Safety and Happiness.
>
> Declaration of Independence, 1776

In order to effectively understand the role, purpose, and potential power of African Americans in the American political system, it is important to establish a clearly defined framework that details the tenets, structures, and systems that influence and shape democracy in America. To be certain, there are several tenets that shape American democracy. By democracy, we refer to a system of government (a hierarchical system of decision and policy-making that maintains societal order through mutually beneficial systems wherein citizens consent to be governed through representatives) whereby "We the People" elect men and women to serve as proxies of political, economic, and sociocultural interest.

The term democracy is derived from two Greek terms – "demos" and "kratia" – and means rule of or by the people. In theory, rule of or by the people has been established in that every two, four, or six years people are able to exercise their choice by campaigning, voting, participating in elections, and exercising their political rights as detailed in the first ten amendments to the US Constitution. In practice, however, American democracy, especially the universal incorporation and participation of African Americans in the political system, has been obstructed by several factors. First, African Americans have endured the persistence of institutional limitations such as the refusal of certain states to recognize their rights as guaranteed in the US Constitution, established via Supreme Court rulings, and implemented through both the executive and legislative branches of government. Second, African American political involvement and incorporation has also been obstructed by man-made fear and intimidation tactics. It is widely known that during the era of the Black Codes and Jim Crowism, extra-legal fear and intimidation methods such as the hanging of nooses and cross-burnings were common instruments used to keep Black people oppressed and afraid to exercise their political

Table 2.1 Mean length of state sentencing by race (felonies)

	White	Black
All offenses	37 months	40 months
Violent offenses	71 months	84 months
Robbery	85 months	100 months
Aggravated assault	41 months	48 months
Murder	221 months	254 months

Source: Bureau of Justice Statistics, 2004

and legal rights (Franklin and Moss, 2000; Barker, Jones, and Tate, 1998; and Walton and Smith, 2007).

Given the historical legal and extra-legal tactics used to suppress and subvert African American political involvement, some contend that African Americans have operated under a facade of democracy in America. In this context, a facade represents the superficial and symbolic presentation of equality which distributes markedly different democratic tenets such as liberty, freedom, and justice. One controversial facade of democracy that persists is in the criminal justice system where African American criminal defendants receive harsher and longer sentences for crimes in spite of the claim that the justice system, and more importantly the law, is color blind (Mauer, 2006).

If, in fact, democracy is a facade it not only hinders certain groups of people, it also interferes with the primary purposes of government which are to establish justice, insure domestic tranquility, provide for the common defense, and secure the blessing of liberty (US Constitution, 1787). Beyond the ways in which the facade of democracy limits these four purposes of government, the danger of such a system is that it also can determine who actually governs in America.

Who governs in America?

The question of who governs in America is not new. Most notably, two well-known political scientists – E. E. Schattschneider and Robert Dahl – both explored the question of who governs in an effort to shed light on who rules in America. According to E. E. Schattschneider, America operates via a pluralist system that has a very strong "upper class bias." Schattschneider attributes the bias to the lack of participation of lower classes of American citizens. "[A]bstention reflects the suppression of the options and alternatives that reflect the needs of the non-participants . . . *whoever decides what the game is about decides also who can get into the game* . . ." Consequently, "every study of the subject supports the conclusion that non-voting is a characteristic of the poorest, least well-established, least educated stratum of the community" (Schattschneider, 1975: 103).

In contrast to Schattschneider, in a 1967 study of local politics in New Haven, Connecticut, Robert Dahl concluded that all citizens have an opportunity to influence the American political system and subsequently govern. According to Dahl, all groups and classes of people have the ability to participate through involvement with organized interests groups as these groups compete to gain power within the electoral arena through electing people to office as well as shaping public policy on the local, state, and national level (Dahl, 2000). The views of both Schattschneider and Dahl are two of the most widely embraced theories of American governance as espoused through elitism and pluralism. Still, these two dominant views do not capture the full scope of possibilities related to who governs in America. In the next section, we will examine several lenses of analysis related to this critical question in American democracy.

Four lenses of analysis

There are several lenses of analysis that need to be explored in order to effectively address the question of who governs in America. Although a one-dimensional approach to the question can assume that any individual aged 18 years or older (who is a registered voter in America) governs via popular elections and other mechanisms of political participation, even political novices understand that the political system is a little more complicated than one individual casting his or her vote on a modern, computerized voting machine.

A more advanced response to the question, however, suggests that, in America, the question of who governs may be best addressed through an analysis of competing models of political incorporation and empowerment. In this section, we will examine four different models of governance – pluralism, elitism, colonialism, and coalition politics. Although some may contend that coalition politics should be viewed as a subsection of pluralism, we will examine each as an individualized model of governance and assess the benefits and limitations of each theory. Additionally, each model will be reviewed in terms of the ways in which it helps shed light on the political behavior and participation of African Americans, offering insight into the ways in which African Americans as a collective political force mobilize resources and community members to develop a clearly defined, resonant, and substantive political agenda and voice in America.

Pluralism

The pluralist model claims that in a democracy all members of society have an opportunity to use their political mobilization skills and political muscle to influence political outcomes and public policy in America. The pluralist model holds that both individuals and groups (in some instances conflicting individuals and groups) through competitive, democratic processes have an

Table 2.2 An overview of the four models of governance in America

Pluralism	Governmental systems are equal as all people have an equal opportunity to influence political systems through organized groups
Elitism	Government is controlled by a small group of powerful, wealthy, and influential group of key leaders and economic/business stakeholders
Colonialism	Governmental systems are maintained by a dominant group of people who exert power, control, and influence over a subordinate group of people
Coalitions	Governmental systems are influenced by the cooperative and strategic alliances of diverse groups which unite around common issues and causes

equal opportunity to sway political outcomes by lobbying key political leaders and decision-makers on behalf of their group interests. In his examination of the power structure of New Haven, CT, Robert Dahl concluded that the pluralist model worked. He reached this conclusion because there was no single group of power brokers controlling policy outcomes in the city. In fact, Dahl's research highlighted the positive effect of competing spheres of interest on local government decision-making and political participation.

The impact of pluralism on African American political participation can be traced back to the late 1960s and early 1970s and the rise of Black electoral politics on the local level. Most notably, the use of coalition or rainbow politics has been most evident in cities like Cleveland and Gary where some of the nation's first Black mayors were elected into office. The Black, Brown, White, and female coalitions responsible for using their collective influence to change the faces in electoral politics on the local level were undoubtedly instrumental in boosting the impact and significance of descriptive representation in America. In this regard, the most profound benefit of the pluralist model is its ability to garner the collective resources of diverse people and groups (groups who historically have been in competition with each other) to transform old political systems, machines, and institutions that have been historically closed to African American faces and leaders and members of the community that work to "influence" Black interests.

Limitations of the pluralist model

While, on the surface, the pluralist lens provides an interesting explanation for the ways in which groups – no matter how far removed from the political system – are able to gain access to the decision-making arena, upon closer examination, the pluralist model is limited in its ability to effectively provide tangible political incorporation and empowerment for African Americans.

The first limitation of the pluralist model is that it fails to effectively take into consideration long-standing institutional and structural barriers. As Barker, Jones, and Tate (1998) assert, pluralists fail to examine the historical legacy of slavery, Jim Crow laws, separate but equal laws, and extra-legal fear and intimidation tactics in Black political participation. In other words, an examination of pluralism that only speaks to incorporation in the post-civil rights era does not effectively address the centuries of purposive, manmade, and government instituted exclusion and non-incorporation of Black interests on the local, state, and national level.

Further, the pluralist model as an effective model of African American political access and incorporation is limited because a system designed around the notion of access is not effective if and when one's political rights are usurped, hindered, or harassed as was the case during the 2000 presidential election. Arguably, when thousands of African Americans were denied the right to vote as a result of fallacious claims of improper identification as well as a host of other smoke-and-mirror tactics, including voter intimidation and obstructionist tactics, pluralism is no longer effective as a tool of political incorporation. In this regard, the pluralist model fails to acknowledge the subtle influence of both institutional racism and modern-day Jim Crow techniques designed to frustrate and alienate African American voters from participating in politics at all levels.

Moreover, pluralism as a model of African American politics is limited in that it does not clearly delineate the strong influence of interest groups and "good old boy" networks on politics. In other words, the pluralist model fails to account for the impact of pre-established institutional networks, political relationships, and the roles of power and wealth which extend far beyond the parameters of the theoretical model. In this regard, pluralism does not take into account the long-standing history of "junior partnerships" and "second-tier" political and economic relationships African Americans have been subjected to in cities such as Atlanta, Cleveland, and Los Angeles (Stone, 1989). Moreover, pluralism fails to adequately address the fact that part of the reason traditionally disenfranchised groups still choose not to participate in politics is that, beyond the rhetoric of "every vote counting," in practice some people remain convinced based on past patterns that (1) pluralism still has a way to go before all groups have an equal opportunity to influence outcomes; (2) pluralism remains limited because of the strong impact and influence of multinational corporations and business entities that are more powerful and influential than organized groups; and (3) pluralism has failed to adequately overcome the long history of uneven political, economic, and sociocultural enfranchisement of African Americans.

Elitism

Another well-known model of analysis related to who governs in America is elitism. Elitism asserts that democracy in America is controlled by a small group of wealthy and influential individuals who use their positional power to influence and control public policy and high-level decision making. According to C. Wright Mills (1956), America's power elite consists of a small group of military, business, and political influencers that implement domestic and foreign policy decisions for the nation. In sum, elitism holds that power in America is maintained by a few influential individuals/corporations and not the masses through organized interests. In effect, elitism is the complete opposite of pluralism in that the model only allows a predetermined, predominantly economic minority to govern American institutions, determine public policy, and implement democratic ideals.

Limitations of elitism

Although elitism has not been complementary to African American political participation, it is necessary to examine the model, especially given all the political correctness of the 1990s and the open-and-closed door conversations by many political pundits, commentators, media outlets, chat rooms, and bloggers who maintain that racism is a thing of the past and that America is the land of equal access and opportunity for all people. The history of African American political power details the limited influence and infiltration of Blacks in key economic, political, and sociocultural institutions and organizations. Even in instances when African Americans have been a part of "elite" administrations and organizations, they have tended to operate in highly symbolic, top-down organizational networks where real decision-making abilities appear non-existent or limited at best.

In *We Have No Leaders: African Americans in the Post-Civil Rights Era*, Robert C. Smith and Ronald Walters detail the purposive decision of President Reagan's Black political appointees to separate themselves from promoting or supporting an African American agenda. In an effort to distance the executive branch from previous administration political appointees, the four African Americans appointed during President Reagan's tenure in office "would carry out their official responsibilities and would not as Blacks seek to shape administration policies on race issues unless such issues came within the purview of their official duties" (Smith and Walters, 1996: 154). In other words, there was to be no collective action by Blacks in the Reagan administration on behalf of Black interests.

Moreover, as evidenced in C. Wright Mills's definition of the "power elite," the problem with elitism is that it appears to represent a "closed" circle of pre-established political influencers and power players. According to Marcus D. Pohlmann, elite theorists recognize a certain degree of competition between interest groups; however, they reach very different conclusions about just how open and fair it all is.

> While power does not always equate precisely with one's amount of power resources, the
> two correlate often enough to allow the conclusion that those with the most political

power resources generally will dominate governmental decisions. Thus, a combination of resource-rich corporate elites and governmental officials, most drawn from the white upper strata of society, will share many interests and work in unison to frame the political agenda in a way that will guarantee that their interests will be served (Pohlmann, 1999: 24).

Given its exclusive, top-down system of governance, elitism does not work as an effective model of African American political participation.

Colonialism

Another lens of analysis to examine the question of who governs in America is colonialism. The colonial model asserts that there are two distinct groups of people – a dominant group and a subordinate group; the powerful and the powerless. The powerful (dominant group) are able to control the powerless (subordinate group) through force, if necessary, as well as through the use of punishment (loss of life, employment, status) and sanctions. Those who operate through the use of the colonial model also use government legitimacy and authority to maintain existing power relationships by manipulating and controlling the political, economic, and sociocultural structures of the nation as well.

By some accounts, the connection between African Americans and colonialism extends back to the mid-1400s and included Dutch, Portuguese, and British control and usurpation of power throughout the continent of Africa. The goal of these groups was to further expand the industrial and economic empires of their nations through the exploitation and sale of the continent's natural resources of gold, diamonds, cocoa, coffee, tea, and massive amounts of cheap labor (Markovitz, 1987). In terms of African American politics, colonialism was widely introduced during the 1960s through the Black Panther Party and other Black liberation groups who claimed that Blacks in America were being dominated by the powerful through segregation, discrimination, and institutional racism. In *Black Power: The Politics of Liberation*, Carmichael and Hamilton assert that Blacks in America existed in a colonial state of domination and oppression.

> There is no American dilemma because black people in this country form a colony, and it is not in the interests of the colonial power to liberate them. Black people are legal citizens of the United States with, for the most part, the same legal rights as other citizens. Yet they stand as colonial subjects in relation to the white society. Thus institutional racism has another name: colonialism. (Carmichael and Hamilton, 1967: 5)

Perhaps even more insulting to African Americans during this era was the fact that in the midst of their ongoing struggle for basic human rights they watched helplessly as former colonized nations such as Ghana gained their independence while American leaders rallied around "with-all-deliberate-speed" ideologies which translated into as slow as possible in relation to African American economic, political, and voting rights. As Dr King stated:

> It would be fortunate if the people in power had sense enough to go on and give up, but they don't do it like that. It is not done voluntarily, but it is done through the pressure that comes about from people who are oppressed. If there had not been a Gandhi in India with all of his noble followers, India would have never been free. If there had not been an Nkrumah and his followers in Ghana, Ghana would still be a British colony . . . there are always those people in every period of human history who don't mind getting their necks cut off, who don't mind being persecuted and discriminated and kicked about, because they know freedom is never given out, but it comes through the persistent and the continual agitation and revolt on the part of those who are caught in the system. Ghana taught us that. (Carson, 1998: 30–1)

As both India and Ghana proved, there are instances when the subordinate group, depending upon its level of group consciousness and efficacy, will rise up and rebel against the dominant governing system as African Americans ultimately did during the civil rights movement of the 1950s and 1960s.

Limitations of the colonial model

The main limitation of the colonial model is that most power players (including elites) dismiss it as nothing more than emotional rhetoric that is not grounded in the truth. The proliferation of an alleged colonial model in America by members of the Black Panther Party can be easily dismissed as divisive race-based politics designed to cause a tear in the beautiful tapestry of the "evidences" of American truth, which include the Declaration of Independence, the US Constitution, and the equal protection clauses of the 5th and 14th Amendments. The reason some elected officials and paid political voices refuse to acknowledge that perhaps two types of government – one of the powerful and one for the powerless – exist is that it may be difficult for some American political leaders and institutional voices to accept the fact that things such as redlining, driving while Black (DWB), and "three strikes and you're out" laws, as well as other institutional mechanisms, have been consciously or unconsciously aimed at African American constituencies.

Moreover, even if modern use and implementation of the colonial model is dismissed, defenders of American liberty and equality are hard pressed to defend the discriminatory practices of the federal government and its denial of federal housing loans to African Americans after the Great Depression. As Dennis Judd and Todd Swanstrom contend in *City Politics: The Political Economy of Urban America*:

> From the 1930s through much of the 1960s, the federal government helped finance a suburban housing boom that was effectively put off limits to blacks. Federal administrators worked hand in hand with local developers and financial institutions to enforce restrictive covenants that prohibited property from being sold to blacks, and they also made it virtually impossible for blacks to secure the federally subsidized mortgages that fueled the suburban booms. (Judd and Swanstrom, 2005: 107).

As the authors maintain, the denial of federal housing loans forced Blacks to live in high rise housing projects (concrete jungles as remixed by hip-hop artists) or to compete over the older, second-class and second-rate homes left behind as a result of White flight to suburban communities.

In spite of the evidence of the persistence of a dominant–subordinate power relationship in major American institutions, it seems as if modern-day discussions of the impact of colonialism continue to be sideswiped by political pundits and other agenda setters who quickly point to the "headlines" of Black political, economic, and sociocultural advances from the 1960s to the present. While the inroads and accomplishments of African Americans in every area of life over the past 50 years is phenomenal, the fact remains that during this same historical time periods both individuals and institutions worked in concert to limit and subject African Americans to a separate, uneven, and, at times, hostile system of governance and political incorporation.

Moreover, even when overt oppressive mechanisms have been absent, many who argue against America's use of colonialism fail to recognize two key ingredients of the model – acquiescence and political repression – both of which have been evidenced throughout the African American freedom movement. As John Gaventa asserted, "A has power over B to the extent that A can get B to do something detrimental to B's best interests" (Gaventa, 1980: 5). Using Gaventa's model to capture the state of African American political incorporation and involvement, it seems that well after the constitutional elimination of separate but equal laws and practices, African Americans still engaged in practices detrimental to their interests until the incorporation of the direct action phase of the civil rights movement.

Coalitions

The final lens of analysis that we will use to offer insight into the question of who governs is the coalition (rainbow) politics model. Although the coalition model is a direct outgrowth of the pluralist model, it is necessary to examine it as an isolated entity as it seeks to go beyond the generality of the pluralist model and specifically focuses on minority group empowerment through majority group alliances and shared power and/or electoral/political alliances. The coalition politics model is based on the belief that racial and/or minority groups with shared ideological predispositions can join forces to positively impact the political arena as well as political decision-makers (Browning, Marshall, and Tabb, 1984; Sonenshein, 1990; Gomes and Williams, 1992; McClain and Stewart, 2005). There are several benefits of the coalition politics model as a governing tool. First, traditional coalitions unite a broad range of groups and interests to influence policy as was evidenced in the nation's most well-known New Deal coalition. Franklin Delano Roosevelt's New Deal was a multidimensional coalition of Catholics, Protestants, Blacks, blue-collar workers, the poor, and the unemployed. The New Deal coalition was responsible for providing a relative amount of symbolic power to African American leaders. For example, President Roosevelt appointed Mary McCleod Bethune as an advisor. Another benefit of the coalition model is that it can eliminate group competition amongst people of similar economic/political/social status by allowing them to rally around a host of valence issues (issues that universally impact voters regardless of socio-economic status) and common community concerns such as crime, violence, electoral representation, and employment opportunities.

The coalition politics model, to be sure, is limited. Namely, the assumption that diverse racial groups will come together in support of a common cause minimizes the impact of group competition which makes interracial and intra-racial coalitions difficult to establish and maintain. Moreover, in times of political or economic scarcity, groups tend to work against, not for, each other. Another limitation of the coalition politics model is that it does not necessarily address the issue of coalitional shifts. If groups coalesce around "issue-specific" agendas, what happens once the issues are resolved? Further, as Hanes Walton and Robert C. Smith contend in *American Politics and the African American Quest for Universal Freedom*, coalition politics models presupposed three things:

1. African Americans share similar interests with other oppressed groups;
2. a viable coalition can be achieved with the haves (powerful) and the have nots (powerless);
3. moral and ethical appeals can sustain coalitions (Walton and Smith, 2007: 83–8);
4. history has shown that coalitions based on these three assumptions are short-lived at best as racial and minority groups tend to focus more on the short-term, "what is in it for me?" objectives instead of long-term, tangible group benefits including substantive policy gains.

Additionally, the coalition politics model fails to consider the negative effects of shifting interests, the tendency of dominant members of the coalition to engage in "father knows best" political paternalism, and the problems that arise when group members infuse politics with issues of morality. One of the dangers and limitations of "moral and ethical" (Walton and Smith, 2007: 86) political coalitions occurs when group members are at odds over the implementation of policy. One area of controversy surrounds churches (group members) connected to the Office of Faith-Based Initiatives – a federally funded program of the Bush II administration that provides grants to religious organizations and interests. Although the Black Church is one of the largest faith-based initiatives beneficiaries, many of these churches were divided in terms of their political support for President Bush. Although President Bush declared war on same-sex marriages, stem cell research, and a woman's right to choose, many African American political and spiritual leaders contend that leaving children behind (referencing Bush's "no child left behind" fiasco) is just as immoral as some of the knee-jerk reaction, traditional Republican-agenda issue items such as abortion.

Coalition politics and the future of who governs in America

In spite of its limitations, I believe the coalition politics model has the greatest potential to be an effective governing model of African American political participation and governance in America. I believe such is the case because the coalition politics model speaks to the heart of African American politics which has always sought to use a variety of political allies and tools to uplift and empower as well as work towards the eradication of injustice and inequality for all groups. Given the growth and influence of the Latino population, I think the coalition model still has the potential to serve as a catalyst for change and genuine political power for groups that have had to overcome a series of failed political models, false political promises, and the resulting facade of democracy which has limited their ability to have their say in the democratic marketplace.

Why examine who governs?

My purpose in examining a variety of models of governance of African American political participation has been several-fold. First, the examination is helpful as it sheds light on the institutional ebbs and flows African Americans have endured to become active participants in American politics. Whereas on the one hand, African Americans are encouraged to "hold these truths to be self-evident that all men are created equal" (Declaration of Independence, 1776) on the other hand, African Americans have had to forge new paths of political incorporation and empowerment because American political institutions and leaders failed to extend the rights and privileges of governance to them.

Second, an examination of who governs highlights the limitations of traditional models of American political participation and behavior. The political history of African Americans details that sole reliance on traditional methods of political participation such as voting have not been an effective means of substantive political incorporation and service delivery. As the 2000 presidential elections showed, voting is not enough. Moreover, modern racialized political issues such as the Georgia voter ID law also speak to the need to broaden and expand their political allies. In this regard, African Americans must diversify their political interests and continue to diligently seek both traditional and non-traditional methods of political incorporation and empowerment.

Finally, an examination of competing models of governance highlights the gap between theory and practice that continues to plague the African American political experience in America especially as it relates to the nation's most prized and praised political tenets.

The gap between theory and practice

Arguably, one of the greatest tragedies of American democracy is that, in spite of the greatness of the nation's political tenets, there still remain significant gaps between theory and practice as it relates to the overall application and extension of rights to all of America's beloved sons and daughters. The first gap between theory and practice lies within the language of the Emancipation Proclamation. The Emancipation Proclamation declared that all persons categorized as slaves were free and that their freedom would be both recognized and maintained by the executive government.

> And by virtue of the power, and for the purpose aforesaid, I do order and declare that all persons held as slaves within said designated States, and parts of States, are, and henceforward shall be free; and that the Executive government of the United States, including the military and naval authorities thereof, will recognize and maintain the freedom of said persons. (Emancipation Proclamation, 1863)

The post-Civil War history of Blacks in America, however, portrayed a different story of executive branch behavior. Although President Lincoln did commit to protecting the interests of Blacks, the majority of his executive branch promises ultimately translated into powerful political rhetoric that did not, in practice, reflect what was promised to Blacks in the language of the Emancipation Proclamation. It must be noted that President Lincoln's initial response to the growing tensions amongst the races was to engage in a Black colonization project in Central America. He wrote, "There is an unwillingness on the part of our people, harsh as it may be, for you free colored people to remain with us . . . It is better for us both . . . to be separated" (Hammond, Hardwick, and Lubert, 2007).

Beyond President Lincoln's attempt to relocate former slaves to Central America, many Blacks were denied the full scope of the proclamation as slave owners engaged in a variety of insidious acts designed to overturn Lincoln's executive order. Additionally, thousands of Black soldiers, especially in the South, were denied "equal" pay and were not received well by some of their White military counterparts.

> And I hereby enjoin upon the people so declared to be free to abstain from all violence, unless in necessary self-defense; and I recommend to them that, in all cases when allowed, they labor faithfully for reasonable wages. And I further declare and make known, that such persons of suitable condition, will be received into the armed service of the United States to garrison forts, positions, stations, and other places, and to man vessels of all sorts in said service. (Emancipation Proclamation, 1863)

Arguably, it is one thing to be "received" into the armed services and an entirely different thing to benefit from the rights and privileges offered by the institution. The military experiences of Blacks reflected the unwillingness of the armed services to extend institutional courtesies to its darker-hued comrades and further reinforced the political symbolism of certain political acts.

Another gap between theory and practice can be found within the language of the United States Constitution. Although it can be argued that the theoretical nature of the language of the Constitution was never intended to be "literally" interpreted, the fact remains that there is an enormous gap related to the political, economic, and sociocultural incorporation of African

Table 2.3 The Civil War Amendments

Amendment XIII
Section 1: Neither slavery nor involuntary servitude, except as a punishment for a crime whereof the party shall have been duly convicted, shall exist within the United States, or any place subject to their jurisdiction.
Section 2: Congress shall have power to enforce this article by appropriate legislation.
Amendment XIV
Section 1: All persons born or naturalized in the United States, and subject to the jurisdiction thereof, are citizens of the United States and of the State wherein they reside. No State shall make or enforce any law which shall abridge the privileges or immunities of citizens of the United States; nor shall any State deprive any person of life, liberty, or property, without due process of law; nor deny to any person within its jurisdiction the equal protection of the laws.
Amendment XV
Section 1: The right of citizens of the United States to vote shall not be denied or abridged by the United States or by any State on account of race, color, or previous condition of servitude.
Section 2: The Congress shall have power to enforce this article by appropriate legislation.

Source: US Constitution

Americans. The gap is couched within the first 50 words of the Constitution of the United States of America: "We the people of the United States, in order to form a more perfect Union, establish Justice, insure domestic Tranquility, provide for the common defense, promote the general Welfare, and secure the Blessings of Liberty to ourselves and our Posterity, do ordain and establish this Constitution for the United States of America" (US Constitution, 1787). The founders stated that the Constitution was established in order to "form a more perfect Union, establish Justice, and insure domestic Tranquility." The fact remains, however, that the practices (i.e., the continuation of slavery) cancelled out the true intentions of their political tenet as the maintenance of the institution of slavery (and the well-known fact that it was one of the great silences of the Constitution) proves that the practices of the founding fathers were in direct conflict with the tenets of justice and tranquility etched in the preamble.

The final gap between theory and practice is found within the language of the 13th, 14th, and 15th Amendments – also known as the Civil War Amendments. These three amendments, passed over a five-year period (1865–1870), were designed to politically empower African Americans after the highly divisive Civil War. The amendments clearly establish a framework for the elimination of slavery, the extension of citizenship and due process to African Americans, and voting rights for African American males. However, the practical application of these laws was delayed upwards of 100 years as

Black Codes, Jim Crow laws, landmark Supreme Court cases such as Plessy vs. Ferguson, separate-but-equal, and fear and intimidation tactics were used to keep the Negro in his place.

In short, the Civil War Amendments did not protect African Americans from manmade and extra-legal (above and beyond the law) tactics such as the grandfather clause, poll taxes, court order sanctions, and even death for refusal to end Negro agitations and engaging in rabble-rousing. The aforementioned examples of the gaps between theory and practice in American political tenets and policies are just a glimpse of the ways in which the Lockean "natural rights" of African Americans were denied and/or abridged in an effort to maintain a system of domination and subordination in the United States.

Symbolic versus substantive representation

One of the most compelling arguments in support of African American inroads in the post-civil rights era has been the highly visible profiles of Blacks in every major arena of American life. Over the past 40 years, African Americans have gone from the backburner to the forefront of American political life. Whereas Fannie Lou Hamer was shut out of the Democratic National Convention in 1964, Barack Obama and Al Sharpton were headliners at the 2004 Democratic National Convention in Boston. African American political inroads are not limited to the Democrats. President Bush's appointment of Condoleezza Rice (National Security Advisor) and Colin Powell (Secretary of State) were seen as significant efforts on the party of the Republican Party to solidify their openness to Black leadership as well as to develop relationships with and court the African American vote. Without a doubt, African Americans have experienced increased levels of political visibility on the local, state, and national scene. The question remains, however, if such visibility has translated into substantive political power and service delivery for the subset.

Symbolic politics

One of the dangers in having a highly visible cohort of African American political leaders and influencers is that it may be assumed, given their airtime and ad space coverage, that Blacks in America are doing well. And, for the most part, African Americans have progressed tremendously since the John Kerryesque flip-flopping of former President Lincoln. In particular, the political strides of African Americans in the post-civil rights era have been phenomenal with more than 4,000 Black elected officials serving at the local, state, and national levels of government. The political inroads of African Americans are not limited to the Democratic Party. No one failed to recognize the history making presidential appointments of George H. W. Bush in his landmark appointment of two African Americans until Rice's subsequent replacement of Powell as Secretary of State upon General Powell's resignation from office.

If one were to base African American political, economic, and sociocultural incorporation and empowerment based on the high profile nature of Black presidential appointments, elected officials, and politically engaged artists and entertainers like Sean "P. Diddy" Combs, it would be logical to conclude that African Americans in the post-civil rights era have "overcome."

The reality, however, as recently expressed by *New York Times* guest columnist Henry Louis Gates, is that the symbolic status of Blacks, including the high-profile appointments of Colin Powell and Condoleezza Rice, does not translate into Black substantive representation. If in fact, symbols represent something that may not actually exist, it can be very dangerous, especially from a political standpoint, to translate African American visibility (symbolism) in certain arenas into actual (substantive) political, economic and sociocultural incorporation and empowerment in America.

Undoubtedly, political symbolism can be an effective means of appeasing the masses as well as fostering inclusion and diversity. According to David Easton (1953), political symbolism is one of the tools used by institutional systems to maintain institutional norms and stability. Easton contends that in certain instances the government can engage in policy that gives an illusion of change when in fact nothing other than a facade has been created to mask the truth. The Humphrey-Hawkins Full Employment Act of 1978 serves as an excellent example of symbolic politics at its best. Birthed on the heels of the Urban League's first national post-civil rights era Black agenda conference, the initial legislation was designed so that "adult Americans able and willing to work have the right to equal opportunities for useful paid employment; that the federal government is responsible for guaranteeing this right and for assuring that national full employment is attained and maintained; and that other national economic goals shall be pursued" to level the economic playing field and ensure "full employment" opportunities for historically underrepresented groups of people including African Americans (Pub. L. 95-523, October 27, 1978, 92 Stat. 1887, 15 USC, 3101).

Additionally, the Act was designed to eliminate income disparities resulting from higher rates of unemployment for Blacks. By the time former President Jimmy Carter endorsed the Humphrey-Hawkins Act, this "full employment" legislative act was a mere skeleton of its original intent and character. As Robert C. Smith and Ronald W. Walters contend,

> The final version of the bill endorsed by Carter retained the language guaranteeing full employment as a right and a 4 percent target goal for adults; but in exchange Carter got language included that put controlling inflation on equal footing with reducing unemployment, and authority for the president to modify the bill's goals or timetables in the third year after passage. It also removed any language dealing with direct authorization of expenditures . . . by the time the bill reached the floor of the House for debate it was largely symbolic. (Smith and Walters, 1996: 201)

The highly symbolic nature of Black legislative agendas is a by-product of several factors including the absence of a genuine rainbow coalition on Capitol

Table 2.4 Cost-benefit analysis of symbolic and substantive representation

Costs	
Symbolic representation	Does not translate into real political, economic, or sociocultural value; can represent an image or illusion of power; does not provide a long-term solution for the tangible and transformative access, power, and influence in the political system; geographic districts may be manipulated in order to elect descriptive representatives
Substantive representation	Representatives may not descriptively look like those they represent; fewer racial, ethnic, and gender minorities may be visibly present in elective offices; certain group members may be unwilling to participate in politics as they do not feel and/ or believe they are adequately represented
Benefits	
Symbolic representation	Powerful source of group consciousness, racial identity, and representation as people see images of self and are motivated/inspired to participate in politics; electoral numbers/demographics of racial, ethnic, and gender minorities increase; all groups are being represented in American politics and reflect democratic tenets of equality, justice, and due process
Substantive representation	Tangible public policy and legislative benefits are provided to racialized electoral districts; representatives engage in transformative not transactional politics as they usually have the support of a broad coalition of interests in their home district and engage in strategic alliances on both sides of the political aisle on Capitol Hill

Hill to broker the holistic legislative needs of minority groups. In spite of the limited nature of many aspects of symbolic politics, some political scientists argue that it is a necessary component of the African American ascension from protest to politics. Specifically, Dr Katherine Tate argues that the symbolic presence and representation of Black faces and interests in Congress are an essential component of the Black political agenda and essential to the long-term viability and inclusion of the Black agenda within American politics.

> Without Black members taking part in the legislative process, the symbolic interests, such as the congressional medals to Rosa Parks, would not be there. Martin Luther King's birthday becoming a national holiday symbolized the role he played in transforming the country into a true democracy. As a national holiday, it becomes difficult to diminish his place in history and the role of African Americans generally in America. Their absence would contribute further to the symbolic marginalization of Blacks' place in American society and in history. (Tate, 2003: 110)

The impact of symbolic politics on African American political behavior is certain. African Americans tend to vote for candidates who symbolically appear to represent their collective interests (Swain, 1993; Tate, 1993, 2003). Perhaps an extension of the rise of New Black Politics (Black electoral politics focused on unifying the Black vote, especially the Black underclass vote), symbolic politics, including Black-elected officials and political appointees, does impact Black voter turnout and Black voting behavior. The two presidential bids of Jesse Jackson represent one example wherein a wide variety of economic and politically divergent African Americans rallied together around the collective agenda of a Black man running for the highest office of the land. Some contend that the presidential success of Senator Barack Obama is yet another example of the positive impact of political symbols as Obama's campaign touched a broad range of issues that appealed to a cross-section of interests. Still, many wonder what course of action President Obama will take to address issues specific to the African American community as his presence alone does not change the economic, political, and sociocultural difficulties that have been a part of the Black experience in America. It must be noted, however, that political theorist Hanna Pitkin (1972) devalues the use of political imagery and symbolism and contends that citizens are best represented when elected officials act in their best interests as opposed to merely descriptively representing them (Swain, 1993).

Where do we go from here?

The struggle for Black political representation in America continues. Although the obvious "signs" of separation are long gone, African American political incorporation and empowerment remains limited at best. One of the greatest challenges African Americans have faced is the inability to use traditional models of governance to gain access to the political system. Both pluralism and elitism have proven to be effective models of political empowerment and incorporation and, in some respects, have subtly worked against Black incorporation. Ironically, in spite of overt denials of such a system of governance, it seems that in America, African Americans have been subjected to a system of colonialism that has either denied access to this group of citizens and/or changed the rules of the games just as Blacks were about to benefit from the purposes and tenets of American government. It seems that the most beneficial model of governance for African American political incorporation has been the coalition (rainbow) model of politics which unites divergent groups around a collective theme of valence issues and concerns. It was the Franklin D. Roosevelt New Deal Coalition of the 1930s, the Civil Rights Coalition of the 1950s and 1960s, the Jesse Jackson Rainbow Coalition of the 1980s, and the New Millennium Coalition of 2008. President Barack Obama has brought issues of fairness, equality, justice, and tangible incorporation of African American political and economic interests to the forefront of our nation. Still, African Americans are expected to be simultaneously cognizant and transcendental of the race and the race-based nature of American politics.

The failure of the American political system to, in actuality, create a true space and place for Black interests is reflective of the bittersweet relationship between this political subset and the nation. In the final analysis, the potential of Black political interests and political alignments is contingent upon the ability of America to self-correct some of its "ugly ways" related to its tendency to engage in top-down, dominate–subordinate models of political behavior. The reality is that until an earnest effort towards collective consciousness and "win-win" coalition politics is pursued, the interests of out-groups will continue to ebb and flow without any significant ability to spring forth into new rivers of political, economic, and sociocultural realities.

POINTS TO PONDER

1. What are some of the key components of democracy?
2. In what ways have democratic institutions helped and hindered African American political participation?
3. Briefly detail the four lenses of who governs and how they impact African American political participation and behavior.
4. What are the major differences between symbolic and substantive representation? Do you believe that both add value to the overall African American political experience? Elaborate.

KEY PHRASES AND PEOPLE

democracy	symbolic politics	colonialism
coalitions	elitism	pluralism
Fannie Lou Hamer	substantive politics	the power elite
		the Civil War Amendments

3

African Americans and Dollars and Sense

Dollars and sense

July 2, 1964 was a landmark day in the lives of Black Americans throughout the United States of America. On this day, the President of the United States of America – Lyndon Baines Johnson – signed into law the nation's first significant piece of civil rights legislation. Under the joint leadership of both the president and the Congress, the Civil Rights Act of 1964 (the CRA) became the official "leveler" of rights for African Americans and other unprotected minority groups from a variety of injustices, double standards, and ineffective theoretical models of governance. Although the language of the Act was full of legalese, it clearly detailed the protection of rights in six key areas and provided broad language to extend its use when necessary. The main sections of the Civil Rights Act of 1964 (P.L. 88-352, 78 Stat. 241) are designed to do the following:

1. enforce the constitutional right to vote;
2. confer jurisdiction upon the district courts of the United States to provide injunctive relief against discrimination in public accommodations;
3. authorize the Attorney General to institute suits to protect constitutional rights in public facilities and public education;
4. extend the Commission on Civil Rights;
5. prevent discrimination in federally assisted programs;
6. establish a Commission on Equal Employment Opportunity.

The passage of the Civil Rights Act of 1964 made sense both politically and socioculturally. From a political standpoint, the passage of the CRA was beneficial as the Black community was growing increasingly weary with the false promises, half truths, and partial implementation of federal government legislation and equal protection of minority rights. African Americans had been championing their right to vote throughout the South in a concerted effort for years. As Dr Martin Luther King, Jr shared in his "Give Us the Ballot" speech, "in the midst of the tragic breakdown of law and order, the executive branch of the government is all too silent and apathetic. In the midst of the desperate need for civil rights legislation, the legislative branch is all too stagnant and hypocritical" (Carson and Shepard, 2001: 49).

Dr King's criticism of both the executive and legislative branch was merited as many African Americans felt betrayed by the nation's slow and "deliberate"

Plate 3.1 *Dr Martin Luther King, Jr, pastor, civil rights leader, and youngest recipient of the Nobel Peace Prize*

failure to substantiate the Brown vs. Board of Education Supreme Court ruling throughout the South. Moreover, many members of the civil rights establishment (both leaders and followers) were still cautious of government promises as prior administrations failed miserably to deliver substantive policy to the Black community in spite of very powerful, convincing, and overtly symbolic gestures to the contrary. One of the most notable failures was President Dwight D. Eisenhower's lackluster commitment to the protection of civil rights as notably displayed in his unwillingness to use executive power to enforce the Supreme Court's ruling in Brown vs. Board of Education (347 U.S. 483 (1954)). Thus, in 1957, when Dr King spoke out about the betrayal of the executive and legislative branches as well as both political parties, he declared that the time had now come for African Americans to take care of their own needs. As Walter Fauntroy, former director of the Washington, DC Southern Christian Leadership Conference, detailed, "[Dr King taught me] politics is the process of determining who gets how much of the whats, whens, wheres, and hows in five areas: income, education, healthcare, housing, and justice" (Carson and Shepard, 2001: 44). The political frustration of the African American community, undoubtedly, would swell into frustrations both economically and socio-culturally as many would be hard pressed to believe that any aspect of their being was respected, given the terrible treatment received politically. As such, the passage of the Civil Rights Act of 1964 made sense from a sociocultural standpoint as well as many Blacks soon realized that "not now" translated into "never." As such, Black leaders could no longer guarantee passive resistance and patience while the United States' government feigned trying to work out a custom-fit civil rights agenda.

Moreover the prominence and popularity of the Nation of Islam, the honorable Elijah Mohamed, and the most fiery and radical proponent of "by any means necessary," Malcolm X, sent a strong message to the nation that the social consciousness of the Black community was changing and perhaps moving in the direction of violent revolution or revolt. Given the radical shift in the social climate of America circa 1962, the language and tone of President Johnson's announcement of the passage of the Civil Rights Act of 1964 should not have come as a surprise.

In his address, President Johnson was careful to point out the gap that existed between the language of the US Constitution and the manmade practical application of an individual's right to equal protection, justice, and liberty under the law.

> We believe that all men are created equal. Yet many are denied equal treatment. We believe that all men have certain unalienable rights. Yet many Americans do not enjoy those rights. We believe that all men are entitled to the blessings of liberty. Yet millions are being deprived of those blessings – not because of their own failures, but because of the color of their skin. The reasons are deeply imbedded in history and tradition and the nature of man. We can understand – without rancor or hatred – how this all happened. But it cannot continue. Our Constitution, the foundation of our Republic, forbids it. The principles of our freedom forbid it. *Morality forbids it. And the law I will sign tonight forbids it.* (Johnson, 1965: 842–4; italics in original)

The televised speech revealed the president's disagreement with the inequalities that were birthed and reinforced by the dubious mistreatment of African Americans. More importantly, President Johnson vowed to end the separate and unequal system of governance that was responsible for the absence of genuine African American political, economic, and sociocultural empowerment in the United States.

Today

It has been more than forty years since the passage of the landmark Civil Rights Act of 1964. In spite of the courageous leadership of President Johnson (and Congress) and the subsequent passage of both the Voting Rights Act of 1965 and the Fair Housing Act of 1968, it is still difficult to make "sense" out of what has happened to African Americans in the post-civil rights era. In particular, Dr King's attention to the whats, whens, wheres, and hows has not translated into significant substantive gains and political inroads for the overwhelming majority of the African American community in the twenty-first century. In short, African Americans have still not reached a level playing field as compared to their White counterparts in a variety of socio-economic arenas that have been traditionally used to measure progress and success in the US.

In arenas ranging from education to investments, African Americans still lag behind their White counterparts economically. While there are myriad explanations as to why Blacks are not doing as well as Whites, including globalization, outsourcing, the after-effects of 9/11, the war in Iraq, the sluggish US economy, escalating gas prices, and the recent mortgage industry crisis, the fact remains that it is difficult to make sense of why African Americans are so far behind, especially given all of the positive legislation enacted to correct the historical legacy of discrimination in America. In this chapter, we will examine the gap between theory and practice as it relates to African American socio-economic progress as well as the ways in which traditional models of governance have proven to be ineffective sources of economic, social, and political empowerment for African Americans.

Rewind: the Poor People's Campaign

In 1967, Dr Martin L. King, Jr and the staff of the Southern Christian Leadership Conference met to strategize about the next phase of the civil rights agenda as the passage of both the Civil Rights Act of 1964 and the Voting Rights Act of 1965 were major milestones for the movement. It was during this meeting that King and his supporters overwhelmingly agreed that the next phase of the movement should focus on economic rights and the passage of federal government legislation for a guaranteed minimum living wage. Known as the Poor People's Campaign, Dr King launched a multi-racial coalition of the "haves," "have nots," men, women, Northerners, Southerners, and all concerned with American domestic policy. Participants in the campaign were to bring the horrific conditions of poverty in America to the forefront of the consciences of the nation's leaders. Plagued by the reality that it was self-defeating for a person to have the right to eat and lack the financial means to engage in such a basic human right, Dr King called for people to join him in Washington, DC in June of 1968 to "sleep in" and lobby federal agencies until Congress enacted legislation to aid the nation's poor and provide a living wage whereby men and women could enjoy the basic freedoms of America.

Dr King launched the Poor People's Campaign in Memphis, Tennessee. A city infamous for its wage inequities for Blacks, Dr King specifically chose Memphis because he believed that the economic disparities of Memphis were reflective of the nation as a whole. Unfortunately, Dr King never lived to see the fruition of the Poor People's Campaign as he was assassinated prior to its launch. Nonetheless, the principles behind the Campaign – "livable" employment and economic opportunity for all – still permeate today.

In many respects, the principles of the Poor People's Campaign are timeless as race-based economic inequalities still persist and continue to impact a

Plate 3.2 *An African American family*

variety of quality-of-life issues related to African Americans. African American gaps in socio-economic status inevitably impact quality-of-life issues. As Andrew Hacker (1992) suggested, the end result of America's misdirected policy agenda is the maintenance of "two nations: black and white, separate, hostile, and unequal." Moreover, even if critics dismiss the call to conscience of Dr King and the concern of Andrew Hacker, Hurricane Katrina clearly articulated the perilous impact of the gap between those who have economic and sociocultural means and those who do not.

Undoubtedly, the unresolved racial tensions of this nation, coupled with an ever-increasing economically centered class divide, have maintained and, in some instances, exacerbated a perilous cycle of poverty, neglect, and disregard for African Americans and poor people alike.

In the next section, a variety of quality-of-life areas will be examined in an effort to assess how well African Americans are doing in the post-civil rights era of greater political, social, and economic opportunity.

Home ownership

One of the fundamental tenets of the "American dream" has been home ownership. The dream of owning one's home has been as much a part of the American democratic fabric as has voting. Home ownership affords one many "social" badges of acceptance and financial acumen. Additionally, home ownership provides a sense of belonging, accomplishment, and personal satisfaction. According to a 2003 Fannie Mae National Housing Survey, an overwhelming majority of Americans (n = 96%) have had a positive experience with home ownership. Ninety-three percent of African American and Latino households share in the positive experiences of home ownership. According to the findings, both African Americans and Latinos cited "having the feeling it is something of your very own" as a determining factor in purchasing their homes. In spite of the overwhelming sense of satisfaction in home ownership, only 12% of those "seeking" to purchase a home were African American. Some of the possible reasons for such a low percentage of African American seekers are affordability/upkeep (39%), credit scores/ratings (42%), complicated home-buying processes (25%), and temporary living conditions (22%) (Fannie Mae National Housing Survey, 2003). Additionally, the survey instrument reported that minorities view credit challenges as the most pressing obstacles to home ownership. Surprisingly, poor credit scores/ratings are seen as an even greater threat to home ownership than affordability.

In spite of Fannie Mae's efforts to create 6 million new homeowners through its "American Dream Commitment" program, there still remain four critical gaps that need to be addressed in order to reach its goal of 1.8 million minority homeowners in the US. Interestingly, in all four areas there are significant differences between the general public and minority groups in regards to information, affordability, credit, and confidence in the home-buying processes. As compared to one-third of the American population, only 18% of African Americans believe they have an "above average" understanding of the home-buying process. An information gap is evident both in employment history and length of mortgage. Whereas 65% of the general public knows that you do not have to be employed by the same employer for at least five years in order to qualify for a mortgage, only 51% of African Americans are knowledgeable of such information.

In terms of length of mortgage, 74% of the general public knows that a 30-year mortgage commitment is not necessary compared to only 64% of the African American community. In spite of these gaps, home ownership aspirations offer a glimpse of hope as 63% of African American renters responded that they are "optimistic" about purchasing a home in the next three years. In terms of actual purchasers, the rate of African American home ownership has fluctuated between 44% and 49% over the last nine years with the greatest increase in ownership occurring in the last four years. Still, African American home ownership is at least 25% less than their White counterparts. Moreover, the rate of African American foreclosure is at an all-time high around the nation.

Poverty

In his final work, *Where Do We Go from Here: Chaos or Community?*, Dr Martin L. King, Jr (1967) provided a detailed examination of the triple evils crippling America. The triple evils of poverty, racism, and war, according to King, were the cornerstone problems of the twentieth century ailing both America and

Table 3.1 Home ownership by race, 2005–1996

	2005	2004	2003	2002	2001	2000	1999	1998	1997	1996
African American	48.2	49.1	48.1	47.3	47.4	47.2	46.3	45.6	44.8	44.1
White (Non-Hispanic)	75.8	76.0	75.4	74.5	74.3	73.8	73.2	72.6	72.0	71.7
Asian	60.1	59.8	56.3	54.7	53.9	52.8	53.1	52.6	52.8	50.8
Hispanic	49.5	48.1	46.7	48.2	47.3	46.3	45.5	44.7	43.3	42.8

Source: US Census Bureau

Table 3.2 Poverty rates by race, 2005–6

	2005	2006
African American	24.9	24.3
White (Non-Hispanic)	8.3	8.2
Asian	11.1	10.3
Hispanic	21.8	20.6

Source: US Census Bureau

the world. King defined poverty *as materialism, unemployment, homelessness, hunger, malnutrition, illiteracy, infant mortality, and slums.* King also recognized the dilemma faced by many hard-working, dedicated, and committed people who were caught in the vicious web of "not enough" food and finances as a result of the triple evils. "I have the audacity to believe that peoples everywhere can have three meals a day for their bodies, education and culture for their minds, and dignity, equality, and freedom for their spirits. I believe that what self-centered men have torn down, other-centered men can build up" (King, 1965: 165).

Yet more than 40 years after Dr King's untimely assassination, America's evil of poverty persists. According to the US Census Bureau, the official poverty rate in 2003 was 12.5%, an increase from 2002 (12.1%). In 2003, the number of people in poverty rose by 1.3 million to 35.9% of the overall population. Additionally, the poverty rate of children increased from 16.7% in 2002 to 17.6% in 2003. The poverty rate of African Americans was 24.4% in 2003. Interestingly, for African Americans the poverty rate, or the number of those in poverty, changed from 2002 to 2003. Moreover, between 2005 and 2006, the percentage of African Americans in poverty averaged around 24.6% according to US Census Data.

Additionally, Census data information that includes additional variables of age and sex presents an even more alarming picture of African American poverty. 30.2% of African Americans aged 17 and under live in poverty as

Table 3.3 Percentage of families in poverty, 2005–6

	2005	2006
African American	24. 9%	24.3%
White (Non-Hispanic)	10.6%	10.3%
Hispanic	21.8%	20.6%

Source: US Census Bureau

compared to 9.5% of non-Hispanic Whites. For Black males 17 and under, 29.7% live in poverty as compared to 9.6% of non-Hispanic Whites and 30.7% of Black females as compared to 9.5% of their counterparts. As the data indicate, Black youth are three times more likely to live in poverty and poor areas than White children.

One of the highest rates of poverty has been found in Black single-headed households. In 2001, 1.8 million homes headed by African American women fell below the poverty line. African American female households have a 35% poverty rate as compared to Hispanic White families (16%). Moreover, African American families have a higher rate of poverty than White and non-Hispanic Whites (21% compared to 6%). For married couples, African Americans also have experienced a greater rate of poverty as compared to their non-Hispanic White families (8% as compared to 3%).

Income

Historically, African American income levels have lagged behind their White counterparts. Given the legacy of slavery, Jim Crowism, and separate but equal doctrines of the country, coupled with institutional racism, it is not surprising that, in an effort to level the economic playing field of the nation, the Southern Christian Leadership Conference (SCLC) launched "Operation Breadbasket," an economic pressure and divestment campaign designed to force companies such as Wonder Bread and Sealtest not only to hire African American employees but also to reinvest dollars in Black banks and communities (Carson and Shepard, 2001: 175–80). In spite of the relative success of Breadbasket's "if you respect my dollar, you must respect my person" campaign, in the post-civil rights era, African Americans still have not experienced the economic success of other groups in America. In fact, the most recent US Census data show that African American median income levels lag behind every minority group in the nation, even Hispanics.

In 2003, the median household income of African Americans was $29,700 as compared to Whites ($47,800) and Asians ($55,300). In 2003, Hispanic median household income was $33,000, roughly $3,300 more than African Americans. In 2005, real median income increased for all races for the first time in seven years. In spite of the positive trajectory, African American households had

Table 3.4 Median income by race: three decades

Race	2006	1995	1985
African American	$31,969	$28,485	$25,642
White	$50,673	$45,496	$43,100
Hispanic	$37,781	$29,079	$30,221

Source: US Census Bureau

the lowest median income in 2006, $31,969 compared to $50,673 for their White counterparts. According to US Census Bureau data, in terms of income, African Americans have lagged behind every other racial and/or ethnic group except Native Americans for the past four decades.

The income levels of African Americans over the past three decades are troubling. On the one hand, the numbers can be explained away due to lower labor force participation rates, a higher proportion of blue collar and service industry occupations, lower educational levels, and high school gradua-tion rates. On the other hand, however, it does not make sense that African Americans continue to be on the lowest rung of America's economic ladder. It is difficult to explain and make sense of the fact that African Americans are not as economically prosperous as their counterparts in a day and age where government intervention and legislation to elevate the undue burden of race in education, employment, and hiring practices is widely documented and well known. The fact remains, however, that something is terribly out of bal-ance educationally, occupationally, and perhaps even institutionally in that, although legislation has been enacted, racial discrimination and institutional biases such as redlining, zip code discrimination, and pay inequity based on gender and race still exist in America.

The question remains, why is it that African Americans in the post-civil rights era still remain, as Dr King articulated, in the "basement of our great society" (Carson and Shepard, 2001: 82)? Moreover, what factors can be attributed to the apparent multigenerational trend of unequal economic access and success in the African American community? Some contend that the economic lack in the African American community is a direct result of the colonial model of gov-ernance. As chapter 2 discussed, the colonial model of governance is designed to maintain a powered relationship wherein those with power dominate those who have been either shut out of or relegated to the lowest rungs of power. In this regard, perhaps another explanation of the poor economic inroads of African Americans can be attributed to the illusion of inclusion that has been over-emphasized in the post-civil rights era of symbolic politics: highly visible political appointments absent genuine political power, African American busi-ness/corporate appointments and contracts that do positively impact the over-all community, and the over-saturation and obsession with all things "bling" as the most significant aspect and achievement of the hip-hop community.

Table 3.5 Labor force statistics, 1984–2004

	1984	1994	2004
African American	62.2%	63.4%	63.8%
White	64.6%	67.1%	63.3%
Hispanic	64.9%	66.1%	68.6%

Source: US Department of Labor

Labor force participation

African Americans have always participated in the workforce of America. From slavery through freedom, Black people have been an integral part of the economic underpinnings of the nation. In the post-civil rights era, African American labor force participation has been on a par with its counterparts. Both African American males and females participate at an average rate of 66.7% and 61.5% respectively.

Interestingly, although African American labor force participation in the last three decades has been relatively parallel to their White, Asian, and Hispanic counterparts, as detailed earlier, they still lag behind economically. In some respects, the gap between the labor force participation rates of African Americans and their subsequent economic payoffs speaks to the proven gap between theory and practice as it relates to the full incorporation of African Americans in the American political system. Moreover, the inconsistency in African American labor force participation rates in comparison to their income levels may also shed more light on the ways in which the pluralist model fails as a tool of African American political incorporation as African Americans have not been able to use their collective interests to influence economic policies in their favor.

Education

African American educational achievement in the post-civil rights era has been phenomenal. The majority of the credit for African American educational success must be given to the National Association for the Advancement of Colored People (NAACP) Legal Defense Fund and its historic work to overturn discriminatory separate but equal practices in both elementary, secondary, and higher education. Some of the historic Supreme Court cases dealing with educational inequalities the NAACP Legal Defense Fund brought before the Court include Brown vs. Board of Education (1954), McLaurin vs. Oklahoma (1950), Missouri ex. rel. Gaines vs. Canada (1938), and Sweatt vs. Painter (1950). In many respects, the work of the NAACP Legal Defense Fund was a direct attack on the system of elitism in America which reinforces a model of governance where a small, wealthy, and influential group of people

Table 3.6 50 years of educational attainment by race (% of earned 4-year degrees)

	African American	White	Hispanic
1950	2.2%	6.6%	–
1960	3.5%	8.1%	–
1970	6.1%	11.6%	–
1980	7.9%	18.4%	7.6%
1990	11.3%	23.1%	9.2%
2000	16.6%	28.1%	10.6%

Source: US Census Bureau

control the political decision-making and public policy process. Using both the 5th (Due Process Under the Law) and 14th (Equal Protection Under the Law) Amendments as ammunition against the discriminatory educational practices that existed throughout the United States, the NAACP Legal Defense Fund was successful in proving that the elitist model of separate but equal was in fact separate and unequal and placed undue burdens on African Americans seeking to obtain quality education.

In spite of these inroads, African American educational achievement continues to lag behind its White counterparts. Since the passage of the Civil Rights Act of 1964, the number of African Americans who have earned at least a bachelor's degree has increased but it is still not comparable to Whites who earned twice as many degrees as African Americans. In fact, in a fifty-year US Census longitudinal study, the data showed that the gap in number of bachelor degrees earned for Whites and African Americans has decreased from a rate of 3:1 in the 1950s to a rate of 2:1 since the 1970s. Clearly, the rise in affirmative action policies in the 1970s played a role in eliminating some of the educational gap between the races. Out of all the groups surveyed, Hispanics still lag behind earning bachelor degrees at a rate of almost 3:1 compared to their White counterparts and not quite 2:1 compared to their African American counterparts.

In *The State of Black America 2005*, the National Urban League offered ten policy-specific recommendations to address the widening disparities within the African American community. The Urban League's "Prescriptions for Change" are as follows:

1. Congress must extend the Voting Rights Act which expires in 2007.
2. Raise the minimum wage from $5.15 to $7.25 per hour and tie future increases to an objective standard. The minimum wage must be a living wage, not a poverty wage.
3. Close the home ownership gap by lowering down-payment requirements and making mortgages more available and affordable to all. Strengthen the Community Reinvestment Act which has helped to guide the banks

in this area.

4. Increase business development and entrepreneurship in the African American and other urban communities by doubling the size of the New Markets Tax Credit Program.
5. Strengthen and improve the Community Block Grant program and other urban economic opportunity and job training programs.
6. Expand job training and career counseling efforts with a focus on young urban males.
7. Make full-day access to quality pre-school education mandatory for every child starting at age three years old.
8. African Americans must energize their focus on savings, investing, and estate planning.
9. African Americans, especially the African American middle class, should increase their commitment to "civic tithing." Civic tithing means financially supporting as well as giving volunteer time to African American institutions, churches, civil rights organizations, and community programs.
10. Urge Congress to support policies that increase access to affordable and preventable healthcare for African American and other communities of color.

The recommendations of the Urban League represent the first of many steps that must be taken to address African American socio-economic inequality. Unlike other policy specific recommendations that have been made in the almost forty years since the Poor People's Movement, the recommendations of the Urban League provide realistic, practical, and easily implemented action steps that should begin to shift the status of African Americans in some of the socio-economic areas where they lag behind other racial and ethnic groups in America.

Where do we go from here? The great vaults of opportunity

In his famous "I Have a Dream" speech, Dr Martin Luther King, Jr reminded his more than 250,000 listeners gathered on the lawn of the Lincoln Memorial that America was home to the greatest vaults of opportunity in the world. In his address, King told his audience that those African Americans gathered on that sweltering August 1963 day were there to make good on the check of "the riches of freedom and the security of justice." The importance of this was the fact that the first time the "Negro community" attempted to cash the check, it was returned and stamped "insufficient funds." In effect, Dr King's reminder of America's initial bad check to the Negro community would not stop their demand for equal protection and rights in America. As King declared, "America has given the Negro a bad check . . . but we refuse to believe that the bank of justice is bankrupt. We refuse to believe that there are insufficient funds in the great vaults of opportunity in this nation" (Carson and Shepard, 2001: 82). Still, more than forty years after Dr King's landmark speech at the March on Washington, African Americans have not holistically benefited from the great vaults of opportunity in America. In fact, it seems as if they have been penalized and, in some instances, sidelined by a mirage of political leadership and policy enactment double-faults.

Perhaps one of the most seismic and schizophrenic policies of the American government that has negatively impacted the African American community has been affirmative action. Affirmative action is a federal policy designed to ensure that companies, educational institutions, and organizations that receive federal funds take steps (affirmative or positive actions) to make sure that groups historically discriminated against are free of any type of racial, sexual, or physical disability bias in hiring and employment practices. Introduced by President Kennedy in 1961 and signed into law by President Johnson in 1965, affirmative action has been more than problematic for African Americans as they have been made to be the scapegoats and symbolic representatives of everything bad about affirmative action, especially quotas.

The problem with affirmative action is that it overshadowed all government conversations about genuine equal opportunity and became the poster child of inclusion in the post-civil rights era. Moreover those who Dr King advocated on behalf of were never included. Finally, those African Americans who have benefited from affirmative action over the past 40 years still do not outnumber the even greater number of White women who benefited from the government policy. As Thomas M. Shapiro articulated,

> The twisted, politically narrow, and bureaucratically unfortunate notion of "affirmative action" substituted for equal opportunity by century's end, and affirmative action continues to frame our hopes and distrust regarding race. Even though the struggle for equal opportunity is far from completed, the single-minded and narrow focus on affirmative action forces compromises with our past, obscures our present understanding of racial inequality, and restricts policy in the future. (Shapiro, 2004: 6)

The over-emphasis on symbolic race-based policies like affirmative action has led to a substantive policy schism which subconsciously ignores other areas where African Americans have not been able to benefit from the great vaults of opportunity in this nation. Some of the other areas where African Americans continue to experience overwhelming inequality are in asset accumulation, generational wealth, stocks and bonds, trade purchases, home ownership, credit worthy FICA scores and credit ratings, 401(k) and Roth IRA plans/accounts, and even basic checking and savings accounts. The end result of such a policy schism is that, similar to the twentieth century, the problem of the twenty-first century is also the color line, the difference being that today not only are African Americans faced with a persistent color line, they are also faced with a rapidly crystallizing economic class line that is no longer distinguishing who has "big things poppin'" solely based on race. As such, the question becomes, is it even necessary to try to make sense out of the last-place status of African Americans in a variety of socio-economic indicators of success in America?

In the remaining chapters we will examine the impact of African American absence of access to economic, political, and sociocultural opportunities and the impact this has had on Black political behavior, voting strength, and transformative politics in the post-civil rights era.

POINTS TO PONDER

1. What was the significance of the Civil Rights Act of 1964? Do you think it paved the way for subsequent civil rights legislation?
2. In your opinion was Dr King an effective leader of African Americans? Please elaborate.
3. In what ways do the four models of governance impact African American access in the post-civil rights era?
4. In what ways have African Americans achieved the "American dream"? In what areas are improvements needed?

KEY PHRASES AND PEOPLE

Dr Martin L. King, Jr.   The Civil Rights Act of 1964   NAACP Legal Defense
affirmative action   President Lyndon B. Johnson   Fund
median income   equal opportunity   The Poor People's
home ownership   Movement

4

African Americans and Voting Behavior

In the previous chapter we examined some of the socio-economic indicators of success in America to determine how well African Americans in the post-civil rights era are doing. In a variety of areas, the data indicates that in spite of the civil rights legislation of the 1960s (The Civil Rights Act of 1964, The Voting Rights Act of 1965, Executive Order 110426 – Affirmative Action, and The Fair Housing Act of 1968), African Americans are out-earned, -employed, and -housed by both their White and Hispanic counterparts. Perhaps even more interesting is the fact that, in spite of a more than 70 percent work-force participation rate (US Labor Department Statistics), African Americans have remained on the lowest rungs of the income, education, and asset accumulation indexes in the nation. As we broaden our discussion of African American politics, it is important to examine the relationship between African American voting behavior and socio-economic, cultural, and political factors that impact their levels of political participation in America. In this chapter, we will explore the intimate relationship between African Americans, voting behavior, and political participation. Additionally, we will examine the impact of political culture, political socialization, and the politics of hip-hop on African American voting behavior.

Political behavior in America

Political behavior is the study of the rational actions and decisions of individuals and/or groups to determine their beliefs and opinions about a variety of personal and public policy issue items such as abortion, education, taxes, and federal government spending as well as the role of the government in responding to or resolving such issues. The individual and/or group patterns that are captured in models, predictors, and measures of political behavior are used to make assertions about future political outcomes and events including elections. In other words, we can examine the voting patterns of an individual and group to make projections and predictions about how he or she will think and act in a variety of arenas that impact his or her economic, political, and sociocultural status. As shared by Dr King in chapter 3, if politics is about the whos, whats, whens, wheres, and hows, voting behavior sheds light onto "how much" of the five "w"s individuals and groups receive.

In the study of political behavior, political behavioralists (those who study the political actions of individuals and groups both sociological and psychologically) examine the impact of individuals and aggregate groups on political institutions and organizations. These social scientists seek to understand the ways societal, structural, and psychological factors such as age, race, gender, socio-economic status, religion, and family background persuade or dissuade people from participating in political acts such as campaigns, elections, and voting. Moreover, political behavioralists seek to develop rational models or predictors of participation that supersede traditional obstacles and barriers of participation. In sum, it may be argued that political behavioralists seek to create a political environment wherein the tenets of American democracy can be fully utilized to create the "good life" that Kanye West and T-Pain rap about.

African American political behavior

For the majority of the first half of the twentieth century, African American political behavior was virtually ignored. A major reason why African American political behavior was kept off of the radar was that their right to vote was constantly being manipulated and usurped by the separate and unequal systems of segregation, racism, and Jim Crowism which vehemently violated federal laws extending personal and political rights to Blacks. It is important to note that, although mainstream social scientists ignored Black political activity and participation, it cannot be assumed that Blacks were not politically active. Dating back to the political activity of Frederick Douglass, Sojourner Truth, Harriet Tubman, Booker T. Washington, Mary McCleod Bethune, and W. E. B. Du Bois, the African American community has always had a robust fleet of traditional and non-traditional political actors and participants who have "agitated" the American political system for freedom and liberty.

The importance of the political and social conscious activities of African Americans in the pre-civil rights era reflects both individual and aggregate behavior designed to gain access to and develop voice and leadership within a variety of governmental institutions and organizations. Moreover, the predominantly non-traditional political behavior of these men and women debunks the belief that, prior to the end of the civil rights movement, African Americans did not display or engage in activities worthy of being classified as political behavior. The Niagara Address of Frederick Douglass is one of a host of examples that showcased the political consciousness, involvement, and aptitude of Black leaders and their earnest desire to correct the injustices of slavery and Jim Crowism.

African American leaders like Frederick Douglass were also assisted by the political activity and behavior of organized groups and interests such as The National Association for the Advancement of Colored People (NAACP), the Black Pullman Porters, the Congress of Racial Equality (CORE), and the

Box 4.1 Frederick Douglass – West India Emancipation Speech, August 3, 1857

If there is no struggle there is no progress. Those who profess to favor freedom and yet deprecate agitation are men who want crops without plowing up the ground; they want rain without thunder and lightning. They want the ocean without the awful roar of its many waters. This struggle may be a moral one, or it may be a physical one, and it may be both moral and physical, but it must be a struggle. Power concedes nothing without a demand. It never did and it never will. Find out just what any people will quietly submit to and you have found out the exact measure of injustice and wrong which will be imposed upon them, and these will continue till they are resisted with either words or blows, or with both. The limits of tyrants are prescribed by the endurance of those whom they oppress. In the light of these ideas, Negroes will be hunted at the North and held and flogged at the South so long as they submit to those devilish outrages and make no resistance, either moral or physical. Men may not get all they pay for in this world, but they must certainly pay for all they get. If we ever get free from the oppressions and wrongs heaped upon us, we must pay for their removal. We must do this by labor, by suffering, by sacrifice, and if needs be, by our lives and the lives of others.

Source: http://www.blackpast.org/?q=1857-frederick-douglass-if-there-no-struggle-there-no-progress

National Urban League, all of whom have worked behind the scenes to legitimate Black political behavior and political activity in the United States by utilizing the demographic strength, collective concerns, and consciousness of African Americans. The efforts of the NAACP, the Urban League, and others were responsible for the overturn of Supreme Court rulings upholding racial segregation, the formation of Presidential Commissions on Race, and the modern-day civil rights movement. Still, the question remains, what is African American political behavior?

In my opinion, one of the most comprehensive and in-depth explanations of African American political behavior is offered by Dr Hanes Walton, Jr in his explanation of the symmetric intricacies of Black political behavior and activity which are both beautiful and repulsive. According to Dr Walton, Black political behavior is the sum total of a variety of factors and influences that shape the community's political perceptions and realities.

> Black political behavior is a function of individual and systemic forces, of "inner" and "outer" forces, of intrapsychic and societal realities, of things seen and unseen, of sociopsychological and material forces, of micro and macro influences . . . [it] is a variety of political patterns, experiences, and activities. It is heterogenous, at times and in some places more factionalized than unified, more conflictive than cooperative, and more discordant than harmonious. These differences arise from the numerous divisions in the black community, divisions of class, ideology, politics, and culture. Moreover, black political behavior is not monistic, static, or time-bound. It undergoes cycles of stagnation, deviation, and regeneration. The flux of social growth and decay affects the black political milieu as it does any sociopolitical milieu. In short, the current realities of black political patterns might not be the same tomorrow. (Walton, 1985: 7)

The beauty of Dr Walton's explanation of Black political behavior is that he is careful to point out that it is no different than the political behavior of other groups of Americans. As he clearly details, the societal issues of the day – the economy, public education, and healthcare – impact the African American community in the same ways that it impacts the White community in America.

Moreover, Dr Walton's explanation of African American political behavior addresses the unspoken issue of the resilience of collective group action and consciousness in that it speaks to the ability of a political cadre to sustain and revitalize itself in the midst of purposive and systematic exclusion by government agencies, institutions, and actors. In theory the latter are supposed to represent one's interests, although in practice these workers of inequity create barriers and enforce biased practices designed to politically misalign the African American community.

In spite of these efforts, African Americans have been able to develop their own political community and voice, reflecting distinct features and attributes that are uniquely associated with models of group consciousness, socio-economic status indexes, and fear/threat models of political participation. Moreover, African Americans have been able to develop a socially conservative and economically liberal political ideology that has shaped their behavior and views on a variety of salient policy issues such as the war in Iraq, federal government assistance in the aftermath of Hurricane Katrina, and the most recent mortgage industry crash which has caused an alarming number of first-time African American homeowners to lose their American dream as a result of bank foreclosures.

Three indicators of African American political behavior and participation

In terms of African American political behavior and participation, there are three major areas of study that detail the political actions and outcome of the community. The most well-known indicator of African American political behavior is the group consciousness, linked fate, or Black utility heuristic model of participation (Barker, Jones, and Tate, 1998; Dawson, 1995). The linked-fate status of African Americans has, in many respects, created a political climate characterized by Black group consciousness or race consciousness. As Barker, Jones, and Tate (1998) articulate, "Race consciousness has been shown to promote Black political participation. Blacks' self-awareness as a discriminated and disadvantaged group in society leads them to be more politically active than other disadvantaged groups who lack a comparable collective identity" (Barker, Jones, and Tate, 1998: 238). In other words, African Americans vote in bloc as a result of their collective historical experiences as well as their present reality of not doing as well as their White and Latino counterparts in a variety of socio-economic indices of success.

Moreover, as Michael C. Dawson (1995) detailed in *Behind The Mule: Race and Class in African American Politics*, African American political culture and behavior has tended to focus on "group interests" as "the information networks in the black community – the media outlets, kinship networks, community and civil rights organizations, and especially the preeminent institution in the black community, the Black Church – would all reinforce the political salience of racial interests and would provide information about racial group status" (Dawson, 1995: 10). Also defined as the Black utility heuristic, group-based political culture and political behavior has been a distinctive characteristic of African American politics that can be traced back to the historic subjugation of the race. Moreover, according to R. Drew Smith, there are several "core" Black issues that unite the community politically and mobilize the Black vote. These core issues include a broad range of "civil rights" such as affirmative action, criminal sentencing and other policing issues, community development, employment and education opportunities. These core issues impact Black political behavior – African-American collective thought and decision-making related to politics and public policy. As such, the collective consciousness of African Americans causes them to engage in political activity and behavior that is predominantly based on race as understood as linked fate and not in terms of issues of class and/or individualized American status.

In some respects, the linked fate/group consciousness/Black utility heuristic (Dawson, 1995) model closely resembles the coalition model of governance of chapter 2. Both models are effective in the organization and mobilization of individuals and groups based on their concentric spheres of interests and historical patterns of economic, political, or social usurpation of rights. In organizing individuals and groups around shared interests, both models effectively address challenges that arise as a result of either pre-established or unintended structural obstacles and barriers that have tended to work in favor of those with traditional and long-standing access to power while simultaneously working against those who have been denied access to the same governmental institutions.

The second model of African American political behavior and participation focuses on the socio-economic status of group members. In this regard, it is believed that the higher one's socio-economic status, the more likely an individual is to participate in the political and electoral arenas including engaging in activities such as registering to vote and participating in elections (Verba and Nie, 1972; Barker, Jones, and Tate, 1998; Dawson, 1995; Walton, 1985, 1994). The socio-economic status model is based on the belief that those who have a more vested interest in political outcomes due to their educational and economic investments are more likely to be involved in politics and political decision-making because they have some personal interests at stake. The additional benefit of having an invested electorate is that over time the costs associated with voting (which traditionally limits and/or excludes those of lower socio-economic status) are minimized as those with higher

Table 4.1 African American degree completion percentages

Year	Bachelor's Degree	Masters/PhD
2004	14.1%	3.0%
2003	15.0%	2.6%
2002	15.6%	2.4%
2001	15.5%	2.3%
2000	14.2%	3.7%
1998	13.0%	2.8%
1995	13.0%	1.8%

Source: US Census Bureau

socio-economic status connect voting and other forms of political activity with a sense of civil duty and responsibility. In this regard, the number of "invested" African American voters continues to increase as their level of secondary and post-secondary earned degree status increases.

In spite of the positive impact of socio-economic indicators on African American voting behavior, there are to be sure, some challenges with this model of participation. Specifically, the socio-economic status model as a predictor of African American voting behavior is extremely problematic in the post-civil rights hip-hop era as many of those most well-known faces of the hip-hop community cannot vote due to prior felony convictions. Although these entertainers are in some of the highest socio-economic brackets in the world, their economic status does not have anything to do with their ability to transfer such to the political realm as their voting rights have been revoked.

Beyond the hip-hop icons that cannot vote because of prior felony convictions, there is also a very large portion of the economically well-off hip-hop community who simply do not participate in politics in meaningful and transformative ways as P. Diddy's "Vote or Die" campaign embarrassingly displayed. In spite of the highly symbolic "Vote or Die" campaign where Diddy utilized many of his celebrity friends to appear in public awareness ads sporting his $35.00 "Vote or Die" T-shirt, a large number of his celebrity endorsees did not even participate in the 2004 presidential election or the 2006 midterm election.

Moreover, in spite of Diddy's highly publicized celebrity status at both the Democratic and Republican National Conventions, Diddy, in my estimation, failed to actualize the opportunity as he never publicly endorsed or discussed his issue agenda with his extremely loyal, energetic, and youth-based hip-hop consumer population. Unlike Harry Belafonte and James Baldwin who utilized their celebrity status to engage in transformative acts of African American political behavior in the 1960s, P. Diddy seemingly has not utilized his status as an entertainer and business mogul to galvanize and connect the linked-fate

Plate 4.1　*Sean "P. Diddy" Combs – hip-hop mogul*

status of his diversified yet overlapping political interests and populations. In 2008, however, P. Diddy remedied this and put his entire entertainment and fashion conglomerate behind the successful election oof President Obama. As such, it is not necessarily accurate or in the best interests of the entire African American community to base voting behavior and participation on socio-economic status.

In many respects, the socio-economic model of Black political participation is limited by some of the same challenges of the pluralist model of governance in that it does not guarantee equal results or outcomes for group participation and fails to take into account institutional, structural, and legal restrictions that prohibit people desirous of participating in politics the ability to do so. Additionally, the socio-economic status model fails to account for those who have the indicators of participation (education, wealth, or both) but do not participate for a variety of reasons including apathy, disconnection from political leaders and institutions, or because they do not feel like their vote counts.

The final area of African American political behavior and participation is the perceived fear/threat model. The perceived fear/threat model asserts that African Americans do not participate in politics because of concerns that retaliatory measures will be instituted against them to both dissuade them from engaging in acts of political behavior and/or to keep them in their place as it relates to them not mobilizing to disrupt the current political and economic systems (Franklin and Moss, 2000; Leighley and Vedlitz, 1999). An excellent example of the fear/threat model of participation in practice was in Birmingham, Alabama. During the Easter weekend of 1963, the Southern Christian Leadership Conference and the Alabama Human Rights Commission engaged in an economic boycott of the downtown central business district store merchants who refused to speak out against segregation in the city. Seen as outsiders who came to Birmingham to agitate the "good Negroes" of the city, Dr Martin L. King, Jr (SCLC) and Rev. Fred Shuttlesworth (AHRC) were threatened with physical harm if they did not call off the boycott immediately.

In his "Letter from Birmingham Jail," King responded to his critics by highlighting the unjust and racially incised treatment of African Americans which was designed to create a community of fear.

> There can be no gainsaying the fact that racial injustice engulfs this community. Birmingham is probably the most thoroughly segregated city in the United States. Its ugly record of brutality is widely known. Negroes have experienced grossly unjust treatment in the courts. There have been more unsolved bombings of Negro homes and churches in Birmingham than in any other city in the nation. These are the hard, brutal facts of the case. (Martin Luther King, Jr Papers Project, www.kingpapers.org)

The civil disobedience of African Americans in Birmingham spoke yet again to the power of the linked-fate model of political behavior as a means of overcoming legal and extra-legal fear and intimidation tactics which were designed to dissuade the Black community from engaging in protest politics. Interestingly, the fear/perceived threat model of African American political behavior is reminiscent of the colonial model of governance in that powered relationships are manipulated and a variety of carrot and stick mechanisms are utilized to keep the powerless in lower economic, political, and sociocultural arenas.

African American political culture

In order to effectively understand African American political behavior, the relationship between political culture and socialization must be clearly understood. In very broad terms, political culture is defined as a set or series of attitudes, beliefs, and patterns of thought related to politics and political events. These beliefs have a tendency to shape and influence one's outlook and perceptions about all things political. In the context of African American politics, political culture can be more narrowly defined as the attitudes and beliefs that tend to shape the collective political experiences and thoughts of Blacks in America. According to Smith and Seltzer (2000), there are three distinct components of African American political culture. The collective experiences of African Americans have produced a political culture that tends to be more liberal, religious, and distrustful of government. In the next section, we will utilize the 2004 presidential election to more closely examine African American political behavior.

Black political behavior, election 2004, and beyond

According to the 2004 National Opinion Poll conducted by the Joint Center for Political and Economic Studies, African Americans were not pleased with the job performance of the Bush administration. In particular, 76% of Black respondents gave the president "fair or poor" job performance ratings compared to 59% in 2000. It seems apparent that the president's negative approval rating has been impacted by the administration's absence of substantive policy linkage and political relationship with the broader African American community. Bush fared best with both secular and Christian Black conservatives receiving job performance ratings of 33% and 35% respectively. Perhaps the positive approval rating of President Bush from secular and Christian Black conservatives is a result of his conservative African American political appointments (most notably Colin Powell and Condoleezza Rice) as well as his Faith-Based Initiatives which have directly benefited key Black Church leaders and churches.

Bush vs. Kerry

In a "mock" presidential election question, the Joint Center asked respondents, "Suppose the 2004 presidential election were being held today . . . who would you like to see win?" Only 18% of the African American respondents were in support of a Bush ticket with an overwhelming majority of the respondents (69%) in support of Kerry. A CNN.com election "exit poll" solidified the sentiments of the Black community as 88% of African American respondents surveyed voted for Kerry compared to 11% who voted for Bush. African American anti-Bush voting behavior and sentiments were compounded during the Hurricane Katrina fiasco. Shortly after the hurricane, an NBC/Washington Post poll showed a 2% approval rating of President Bush from African Americans compared to 45% of White respondents and 36% of Hispanic respondents. Although some questioned the accuracy and margin of error of the poll, which is usually plus or minus 3%, the fact remained that the numbers were some of the lowest in the recordable history of the nation.

As Democratic pollster Peter D. Hart stated in a WashingtonPost.com interview, "African Americans were not supporters, but I don't think that they outright detested him – until now," Hart said. Perhaps like the sentiments of Kanye West and his infamous "Bush Don't Like Black People" monologue, according to Hart, "The actions in and around Katrina persuaded African Americans that this was a president who was totally insensitive to their concerns and their needs."

In the aftermath of Hurricane Katrina, the president's approval rating was at an all-time low in the African American community. Perhaps what proved to be of more interest, however, was the faltering approval rating of the president as a result of a series of misguided, seemingly egocentric, and hostile moves directed towards both the domestic and global communities. The difference, however, is that a majority of Americans, regardless of race, disapproved of the president's leadership. According to an October 31, 2007 Rasmussen Report, only 38% of the US population approved of the job the president was doing compared to 60% of the population who disapproved of the president. Some of the issues that impacted the president's approval rating were the war in Iraq, the crisis in the mortgage industry, and the US economy.

Opinion divide

There is a great deal of research that documents the major differences of opinion between African Americans and other racial/ethnic groups. Although the opinion divide can be attributed to a variety of factors, I believe that the political ideology of African Americans plays a major role in their perceptions of politics which in turn impacts their political behavior. As such, I think it is important for us to examine the impact of African American political ideology on voting behavior. In this regard, political ideology is defined as the beliefs and opinions an individual has about politics and public policy. Usually, an individual's political ideology is strongly influenced by a variety of political socialization agents including family, friends, socio-economic status, education, religion, race, gender, and geographic areas. In the next section, we will continue to examine African American political ideology by examining survey responses to the 2004 Joint Center for Economic and Political Studies data. The Joint Center survey tapped into African American political ideology by highlighting areas they deemed "the most important" problem or issue facing African Americans.

In terms of the survey results, the most notable shift was in the respondents' rankings of the "most important" problem facing the nation. Whereas in the year 2000 the majority of African Americans surveyed stated that education was the most important problem facing the United States (26% of respondents), in 2004, only 7% of African American respondents said that education was the top issue facing the US. The 2004 Joint Center survey revealed that African Americans believe that the economy (jobs, poverty, homelessness, and hunger) is the top issue facing the US. The shift from education to the economy can be attributed to several political and economic events that occurred during the four-year time interval between the surveys. In particular, the impact of September 11, 2001 and America's subsequent war on terror, the ongoing war in Iraq, the financial scandals of major business corporations including Enron, Tyco, and WorldCom, and the rising costs of healthcare for all Americans have precipitated the change in perspective.

Interestingly, in 2004, concerns about the economy, the war in Iraq, and terrorism more closely connected the "priorities" of all respondents. Still, according to Martin Kilson (*The Black Commentator*, 2004), Harvard professor of political science, there remains strong consensus in the Black community surrounding issues of "housing, jobs, education, criminal justice, and an overall proactive federal role in ending racism's impact in these areas through affirmative action and related policies."

> African Americans remain in remarkable, consistent agreement on political issues, a shared commonality of views that holds strongly across lines of income, gender and age. The Black Commentator's analysis of biannual data from the Joint Center for Political and Economic Studies confirms the vitality of a broad Black Consensus. Most importantly, the data show that Black political *behavior* has not deviated from recent historical patterns, nor is any significant Black demographic group likely to diverge from these patterns in the immediate future. (Kilson, 2004, www.blackcommentator.com)

During the 2004 presidential election, African American public opinion and political behavior on key issues impacting the Black community remained solid. For example, 63% of African Americans expressed concern about whether their vote would be properly counted given the controversy surrounding the 2000 presidential election. Also, President Bush's "No Child Left Behind" education initiative fared poorly with African Americans. "Among African Americans, almost three times as many gave the program fair or poor grades (67%) as gave it excellent or good grades (23%)." Similarly, 72% of African Americans surveyed disapproved of the president's handling of the Iraq war and 66% of the respondents believe that the war has negatively impacted American's broader war on terrorism.

Shifting to the issue of "gay marriage," African Americans tend to be more conservative than the general population. In particular, "46% of African Americans supported no legal recognition of gay relationships. Among Black subgroups, those most opposing any legal recognition were Black Christian conservatives (62%) and those living in the South (57%)." In a 2007 opinion survey poll of the NAACP, a little less than 25% of their African American respondents stated that they would support a presidential candidate that favors either gay civil unions or same sex marriages. Interestingly, both African American and White respondents had similar ideological perspectives on these issues.

The 2007 NAACP opinion poll provided an interesting prospective of the future of African American political behavior and thought as an overwhelming majority of its respondents identified universal healthcare, affirmative action, school vouchers, and felony re-enfranchisement as some of their top areas of political interest and support. More than 80% of African American respondents stated they would support a candidate that campaigned for both universal healthcare and affirmative action policies. Additionally, a little less than 70% of African American respondents stated they would support a candidate that proposed felony re-enfranchisement.

Table 4.2 2007 NAACP opinion poll

Q: Would you support a presidential candidate who "supported . . ."?	
Affirmative action	80%
Felony re-enfranchisement	65%
Defense spending	38%
Same sex marriage	21%
School vouchers	65%

Where do we go from here?

Over the past 50 years voting in America has been on the decline. There are many research articles that detail the factors that have contributed to the declining electorate which includes the costs associated with voting, the decline of generational party loyalists, and an increasing sense of apathy and disconnect among Generation Xers who do not feel connected to government and politics. In addition to the absence of historical indicators of voting behavior and political participation such as card-carrying members of the two major political parties, the American electorate has been on the decline as a result of a rise in the number of independent voters, political malfeasance, corruption, and scandal at the local, state, and national level, and the absence of major political, social, and/or economic events to galvanize the voting public. Moreover, a large number of the eligible American voting-age population simply is not involved in politics because they feel as if their vote and voice do not count.

Interestingly, the overall disconnect which has led to a decline in the voting behavior of the American electorate has not spread to the African American community. Since 2000, African American voting behavior and participation has steadily increased and was predicted to be at an all-time high during the 2008 electoral season. The increase in African American voting behavior can be attributed to many factors; however, it seems that the number-one motivator was the pending election of President Bush in 2000 – in particular his seemingly anti-African American policy stance as compared to the then Democratic frontrunner Al Gore – and his subsequent re-election in 2004 that motivated and inspired people who never participated in politics to cast their vote in hope of change.

In 2004, African Americans cast 14.6 million votes in the presidential election compared to 10.5 million votes in the 2000 election. The increase of a little more than 2% can be attributed to the rise in the number of men, women, and youth voters from 2000 to 2004. In terms of women, the percentage of African American female voters increased from 56% in 2000 to 60% in 2004. The number of African American male voters also rose from 40% in 2000 to 42% in 2004. Finally, the number of young people between the ages of 18 and 29 who participated in the presidential election also increased from 2.1 million voters in 2000 to 3.7 million voters in 2004 which indicates that the voter registration and mobilization efforts of the Hip-Hop Action Network, the NAACP, the Urban League, and a host of other civil rights and grassroots organizations that targeted young people and first-time voters were relatively successful.

In terms of where the African American community goes from here, it seems that the recent efforts to galvanize the Black voting age population should be continued and built upon in an effort to increase the number of African American voters – especially African American males who still participate at a rate of less than 50%. I believe if efforts similar to those targeting African American and urban youth are utilized to target African American men, the number of men who participate and cast their ballot on the local, state, and national level should increase. Additionally, I believe that the efforts of the NAACP and other organizations to re-enfranchise felons also may increase the number of African American males who participate in politics as those who are convicted felons are currently ineligible to vote in a majority of states without going through a lengthy and tedious process. The challenge, however, with re-enfranchisement efforts of convicted felons is in determining what types of prior convictions are worthy of being considered for re-enfranchise-ment and the consequences associated with a re-enfranchised felon if he or she is convicted of another crime in his or her lifetime.

Overall, however, it appears that African American political participation is moving in the right direction as the numbers of those who are politically connected and have strong feelings on a variety of important issues impact-ing the Black community continue to increase. Additionally, the increase in the number of African American elected officials, the rise in the number of African American voters, and the efforts of major political candidates to reach out to key members of the Black community are positive signs of potential transformative change. Moreover, the recent efforts of African American radio personality Michael Baisden calling for a march in Jena, LA, to protest the unfair legal treatment of six African American males known as the Jena Six, led to one of the largest African American rallies for justice, freedom, and equality of the last twenty years. As such, I think it is important to consider the use of non-traditional political mediums and mechanisms which include entertainment radio and a host of visually driven internet websites such as www.myspace.com, www.facebook.com, www.youtube.com, and godtube. com to mobilize, organize, and inspire African Americans to participate in politics.

Finally, Barack Obama's historic election as president in 2008 will undoubt-edly usher in a new wave of African American behavior and culture as he has seemingly positioned himself as a post-civil rights change agent who is unwilling to position himself in race-specific and/or civil rights movement/leader terms.

Points to ponder

1. What is political behavior? In what ways have African Americans been politically involved and active?
2. What factors contribute to African American group consciousness? Can these factors be used to explain similar behavioral patterns with other racial, ethnic, or religious minorities?
3. What impact do hip-hop artists have on African American voting behavior? Do you agree or disagree with this impact?
4. What factors contributed to the rise of African American voters in the 2000 and 2004 presidential elections?
5. In what ways can African Americans improve their political participation and voting behavior?

Key phrases and people

Frederick Douglass	Sojourner Truth	Rev. Fred Shuttlesworth
Black utility heuristic	political behavior	socio-economic model
linked fate	political culture	fear/threat model
group consciousness	political ideology	felony re-enfranchisement

Part II

5

African Americans and Congress

Congress is one of the most powerful and structurally important organizations in the US government. Historically rooted in the First Continental Congress of 1774 which created the nation's first unicameral legislature, the most powerful branch of government has been restructured throughout the nation's history in an effort to provide a host of legislative policy to constituents as well as institutional checks and balances for the other branches of government. These dynamic changes and challenges have been responsible for the evolution of Congressional power, oversight, and legislative influence over time. In this chapter we will examine the institutional role, scope, and functions of Congress and its impact on African Americans in the political system. In particular, we will look at institutional mechanisms designed to hinder African American Congressional inroads, the rise of African American Congressional influence and power over time, the role of the Congressional Black Caucus, and the future of African American Congressional power.

Historical overview of Congress

The legislative authority of the federal government is outlined in the US Constitution. Article I, Section 1, establishes the legislative scope and authority of Congress and details the formal structure of the law-making body. The first section of the Constitution is clear as it established Congress as the lead law-making branch of government.

ARTICLE I, SECTION 1

All legislative Powers herein granted shall be vested in a Congress of the United States, which shall consist of a Senate and House of Representatives.

In addition to vesting "all legislative power" in Congress, Article I, Section 1 also details the structure of the bicameral legislature. The Congress consists of a two-chamber legislative assembly: the House of Representatives, which consists of 435 members elected every two years based on census apportionment data, and the US Senate, which consists of 100 members (2 members per state) that are elected for six-year terms based on the electoral demands of their entire state. Article I, Section 2, Clause 1 and Article I, Section 3, Clause 1 detail the composition and qualifications requirements of members of the United States Congress.

Table 5.1 The US House of Representatives and Senate at a glance

House	Senate
435 members	100 members
2-year terms	6-year terms
Less prestige	More prestige
Smaller staff	Larger staff
Specific constituency	Broad constituency

ARTICLE I, SECTION 2, CLAUSE 1

The House of Representatives shall be composed of members chosen every second year by the people of the several states, and the electors in each state shall have the qualifications requisite for electors of the most numerous branch of the state legislature.

ARTICLE I, SECTION 3, CLAUSE 1

The Senate of the United States shall be composed of two Senators from each State, chosen by the legislature thereof, for six years and each Senator shall have one Vote.

Although power is shared between both chambers of Congress, the constitutional requirements to hold office in the House of Representatives and US Senate differ. Whereas in the House of Representatives elected officials must be a minimum of 25 years of age, a citizen of the United States for at least seven years, and a resident of the state in which he or she is seeking to gain electoral office, in the United States' Senate elected officials must be a minimum of 30 years of age, a citizen of the United States for at least nine years, and a resident of the state in which he or she is running for office (US Constitution, Article I, Section 2, Clause 2, and Section 3, Clause 3). Another difference between the US House of Representatives and the US Senate is in the area of prestige. It is widely known that members of the Senate have more exclusive perks and privileges including larger staffs, more committee assignments, greater leadership and committee influence, longer terms, and sole responsibility in both appointment confirmations and impeachment trials. In spite of the Senate's higher ranking, both the House and the Senate maintain similar leadership structures in terms of party leadership, must provide mutual consent in order for a bill to become a law, and hold members to the same ethical standards.

Power and responsibilities: Members of Congress

The powers of Congress are clearly outlined in Article I, Section 8 of the Constitution. Known as the "expressed" powers, both chambers of Congress are given the power to tax, coin money, regulate commerce, establish post offices and roads, and declare war. Congress also has the constitutional power of oversight which allows it to serve as a watchdog of other federal government

Box 5.1 Congressional Powers (Article I, Section 8)

The Congress shall have Power to lay and collect Taxes, Duties, Imposts, and Excises, to pay the Debts and provide for the common Defense and general Welfare of the United States, but all duties, imposts and excises shall be uniform throughout the United States;

To borrow Money on the credit of the United States;

To regulate Commerce with foreign nations, and among the several states, and with the Indian tribes;

To establish an uniform Rule of Naturalization, and uniform Laws on the subject of Bankruptcies throughout the United States;

To coin Money, regulate the value thereof, and of foreign coin, and fix the Standard of Weights and Measures;

To provide for the Punishment of counterfeiting the Securities and current Coin of the United States;

To establish Post Offices and Post Roads;

To promote the Progress of Science and useful Arts, by securing for limited Times to Authors and Inventors the exclusive Right to their respective Writings and Discoveries;

[. . .]

To declare War, grant Letters of Marque and Reprisal, and make Rules concerning Captures on Land and Water;

[. . .]

institutions and agencies in an effort to curtail malfeasance and political abuse. Congress's primary area of oversight, however, focuses on executive branch agency decision-making and policy implementation. Congress's oversight role should not come as a surprise given the fact that Article I, Section 8 gives Congress exclusive power to determine and authorize spending, including executive branch spending, in that every year the president must submit his proposed budget to Congress for approval.

The most powerful constitutional provision of Congress is known as the "elastic" clause. Article I, Section 8, Clause 18 provides members of Congress the ability to "make all Laws which shall be necessary and proper for carrying into Execution the foregoing Powers, and all other Powers vested by this Constitution in the Government of the United States, or in any Department or Officer thereof." Additionally, Congressional responsibilities include the power to set the Congressional agenda in terms of what legislation is pursued and enacted, to engage in Congressional hearings and investigations, to impeach and remove members of the legislative, executive, and judicial branch leaders, and to advise and consent in the area of treaties and presidential cabinet other key leader appointments, including Supreme Court appointments and ambassadorships.

Congressional representation

As has been detailed in the previous section, Congress must balance a variety of constitutional powers and roles. Although many of these roles and responsibilities are constitutionally ascribed, there are many other Congressional

> **Box 5.2 Edmund Burke's Speech to the Electors of Bristol (delivered November, 1774)**
>
> Certainly, gentlemen, it ought to be the happiness and glory of a representative to live in the strictest union, the closest correspondence, and the most unreserved communication with his constituents. Their wishes ought to have great weight with him; their opinion, high respect; their business, unremitted attention. It is his duty to sacrifice his repose, his pleasures, his satisfactions, to theirs; and above all, ever, and in all cases, to prefer their interest to his own. But his unbiased opinion, his mature judgment, his enlightened conscience, he ought not to sacrifice to you, to any man, or to any set of men living. These he does not derive from your pleasure; no, nor from the law and the constitution. They are a trust from Providence, for the abuse of which he is deeply answerable.

responsibilities that have evolved and/or became accepted over time. Perhaps the most important role of Congress is the one it plays when serving in the capacity of a "representative" of the people. First introduced by Edmund Burke (1774) and widely accepted and taught in political science and politics classes throughout the nation and world, the representation styles of elected officials as identified by Burke were designed to shed light on the ways in which elected officials were to behave in light of the wishes of their constituents and their own divine intellect, insight, and wisdom. In this regard, members of Congress may serve in the role of a trustee, delegate, or politico.

An elected official that engages in the trustee style of representation employs his or her own judgment in the legislative decision-making process. In this regard, as Burke contended in his address, these men and women seek to employ their unbiased opinion and enlightened conscience as has been entrusted to them by God. Additionally, Burke seemed to infer that misuse and abuse of the trustee style of representation was answerable to Providence.

In contrast to the trustee model is the delegate style of representation. An elected official that operates out of the delegate style of representation seeks to honor and closely adhere to the expectations, wishes, and desires of his constituency base. As such, the delegate's legislative decision-making relies solely on the interests of "their business." The delegate, in many respects, truly is a representative of the people who serves as a proxy of the will of the people who have elected those that represent them.

The final representation style we will discuss is the politico. An elected official that serves as a politico seeks to combine the responsibilities of being elected by the popular demands and trust of the people to legislate their business and interests with the independent intellectual knowledge, sound judgment, and rational ability given to each human being to make effective decisions and leadership choices. The politico, then, is a combination of both the trustee and delegate styles of representation. The elected official operating out of the politico style of representation can vote in accordance with his or

her best judgment (which may include prior knowledge, experience, or expertise in an area) or yield to the desires of his or her constituents.

In addition to the trustee, delegate, and politico styles of representation,
elected officials, specifically members of Congress, also engage in what Robert
Fenno (1978) has popularized as "home style." According to Fenno, home style
details the nature of the relationship between elected officials, their constituents, and an elected official's behavior in the home Congressional district as
a measure of re-election success. Some home style behaviors include meeting
with constituents, public appearances in the district, pork-barrel legislation
(funds directly targeted towards specific needs within the district), and other
communication activities including newsletters and mailers. In contrast,
yet complementary to an elected official's home style, is his or her hill style
(Fenno, 1978). Hill style characterizes the behavior of representatives while
in Washington, DC and includes committee work, floor debate, voting, and
meetings with a variety of interested parties including voters from their home
districts. An effective member of Congress understands the importance of his
or her many faces and seeks to bring balance to personal expectations and the
expectation of constituents while simultaneously handling the responsibilities
of both home (Congressional district interests) and Capitol Hill. In the next
section, we will examine the history of African American Congressional challenges and inroads. It is my hope that a historical overview of both the obstacles
and opportunities experienced by African American members of Congress will
shed light on the promise and great responsibility of the leading branch of
federal government legislation, policy implementation, and oversight.

The roles and challenges of African American Members of Congress

African American members of Congress are in a unique position. In addition
to fulfilling their constitutional and constituency roles and responsibilities,
they are also expected to be role models, community activists, leaders, symbolic and substantive representatives of the entire Black race (Tate, 2003;
Swain, 1993). In short, African American representatives, in large part, due
to the post-civil rights leadership vacuum, are expected to be all things to all
people. Clearly such expectations are in large measure impossible but moreover unreasonable given the enormity of their other Congressional responsibilities. In this regard, many African American members of Congress find
themselves short-staffed, overworked, and underpaid because of the extreme
demand placed on them by what can very well be all of Black America.

The collective demands placed on African American members of Congress
can be limiting for a variety of reasons. First, the expectation of African
American members of Congress to be conscious of and responsive to the
collective "Black agenda" can detract many of them from focusing on the
specific needs of their district or state-wide constituency base. An example of

this occurred recently in Jena, Louisiana where six African American males received extremely harsh punishments for beating up a White man who was one of three young men who hung a noose from a tree at the local high school. One of the major issues surrounding the Jena Six case was the fact that the three White males received a three-day suspension for displaying a symbol – the noose – which is historically known to represent the worst vestiges of hate, racism, and antipathy towards African Americans. During the Jena Six rallies and subsequent demonstrations which included a march on the United States Justice Department, African American members of Congress including Maxine Waters, Sheila Jackson Lee, and others have been put on the frontlines to bring this to the attention of their fellow members of Congress – some of whom represent the area but have failed to act – as well as the nation as a whole. It should come as no surprise then to find a large number of African American members of Congress speaking and advocating on behalf of a wide array of causes and issues that do not have a direct link or impact in their own Congressional districts (Tate, 2003).

Another challenge to a collective African American congressional agenda is that Black legislators can be engaged in race-specific policy agendas to the detriment of more consensus building, race-neutral, valence issues that have the potential to impact an even broader constituency base (Walton and Smith, 2007; McClain and Stewart, 2005; Tate, 2003; Swain, 1993). In this regard, the collective consciousness and linked-fate models of voting behavior can be used against African American legislators who can be labeled as "not Black enough" or "down with the cause" if and when they pursue policy agendas that are outside of the realm of what has been perceived as African American issues and interests. In spite of having to wear their dual consciousness as both legislators and African Americans close to their respective sleeves, the overwhelming majority, if not all 43 members of Congress, have risen to the occasion and continue to work diligently to ensure the progress of the Black legislative agenda.

Still, African American members of Congress are in an uphill battle as they have yet to reach proportional representation in the House or Senate. One of the greatest challenges faced by African American members of Congress has been the inability to attract and maintain a diverse constituency base (Smith and Walters, 1996; Tate, 2003). It has been asserted that a large part of the disproportional representation of Black elected officials in Congress is directly correlated to underlying thoughts and issues of race wherein voting is still largely based on perceptions of competency, familiarity, and deep-seated, knee-jerk reactions that judge Whites to be more skilled than Blacks in areas of governance and leadership (Sniderman and Piazza, 1993; Kinder and Sanders, 1996). An overwhelming number of White voters still do not vote for African American political candidates and do not know how to effectively submit to Black leadership. As such, the scar of race remains unhealed and does not appear to be on its way to recovery any time soon.

By no means is this discussion designed to remove attention away from the winner-take-all system of governance. African American proportional representation in Congress is still severely limited by the absence of a proportional representation model (Barker, Jones, and Tate, 1998). In effect, America's winner-take-all system does not appear to serve the collective best interests of the African American community. Still, African American Congressional representation was assisted by the one-person, one-vote ruling of Baker vs. Carr which has been extremely beneficial in increasing the actual number of Black elected officials on the local, state, and national level and protecting Black voting rights (especially in the South).

A historical overview of African American ascension to Congress

The passage of the Civil War Amendments (the 13th, 14th, and 15th Amendments), along with newly freed slaves understanding their full rights and responsibilities as established in the Emancipation Proclamation, ushered in a new wave of electoral opportunity for Blacks for the first time in American history. The new wave of electoral opportunity was reinforced by the passage of the Civil Rights and Reconstruction Acts of 1866 which required all Southern states, excluding Tennessee, to extend citizenship to African Americans. Any state that refused to acknowledge Blacks as full citizens with voting privileges forfeited their right to be recognized by the United States Congress. The two acts – The Civil Rights Act and Reconstruction Acts of 1866 – were responsible for the election of the largest number of Black representatives prior to the full-scale political empowerment of African Americans in the post-civil rights era (Foner, 2002; Tate, 2003).

In Mississippi, Louisiana, and South Carolina, new Black voters were responsible for the election of a host of Black legislators including the first Black member of the House of Representatives – Joseph Rainey in 1870 – and the first Black member of the US Senate – Hiram Rhodes Revels (Franklin and Moss, 2000).

In several states, Blacks, who constituted the largest demographic constituency, controlled the state legislatures. For the first time since their arrival in America in the 1600s, former slaves were exercising their rights to engage in a host of American institutions, amenities, and opportunities as they pleased. During this era of Black Reconstruction, African Americans not only participated in electoral politics, they also reasserted their independence and self-determination by breaking away from the oftentimes racist and segregationist White church (some of whom advocated slavery as the will of God), they opened their own businesses, bought property, and asserted themselves as full-fledged citizens to the disdain of many of their White community members (Franklin and Moss, 2000).

During the Black Reconstruction Era, African American leadership of the

Box 5.3 Black Reconstruction Era Congressional Legislators

Representative   **Joseph H. Rainey** (Republican, South Carolina) 1870–1879
Representative   **Jefferson F. Long** (Republican, Georgia) 1870–1871
Representative   **Robert C. DeLarge** (Republican, South Carolina) 1871–1873
Representative   **Robert B. Elliott** (Republican, South Carolina) 1871–1874
Representative   **Benjamin S. Turner** (Republican, Alabama) 1871–1873
Representative   **Josiah T. Walls** (Republican, Florida) 1871–1873, 1873–1875, 1875–1876
Representative   **Richard H. Cain** (Republican, South Carolina) 1873–1875, 1877–1879
Representative   **John R. Lynch** (Republican, Mississippi) 1873–1877, 1882–1883
Representative   **James T. Rapier** (Republican, Alabama) 1873–1875
Representative   **Alonzo J. Ransier** (Republican, South Carolina) 1873–1875
Representative   **Jeremiah Haralson** (Republican, Alabama) 1875–1877
Representative   **John A. Hyman** (Republican, North Carolina) 1875–1877
Representative   **Charles E. Nash** (Republican, Louisiana) 1875–1877
Representative   **Robert Smalls** (Republican, South Carolina) 1875–1879, 1882–1883, 1884–1887
Representative   **James E. O'Hara** (Republican, North Carolina) 1883–1887
Representative   **Henry P. Cheatham** (Republican, North Carolina) 1889–1893
Representative   **John Mercer Langston** (Republican, Virginia) 1890–1891
Representative   **Thomas E. Miller** (Republican, South Carolina) 1890–1891
Representative   **George W. Murray** (Republican, South Carolina) 1893–1895, 1896–1897
Representative   **George Henry White** (Republican, North Carolina) 1897–1901
Senator   **Hiram Rhodes Revels** (Republican, Mississippi) 1870–1871
Senator   **Blanche K. Bruce** (Republican, Mississippi) 1875–1881

political, economic, and sociocultural arena was historic in that the same people who had been labeled by many as incapable of engaging in rational decision-making were in some Southern states like North Carolina the leaders of the legislature. The prominence of African Americans in a host of American institutional pillars was unsettling to many and proved to be one of the determining factors in the waves of violence initiated against freed men, women, and families as well as the steady yet pronounced retreat of the United States government – in particular the Freedmen's Bureau – as a guarantor of African American freedom and protection. The short rise to power of African American leaders was both aided and ended by the Republican Party and its inability and unwillingness to put it all on the line for its Black electoral population (Weiss, 1983; Barker, Jones, and Tate, 1998).

In addition to the betrayals of the Republican Party which will be examined in the next section, the Black Reconstruction Era was short-lived due to the decisions of the Supreme Court to uphold racist and segregationist practices designed to reinforce the Black Codes of slavery. Put into effect after the Civil War and the subsequent passage of the 13th Amendment, the Black Codes, which were adopted by Southern states, legally defined the rights and privileges of citizenship of freedmen. In many respects, the Black Codes amounted to a re-articulation of slavery as some of the legalese used words such as "servant" to define freed Black men and women and "master" to define owners of land. As such, the Black Codes, which later evolved into Jim Crow laws, continued legal discrimination against Blacks. Although they were no longer called "Black Codes," the close of the nineteenth century, along with the US Supreme Court ruling in Plessy vs. Ferguson, introduced African Americans to yet another barrier in the quest for complete legislative participation and policy articulation – Jim Crow laws.

Clearly, Jim Crow laws were just as harsh, restrictive, and backward as Black Codes which barred African Americans from participating in electoral politics, owning businesses or weapons of any kind without permission, or gathering without at least one White person present. The difference between the Black Codes and Jim Crow laws, however, was that the latter gave the appearance of inclusion in that they were instituted under the Supreme Court guise of "separate but equal" which stipulated that races of people could be segregated by race so long as the accommodations of the groups were equal. The danger of both the Black Codes and Jim Crow laws was that they reinstituted a system of African American inferiority and dependency on power structures similar to those discussed in the colonial model of governance in chapter 2 of this book.

The betrayals of the party of Lincoln

While the electoral success of Blacks during the Reconstruction era was unprecedented, perhaps even more astounding was the betrayal of the Party of Lincoln, also known as the Republican Party. In an interesting but predictable turn of fate, the Republican Party – the party so supportive and instrumental in the initial stages of Black electoral leadership – in a backroom deal to return power to White Southerners betrayed its Black party members in two politically shattering ways. The betrayal of the Republican Party, arguably, should have been expected as the Party of Lincoln never completely abolished slavery in the United States when given the opportunity to do so. And, similar to his Democratic compatriot of the twenty-first century, President Lincoln had an issue or two with flip-flopping as he continued to go back and forth on the issue of slavery from a pragmatic political perspective. Still, as mentioned, the Republican Party's failure to act effectively, rendered two significant blows to African American Congressional power which would leave this group lifeless until the subsequent rise of Black politics during the 1950s and 1960s (Dawson, 1995).

The first political blow occurred when the Party of Lincoln withdrew federal troops which served as a buffer and protector of Black political, economic, and sociocultural interests in the aftermath of the Civil War (Barker, Jones and Tate, 1998). The removal of Freedmen's Bureau troops spoke volumes in terms of party support for Southern plantation owners, many of whom feared for both their livelihoods and lives as a result of the passage of the Civil War Amendments. The second political blow to African American political incorporation and enfranchisement occurred when the Republican Party acquiesced and withdrew support and protection of critical Civil War legislation (the Reconstruction Act and the 13th, 14th, and 15th Amendments) which prohibited the obstruction of Black citizenship rights, due process, and voting rights (Foner, 2002). For example, the Supreme Court declared in the Civil Rights Cases of 1883 (a combination of five separate cases) that it had no jurisdiction to outlaw racial discrimination by private individuals and groups. These betrayals, coupled with the era of Jim Crowism opposition, led to the death of Black Congressional participation and presence for almost three decades. To be exact, during the era of Jim Crowism, there were no Black elected officials. The Black Congressional vacuum lasted 27 years and subsided with the election of Oscar DePriest (R-IL) in 1928.

Black Congressional inroads in the twentieth century

From the end of the Black Reconstruction era to the passage of the Voting Rights Act of 1965, only seven African Americans were elected to Congress. The seven African American members of Congress were: Oscar De Priest (R-IL), Arthur W. Mitchell (D-IL), William L. Dawson (D-IL), Adam C. Powell, Jr (D-NY), Charles C. Diggs, Jr (D-MI), Robert N. C. Nix (D-PA), and Augustus F. Hawkins (D-CA). Interestingly, all of these men served in the US House of Representatives and represented more progressive electoral regions of the Midwest and East and West Coasts. The relatively dismal number of Black elected officials was reflective of the failure of all three branches of government to protect Black electoral interests including the right to vote absent Jim Crow-era techniques such as the grandfather clause, poll taxes, and literacy tests, one-person, one-vote procedures, and reapportionments based on 10-year census guidelines.

The increase in the number of Black Congressional members can be directly attributed to the passage of the historic Voting Rights Act of 1965 (Tate, 2003; Pohlmann, 1999). According to the Act, it is unlawful to prohibit and/or deny African Americans the right to vote and/or to use any discriminatory or obtrusive measures to hinder their right to vote. The Act was primarily targeted towards Southern states deeply immersed in segregation and also made voting requirements such as the grandfather clause illegal. After the passage of the Voting Rights Act of 1965, the number of Black elected officials on the national, state, and local level dramatically increased as the electoral participation of Black voters increased by upwards of 50 percent nationwide. Some Voting Rights Act Black Congressional milestones include the election of the first African American female member of Congress (Shirley Chisholm, D-NY) in 1969, the election of the first African Americans representing the South since the Black Reconstruction era (Barbara Jordan, D-TX and Andrew Young, D-GA), and the political realignment of African American voters and representatives with the Democratic Party.

Plate 5.1 *Members of the Congressional Black Caucus*

Today, there are 43 African American members of the US Congress. Although these men and women are effective descriptive representatives of their constituency bases in that they represent a variety of race-specific issues and interests, these men and women are still significantly underrepresented as they do not even comprise 1 percent of the 535 members of the House of Representatives and US Senate. Further, African American members of Congress, especially those in leadership positions, must focus on valence issues as many of their seniority-based committee assignments deal with appropriations, the judiciary, and ways and means none of which are race-specific and/ or directly deal with African American interests. According to Katherine Tate (2003), a large majority of African American members of Congress focus on committee assignments that provide some form of constituency service as a means of aiding their home bases. In this way, African American members of Congress seek to be descriptive representatives who provide substantive policy and financial aid to their majority-minority constituency districts.

Reapportionment and racial redistricting

According to the US Constitution, Congressional districts must be reapportioned every ten years based upon demographic shifts as reflected in Census Bureau data (which occur every ten years). Known as apportionment, every ten years US House of Representative seats are redistributed based on population shifts throughout the 50 states. The problem with apportionment is that it can be manipulated to give an unfair advantage to certain parties. Gerrymandering, which is the manipulation of electoral districts to provide an unfair advantage to a political party and/or candidate, has long been used as a tool of political manipulation and suppression to hinder the African American vote as well as to provide an unfair advantage for competing interests and groups.

Although the initial history of gerrymandering was not race-based in its intent, the subsequent use and practice of gerrymandering, specifically the tactics of packing and stacking minority Congressional districts, has been extremely racialized in the post-civil rights era (Swain, 1993; Gilliam, 2002; Lublin, 1997). During the 1960s, the Supreme Court ruled in the landmark Baker vs. Carr case that voting disadvantages based on malapportionment (the distribution of state and federal legislative districts with unequal numbers of constituents) were no longer outside the jurisdiction of the highest court of the land and violated the due process and equal protection of minority voters. In effect, racial gerrymandering – which occurs when state or federal legislative districts are drawn to negatively impact the Black vote – was against the law.

In an effort to remedy past discriminatory efforts, Congress reinforced and strengthened the Voting Rights Act of 1982 (an extension of the VRA of 1965) by making electoral districts which weakened minority voting illegal. Some contend that the additional language in the Voting Rights Act of 1982 led to the creation of majority-minority districts that were based on packing districts, with African American voting majorities of upwards of 80–90% of the African American voting age population that sometimes spanned the entire geography of the state. Identified by some as odd, eccentric, and unintelligible districts based solely on race, in 1993, the Supreme Court ruled against the creation of majority-minority districts which used race as the sole criterion of their creation.

In my opinion, the Supreme Court ruling in Shaw vs. Reno (509 US 630 (1993)) was a short-term remedy and quick fix, knee-jerk racial reaction to a problem – a disproportionate number of African American elected officials especially on the federal level – that still has not been remedied and ails the effective political representation and policy inputs/outputs of Blacks in America. In effect, it seems as if the Supreme Court used Shaw vs. Reno to further penalize African American voting interests in that the majority of the Court left remedying the problems of minority voting bias, vote dilution, and low levels of African American descriptive representation in the hands of Congress – the same institution that had failed to legislate on behalf of those people it was theoretically designed to represent. As such, the paltry number of African American members of Congress, in my estimate, stems from the failure of Congress and the Supreme Court to effectively act to find substantive solutions to the short-term, albeit temporarily effective, symbolism of majority-minority legislative districts. The failure of two of the nation's leading institutions – the US Congress and the United States Supreme Court – to act, coupled with state-led initiatives to enforce mandatory voter ID legislation continues to make the African American vote vulnerable. Thus, even with the election of the first African American president and his impending

Supreme Court nomination, we still must ask how much progress has been made when there are almost an equal number of African American legislators now as there was during the Black Reconstruction Era of 1865. Moreover, what is the point of the Voting Rights Act of 1965 and its subsequent extensions if in 2008 individuals must by law provide proof of residency in a state in the form of picture identification before they can participate in democratic elections?

The Congressional Black Caucus

The Congressional Black Caucus is an umbrella organization of the 43 African American members of Congress. The CBC is a policy-specific, interest- and advocacy-based voice for the collective Black agenda in the United States (Singh, 1998). Although there were a variety of issues that led to the formation of this Congressional advocacy arm, most scholars agree that the three main factors that led to the development of the CBC were (1) the leadership vacuum caused by the assassination of Dr Martin L. King, Jr; (2) the rise in the number of Black Congressional members as spurred by the passage and enforcement of the Voting Rights Act of 1965 as well as landmark Supreme Court rulings including Baker vs. Carr (1962) and Reynolds vs. Sims (1964); and (3) the election of Richard Nixon who was a strong supporter of the Southern Strategy – a Republican Party initiative to gain election by appealing to White voters through anti-civil rights campaigns.

The Congressional Black Caucus was formally established in 1971 although the early informal gathering of the CBC in the form of the Democratic Select Committee began in 1969 (Smith and Walters, 1996; www.congressionalblack-caucus.net/history). Renamed the Congressional Black Caucus during the 92nd Congress, the 13 founding members of the CBC represented a variety of Black interests and constituencies around the nation. The mission of the CBC has been to provide substantive policy and legislation for African Americans, as well as an action network for those who may not have the political clout or acumen to express their political, economic, education, healthcare, or employment needs (www.congressionalblackcaucus.net).

The Congressional Black Caucus has evolved from a highly symbolic, reactionary organization to a stable and effective insider player. Currently, there are 43 members of the CBC who provide a cross-section of Black representation, coming as they do from urban, rural, and suburban areas to represent a variety of socio-economic constituencies and geographic areas. Throughout the years, the CBC has been an outspoken critic of apartheid, the US's treatment of Haitians, the Rwandan conflict, and most recently the failure of the Bush administration during the Hurricane Katrina fiasco and its failure to act related to the atrocities in Darfur, Sudan. Although the CBC has not been able to provide as much substantive legislation to its constituents, its members, through a range of bill co-sponsorships, have been able to pair up with members on both sides of the legislative halls to produce a relative amount of service delivery to its voters (Tate, 2003). The CBC has also been able to use its strong Democratic influence to partner with Congressional Republicans to block executive branch power, including the 1993 alliance to block President Clinton's line-item veto power.

The CBC works with the Congressional Black Caucus Foundation (CBCF), its non-partisan, non-profit arm which serves to "broaden and elevate the influence of African Americans in the political, legislative, and public policy arenas" (www.cbcfinc.org). The CBCF sponsors a variety of policy, leadership, and educational programs including its Annual Legislative Conference (ALC) which allows its members a platform to share their Congressional work, solicit support, and discuss/develop policy positions on a variety of issues that directly impact the Black community. In spite of its visibility and voice on certain issues, for more than 30 years it seems as if the CBC has remained a largely symbolic, intensively partisan, political group that has been effectively neutralized by both the Democratic and Republican Party apparatus.

African American inroads in Congress have been small yet somewhat effective as models of both descriptive and substantive representation. Moreover, given the passage of the Civil Rights Amendments, African American members of Congress have also been blessed to witness a generational effect as some African American leaders as well as members of Congress have witnessed their offspring pick up the torch of Black political, economic, and sociocultural empowerment they began. In the next section we will examine the generational impact of Harold Ford, Jr and Jesse Jackson, Jr. Both of these African American Congressmen come from rich civil rights families and have carved out their own niche of influence and empowerment by utilizing the most powerful branch of government as their soapbox.

Following their father's generational lead: Harold Ford, Jr and Jesse Jackson, Jr

The inroads of African American legislators in the post-civil rights era has allowed for a new era of generational leaders to either walk directly in their family members Congressional footsteps or pave new federal policy inroads beneficial to the African American collective agenda on the local, state, and national level. In this regard, two men who have continued the activist legacies of their fathers are Harold Ford, Jr and Jesse L. Jackson, Jr. Both of these men carved out their own agenda of legislative activism and leadership in the United States House of Representatives that first began with the inroads of their fathers – both history makers in their own right.

Harold Ford, Jr

Harold Ford, Jr (D-TN) is no stranger to politics. He is the son of Harold Ford, Sr – the first African American member of the House of Representatives in the twentieth century. Harold E. Ford, Jr entered the US House of Representatives at 26 and has served the 9th district of Tennessee for five consecutive terms. It is well known that Ford, Sr groomed his son to take over his Congressional safe seat after serving 11 terms in office. In his efforts to redirect some of his often-times controversial and in-your-face politics (many of which alienated his White constituents), Ford, Sr steered his son in a clearly Democratic-centered, policy-centrist position in an effort to garner a re-emerging White vote in the majority-Black 9th Congressional district of Tennessee.

As planned, Harold Ford, Jr branded himself as a moderate Democrat with strong family values. In this regard, his voting record documented his moderate leanings as he voted in support of the war in Iraq, opposed same-sex marriage, voted against partial birth abortion, and advocated for universal healthcare coverage for all American citizens. In his ten years of Congressional service, Ford served on a variety of committees, including the Budget Committee and the House Committee on Financial Services. He also co-chaired the Congressional Savings and Ownership Caucus and the Community Solutions and Initiatives, and was a member of the Department of Defense's Transformation Advisory Group and the Blue Dog Coalition (www.haroldfordjr.com).

In 2006, Congressman Ford expanded his electoral horizons and unsuccess-fully ran for the US Senate. "Ford for Tennessee" was the Congressman's cam-paign motto and focused on a variety of critical issues that impact not just his constituents but all Americans. Some of the noteworthy issues Ford advocated on behalf of was the ASPIRE Act which seeks to provide investment savings accounts for all children born in America, affordable healthcare, education, and national security. Although his bid for the US Senate was unsuccessful, Harold Ford, Jr received a great deal of support from women and college stu-dents throughout the state of Tennessee (Women for Ford and Team Ford) alike and was endorsed by the region's most well-known newspaper – *The Tennessean* – and a host of local- and state-level economic, political, and religious leaders. While in the House, he was known as consensus builder who worked on both sides of the aisle to provide pragmatic solutions for not just African Americans but all Americans. At present, former Congressman Ford is the chairman of the Democratic Leadership Council (www.haroldfordjr.com).

Jesse L. Jackson, Jr

Jesse Jackson, Jr entered the 104th Congress with a rich array of group mobili-zation and organizing skills under his belt. No stranger to the political world, Jesse L. Jackson, Jr grew up under the enormous grassroots mobilization and civil rights legacy of his well-known father, Jesse Jackson, Sr, the oftentimes controversial, rhyming, two-time Democratic Party presidential candidate and civil rights activist known worldwide for his negotiating skills on behalf of US troops and hostages.

Prior to his electoral success, Jesse L. Jackson, Jr served as the national field director of the Rainbow Push Coalition – the civil rights organization founded and led by his father, Jesse Jackson, Sr. As the national field director, he successfully registered more than a million new voters. Additionally, Jackson, Jr was heavily involved in efforts to end the segregationist system of apartheid in South Africa and even spent time in jail for his activist effort surrounding the issue (jessejacksonjr.org).

As a five-term member of the United States House of Representatives, Jesse L. Jackson, Jr is a member of the Appropriations Committee. He is also the fifth-ranking Democrat on the subcommittee on Labor, Health and Human Services, and Education and is the second-ranking Democrat on the Subcommittee on Foreign Operations, Export Financing, and Related Programs. Under the leadership of Jackson, Illinois's 2nd District has received more than 400 million dollars in federal grant awards to provide a wide array of facade redevelopment and concrete service delivery to constituents. Congressman Jackson is extremely interested in issues of fairness and equality and was a vocal supporter of the renewal of the Voting Rights Act of 1965. Jackson has continued his emphasis on fairness and equality and introduced 13 legislative bills covering a wide array of issues including the right of all US citizens to public education, healthcare, affordable housing, and full employment.

Having her say: Cynthia McKinney

Introduced to the political arena by her father, former Georgia state representative Billy McKinney, Cynthia McKinney's first political experience came as a write-in candidate in 1988. During her tenure in the Georgia General Assembly, McKinney was responsible for a rule change which had previously banned women from wearing pants in the legislative hall. After a successful bid on the state level, in 2000, McKinney ran and won Georgia's racial gerrymandered 11th district – a newly created majority-minority district that McKinney helped to formulate which stretched from Atlanta to Savannah – a close to four-hour drive by car. As Georgia's first African American female member of Congress, McKinney developed a strong track record of being pro-union, an advocate of education, against the death penalty, and in favor of tax cuts for the wealthy proponent. Considered an impenetrable incumbent, McKinney's smooth sailing experienced rough seas when in the aftermath of the September 11, 2001 crisis she engaged in open criticism of President Bush, claiming that he had prior knowledge of the attacks and allowed such to happen to benefit his personal and family financial interests (cynthiafor-congress.org).

According to her critics, Congresswoman McKinney's unseemly behavior did not stop there. She also personally wrote Saudi Prince Alwaleed and offered to accept 10 million dollars in aid refused by former New York City Mayor Rudolph Giuliani. The final crashing wave to McKinney's solid rock cruise liner of success occurred when her father blamed the problems of Black America on Jews during an evening television broadcast. These events led to McKinney's first Congressional defeat as a ten-year Congressional incumbent to freshman legislator Denise Majette. Majette, a former judge who was heavily bankrolled by anti-McKinney supporters, defeated the Congresswoman by a voting margin of 16% (Majette received 58% of the vote compared to McKinney's 42%).

In spite of what many contended was the good tidings of a bad representative of the state of Georgia, McKinney regained her Congressional seat in 2004 when it became open because Majette decided to run for the US Senate. In April of 2006, however, McKinney found herself in the spotlight again for assaulting a Capitol Hill police officer. The incident, coupled with her unbridled criticism of President Bush and the frustration of many of her constituents related to her increasingly haphazard behavior, caused many McKinney loyalists to shift their support to long-time Dekalb County Commissioner Hank Williams who challenged the Congresswoman. Although McKinney was ahead during the primary, she was defeated by Williams in the run-off when he garnered 59% of the vote compared to only 41% garnered by McKinney. Labeled a time bomb by many, her defeat has been championed as an end of an era of embarrassment and political malfeasance for both the state of Georgia and African Americans in general.

In all actuality, however, the political contributions of the female Congresswoman cannot be dismissed as she was responsible for a host of legislative agendas designed to provide substantive policy to African Americans in her home state and throughout the nation. Known as the voice for the voiceless, during her five terms in Congress McKinney was responsible for having the rural parts of her district designated as an Empowerment Community, was a member of the House Armed Services Committee and of the House International Relations Committee. Her track record for rolling up her sleeves to work with "the least of these" is impressive and undoubtedly has been generated by misunderstood and perhaps even ill-timed political passion, courage, symbolic and substantive representation that has yet to be duplicated in the Congress.

In profile: Barack Obama

US Senator Barack Obama is the second African American to represent the state of Illinois and the first to hold the highest office in the land. A Harvard Law School graduate, Obama has been a committed civil rights attorney, community organizer, and Illinois state senator. During his seven-year career in the Illinois state senate, Senator Obama worked with both Democrats and Republicans to fight for the rights of children and families. Some of his successes included the state-wide Earned Income Tax Credit program and early childhood education initiatives (www.barackobama.com).

Box 5.4 Senator Barack Obama Speech – The National Council of La Raza, July 22, 2007

"The real reason that so many people are coming out and signing up is because they see in this campaign the potential for the change Americans are so hungry for. It's not just the kind of change you hear about in slogans from politicians every few years; it's the kind of bottom-up, grassroots movement that can transform a nation . . . it won't be enough to change parties in this election if we don't also change a politics that has tried to divide us for far too long. Because when we spend all our time keeping score of who's up and who's down, the only winners are those who can afford to play the game – those with the most money, and influence, and power."

Source: http://www.barackobama.com/2007/07/22/remarks_of_senator_barack_obam_21.php

---

As a US Senator, Barack Obama was an outspoken voice for truth and empathy in politics and championed a variety of issues including relief efforts for the victims of Hurricane Katrina, the crisis in Darfur, Sudan, homeland security, the environment, immigration, healthcare, education, and ethics and lobbying (www.barackobama.com). In addition to providing an array of constituency services, including coffee with the Senator, Obama served on several important Senate committees including Veterans Affairs, Foreign Relations, and Environmental and Public Works. He also served on several subcommittees including African Affairs, East Asian and Pacific Affairs, International Economic Policy, Clean Air, Climate, and Nuclear Safety.

Obama is well liked and respected throughout the nation and the world and is seen as a beacon of hope for many. The president's book, *A Time for Hope,* was identified as a Democratic Party blueprint for regaining the White House and many, including Oprah Winfrey, endorsed the Senator in his 2008 presidential election bid. The Senator ran on a platform aimed at strengthening America both at home and abroad by implementing a bipartisan agenda of change focused on galvanizing the 18–29-year-old voters, women, and minorities. To his credit, Obama drew crowds with upwards of 10,000 listeners eager to learn more about his holistic agenda of family, health, finances, education, faith, and environmental improvements and clean-ups.

Although some contended that Barack Obama lacked the necessary political experience to occupy the highest office in the land, in his remarks to the National Council of La Raza during the summer of 2007 he countered his pundits by challenging Americans to see through the smoke-and-mirror, divide-and-conquer tactics which seek to use terms like "inexperienced" to skirt the real issues of political balkanization, polarization, and separatist politics which are crippling the nation.

As president, Barack Obama has worked to restore trust, dignity, and respect to the highest office in the land. Along with First Lady Michelle Obama, the First Family has also brought a unique touch and feeling to the executive office by engaging in a host of hands-on and everyday activities including poetry slams, pick-up basketball games, and frequent visits to local DC eateries. Although President Obama has dealt with some right-wing criticism for his legislative and budgetary decisions, he continues to try to unify the country on the issues that matter most, including credit card protection, passage of automobile fuel efficiency laws, and access to education for all Americans.

Where do we go from here?

African American political inroads in Congress have experienced a variety of ebbs and flows from the Civil War to the present. In spite of both the favorable and unfavorable tides of African American inclusion in the legislative branch of government, members of the community have maintained a spirit of activism, group consciousness, and determination that has allowed them to respectfully remind the system that it must be true to what it wrote in the Constitution concerning the ability of all people regardless of race to have their say in the democratic processes of government.

In the post-civil rights era, African Americans have taken advantage of the political opportunities made available through Congress's passage of the Voting Rights of 1965 and have participated and elected into legislative office some of the largest number of Black officials in the history of the nation. Still, in the post-civil rights era there are only 43 African American members of Congress. These small numbers are not reflective of the population percentage of African Americans in the US nor do they truly reflect the spirit of democracy that in theory, at least, supports the notion of all people having equal access to the political system. There seems to be a gap for African Americans in terms of the practical applicability of such as it relates to the election of Black political officeholders.

As such, I believe it is incumbent upon the African American community to actively involve themselves in Congressional level politics in terms of organizing, mobilizing, and getting people out to the polls to support not only African American candidates that fit the descriptive nature of representation but those who substantively have the best interests of the African American community in mind.

In this regard, I think it is critical to the future of African American Congressional politics to focus on the development of bi-racial and multi-racial strategic alliances that seek to foster community building, trust, and common ground based on both race-specific policy agenda items as well as valence issues.

Moreover, African Americans need to develop closer linkages with both political parties, interest groups, and traditional civil rights organization in an effort to begin to select and support those candidates running for elective office that best represent the overall issues and opportunities of the districts they seek to win elective office in. In this regard, African American community organizations and activists may have to engage in issue awareness campaigns to educate the community about the importance of participating in both mid-term and four-year election cycles as well as the significance of electing into office those who will really represent the overall needs of the districts economically, politically, socioculturally, and in terms of the district demographics.

In the final analysis the beauty of the relatively new and healthy relationship between African Americans and Congress is that because of its youth there is still room for it to grow, develop, blossom, and mature into the founding fathers' original intent concerning the most powerful branch of government.

Points to ponder

1. In what ways did Congress as a federal institution fail African American legislative interests?
2. Briefly detail the three legislative styles of representation and the impact you believe they have on African American policy outcomes.
3. What inroads have occurred as a result of the formation of the Congressional Black Caucus? Do you agree with the mission and policy agenda of the Caucus? Please elaborate.
4. What is your position on racial gerrymandering? Is it a necessary evil or a quick-fix remedy?
5. What African American member of Congress profiled in the chapter best represents you and why? Please elaborate.

Key phrases and people

trustee	delegate	politico
Article I, Section 8	Barack Obama	packing
stacking	Cynthia McKinney	slave codes
Jim Crow Laws	Plessy vs. Ferguson (1896)	gerrymandering

6

African Americans and the President

There are many fascinating components of the American presidency. From the scope of presidential power which has dramatically increased over time to the politics of personality that often shapes executive branch decision-making and outcomes, the executive office of the United States of America proves to be one of the most interestingly unpredictable branches of government. In this regard, it is extremely important to keep in mind that the person that holds the "highest office of the land" is both an individual and an institution. As an individual, the president brings his unique personality, perspectives, leadership, and past electoral experiences to bear. As a key institutional player, the president must consider prior institutional precedents, partisan loyalties, and the long-term viability and credibility of the office in his decision-making.

Arguably, it is the unpredictable nature of the most powerful branch of government, coupled with both its individual and institutional considerations, that has shaped the highs and lows of African American political power and progress in the Oval Office. In this chapter, we will explore the scope, influence, and rise of executive office power over time, examine some of the African American policy inroads which were initiated in the executive office, and examine the impact of African American political voice and leadership on executive office decision-making. Moreover, we will explore the politics of personality as it relates to African American substantive policy outcomes via the executive branch, the ways in which partisanship, political ideology, and religiosity impact presidential popularity among African Americans, and offer insight into the future African American executive branch inroads.

Saving the union . . . The institution and the individual

Seemingly, one of the most mythical aspects of American political history has been the portrayal of former president Abraham Lincoln as the great emancipator of African slaves throughout America. For centuries, President Lincoln has been praised for his endorsement of the Emancipation Proclamation and for his seemingly progressive political stance related to the equality of Black people. While some of the political sentiments of President Lincoln were true – from an individualistic standpoint he believed slavery was morally wrong – the sentiments of the president from an institutional standpoint were different in that he could not let his individual perspective cloud the institutional legacy he was elected to serve and protect. From an individual standpoint, President Lincoln was cognizant of the toil the unspoken issue of slavery wrought on the nation.

> If we shall suppose that American slavery is one of those offenses which, in the providence of God, must needs come, but which, having continued through His appointed time, He now wills to remove, and that He gives to both North and South this terrible war, as the woe due to those by whom the offense came, shall we discern therein any departure from those divine attributes which the believers in a Living God always ascribe to Him? ... With malice toward none; with charity for all; with firmness in the right, as God gives us to see the right, let us strive on to finish the work we are in; to bind up the nation's wounds; to care for him who shall have borne the battle, and for his widow, and his orphan – to do all which may achieve and cherish a just and lasting peace, among ourselves, and with all nations. (Lincoln, Second Inaugural Address, 1865)

The remarks shared during President Lincoln's second inaugural address reflect his individual belief that one of his primary duties as the leader of the nation was to bind up the wounds, in particular slavery, which wreaked havoc and death on the country.

From an institutional perspective, however, President Lincoln was clear in understanding his fiduciary responsibility to preserve and protect the interests of the Union.

> My paramount object in this struggle is to save the union, and is not either to save or destroy slavery. If I could save the union without freeing any slave I would do it, and if I could save it by freeing all the slaves I would do it; and if I could save it by freeing some and leaving others alone I would also do that – what I do about slavery and the colored race, I do because I believe it helps to save the union – I do less whenever I shall believe what I am doing hurts the cause – I shall try to correct errors when shown to be errors; and I shall adopt new views so fast as they shall appear to be true views – I have here stated my purpose according to my view of official duty; and I intend no modification of my oft-expressed personal wish that all men everywhere could be free. (Lincoln, Letter to Horace Greeley, 1862.)

Thus, as many political observers note, Lincoln's institutional responsibility outweighed his individual ideology and moral underpinnings. As he shared, his primary objective was to "save the union." In this context, "the union" is the constitutional and institutional mechanisms of the United States of America which include the executive, legislative, and judicial branches, separation of powers, checks and balances, federalism, and the institutional mores that protect and maintain these systems. Although Lincoln has been championed as the "Great Emancipator" of African American people, it may be argued that his greatest role was that of an institutional player who understood the fundamental balance of being both an institution (the leader of the executive branch) and an individual (one who has personal beliefs, ideologies, and thoughts). As such, perhaps Lincoln's greatest gift was that of a cautiously calculated institutional leader who fostered paradigmatic change for African Americans. As Walton and Smith detail, "in his timid, cautious, moderate approach to dealing with the freedom of African Americans, Abraham Lincoln is the paradigmatic president, setting an example – a pattern or model – for the handful of other American presidents who have dealt in a positive way with the African American freedom quest" (Walton and Smith, 2007: 185).

Presidential power

The power of the president is detailed in Article II of the US Constitution. Specifically, Article II, Sections 1 through 4, detail the requirements, roles, and duties of the leader of the executive branch. To begin, Article II, Section 1, Clause 5 details the citizenship and age requirements of the executive branch. Any person wishing to become president of the United States must be a natural-born citizen and at least 35 years of age:

> Clause 5: No Person except a natural born Citizen, or a Citizen of the United States at the time of the adoption of this Constitution, shall be eligible to the Office of President, neither shall any Person be eligible to that Office who shall not have attained to the Age of thirty-five Years, and been Fourteen years a resident within the United States.

Since the election of Arnold Schwarzenegger as Governor of California there has been very loose talk about a possible constitutional amendment to remove the "natural-born Citizen" provision to allow naturalized citizens an opportunity to be elected. In addition to the citizenship and age requirements, Article II, Section 2, Clauses 1–3 detail the roles and responsibilities of the president. Although the power of the president through Article II, Section 2 is rather limited, especially in comparison to the Congress, some presidents have used a loose interpretation of the clause to expand and extend presidential power over time.

The five most widely accepted roles of the president are commander in chief, chief executive, chief diplomat, chief legislator, and head of state (US Constitution, Article II, Section 2, Clauses 1–3). Each role displays a unique yet potentially overlapping function of the executive office. The five roles are detailed below:

Commander in Chief – As commander in chief, the president serves as the head of the United States Armed Forces. In this role, "The President shall be the Commander in Chief of the Army and Navy." The commander in chief has the power to appoint top military executives.

Chief Executive – As chief executive, the president is the head of the federal bureaucracy. In this regard, the president is the symbolic CEO of more than 2 million federal government employees. As chief executive, the president has influence over the Executive Office of the president, the 15 Cabinet Departments, and 60 executive agencies.

Chief Diplomat – As chief diplomat, Article II, Section 2 gives the president the power to make treaties, executive agreements, and to appoint and receive foreign dignitaries. The president is required to engage with the "advice and consent of the Senate" in executing these powers.

Table 6.1 Cabinet level departments

Department of State	1789
Department of the Treasury	1789
Department of Interior	1849
Department of Agriculture	1889
Department of Commerce	1913
Department of Labor	1913
Department of Defense	1947
Department of Housing & Urban Development	1965
Department of Transportation	1966
Department of Energy	1977
Department of Health & Human Services	1979
Department of Education	1979
Department of Veteran's Affair	1989
Department of Homeland Security	2002

Chief Legislator – As chief legislator, Article II, Section 3 details the power of the president to initiate and implement public policy. The most well-known aspect of this presidential role is the Constitution provision for the president to "give to the Congress Information of the State of the Union." Every January, most Americans have at least one of their favorite television hours interrupted as the president details his policy agenda for the year.

Head of State – As the head of state, the president acts in his ceremonial role as the leader of the United States of America. In this role, the president represents the nation both domestically and abroad and participates in a variety of American pastimes such as throwing the opening pitch on the first day of the baseball season. Additionally, as head of state, the president has the power to grant pardons and reprieves as well as appoint federal and Supreme Court judges.

Undoubtedly, African Americans have benefited from some of the roles of the president more than others. Nonetheless, it seems as if the president's role as commander in chief and chief executive have been most beneficial to African Americans as former President Truman integrated the armed forces and the federal bureaucracy continues to employ a large number of African American civil servants. Two other executive branch powers that have provided limited benefit to African American interests are executive orders and the power of appointment. Whereas executive appointments can be limited to presidential reign in office, executive orders can be more lasting as they are in effect executive office policy legislation on a particular issue.

Box 6.1 Executive Order 10925

The contractor will not discriminate against any employee or applicant for employment because of race, creed, color, or national origin. The contractor will take affirmative action to ensure that applicants are employed, and that employees are treated during employment, without regard to their race, creed, color, or national origin. Such action shall include, but not be limited to, the following: employment, upgrading, demotion or transfer; recruitment or recruitment advertising; layoff or termination; rates of pay or other forms of compensation; and selection for training, including apprenticeship.

Source: www.eeoc.gov/abouteeoc/35th/thelaw/index.html

In terms of African Americans, the most well-known and misunderstood executive order was Executive Order 10925 which outlined the policy of affirmative action – executive branch policy prohibiting discrimination in the issuance of government contracts. Executive Order 10925 also set precedent for Executive Order 11246 which extended affirmative action to minorities, women, and the disabled.

As a policy output, affirmative action was signed into law by former President Lyndon B. Johnson and revised by former President Richard M. Nixon. Affirmative action has been extremely controversial as many have unfairly labeled it as a "Black" quota system when in fact the greatest beneficiaries of the program have been White women. Moreover, the policy has been highly divisive as many White Americans feel as if (1) they are being denied jobs, employment, and educational opportunities and (2) they are being blamed for the "sins" of their forefathers. Although affirmative action was signed into law by the president, the US Supreme Court, it seems, will continue to decide the fate of the executive order.

Limited access granted – the executive branch and Black substantive policy

The political influence of African Americans on the executive branch of the United States of America has been at best limited. In spite of the historic influence and "cracked" door access of men and women such as Frederick Douglass (President Lincoln), Booker T. Washington (President Theodore Roosevelt), Mary McCleod Bethune (President Franklin D. and First Lady Eleanor Roosevelt), the Big Six civil rights leaders – A. Philip Randolph (Brotherhood of Sleeping Car Porters), James Forman (Congress of Racial Equality), Dr Martin L. King, Jr (Southern Christian Leadership Conference), John Lewis (Student Nonviolent Coordinating Committee), Roy Wilkins (National Association for the Advancement of Colored People) and Whitney Young, Jr (The Urban League) (President John F. Kennedy and President Lyndon B. Johnson) to presidential administrations, the current reality of Black executive branch political influence and access appears highly symbolic and limited to a few hand-selected

Black presidential political appointees and self-appointed *spiritual* advisors. In this regard, although Black national-level political development and incorporation remains critical to the long-term success of "Black interests," it seems as if an executive office gateway of Black political empowerment and incorporation may remain historic and relatively symbolic. Part of the relative symbolism of the relationship between the executive branch and African Americans may be related to the racist attitudes and mindsets that have shaped many of the individuals elected to office. As Walton and Smith contend, the majority of American presidents have either been racist or race-neutral in terms of the official executive office position on African Americans.

> Of the 43 men who have served as president, very few have been allies in the African American freedom struggle. On the contrary, most have been hostile or at best neutral or ambivalent . . . Twenty-three (more than half) were white supremacists, including as we have said, Abraham Lincoln. Eighteen have also been racists, supporting either slavery (including eight slave owners) or segregation and racial inequality. Thirteen have been neutral or ambivalent in their attitudes toward African American freedom. Nine – Lincoln, Grant, Benjamin Harrison, Truman, Kennedy, Johnson, Nixon, Carter, and Clinton – have pursued anti-racist policies in terms of the emancipation of the slaves and their freedom and equality in the United States. (Walton and Smith, 2007: 190–1)

It should come as no surprise that the majority of African American executive office inroads have occurred in conjunction with the changing of the guard related to the nation's perception and treatment of African Americans which was fueled and influenced through the political, economic, and sociocultural realignment of the civil rights era of the 1950s and 1960s. Arguably, the paradigmatic shift of the movement fostered such an atmospheric change in Black political behavior, ideology, and expectation that holders of the highest office of the land have been forced in some way to respond to the resounding demands of Black political incorporation and substantive policy delivery. The following provides an examination of executive office African American appointments and policy outputs from former President Harry S. Truman through the Bush II administration.

Truman

In spite of the ambivalence, empty words, and pattern of non-decision-making of those executive office leaders before him, former President Harry S. Truman's sometimes bold and pragmatic leadership could have served as a model of executive office Black political incorporation and substantive policy delivery. The political potential of President Truman was enormous as he was the first executive branch leader in more than 50 years to step out and build political associations and relationships with African Americans. In his executive capacity, President Truman used his executive office power and influence to introduce critical anti-lynching and job discrimination legislation (Pohlmann, 1999). Additionally, President Truman was responsible for the passage of two critical executive orders – E. O. 9980 (1948) which established a policy of non-discrimination in government employment and E. O. 9981 (1948) which banned discrimination in the armed forces. Still, the failure of President Truman to move beyond symbolism in relation to his presidential actions towards African Americans proved difficult for African Americans, especially those in the armed services as he refused to integrate their rank in the military which maintained their second-class status. Moreover, similar to Truman's passage of E. O. 9981, the majority of the president's civil rights executive decisions lacked effective implementation and therefore rendered them insufficient as a remedy for past discriminatory actions against African Americans (Barker, Jones, and Tate, 1998). As such, the presidential leadership of Truman was lukewarm at best, as African Americans really did not gain substantive service delivery from the leader of the nation.

Eisenhower

President Dwight E. Eisenhower is perhaps most well known for his decision to dispatch the National Guard to Little Rock, Arkansas to ensure that the Little Rock Nine (the first African American students to be integrated into a public high school in the post-Brown vs. Board of Education ruling) were protected. Although the president's decision may appear to have been supportive of "Black interests," it is a well-known fact that, similar to the decision of President Lincoln on Emancipation, Eisenhower's dispatch of the US National Guard was simultaneously focused on ensuring that the laws of the *union* were upheld by the states (Wicker, 2002).

Like his predecessor Harry S. Truman, Eisenhower also utilized his power of the pen in support of African American interests. In 1953, Eisenhower signed E. O. 19479 into law. The executive order in many respects was a continuation of Truman's two previous orders and stated that a "Government Contract Committee [would be established] to ensure that government contractors and subcontractors comply with non-discrimination provisions in employment" (E. O. 19479, 1953). Similar to his predecessor, President Eisenhower's executive branch actions towards African Americans were highly symbolic in that the president only moved when forced to do so and used as little governmental authority and legitimacy as possible. In an ironic twist of events, President Eisenhower's appointment of Earl Warren as Chief Justice of the United States Supreme Court passively made him a substantive champion of civil rights as the progressive thinking of Warren provided the most substantive policy inroads for African Americans in the history of the United States.

Kennedy

The Camelot presidency of the nation's youngest and extremely charismatic leader – John F. Kennedy – may have been blemished by his reluctance to

Plate 6.1 *President Lyndon B. Johnson and African American civil rights leaders*

aggressively support African American civil rights. Although Kennedy received 75% of the Black vote in the 1960 presidential election, he was very slow to mark his executive agenda with overt gestures in support of African American inter- ests. The majority of Kennedy's actions were highly symbolic. One example of his symbolism was Executive Order 11063. Although E. O. 11063 banned dis- crimination in federally assisted housing, Kennedy took two years to actualize his campaign promise to end housing discrimination in rentals and homes for sale which proved to be the greatest area of inequality for African Americans. In the end, Kennedy's promise to end housing discrimination with the "stroke of the pen" was another in a series of unfulfilled promises that caused prominent civil rights leaders including Dr Martin L. King, Jr to withhold electoral support in the 1960 presidential election (Carson and Shepard, 2001: 149–50).

Johnson

By far, President Lyndon B. Johnson was the most proactive executor of African American civil rights. In his landmark "We Shall Overcome" speech, Johnson clearly defined the terms of his presidency.

> As a man whose roots go deeply into Southern soil, I know how agonizing racial feelings are. I know how difficult it is to reshape the attitudes and the structure of our society. But a century has passed, more than a hundred years since the Negro was freed. And he is not fully free tonight. It was more than a hundred years ago that Abraham Lincoln, a great President of another party, signed the Emancipation Proclamation; but emancipa- tion is a proclamation, and not a fact. A century has passed, more than a hundred years, since equality was promised. And yet the Negro is not equal. A century has passed since the day of promise. And the promise is unkept. The time of justice has now come. I tell

you that I believe sincerely that no force can hold it back. It is right in the eyes of man and God that it should come. And when it does, I think that day will brighten the lives of every American. (Lyndon B. Johnson, 1965)

This heartfelt address revealed Johnson's commitment to right the wrongs of the past. During his tenure, Johnson was responsible for signing three major civil rights bills into law – the Civil Rights Act of 1964 (a comprehensive act designed to eradicate racial discrimination in the public and private sector), the Voting Rights Act of 1965 (eliminating voting restrictions for African Americans and other minorities), and the Civil Rights Act of 1968 (banning housing discrimination). Additionally, President Johnson was the first president to appoint an African American to the Supreme Court (Thurgood Marshall) and engage in a massive program to redirect and address economic inequality through his "war on poverty" efforts.

Still, it must be noted that, in some respects, President Johnson was able to capitalize on the inability of President Kennedy to effectively legislate and as such was catapulted into the limelight of civil rights activism by default. As such, the question of the genuineness of Johnson's substantive policy implementation can never be truly measured as the historical record cannot be reinterpreted absent the Camelot years.

CIVIL RIGHTS ACT OF 1964

Title 2 – Injunctive Relief Against Discrimination in Places of Public Accommodation

Sec. 201: (a) All persons shall be entitled to the full and equal employment of the goods, services, facilities, and privileges, advantages, and accommodations of any place of public accommodation, as defined in this section, without discrimination or segregation on the ground of race, color, religion, or national origin.

VOTING RIGHTS ACT OF 1965

An ACT to enforce the 15th Amendment to the Constitution of the United States, and for other purposes. Be it enacted by the Senate and House of Representatives of the United States of America in Congress assembled, that this Act shall be known as the "Voting Rights Act of 1965."

Sec. 2: No voting qualification or prerequisite to voting, or standard, practice, or procedure shall be imposed or applied by any State or political subdivision to deny or abridge the right of any citizen of the United States to vote on account of race or color.

FAIR HOUSING ACT OF 1968

Sec. 801 [42 U.S.C. 3601] Declaration of Policy: It is the policy of the United States to provide, within constitutional limitations, for fair housing throughout the United States.

Sec. 802 [42 U.S.C. 3602] Definitions:

[. . .]

(b) "Dwelling" means any building, structure, or portion thereof which is occupied as, or designed or intended for occupancy as, a residence by one or more families, and any vacant land which is offered for sale or lease for the construction or location thereon of any such building, structure, or portion thereof.

(c) "Family" includes a single individual.

(d) "Person" includes one or more individuals, corporations, partnerships, associations, labor organizations, legal representatives, mutual companies, joint-stock companies, trusts, unincorporated organizations, trustees, trustees in cases under title 11 [of the United States Code], receivers, and fiduciaries.

(e) "To rent" includes to lease, to sublease, to let and otherwise to grant for a consideration the right to occupy premises not owned by the occupant.

(f) "Discriminatory housing practice" means an act that is unlawful under section 804, 805, 806, or 818 of this title.

(g) "State" means any of the several States, the District of Columbia, the Commonwealth of Puerto Rico, or any of the territories and possessions of the United States.

Nixon

President Nixon was elected on a platform of devolution (returning power back to the states) and "law and order" (Brooker and Schaefer, 2006). The president's strong anti-civil rights campaign seemed to dissipate once in office as he strengthened Executive Order 11246 which "requires government contractors to take affirmative action as a prerequisite to the award of a contract." In revising E. O. 11246 through E. O. 11245, Nixon demanded that reasonable timetables must be established to enact these policies. Additionally, E. O. 11245 was extended to a variety of arenas including employment and education. Ironically, President Nixon inadvertently became a substantive policy champion of African American civil rights in that his "teach a man to fish" ideology empowered a host of African American government contractors, entrepreneurs, and business leaders in spite of his strong, divisive, and offensive anti-civil rights rhetoric. In some respects, Nixon as an institutional leader can be credited with developing a model of African American economic empowerment which served as a means of overcoming past racial discrimination. Still, as an individual, much was to be desired of the man who was known to make derogatory remarks about African Americans, women, and other racial/ethnic minorities.

Ford

Presiding over one of the shortest executive office terms, former President Gerald Ford is most well known for his failure to commit to federal government enforcement of Court-ordered school desegregation through busing. In addition to flip-flopping on the issue of busing, Ford also took a lukewarm position on civil rights, in spite of his personal beliefs that the Republican

Party needed to be more inclusive of racial and ethnic minorities. In spite of his passive executive leadership in the realm of African American public policy, President Ford made history as the first president to appoint an African American to a cabinet position – William T. Coleman (Secretary of Transportation). Still, Ford's relationship with his African American constituency remained symbolic as he never utilized his executive privilege to solidify substantive political inroads and gains for Blacks in America.

Carter

Known as the favorite son of the South, President Carter was responsible for the most visible, high-level African American appointment in the history of the nation. Under his executive office leadership, President Carter appointed Andrew Young – former Atlanta mayor and top aide to Dr Martin L. King, Jr – as the United States Ambassador to the United Nations (Barker, Jones, and Tate, 1998; Walton and Smith, 2007). Carter also appointed a high-profile African American female, Patricia Harris, as the cabinet head of the newly divided Department of Housing and Urban Development (HUD). Additionally, President Carter, like Nixon, appointed a large number of African Americans to a wide array of bureaucratic, sub-cabinet positions (Smith and Walters, 1996). Still, the greatest failure of the Carter administration was its overly symbolic African American appointments which lacked the political power and influence needed to effectively implement social change (Smith and Walters, 1996). Moreover, the Carter administration's development of government agencies such as the Department of Housing and Urban Development without providing the effective oversight, implementation, and financial resources needed to transform the urban communities the agency was designed to assist further substantiated the executive office symbolism of the administration that was elected via a strong Black vote, especially in the South.

Reagan

Without a doubt, the greatest contribution of the Reagan administration to Black interests was the federal King Holiday legislation. In November of 1983, President Ronald Reagan signed Public Law 98-144 which designated the third Monday in January as a federal holiday honoring slain civil rights leader Dr Martin Luther King, Jr. The holiday marked the first time in American history that the nation honored an African American with such a significant distinction.

The Reagan administration was also responsible for four high-level African American appointments. During his reign in office, Reagan was responsible for the appointment of Colin Powell (National Security Advisor), Clarence Pendleton (Chair of the Civil Rights Commission), Samuel Pierce (cabinet head of the Department of Housing and Urban Development (HUD)), and Clarence

Thomas (Chair, Equal Employment Opportunity Commission) (Smith and Walters, 1996; Newton, 2006). In effect, the Reagan administration provided an interesting mix of both symbolic and substantive legislation that would have a lasting effect long after the tenure of the famed actor subsided in the executive branch. Still, President Reagan was clear in his positioning on civil rights as in many respects his highly inflammatory and race-specific language sparked the resurgence of racialized politics, divided government, and the rise of Black neo-conservatism which blamed the fate of Black America on poor choices and the failure of African Americans to embrace the Puritan work ethic.

George H. W. Bush

As the 41st President of the United States of America, George Herbert Walker Bush promised to develop a "fresh" wind of change designed to reach out to African American constituencies. In this regard, Bush I was responsible for the appointment of Louis Sullivan (Secretary of Health and Human Services), General Colin L. Powell (Chair, the US Joint Chiefs of Staff), Condoleezza Rice (Director, National Security Council), and Clarence Thomas (US Supreme Court). Still, in terms of substantive policy initiatives, the Bush I administration did not provide any "kinder and gentler" transformative service delivery to African Americans as the president engaged in a highly symbolic and extremely distanced association with African Americans. As Barker, Jones, and Tate (1998: 311) articulate, the primary difference between the Reagan administration and the Bush I administration was "one of style not substance."

Clinton

William Jefferson Clinton made history in his appointment of four African Americans to top cabinet-level positions as well as his selection of several other African Americans to prominent executive office positions (Smith and Walters, 1996; Barker, Jones, Tate, 1998; Walton and Smith, 2007). During his first term in office, Clinton appointed Ron Brown (Secretary of Commerce), Jesse Brown (Secretary of Veteran Affairs), Mike Epsy (Secretary of Agriculture), and Hazel O'Leary (Secretary of Energy). Additionally, Clinton was responsible for the appointment of Clifton R. Wharton (Deputy Secretary of State), Jocelyn Elders (Surgeon General), Maggie Williams (Chief of Staff), and Alexis Herman (White House Office of Public Liaison). The unprecedented number of Black political appointees marked a significant change in African American executive office influence and policy-making. Clinton also apologized for slavery in America while on a trip to South Africa, organized a blue ribbon panel on Race Relations, and stated his "Mend It, Don't End It" position on affirmative action.

Seemingly, the hyperactivity of the Clinton administration was beneficial to African Americans as the man dubbed the nation's first "Black President" was "so fresh and so clean" that he played his saxophone on the Arsenio Hall Show (Wickham, 2002). In the final analysis, however, President Clinton was perhaps the greatest Democratic Party disappointment of African American substantive policy delivery. In fact, it has been contended that the Clinton administration engaged in a grossly symbolic eight-year campaign of African American policy manipulation that proved to be more detrimental than previous Republican administrations. In particular, during the Clinton administration the effective incorporation of Black interests was highly symbolic, usurped under the guise of proactive policy, and oftentimes relegated to the political realm of indecision and inaction (Smith and Walters, 1996; Walters, 1998).

George W. Bush

In spite of his anti-affirmative action policy stance, President George Walker Bush appointed a significant number of African Americans within the executive branch. Most notably, Bush was responsible for the historic appointments of Colin L. Powell as Secretary of State and Condoleezza Rice, first as National Security Advisor and then as Secretary of State, Roderick R. Paige as Secretary of Education, Alphonso Jackson as Deputy Secretary to Housing and Urban Development, Leo S. Mackay, Jr as Deputy Secretary of Veterans Affairs, Larry D. Thompson as the Deputy Attorney General, and Stephen A. Perry as Administrator of General Services Administration. Bush II was also responsible for the development of the Office of Faith-Based Initiatives, the No Child Left Behind campaign, and Low-Income Tax Credits and Vouchers.

Overall, African American economic and political success did not improve under the war-torn Bush II administration. Moreover, the failure of the housing industry, coupled with rising gas prices and natural disasters around the nation, did not see an increase in Bush II policy responsiveness towards African Americans or Americans in general. As such, the Bush II administration also remained a symbolic wreath-laying administration that has apparently left many, including children, behind.

Executive office symbolism or substance?

The relationship between the executive office and African Americans continues to remain a work in progress. In spite of a historic number of executive office post-civil rights era sub-cabinet and cabinet appointments, advisor positions, and ambassadorships, the majority of the executive branch courtesies extended to African Americans remains largely symbolic in that they revolve around top-level executive office and bureaucratic placements, proclamations, extensions of previously signed laws, and executive orders.

It is not surprising that African Americans have made the most substantive

Table 6.2 Executive Office Substantive Policy support rankings

Democrats	Republicans
1. Lyndon B. Johnson	1. Richard M. Nixon
2. Harry S. Truman	2. Ronald Reagan
3. William Jefferson Clinton	3. Dwight E. Eisenhower
4. Jimmy Carter	4. George Walker Bush

Table 6.3 Executive Office Cabinet Level appointment rankings

Democrats	Republicans
1. William Jefferson Clinton	1. George Walker Bush
2. Jimmy Carter	2. George H. W. Bush
3. Lyndon B. Johnson	3. Ronald Reagan

executive branch policy inroads when a Democrat has been in office. In this regard, President Lyndon B. Johnson leads all Democrats with his passage of three historic Civil Rights bills. Still, the Democrats or Republicans who have occupied the White House have not singularly supported or enacted legislation to provide paradigmatic change in the political, economic, or socio-economic status of African Americans. It seems as if no other president (past or present) has been as committed to improving the substantive economic and political livelihood of African Americans as was the former Southerner who realized that the improvement of African Americans was significant to the overall improvement of the United States of America.

Other Democratic executive office honors extend to former President Harry S. Truman and William Jefferson Clinton. In terms of Clinton, however, it must be noted that although he was dubbed America's first "Black" president, his executive office activity was not as pro-Black as his supporters, the media, and the Democratic Party have led many to believe. One example of the absence of substantive policy adoption – in spite of a historic number of African American cabinet members – was Clinton's 1996 decision to end "welfare as we know it."

In terms of Republican executive office chief executives, whether intentional or not, Richard Nixon provided the most substantive policy legislation with the passage of Executive Order 11245.

African American presidential support

There are many factors that impact African American support of the executive branch. Given the fact that African Americans tend to view the responsibilities and obligations of the government to its constituents differently than Whites, it should come as no surprise that a large amount of African American

Table 6.4 African American top five issues

Issue	Black Population		
	2004	2002	2000
Employment/economy	31%	23%	14%
Education	7%	14%	26%
Healthcare	20%	5%	18%
Terrorism	10%	17%	1%
War in Iraq	22%	6%	–

Source: 2004 Joint Center for Political and Economic Studies National Opinion Poll

Table 6.5 2004 presidential election voter registration and turnout, by race

Race	Reported Registered		Reported Voted	
	Total Pop	Citizen Pop	Total Pop	Citizen Pop
Whites	67.9%	73.6	60.3%	65.4%
African-Americans	64.4%	68.7	56.3%	60.0%
Hispanic	34.9%	57.9	28.0%	44.1%
Asian	34.3%	51.8	29.8%	44.1%

Source: CNN.com

presidential support is derived from a variety of domestic policy responses as well as the overall group success and progress of African Americans collectively. In this regard, African Americans have focused their presidential election support on the candidate that appears to be most committed to the African American agenda which has focused on the following issues: unemployment, education, healthcare, and ending the war in Iraq.

Black partisanship in the 2000 and 2004 presidential election

In both 2000 and 2004, an overwhelming majority of African Americans supported Democratic presidential candidates – Al Gore (2000) and John Kerry (2004). According to a CNN.com 2004 presidential election exit poll, African Americans overwhelmingly supported John Kerry. According to the data, 88% of African Americans who voted cast their vote for Kerry compared to 11% who voted for President Bush. These numbers were impressive given the increase in the number of African Americans who registered and turned out to vote in the national election.

Table 6.6 African American supporters of Hillary Clinton

Rep. Alcee Hastings (D-FL)
Rep. Charles Rangel (D-NY)
Rep. Yvette Clarke (D-NY)
Rep. Greg Meeks (D-NY)
Rep. Edolphus Towns (D-NY)
Rep. Laura Richardson (D-CA)
Rep. Diane Watson (D-CA)
Rep. Sheila Jackson Lee (D-TX)
Rep. Corrine Brown (D-FL)
Rep. David Scott (D-GA)
Rep. Emanuel Cleaver (D-MO)
Del. Donna Christian Chistensen (D-VI)
Attorney Willie A. Gary
Rev. William H. "Bill" Gray, former CEO of United Negro College Fund
Trenton (NJ) Mayor Doug Palmer
Buffalo (NY) Mayor Byron Brown
Former New York City Mayor David Dinkins

Source: hillaryclinton.com

In spite of Rap the Vote, Rock the Vote, and Motor Voter campaigns that increased Black voter registration and participation, African Americans were still unable to put their candidate – John Kerry – in the White House.

There are a variety of explanations as to how and why the Black vote came up short in both the 2000 and 2004 presidential elections. In the 2000 election, arguably the state of Florida with its various forms of chad, tad, and butterfly ballot controversy cost Al Gore the election as thousands of African Americans were disenfranchised. Beyond the controversy in Florida, the African American vote was also usurped in cities around the nation as polling centers closed in spite of the long lines of voters who waited upwards of eight hours to cast their ballots.

In a 2000, CNN.com election survey, African American respondents were asked the following: Do you feel cheated by the outcome of the election? Who would have won if the Florida recount had continued? Will President Bush work hard to represent African Americans? Sixty-eight percent of the African American respondents felt cheated by the election outcomes. Eighty-one percent of respondents believed that Al Gore would be elected if the Florida recount continued. And, seventy percent of African Americans did not believe that President Bush would work hard to represent their interests.

Table 6.7 African American supporters of Barack Obama

Rep. Sanford Bishop (D-GA)
Rep.William Lacy Clay (D-MO)
Rep. John Conyers (D-MI)
Rep. Elijah Cummings (D-MD)
Rep. Artur Davis (D-AL)
Rep. Danny Davis (D-(IL)
Rep. Keith Ellison (D-MN)
Rep. Chaka Fattah (D-PA)
Rep. Al Green (D-TX)
Rep. Jesse Jackson, Jr (D-IL)
Rep. Gwen Moore (D-WI)
Rep. Bobby Rush (D-IL)
Oprah Winfrey, Television Mogul
Massachusetts Governor Deval Patrick
Newark (NJ) Mayor Cory Booker
Richmond (VA) Mayor Douglas Wilder
Professor Cornel West, Princeton University
Michael Eric Dyson, Author
Alice Walker, Author
Rev. Jesse Jackson, Sr., Activist

Source: www.barackobama.com

For the first time in history an African American – Barack Obama – has been elected as president of the United States of America. Although Hillary Clinton made history and garnered more than 18 million votes during the primary season, she ultimately conceded and supported Senator Obama in his Democratic presidential bid.

Where do we go from here?

Clearly, the election of Barack Obama as president of the United States of America is both historic and, for some, unbelievable given the history of Blacks in America. Nonetheless, it is hoped that the new "President of Cool" will usher in a new paradigm of intellectual, racial, gender, and ideological diversity, economic opportunity, and political understanding both domestically and globally.

The one thing to keep in mind, however, is that the election of an African

American president will not automatically translate into substantive African American policy inroads and adoption from the Oval Office. Additionally, as the executive branch is both an individual and an institution, an African American president cannot abandon institutional norms in favor of an African American agenda. As such, the future of African American politics in terms of the executive office will continue to be an evolving partnership which employs a variety of executive office powers and privileges to ensure the continued emancipation of Black interests in America.

POINTS TO PONDER

1. In what ways has the executive branch been an instrument of change for African Americans?
2. Identify and briefly detail the five constitutional roles of the president.
3. What is your opinion on the political leadership of President Abraham Lincoln as both an institutional and individual player?
4. Discuss the executive office leadership of both the Democratic and Republican parties. How do the individual executive office leaders rank?
5. What are your expectations of the nation's first African American president, Barack H. Obama?

KEY PHRASES AND PEOPLE

Executive Order 10925	President Carter	Shirley Chisholm	President Ford
Executive Order 11246	Commander in Chief	President Truman	President Reagan
chief diplomat	President	President Bush	Carol Moseley
Head of State	Eisenhower	President Clinton	Braun
Chief Executive	President Kennedy	President G. H. W.	Jesse Jackson
Chief Legislator	President Johnson	Bush	Al Sharpton
	President Nixon	Fair Housing Act (1968)	Barack Obama

7

African Americans and the Judiciary

On again–off again

African Americans have endured a long, on again–off again relationship with the United States judiciary. In many respects, the tumultuous affair can be characterized as a fling, given the Court's penchant for non-decision-making and laissez-faire justice as it relates to genuine African American due process and equality under the law. In this chapter we will explore the seemingly schizophrenic nature of the American judiciary with regard to African American political incorporation and empowerment. From the insidious comments of former Supreme Court Justice Roger Taney to what some contend was the betrayal and hyperactivity of the Republican-appointed Warren Court, African American liberty and justice through the American legal system continue to be subject to the changing currents of American political leadership, public opinion, and larger institutional and structural tides. In this regard, the question we will examine in this chapter is whether or not the Court has been the best intermediary of African American interests and what, if any, avenues of recourse are available as the Supreme Court, in particular, becomes more and more conservative and possibly anti-civil rights?

African Americans and the US Constitution

As has long been articulated, one of the greatest silences of the US Constitution surrounded the issue of slavery in America. How ironic that one of the most touted international documents of freedom and equality was deafeningly silent on whether a class of people – legally classified as slaves – should be considered citizens of the United States of America and subject to all of the rights and privileges extended to its people. Prior to the ratification of the US Constitution, the framers engaged in persuasive debate about the citizenship status of slaves. One of the biggest concerns related to changing the status of slaves to US citizens was that it would produce an immediate political majority for the South as the demographic head count of its citizenry and its subsequent political power and authority in Congress would automatically increase. To curtail any impending unfair political advantage, the framers of the Constitution reached a compromise as to what to do with slaves. Known as the "Great Compromise," slaves were counted as three-fifths of a person so as not to give the South an unfair political advantage because of their population-based majorities.

The Three-fifths Compromise – Article I, Section 2, Clause 3, US Constitution

The loophole of the Great Compromise was that whereas slaves were considered somewhat a person (3/5s) for the purpose of political and geographic counting, in a rather convenient and self-serving fashion they were not considered persons in terms of the genuine extension of American civil liberties, rights, due process, and equality. One case in point of America's sliding scale of justice and equality was Dred Scott vs. Sandford (60 U.S. 393 (1857)). The case revolved around two issues: first, whether slaves based upon the language of the Constitution were citizens; second, what, if any, power did Congress have over free and slave territories. Dred Scott, a slave, was brought to Illinois (a free territory) by his owner and remained there for four years. Upon his return to Missouri, Scott petitioned the Court for his freedom and was granted citizenship by Missouri's lower court.

Scott's citizenship, however, was overturned by the Supreme Court of Missouri. In 1857, the US Supreme Court heard the case and upheld the Missouri Supreme Court decision. Prior to delving into the infamous ruling of Supreme Court Chief Justice Roger Taney, it must be noted his race-laced opinion was already substantiated within the confines of the Constitution. Both Article I, Section 2, Clause 3 and Article IV, Section 2, Clause 3 were written to protect and reinforce the institution of slavery in America.

ARTICLE I, SECTION 2, CLAUSE 3

Representatives and direct Taxes shall be apportioned among the several States which may be included within this Union, according to their respective Numbers, which shall be determined by adding to the whole Number of free Persons, including those bound to Service for a Term of Years, and excluding Indians not taxed, three fifths of all other Persons.

ARTICLE IV, SECTION 2, CLAUSE 3

No person held to Service or Labour in one State, under the Laws thereof, escaping into another, shall, in Consequence of any Law or Regulation therein, be discharged from such Service or Labour, but shall be delivered up on Claim of the Party to whom such Service or Labour may be due.

In essence, the beautiful language etched in the preamble of the US Constitution which claims to form a "more perfect Union, establish Justice, insure domestic Tranquility, provide for the common defense, promote the general Welfare, and secure the Blessings of Liberty" was never intended for nor extended to slaves and their descendents.

Supreme Court Chief Justice Roger Taney made this crystal-clear in his detailed ruling against Scott. In his ruling Taney wrote,

> The question before us is, whether the class of persons described in the plea in abatement compose a portion of this people, and are constituent members of this sovereignty? We think they are not, and that they are not included, and were not intended to be included, under the word "citizens" in the Constitution, and can therefore claim none of the rights and privileges which that instrument provides for and secures to citizens of the United States . . . they had for more than a century before been regarded as beings of an inferior order, and altogether unfit to associate with the white race, either in social or political relations; and so far inferior, that they had no rights which the white man was bound to respect. (Dredd Scott vs. Sandford, 60 U.S. 393 (1857))

The irony, however, is that in spite of Chief Justice Taney's very strong opinion, Supreme Court Justice McLean wrote in his dissenting opinion that the decision to view and treat slaves as less than human was a matter of choice not law or the Constitution. In the argument, it was said that a colored citizen would not be an agreeable member of society. This was more a matter of taste than of law. Several of the States had admitted persons of color to the right of suffrage, and in this view had recognized them as citizens; and this had been done in the slave as well as the free States.

Thus, the case of Dred Scott vs. Sandford served as a harsh reminder that regardless of the transparency and clarity of the Constitution, specifically the 5th and 14th Amendments, judicial interpretation can muddy and fog up the mirror of justice, equality, and liberty. Moreover, the belief that slaves were considered "things" reinforced both historic and modern interpretations of Blacks as being scientifically inferior, intellectually debasing, and morally corrupt both from a sociocultural, economic, political, and legal perspective. Moreover, the black eye of injustice first rendered by Justice Taney continues to shape African American interaction with the legal system and has led to several miscarriages of justice, including the "three strikes and you're out" law, harsher sentencing for African Americans, and a disproportionate number of African Americans tied up in the legal system. As such, the Court on both the federal and state level may in fact remain the last resort of African American liberty and justice depending on its structure, make-up, political leanings, and loyalties.

The Emancipation Proclamation and Civil War Amendments

The Emancipation Proclamation, along with the three Civil War-inspired constitutional amendments, seemingly turned the tide of the *hands off* approach of political leaders and governmental institutions with the legal authority to set precedent for African American judicial activism in the twentieth century. In particular, the fall-out between the Confederacy and Union related to the spread of slavery into the western territories of America caused President Lincoln to rethink his positioning as both an individual and an institutional leader of the United States.

The actions of Alabama, Arkansas, Florida, Georgia, Louisiana, Mississippi,

Box 7.1 Emancipation Proclamation

That on the 1st day of January, AD 1863, all persons held as slaves within any State or designated part of a State, the people whereof shall then be in rebellion against the United States shall be then, thenceforward, and forever free; and the executive government of the United States, including the military and naval authority thereof, will recognize and maintain the freedom of such persons and will do no act or acts to repress such persons, or any of them, in any efforts they may make for their actual freedom.

North Carolina, South Carolina, Texas, West Virginia, and Virginia, coupled with their subsequent seizure of federal property, prompted President Lincoln to rally Northern troops (as well as slaves who received manumission – citizenship – for serving in the military) to regain control of the South (Franklin and Moss, 2000; Foner, 1995, 2002). Upon restoring order to the extremely divided nation, Lincoln signed into law the Emancipation Proclamation which was perhaps the first proactive protection of Black interests within the scope of law.

There are many significant aspects of the Emancipation Proclamation. First, the executive office document ended slavery and in doing so overturned the scorned opinion of Justice Taney in Dred Scott (1857). Second, the Emancipation Proclamation clarified Lincoln's true position as both an individual and an institution. Although, as an individual, President Lincoln believed that the institution of slavery was morally reprehensible, as the leader of one of the most powerful institutions in America, he had to balance what was in the best interest of the nation as a whole. Lincoln made it perfectly clear that his desire was to do whatever possible to save the Union. As such, his decision to pen the Emancipation Proclamation was ultimately an institutional decision which pragmatically complemented his individual moral beliefs concerning slavery.

As he stated in his second inaugural address,

> One eighth of the whole population were colored slaves, not distributed generally over the Union, but localized in the Southern part of it. These slaves constituted a peculiar and powerful interest. All knew that this interest was, somehow, the cause of the war. To strengthen, perpetuate, and extend this interest was the object for which the insurgents would rend the Union, even by war; while the Government claimed no right to do more than restrict the territorial enlargement of it. (Bartleby, 2001, www.bartleby.com/124/pres32.html)

The political maneuvering of Lincoln is evident in that, even after the signing of the Emancipation Proclamation, substantive service delivery and federal government protection of freed slaves was slow and inconsistent. Moreover, freedmen and women were confined to seek their livelihood in federal government benevolence and good deeds (Cimbala and Miller, 1999). One such institution was the Freedman's Bureau which served as a short-term, highly symbolic measure that was ill equipped and incapable of addressing more than two hundred years of purposive, manmade, government-protected and reinforced oppression and discrimination based solely on race. Given the limited scope and protection of the Emancipation Proclamation, along with the deep-seated anger and retaliatory nature of many constituents of the former Confederate states, the US government was forced to provide other protections to former slaves as freedom alone was not enough to curtail and subdue the swelling flames of Confederate anger and rage that spread throughout the South (Franklin and Moss, 2000).

The passage of the 13th, 14th, and 15th Constitutional Amendments served as a first attempt to positively redirect the political climate in America during the aftermath of both the Civil War and slavery as both issues proved to be the knee-jerk reaction political issues of the day. Clearly, some of the saliency of the issue surrounded the fact that the Democratic and Republican parties did not want to do anything to totally harm the nation and its majority citizenry. As such, the Civil War Amendments were good-faith efforts of legal empowerment that were devoid of legal authenticity and authority because of the failure of the executive, legislative, and judicial branch to enforce the constitutional guarantees. The Civil War Amendments produced an evolutionary change in the perception and views of former slaves as "other" in that they were now granted the protection of the judiciary – the same institutional branch that treated them as concubines for more than 100 years.

Still, the protections extended through the Civil War Amendments were limited at best. Most notably, the freedoms extended to African Americans were usurped through the incorporation of Jim Crow laws and of separate but equal policies that restructured and repressed the freedoms extended and granted through the Civil War Amendments. The reversal of African American universal rights which began with the sliding-scale political incorporation of the legislative and executive branches was further solidified by the failure of the Supreme Court to execute equal justice in its landmark Supreme Court cases of Plessy vs. Ferguson (16 U.S. 537 (1896)), Sweatt vs. Painter (339 U.S. 629 (1950)), Brown vs. Board of Education (347 U.S. 483 (1954)[1] & 349 U.S. 294 (1955)), and Baker vs. Carr (369 U.S. 186 (1962)) which served to encrust the colonial model of governance and the second-class citizenship of African Americans from slavery through the passage of the Civil Rights Act of 1964. In the next section, we will examine some of these landmark cases in an effort to further substantiate the failure of the judicial system to act on behalf of African American interests even when a strict interpretation of the Constitution warranted fairness and equality for them.

African Americans and landmark Supreme Court cases

Plessy vs. Ferguson (16 U.S. 537 (1896))

In the case of Plessy vs. Ferguson, Homer Plessy, a man of one-eighth African blood, violated Louisiana law by refusing to give up his train car seat in the

White section of a railroad car. In challenging the state law, Plessy argued that the law violated his 14th Amendment rights. Interestingly, the Court used the landmark case of Plessy vs. Ferguson (1896) to institutionalize the Jim Crow system of separate but equal. As Justice Brown wrote in the majority opinion, "the object of the amendment [14th] was undoubtedly to enforce the absolute equality of the two races before the law, but, in the nature of things, it could not have been intended to abolish distinctions based on color, or to enforce social, as distinguished from political, equality, or a commingling of the two races upon terms unsatisfactory to either" (Plessy vs. Ferguson, 163 U.S. 537 (1896), Docket 210).

Plessy vs. Ferguson (1896) also served as the cornerstone case used by civil rights advocates to challenge the constitutionality of the separate but equal doctrines that unjustly reinforced African American inferiority until the 1950s. Further, through the judicial codifying of the Supreme Court, the nation which had recently emancipated slaves reinforced and re-established a second-class society for African Americans and sought to blame them and not the institutional players and mechanisms that created such an apartheid-like system in the land of the free and home of the brave, especially in the arena of state-enforced segregation. Moreover, as reinforced by the Plessy decision, Justice Brown argued that any feelings of inferiority were self-induced and therefore not the responsibility of the Court to rectify.

> We consider the underlying fallacy of the plaintiff's argument to consist in the assumption that the enforced separation of the two races stamps the colored race with a badge of inferiority. If this be so, it is not by reason of anything found in the act, but solely because the colored race chooses to put that construction upon it. [The] argument also assumes that social prejudices may be overcome by legislation, and that equal rights cannot be secured to the negro except by an enforced commingling of the two races. We cannot accept this proposition. (Plessy vs. Ferguson, 163 U.S. 537 (1896), Docket 210)

The proposition that the Supreme Court should have been unwilling to accept was the propaganda of Brown and others who consistently ignored the scope of the Constitution and the rights and privileges of citizenship, due process, equal protection, and suffrage that African Americans were supposed to be guaranteed. Moreover, the failure of the Supreme Court to aggressively interpret the law to speak to the evolving status of former slaves, yet provide loose interpretations of the Constitution on other issues that were beneficial to key political and economic stakeholders, further reinforced the on again–off again highly symbolic nature of their relationship with African Americans.

The unwillingness of both Congress and the Supreme Court of the United States of America to protect the interests, citizenship, and suffrage of African Americans caused African Americans to develop creative and ingenious ways to challenge the constitutionality of separate but equal laws by using the 14th Amendment, specifically, the equal protection clause, to challenge the racist and discriminatory nature of segregation during the nineteenth and twentieth centuries.

Missouri ex. rel. Gaines vs. Canada (305 U.S. 337 (1938))

One of the first landmark 14th Amendment equal-protection Supreme Court case challenges occurred in 1938 with the case of Missouri ex. rel Gaines vs. Canada. The facts of the case are as follows: Lloyd Gaines, an African American male, was denied admittance to the School of Law of the State University of Missouri because of his race. The Court ruled against the school's policy of denying Blacks admittance to the law school and instead paying for their tuition at other comparable out-of-state institutions as a means of complying with the separate but equal doctrine of Plessy vs. Ferguson (16 U.S. 537 (1896)). In his ruling, Chief Justice Hughes stated that it was not sufficient for the state to provide alternative educational opportunities because it still violated the equal rights of Negro students.

> The basic consideration is not what sort of opportunities other states provide, or whether they are as good as those in Missouri, but as to what opportunities Missouri itself furnishes to White students and denies to negroes solely upon the ground of color. The admissibility of laws separating the races in the enjoyment of privileges afforded by the state rests wholly upon the equality of the privileges which the laws give to the separated groups within the state . . . the White resident is afforded legal education within the state; the negro resident having the same qualifications is refused it there and must go outside the state to obtain it. That is a denial of the equality of legal right to the enjoyment of the privilege which the state has set up, and the provision for the payment of tuition fees in another state does not remove the discrimination.

Although the Court did not eradicate the doctrine of separate but equal in its decision, it was a step in the right direction as the state with only one institution had to grant admission to all students regardless of race.

Sweatt vs. Painter (339 U.S. 629 (1950))

Another equal protection case dealing with higher education was Sweatt vs. Painter. The facts of the case are as follows: Herman Sweatt was denied admission to the University of Texas Law School solely on the basis of his race. The University claimed that he could attend the newly created law school that was established for its Black student population. With the assistance of the NAACP Legal Defense Fund, Sweatt challenged the ruling of a Texas trial court that declared that the African American law school was comparable. In rendering the majority opinion of the Court, Chief Justice Vinson declared that the Texas court decision which stated that a separate law school for African Americans complied with the separate but equal provisions of Plessy vs. Ferguson (1896) violated the 14th Amendment equal protection clause. In his opinion, Vinson wrote that the Court was hard-pressed to find substantive equality between the two schools based on a variety of factors including the size of the faculty, library, and professional contact experienced at the two schools.

> Whether the University of Texas Law School is compared with the original or the new law school for Negroes, we cannot find substantial equality in the educational opportunities offered white and Negro law students by the State. In terms of number of the faculty, variety of courses and opportunity for specialization, size of the student body, scope of the library, availability of law [339 U.S. 629, 634] review and similar activities, the University of Texas Law School is superior. What is more important, the University of Texas Law School possesses to a far greater degree those qualities which are incapable of objective measurement but which make for greatness in a law school. Such qualities, to name but a few, include reputation of the faculty, experience of the administration, position and influence of the alumni, standing in the community, traditions and prestige. It is difficult to believe that one who had a free choice between these law schools would consider the question close.

In other words, there was no rational or logical way one could conclude that the Plessy decision was upheld and or that any feeling of inferiority experienced by Negroes was self-induced and therefore their responsibility to correct.

As Vinson stated at the close of his opinion,

> In accordance with these cases, petitioner may claim his full constitutional right: legal education equivalent to that offered by the State to students of other races. Such education is not available to him in a separate law school as offered by the State. We cannot, therefore, [339 U.S. 629, 636] agree with respondents that the doctrine of Plessy vs. Ferguson, 163 U.S. 537 (1896), requires affirmance of the judgment below. Nor need we reach petitioner's contention that Plessy vs. Ferguson should be reexamined in the light of contemporary knowledge respecting the purposes of the Fourteenth Amendment and the effects of racial segregation. [. . .] We hold that the Equal Protection Clause of the Fourteenth Amendment requires that petitioner be admitted to the University of Texas Law School. The judgment is reversed and the cause is remanded for proceedings not inconsistent with this opinion.

Brown vs. Board of Education Topeka, Kansas (347 U.S. 483 (1954))

Brown vs. Board of Education is perhaps the most well-known 14th Amendment equal protection case of African American judicial activism as it solidified the "on-again" nature of the relationship between the Court and its concubine. The facts of the case are as follows: Oliver Brown, along with 11 other plaintiffs, challenged a US District Court ruling favoring the decision of the Topeka, Kansas school board which maintained separate but equal elementary educational facilities for Black and White students. At issue for Mr Brown was the fact that his daughter, a third-grade student, had to walk six blocks to get to her bus stop to be taken to her all-Black elementary school when an all-White school was seven blocks from their residence.

Brown was argued before the US Supreme Court by Thurgood Marshall of the NAACP Legal Defense Fund who was later appointed to the United States Supreme Court (1967). In a unanimous 9–0 decision, Chief Justice Earl Warren argued that in separate but equal laws, facilities in the educational arena violated the equal protection clause of the 14th Amendment. He stated that "separate educational facilities are inherently unequal." Moreover, the Court, in one of the most activist moves of the twentieth century, argued that there were detrimental educational as well as psychological impacts of racial segregation in public education that needed to be remedied.

> Segregation of White and colored children in public schools has a detrimental effect upon the colored children. The impact is greater when it has the sanction of law, for the policy of separating the races is usually interpreted as denoting the inferiority of the Negro group. A sense of inferiority affects the motivation of a child to learn. Segregation with the sanction of law, therefore, has a tendency to retard the educational and mental development of Negro children and to deprive them of some of the benefits they would receive in a racially integrated school system. Whatever may have been the psychological knowledge at the time of Plessy vs. Ferguson, this finding is amply supported by modern authority.

Although Brown was severely fought on both the local and state level by mayors, school boards, governors and state senators who were anti-integration, the case ushered in a new wave of hope and possibility as many in the civil rights movement believed it was only a matter of time before the harsh realities of racial segregation and discrimination would subside. Moreover, the case opened the door to Supreme Court equal protection for African Americans for more than a decade.

Baker vs. Carr (369 U.S. 186 (1962))

According to former Supreme Court Justice Earl Warren, Baker vs. Carr was the most important case he ever decided. At issue was the state of Tennessee's failure to reapportion its state's legislative districts in more than 60 years. Mr Charles Baker sued the state on the grounds that his 14th Amendment rights were being violated as the state's failure to redistrict provided an unfair majority to rural residents of the state of Tennessee. In a 7–2 decision led by Justice Brennan, the Court ruled that reapportionment issues were justifiable. Going against former Justice Felix Frankfurter's belief that the Court should remain "outside of the political thicket," Baker vs. Carr opened the door for the Court's "one person, one vote" ruling in Reynolds vs. Sims (1964) which was responsible for the electoral empowerment of African Americans nationwide, especially in the South.

In Profile: Thurgood Marshall

Appointed by President Lyndon Baines Johnson in 1967, Thurgood Marshall became the first African American appointed to the United States Supreme Court. Justice Marshall's appointment was not only historic but it also further solidified the activist nature of the executive branch towards civil rights. Prior to his appointment, Marshall served as the chief counselor of the National Association for the Advancement of Colored People Legal Defense Fund (NAACP-LDF). For more than twenty-five years, Marshall diligently worked to eradicate the horrors of legal segregation and African American alienation through meticulous direct confrontation and exposed the hypocrisy and malfeasance of the 14th Amendment as it related to African American justice and equality (Williams, 1998). Marshall's most well-known victory was the landmark Brown vs. Board of Education (1954) decision. It must be noted, however, that Marshall served in the trenches for years, petitioning and winning favorable 14th Amendment Supreme Court decisions in the area of public education.

A bold articulator of what was prudent and right, Marshall often found himself in the minority as a member of the Court. Even in this most awkward role, given his long history of judicial success, Marshall utilized his dissenting opinion to further inject the collective American psyche with moral, economic, and political truths about what the nation needed to do to remedy hundreds of years of purposive and malicious race-based subjugation and annihilation. In his dissent of Regents of the University of California vs. Bakke (438 U.S. 265 (1978), Docket 76-811), Justice Marshall wrote,

> While I applaud the judgment of the Court that a university may consider race in its admissions process, it is more than a little ironic that, after several hundred years of class-based discrimination against Negroes, the Court is unwilling to hold that a class-based remedy for that discrimination is permissible. In declining to so hold, today's judgment ignores that fact that for several hundred years Negroes have been discriminated against, not as individuals, but rather solely because of the color of their skins. It is unnecessary in twentieth-century America to have individual Negroes demonstrate that they have been victims of racial discrimination; the racism of our society has been so pervasive that none, regardless of wealth or position, has managed to escape its impact . . . the dream of America as the great melting pot has not been realized for the Negro.

The power of Marshall's forthrightness and transparency related to the scar of racism in America – even in dissent – was so powerful that 25 years after this bold dissent, in University of California Regents vs. Bakke, Justice Sandra Day O' Connor referenced Marshall's thoughts in her swing-vote majority opinion in the landmark University of Michigan case (Gutter vs. Bollinger) (for more detail, see pp. 107–9).

Affirmative action: its original intent and aftermath

One of the most controversial issues of the twentieth century is affirmative action. Although initiated in the federal bureaucracy, affirmative action as we know it began under the auspices of the Johnson administration through Executive Order 11246. According to the language of the executive order, affirmative action was designed to remedy past discrimination by providing minorities and women with positive employment, education, and government contract opportunities. Although President Johnson has been credited with the establishment of affirmative action through passage of Executive Order 11246 in 1965, actually President John F. Kennedy was the first executive branch leader to initiate positive steps to correct years of racial discrimination. In 1961, President Kennedy signed Executive Order 10925 which established the Committee on Equal Employment Opportunity. The committee was charged with ensuring that government agencies and contractors take "affirmative action" to eliminate racial barriers in hiring and awarding government contracts. In 1969, President Nixon further strengthened the efforts of both Kennedy and Johnson by initiating the Philadelphia Plan. The Philadelphia Plan was a very forceful plan of minority hiring and government contract awards that had both goals and timetables (Smith and Walters, 1996).

By the mid-1970s, outrage over what many labeled reverse discrimination spilled out around the nation as anti-affirmative action advocates charged that the federal government policy was nothing more than a quota system for unqualified African Americans. The controversy surrounding affirmative action is whether the policy violates the 14th Amendment rights of White people. The 14th Amendment states that "No state shall make or enforce any law which shall abridge the privileges or immunities of citizens of the United States; nor shall any State deprive any person of life, liberty, or property, without due process of law; nor deny to any person within its jurisdiction the equal protection of the laws." The language asserting that no state shall deprive any person is what has been used to challenge affirmative action policies in college and university admissions, the awarding of federal government contracts, employment and hiring practices nationwide.

The most well-known affirmative action challenge occurred in 1978 with the case of University of California Regents vs. Bakke (438 U.S. 265 (1978)). The facts of the case are as follows: Alan Bakke, a White male, applied to the University of California Medical School on two separate occasions and was denied admittance both times in spite of the fact that during the same time period African American applicants with lower MCAT scores and grade point averages were admitted into the program. Bakke sued the University of California, Davis on the grounds that the school's special admissions program for minorities violated his 14th Amendment rights. In a 5–4 decision, the Court ruled in favor of Mr Bakke and granted him admission into the medical program. The Court also ruled in favor of using race as factor in admissions but stated that strict quota systems of race-based admissions programs which excluded certain races of people – specifically White Americans – were unconstitutional as they violated both Title VI of the Civil Rights Act of 1964 and the equal protection clause of the 14th Amendment.

Another highly divisive and extremely controversial higher education affirmative action case occurred in 2003 with the case of Grutter vs. Lee Bollinger (539 U.S. 306 (2003)). The case involved a young lady who was denied admission to the University of Michigan law school only to discover that African Americans and other minorities with lower admission scores were accepted into the school. Ms Grutter sued the university, claiming that the school's admissions policy which gives special consideration to diversity violated her 14th Amendment rights. In a two-prong decision dealing with undergraduate and graduate/law admissions, the Court ruled as follows: In terms of undergraduate admissions policy, the Court in a 6–3 decision ruled against the university's affirmative action program, citing that awarding extra points to racial and ethnic minorities is unconstitutional. In a 5–4 split decision, where Justice Sandra Day O'Connor provided the majority opinion, the Court upheld the law school's affirmative action program that puts special emphasis on matters on diversity.

> It has been 25 years since Justice Powell first approved the use of race to further an interest in student body diversity in the context of public higher education. Since that time, the number of minority applicants with high grades and test scores has indeed increased. We expect that 25 years from now, the use of racial preferences will no longer be necessary to further the interest approved today. (Grutter v. Bollinger, 539 U.S. 306 (2003), Docket 02-241)

As Justice O'Connor clearly detailed, she looked forward to the day when America matured beyond the necessity for racial preferences in public policy. More than three years after the ruling, affirmative action or, as some narrowly see it, African American action still is under the strict scrutiny of many who believe that it is simply a form of reverse discrimination that unfairly benefits unqualified, ignorant, and race card-playing freeloaders.

It is fair to say that the future of affirmative action in America is unknown. In spite of tepid support by former President Bill Clinton as well as the Court, many states including California (Proposition 209), Florida, Texas, and Washington have banned affirmative action in either state hiring and/or college/university admissions policies.

Judicial activism vs. judicial restraint

One of the questions faced by the Court is whether its nine members should actively pursue and accept cases of a political and/or sociocultural nature or if the Court should, as Justice Frankfurter admonished, remain outside of the "political thicket." There are two schools of thought related to the behavior of the Court. The first school of thought is judicial activism. A court that engages in judicial activism believes that the Constitution is a living document that can be adjusted and shaped to fit the needs of modern society. Those who believe and support judicial activism contend that the Court should take advantage of its unique, non-bureaucratic structure and engage in decision-making on issues related to the 1st, 5th, and 14th Amendments which benefit the ever-changing and rapidly modernizing nature of the larger American population (Lewis, 1999; Epstein and Walker, 1998). Although judicial activism goes against the grain of original intent – a school of thought that believes the Court should interpret the Constitution based on the original values and beliefs of the framers – many argue that it has been the activism of the Court, specifically the Warren Court, that must be credited for the enormous political strides of African Americans in the US.

In contrast to judicial activism is the school of judicial restraint. A court that engages in judicial restraint works to remove itself from engaging in and/or soliciting any cases that are political in nature (Kellogg, 2006). Moreover, similar to the school of original intent, proponents of judicial restraint argue against justices interpolating their personal views in the judicial decision-making process. In this regard, the Court tends to also defer to other legislative branches in dealing with questions pertaining to the constitutionality of certain decisions and/or policies unless such legislation directly and explicitly violates the law.

Although judicial restraint is theoretically noble, the fact still remains that the Supreme Court is a highly partisan, presidential-appointment controlled, personality-driven institutional branch laced with individual and global opinions about a range of political, economic, and sociocultural issues.

The Warren, Burger, and Rehnquist Courts

The controversy surrounding judicial activism and judicial restraint oftentimes is best examined in light of the leadership of a particular court. In this section, we will examine three well-known courts – the Warren, Burger, and Rehnquist Courts – and examine their record of judicial activism and/or restraint.

The Warren Court

Undoubtedly, the most comprehensive strides toward African American legal emancipation occurred under the leadership of Supreme Court Chief Justice Earl Warren. Appointed by President Dwight Eisenhower in 1953, Chief Justice Warren relied on pragmatic reasoning and moral rationality based on fairness to rewrite legal precedent which for more than a century relegated African Americans to second-class citizenry (Denton, 1972; Belknap, 2005; Lewis, 2006). Criticized by many for ignoring the original intent of the Constitution as well as crossing the line of the political thicket that the Court, in theory, allegedly remained out of, Chief Justice Warren was able to build both consensus and collegiality among the justices of the Supreme Court in an effort to "do justly, and to love mercy, and walk humbly with thy God." Thus, it came as no surprise that in his Bolling et al. vs. Sharpe et al. (347 U.S. 497 (1954)), Chief Justice Warren referenced the principles of liberty and equality as espoused in the US Constitution.

As long ago as 1896, this Court declared the principle

that the Constitution of the United States, in its present form, forbids, so far as civil and political rights are concerned, discrimination by the General Government, or by the States, against any citizen because of his race . . . Although the Court has not assumed to define "liberty" with any great precision, that term is not confined to mere freedom from bodily restraint. Liberty under the law extends to the full range of conduct which the individual is free to pursue, and it cannot be restricted except for a proper governmental objective. Segregation in public education is not reasonably related to any proper governmental objective, and thus it imposes on Negro children of the District of Columbia a burden that constitutes an arbitrary deprivation of their liberty in violation of the Due Process Clause.

Perhaps best known for his "with all deliberate speed" ruling in the landmark Brown vs. Board of Education (347 U.S. 483) decisions of 1954 and 1955, Chief Justice Warren's most overarching liberation of Black interests actually occurred with his ruling in Baker vs. Carr (369 U.S. 186 (1962)) and the landmark "one person, one vote" ruling which was instrumental in providing for the proper electoral representation of African Americans as well as ensuring the elimination of bias based on geographical location. As Warren shared in his majority opinion, "Legislators represent people, not trees or acres. Legislators are elected by voters, not farms or cities or economic interests . . . A nation once primarily rural in character becomes predominantly urban. But the basic principle of representative government remains, and must remain, unchanged – the weight of a citizen's vote cannot be made to depend on where he lives" (369 U.S. 186 (1962)). Warren's rulings, which usually focused on the sociological and psychological realities of the day, were responsible, as in the case of Baker vs. Carr (1962), for sweeping changes in the ways African Americans were able to participate in every area of American life. The end result of the Warren Court's ruling in Baker vs. Carr (1962) was both an increase in the number of Black elected officials nationwide and the guarantee of equal representation in both urban and rural areas.

Under the leadership of Chief Justice Earl Warren, the "Warren" Court engaged in a floodgate of civil rights policy implementation which included a reversal of the Plessy vs. Ferguson (163 U.S. 537 (1896)) decision, banned racial discrimination in education, clarified and extended voting rights, provided rights for the criminally accused, and provided a host of civil liberties to African Americans. Some of the cases decided under his leadership were as follows:

Baker vs. Carr (369 U.S. 186 (1962))
Reynolds vs. Sims (377 U.S. 533 (1964))
Gideon vs. Wainwright (372 U.S. 335 (1963))
Escobedo vs. Illinois (378 U.S. 478 (1964))
Miranda vs. Arizona (384 U.S. 436 (1966))

Clearly the activism of the Warren Court was not widely received. In fact, President Eisenhower allegedly lamented that his appointment of Warren was the biggest political mistake of his life as the Warren Court activism was seen as a direct affront to the highly symbolic and most often forced intervention of his presidential administration (Sabin, 1999). It has been argued that the actions of Chief Justice Warren did more for African American interests than the executive and legislative branch combined in that even the subsequent legislation of both Congress and presidential administrations were first mitigated by the actions of the Court. In effect, it seems that champions of Warren purport that absent Brown vs. Board of Education (1954) there would not have been key policy in favor of African American interests including the Civil Rights Act of 1957, the Civil Rights Act of 1964, the Voting Rights Act of 1965, the Fair Housing Act of 1968, or affirmative action.

In the final analysis, the progressive opinions of the Warren Court, in spite of a few missteps as was the case in the Court's second ruling of Brown which allowed lower state courts to implement school integration plans, provided a major step in the right direction of African American equal justice and equality and set precedent for a changing of the sociocultural and political guard as it related to the sociological and psychological treatment of this race of people in America.

The Burger Court

Supreme Court Chief Justice Warren Earl Burger was sworn into office by the then president Richard Nixon in 1969. Appointed to replace activist Chief Justice Earl Warren, Burger initially had many in the civil rights community up in arms as the strict constructionist became one of the loudest critics of the activism of the Warren Court. Interestingly, the Burger Court was responsible for one of the most decisive civil rights cases in the nation's history (Schwartz, 1998). In Swann vs. Charlotte-Mecklenburg Board of Education (1971), the Court unanimously ruled in favor of busing African Americans to curb de facto segregation. The Burger Court was also responsible for the landmark Roe vs. Wade case which extended a woman's right to privacy related to abortion. Some other landmark decisions under the Burger Court are as follows:

Furman vs. Georgia (408 U.S. 238 (1972))
United States vs. US District Court (407 U.S. 297 (1972))
Gregg vs. Georgia (428 U.S. 153 (1976))

The Rehnquist Court

Perhaps most well known for presiding over the presidential impeachment trial of William Jefferson Clinton, Chief Justice Rehnquist is known for his conservative, pro-state's rights positions. Sworn in as Chief Justice under the not-so-compassionate Reagan administration, Rehnquist was responsible for ushering in a wave of anti-civil and women's rights conservatism that has changed the nature of the illicit relationship between African Americans and the Court for ever. In a seemingly endless off-again swing, there have been glimmers of hope that these romancers still have not lost that lovin' feeling as was the case with Gutter vs. Bollinger (2003). Some other cases decided under the Rehnquist Court are as follows:

United States vs. Lopez (514 U.S. 549 (1995))
United States vs. Morrison (529 U.S. 598 (2000))
Zelman vs. Simmons-Harris (536 U.S. 639 (2002))

In spite of the conservative nature of the Rehnquist Court, interestingly, over the past 50 years the collective Court and its varied leadership has addressed a variety of issues that directly impact the political and economic livelihood of African Americans, including the integration of educational and public facilities, the right to privacy, the rights of the criminally accused, a woman's right to choose, affirmative action, busing, racially gerrymandered districts, and even election 2000.

Although, most believe the Court could have done a better job in executing justice in some of these decisions, the harsh reality is that absent the activism, good will, and collective conscious of these nine insular and politically tenured men and women, the struggle for African American equality and justice could be something that "deep in our hearts, we still believe."

Where do we go from here?

In spite of the civil rights era activism and good will of the US Supreme Court, many African American leaders are concerned with what appears to be side-stepping or a return to dark-age thinking as the Court, and particularly local and state courts and law enforcement agencies, have engaged in a host of suspect judicial actions and rulings that grossly misrepresent equity in the legal treatment and sentencing of African Americans. A case of particular note was the Georgia Supreme Court's recent overturning of the ruling in the Genarlow Wilson case. Wilson, who at age 17 engaged in a sexual act with a consenting 15-year-old, was sentenced to the mandatory minimum for sexual predators and served more than three years in prison for refusing to accept a plea deal which would have forced him under Georgia law to register as a sex offender and be unable to live in the same household as his adolescent sibling. In its decision, the Supreme Court of Georgia, led by Leah Ward-Sears, an African American female, ruled that the sentencing in the Wilson case was a "gross misrepresentation of justice." The Wilson case, the Jena Six case, and others seem to illuminate the fact that the Court and the US Justice Department have taken a laissez-faire approach perhaps to the detriment of the guarantees of the 5th and 14th Amendments.

As such, it seems as if the Court owes it to the entire American citizenry in general and African Americans in particular to address the issues surrounding sentencing disparities, the death penalty, and "three strikes and you're out" laws, all of which unfairly penalize and stigmatize African American and Latino men. Still, the relationship between African Americans and the Court has come a long way since the days of Chief Justice Taney and his narrow-minded belief that slaves had no rights that Whites were bound to respect. In terms of the future of African Americans and the judiciary, it may be necessary to return to the protest politics model of direct action as mere legislative and executive voice may not be enough to sway the intra-community network of the insular inner-working of the nation's High Court.

Points to ponder

1. In what ways was the decision of Chief Justice Taney in Plessy vs. Ferguson mitigated by racial intolerance and not a strict adherence to the letter of the law?
2. Explain the major differences between judicial activism and judicial restraint. What legal philosophy do you prescribe to and why?
3. In what ways did the activism of the Warren Court assist the political emancipation of African Americans in the political system?
4. In recent years what role has the Supreme Court played in leveling the playing field as a means of remedying past racial discrimination?

Key phrases and people

The Emancipation Proclamation
Dred Scott vs. Sandford (1857)
Plessy vs. Ferguson (1896)
The Civil War Amendments

Justice Roger B. Taney
Chief Justice Earl Warren
Thurgood Marshall
Reynolds vs. Sims

The Freedman's Bureau
Baker vs. Carr (1962)
The Burger Court
The Rehnquist Court

8

African Americans and Political Parties

One of the greatest misunderstandings of African American political behavior is the belief that African Americans have pledged undying loyalty and electoral support to the Democratic Party machine in America. Although it is not an uncommon occurrence to encounter network, cable, talk radio, and internet political commentators and pundits reflecting in terms of monolithic Democratic Party allegiance, the African American community has never been singularly focused on the party of the donkey. Although it has been reported that upwards of 85 percent of the African American community support the Democratic agenda, African Americans have always and will forever remain connected and somewhat politically aligned with the Republican Party (which is affectionately known as the Party of Lincoln).

In this regard, it is important to understand two phenomena. First, African American conservative agenda support is rooted in a long-standing traditionalistic viewpoint that has been a cornerstone of the African American experience in America – especially as espoused in the Black Church. Second, African American political alliance with the Democratic Party is also rooted in a long-standing belief in government intervention and involvement in the economic and social well-being of its citizens. In spite of the long-standing history of the African American community with the two major political parties in America, the instability of the relationship between the entities has been a source of political challenge and confusion throughout the years as African Americans have had to rely on other political institutions and mechanisms to ensure their electoral representation and voice in the American political system. On a more positive note, as African American political power has increased and expanded, both parties have been forced to reconsider and rethink their political strategies and outreach towards African Americans in an effort to court this vital electoral constituency base. In this chapter, we will examine the history of political parties in America, the impact of African American issues and interests on party formation, the impact of both the Democratic and Republican agendas on African American policy interests, and the increased number of Black Elected Officials (BEOs) in the post-civil rights era. Additionally, we will examine the future of African American politics and the role political parties will have in their continued political incorporation and empowerment.

"Federalist #10" and party formation in America

Although there is no Constitution authorization of language addressing the formation of political parties in America, it is widely known that many of the nation's founding fathers – especially James Madison – envisioned America as a nation of people that would wrestle and fight over competing issues and interests which were vital to their political access and influence in the nation. Thus, although there is not a formal impetus for political party formation in America, it can be argued and ascertained that party politics in America was intended to be a fundamental apparatus in the development and maintenance of democracy in America. As Madison detailed in "Federalist #10," an essay in a collection that advocated the ratification of the US Constitution, political party formation was a necessary evil to address the divided interests of humankind and its myriad passions.

> A zeal for different opinions concerning religion, concerning government, and many other points, as well of speculation as of practice; an attachment to different leaders ambitiously contending for preeminence and power; or to persons of other descriptions whose fortunes have been interesting to the human passions, have, in turn, divided mankind into parties, inflamed them with mutual animosity, and rendered them much more disposed to vex and oppress each other, than to cooperate for their common good.

In essence, Madison's writing reinforced the political philosophy of the self-interested man, as suggested by Thomas Hobbes, who would self-destruct absent political and institutional mechanisms designed to effectively channel his personal interests and concerns. Seemingly, it can be posited that political parties developed out of the manmade passions of men to protect and represent their agricultural, economic, and property interests. It must be noted however, that political party formation in America seems to go against Mancur Olson's (1971) belief that groups will not organize to advocate on behalf of public goods as today political parties advocate on behalf of a wide array of public interests and policy concerns. Perhaps this is the case because, unlike interest groups, parties operate under a broad range of party-issue and platform items which force them to embrace a more universal agenda of political change.

Why parties?

In spite of the founding fathers' reservations and concerns about political parties, these American entities are now widely accepted and viewed as cornerstone players in the American political system. Still, an accurate definition of political parties is rather difficult to come by as there are many explanations of political party proliferation in America. As such, from a theoretical perspective, the number one justification of political party formation in America is to provide organized mechanisms of governmental access, influence, and control for a broad range of constituencies and issue advocacy concerns. In this regard, political parties serve as nationwide umbrella networks of political candidacy which provide a variety of perks to group members including elected officials, elective office, legislation, and public policy which reflect member preferences and policy positions. In this regard, the political party serves as an organized apparatus of electoral control and advocacy for members who have common ideological perspectives.

A more pragmatic approach to political party formation identifies the efforts of political parties as designed to gain access to elected office in an effort to control government and public policy. In this regard, political parties organize to win elections on the local, state, and national level. In engaging in efforts to gain electoral victory, one of the primary purposes and benefits of political parties is their ability to provide communication and organization networks of information as a means of connecting party candidates to constituency groups across the nation. These formal networks of connection provide a lifeline of support to both incumbents and those running for office as the party apparatus can inform members of upcoming events, meet and greets, fundraisers, and the like at the click of a button through the use of technology and the internet.

In addition to the ultimate goal of winning elections in hopes of controlling the government, political parties also engage in a variety of activities vital to the maintenance and proliferation of fair, balanced, and accessible political participation in America. In this regard, political parties function in a variety of arenas that are essential to the American political system:

Organize elections   Political parties play a key role in organizing and determining the timing, requirements, and selection of candidates who are qualified to run for political office.

Develop political platforms   Political parties develop party agendas and issue action items that are designed to provide the electorate with a clear understanding of the party agenda, party issues, and party leadership dedicated to advocating on behalf of such issues.

Inform and connect with the electorate   Political parties use a variety of electoral strategies including mailers, email blasts, door-knocking campaigns, and town hall meetings to inform and connect with the voting population in America in hopes of strengthening its base of party loyalists as well as recruiting new members.

Recruit, develop, nominate, and run candidates for elected office   Political parties are heavily involved in the recruitment and development of viable electoral candidates who have what it takes to earn the party label as an endorsed candidate who can win electoral office for the party. In this regard, the party also tries to screen undesirable candidates as well as informally regulating the timing of those interested in running for office.

Win elected office on the local, state, and national level   The ultimate goal of political parties is to win electoral office on all three levels of government in an effort to control policy outcomes that impact the nation. As such, the party organization is a critical connector of party members and a key distributor of party interests and issues to complementary state and local party organizations.

In addition to the various functions of political parties in America, these vital instruments of political power in America also exercise their influence via a variety of "faces." By faces, we are referring to the three widely known views of political party operation. Popularized in the 1950s through V. O. Key and Frank Sorauf, the tripartite view of parties refers to the distinct yet interrelated aspects of the party as an institution, the party as a leader, and the party as an extension of the everyday person. In the next section, we will examine the three faces of political parties – the party organization, the party in the government, and the party in the electorate.

The party in the government   The party organization consists of the members of the political party at the local, state, and national level that are elected under the auspices of the party label/apparatus. On the national level, the party organization consists of the members of Congress that identify with a particular political party, vote in line with party preferences on an issue, participate in party leadership and network associations, and engage in activities to foster the party organization both on Capitol Hill as well as in their home district.

The party organization   In many respects, the party organization is the corporate face of the party. In this regard, the party organization is the official party umbrella organization that represents the party leaders, interests, and financial interests. In America, the two most well-known and recognized party organizations are the DNC (Democratic National Committee) and the RNC (Republican National Committee). Both the DNC and RNC are responsible for the connection of all things party-related to the lesser known state, county, and local level affiliates.

The party in the electorate   The party in the electorate consists of each and every American voter who identifies with a particular political party. The party in the electorate consists of both card-carrying party loyalists as well as those who vote along party lines on issues. In this regard, the party in the electorate consists of the young, old, rich, poor, educated, uneducated, male, female, religious, and non-religious cross section of all Americans.

The concentric nature of all three faces of the political parties provide a great deal of cross-marketing and name recognition for party candidates and platforms as every area of American life is either directly or indirectly influenced by party "talk" and activity. The end result of the complementary actions of

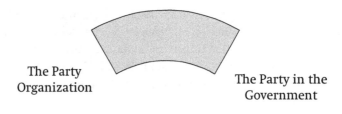

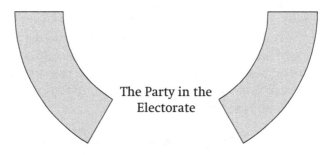

Figure 8.1 *The three faces of political parties*

the party in the government, the party organization, and the party in the electorate is a well-educated, informed, and partisan electorate that will do what is necessary to make sure the candidate of their choice is elected into office on the local, state, and national level.

The formation of African American political party identity

The historical record on the formation of political parties in America is extremely limited in terms of the role and impact of African Americans. Obviously, the almost invisible discussion, inclusion, and impact of African Americans is not surprising given the historical time period of the development of the nation's first political parties. The Federalists and Anti-Federalists did not have any substantive discussion or debate around substantive issues directly tied to the Black agenda. It seems that the primary reason was that, prior to the Black Reconstruction era, discussion of Black interests revolved around the issue of slavery and what to do with the "persons held to Service or Labor in one state"(US Constitution).

It is well known that the Republican Party – the party of the "Great Emancipator" Abraham Lincoln – was the most active advocate of Black political and economic interests in that it supported the abolitionist movement, the Emancipation Proclamation, and the Civil War Amendments (Foner, 1995). Given the Republican Party affections, naturally African Americans supported the Party of Lincoln once given the vote. The Republican Party activism of the late nineteenth century undoubtedly had a significant impact on the early formation of African American political party affiliation as African Americans consistently voted for the Republican ticket and party platform as it was most responsive to the issues of Black group consciousness and the linked-fate model of political participation. The arguably monolithic African American support of the Republican Party was in effect until the shift in party loyalty of Black interests which was solidified with the betrayal of former President Rutherford B. Hayes who gave in to Southern demands to restore the South back to its racist and segregationist ways in 1876 (Foner, 2002).

Prior to President Hayes's devastating political sell-out, emancipated slaves thrived as a result of several political acts spearheaded by Republican leadership including the "radical" Republicans who focused on Black economic opportunity. The most significant effort of the Republican Party was the formation of the Freedmen's Bureau – a federal government agency designed to assist, educate, and protect Southern Blacks. Additionally, the Republican-controlled 39th Congress was instrumental in the passage of the Civil Rights Act of 1866, the 14th Amendment, and the Reconstruction Act of 1867 which created the largest number of Black elected officials in the history of America. As Marcus D. Pohlmann contends,

> It is not difficult to understand why early allegiance went to the party of Lincoln, the Republicans, and not the southern-based and blatantly racist Democrats. Not only did the Republicans lead the "good fight" of abolition during the Civil War, the party subsequently produced the 13th, 14th, and 15th Amendments (The Civil War Amendments), Radical Reconstruction of the South, and the 1866 Civil Rights Act. (Pohlmann, 1999: 167)

Moreover, according to Eric Foner (1995, 2002), the Black Reconstruction era produced approximately 2,000 African American Congressmen. The partisan leadership cadre of African Americans spanned the South and included representatives of former confederate states including Alabama, Georgia, Louisiana, and South Carolina.

President Hayes's sell-out abruptly ended African American political party activity and reinforced a modern-day slave state through the implementation of Jim Crow laws which restricted African American political power and voice by the institutional adoption and enforcement of separate and unequal political, economic, and sociocultural laws as well as a host of disenfranchisement tactics such as the grandfather clause, poll taxes, and literacy tests which were all designed to exclude Blacks from access to and procurement of leadership positions in the American political system.

The best thing yet . . . African Americans and the Democratic Party

Arguably the betrayal and let-down by the Republican Party was the best thing for long-term African American political party inclusion and incorporation. The Democratic Party was forced to reconsider its staunch racist practices

Box 8.1 Franklin D. Roosevelt New Deal Coalition Relief Programs

The Agriculture Adjustment Act
The Civil Conservation Corps
The Emergency Banking Act
The Federal Deposit Insurance Corporation
The Federal Emergency Relief Administration
The National Youth Administration
The Tennessee Valley Authority

and the nation had to take a good look in the mirror as the issue of slavery all but demolished the credibility and integrity of the nation as a purveyor of freedom and justice. As such, the Democratic Party, in an effort to gain control of the national government, was forced to slowly begin to reach out to Blacks through a variety of formal and informal (sometimes even illegal) political strategies and tactics including machine politics and political patronage.

Although Blacks did not immediately exit the Republican Party, it was only a matter of time before the Democratic Party gangsta-like hard press of Black interests occurred. Most notably, the election of Franklin Delano Roosevelt and his "New Deal" political realignment strategies provided an all-inclusive, "come one, come all" multi-racial, ethnic, and interest-based coalition that provided the answer to African American Republican Party discontent. In the aftermath of the Great Depression of the 1930s, President Roosevelt's New Deal policies of government relief coalesced a motley crew of divergent interests including the poor, blue-collar laborers, union workers, racial, ethnic, and religious minorities (most notably African Americans, Catholics, and Jews), and Southern Whites. The Roosevelt administration provided a variety of relief efforts and government intervention and aid programs targeted at key constituency groups and New Deal Coalition members which caused a majority of eligible Black voters to support it (Weiss, 1983).

For 16 years, Roosevelt – the first president ever to be elected to four consecutive terms – provided a wide variety of government relief and aid. President Roosevelt's helping hand legacy of national government intervention was continued by several of his Democratic brethren, most notably Lyndon B. Johnson and his "Great Society" programs of the 1960s. Undoubtedly, the substantive policy enactments of Democratic Party leadership – especially the efforts of Roosevelt, Truman, Kennedy, and Johnson – sealed the deal of African American party loyalty – a loyalty which at times has been reminiscent of a "stand by your man" country tune mixed with some of the ride-or-die faithfulness of a heavy hitting hip-hop track. Additionally, African American realignment with the Democratic Party was also part of a larger political alliance based on the principles of the coalition model of government outlined in chapter 2. In particular, African American Democratic Party allegiance is based on a mutually beneficial, tangible, substantive policy and service delivery win-win model of governance (Browning, Marshall, and Tabb, 1984:

990). The unwavering support of African Americans has been responsible for the election of many Democratic Party leaders into office, including Ulysses S. Grant, Franklin D. Roosevelt, John F. Kennedy, Lyndon B. Johnson, Jimmy Carter, and William J. Clinton.

Moreover, the Democratic political leanings of the African American community have also been evidenced in the five African American presidential candidacies of the twentieth and twenty-first centuries. All five candidates – Shirley Chisholm, Jesse Jackson, Al Sharpton, Carol Moseley Braun, and Barack Obama – have been significantly connected to the Democratic Party organization and used their long-standing political and civil rights notoriety to influence the members of the party in the government and the party in the electorate.

The history of African American political party formation and involvement has not been the most beneficial relationship in terms of the substantive policy outputs they have garnered from either of the nation's two major political parties. Whereas the Democrats have treated African Americans as a "concubine" according to Congressman Charles Rangel (D-NY), the Republican Party's commitment issues have led the party of Lincoln to treat its former political interest as a "chick" on the side. As such, the question that must be further explored is what impact has Democratic Party neglect and Republican Party acquiescence had on African American political party access and incorporation?

The DNC, RNC, and African American political interests

As discussed, one of the most instrumental faces of the political party is its party organization activity. In this regard, both the Democratic National Committee (DNC) and the Republican National Committee (RNC) represent the organization and business function of the two major political parties in America. In this capacity, the DNC and RNC work to advance the platform of the party, raise campaign funds for party-endorsed candidates, engage in a variety of issue-oriented activities to inform the electorate, and engage in year-round voter mobilization, organization, volunteer, and registration initiatives.

The majority of the work done by the Democratic National Committee and Republican National Committee occurs before and after the staged and scripted national party conventions. The national party conventions happen every four years in different metropolitan areas around the nation and are the primary vehicle the two political parties use to formally announce the party's presidential and vice-presidential candidates. The other important aspects of the national conventions are the casting of national convention delegate votes, the introduction and adoption of the party platform, and selection of national party officers.

In terms of African Americans, both the DNC and RNC have made major inroads in their efforts to include Black convention delegates as well as to consider race-specific policy interests. The DNC inclusion of African American interests is perhaps most well known because of the efforts of Fannie Lou Hamer and the Mississippi Freedom Democratic Party. In 1964, Ms Hamer and the MFDP refused to accept two symbolic seats when their entire party was refused seats at the Democratic convention (Barker, Jones, and Tate, 1998). As a result of her tenacity, in 1968 the entire MFDP sat at the DNC Chicago convention. The efforts of Ms Hamer sparked many of the reforms of the DNC led by George McGovern. Senator McGovern and Congressman Fraser were responsible for the implementation of a new nomination process which provided for the pro-portional representation of African Americans at the party convention. Many suggest that these reforms led to an increase in African American participation and leadership within the party organization which was illuminated by the nomination of Ronald Brown as chair of the DNC in 1989, the appointment of Donna Brazile as Al Gore's Election 2000 campaign manager, and the position-ing of younger African American Democrats such as Mayor Kwame Kilpatrick who hosted the 2006 African American Leadership Summit in Detroit.

In contrast, the outreach of the Republican Party and the RNC has consist-ently been tepid and still remains largely symbolic and limited. Seemingly the party of Lincoln has not made significant strides to increase its number of African American convention delegates and party leaders. Consciously aware of the bad rap the RNC has received from African American critics, in 2004 NC Chairman Ken Mehlmann made an effort to engage in a host of consensus-building and outreach initiatives with key African American leaders and organizations. Moreover, African American Republican Party candidacies are on the rise. Most notably, three African Americans ran for office as official Republican Party candidates. Kenneth Blackwell, the former Ohio Secretary of State, ran an unsuccessfully gubernatorial bid in the state, Michael Steele, former Lieutenant Governor of Maryland, ran an unsuccessful bid for an open US Senate seat, and former all-pro running back Lynn Swann lost his Pennsylvania gubernatorial bid in spite of garnering an impressive 40 percent of the vote to incumbent Ed Rendell. On a lighter note, it is rumored that even famous rapper 50 Cent has allegedly gone on record stating that if he could vote he'd support the Republican Party agenda.

Whereas the DNC faced major public challenges to its exclusive, old boy mentality of politics which led to the paradigmatic changes of the 1972 con-vention, it seems as if the RNC and the Republican Party, in general, is shifting as a result of the rising number of Black conservatives who believe the party of the elephant best represents their holistic needs. Interestingly, both the DNC and the RNC 2008 party platforms shed light on the inroads both organiza-tions have made to provide a more inclusive agenda as both parties touch on issues that impact Black public opinion and political behavior including the economy, education, the war on terror, and healthcare. Moreover, in 2009, both political parties made history as Barack Obama became president and

Table 8.1 2008 Democratic Party Platform – Renewing America's Promise

I Renewing the American Dream
Affordable healthcare
II Renewing American Leadership
Ending the Iraq War
III Renewing the American Community
Stewardship of our planet and natural resources
IV Renewing American Democracy
Voting rights

Table 8.2 2008 Republican Party Platform – Country First

I Defending Our Nation
Homeland security
II Economy
Rebuilding home ownership
III Education
Higher education
IV Values
Preserving traditional marriage

Ken Blackwell became the first African American Chairman of the RNC. Some of the highlights of both party platforms are listed in the charts detailed below.

The Congressional Black Caucus

"Black people have no permanent friends, no permanent enemies . . . just permanent interests."

Congressional Black Caucus motto

The Congressional Black Caucus (CBC) was founded in 1971 by thirteen members of Congress (Representatives Shirley Chisholm, William Clay, George Collins, John Conyers, Ronald Dellums, Charles Diggs, Augustus Hawkins, Ralph Metcalfe, Parren Mitchell, Robert Nix, Charles Rangel, Louis Stokes, and DC Representative Walter Fauntroy) (Singh, 1998). Currently, all 43 members of the CBC are African American and members of the Democratic Party. The current chair of the CBC is Barbara Lee. The purpose of the CBC is to provide an umbrella organization of support for African American interests both domestically and globally.

Box 8.2 Congressional Black Caucus 111th Congressional Agenda

Empowerment through Development

An initiative designed to strengthen pipelines of leadership for young people of color on Capitol Hill as well as connect young people of color to the legislative process and civic engagement trainings.

Empowerment through Action

An initiative to prioritize legislation and funding fundamental to the quality of life of America's youth (education, job training, healthcare, etc.) as well as engage young leaders in the 2008 elections by connecting to voter registration, education, and campaign opportunities.

Empowerment through Dialogue

An initiative to host intergenerational dialogues via the internet and symposia on youth-centered policies.

Outreach through Civic Engagement

An initiative to work with progressive civil rights organizations to register 100,000 new voters by October 2008.

Outreach through Issue Education

A programme hosting six 1½-day issue-based sessions throughout the country and eight CBC Symposia on Capitol Hill focused on CBC priorities as well as utilize Black media outlets in outreach efforts.

According to Robert C. Smith and Ronald Walters (1996), the CBC has been seen as "an institution that would organize and represent in Washington the interests of the national Black community." In this regard, the CBC has been an outspoken critic of apartheid, the US's treatment of Haitians, the Rwandan conflict, and most recently the failure of the Bush administration related to the Hurricane Katrina fiasco and its failure to act related to the atrocities in Darfur, Sudan.

The CBC works with the Congressional Black Caucus Foundation (CBCF), its non-partisan, non-profit arm, which serves to "broaden and elevate the influence of African Americans in the political, legislative, and public policy arenas"(www.cbcf.com). The CBCF sponsors a variety of policy, leadership, and educational programs including its Annual Legislative Conference (ALC) which allows its members a platform to share their Congressional work, solicit support, and discuss/develop policy positions on a variety of issues that directly impact the Black community. In terms of the 111th Congress, the Congressional Black Caucus is committed to focusing on youth empowerment, international internet presence, increasing its outreach initiatives, and impacting the alternative energy discussion. The CBC hopes to mobilize members and supporters around its theme which is "Change Course, Confront Crises, and Continue the Legacy."

Although promising, the theme and issue agenda of the Congressional Black Caucus appears to be reminiscent of past unfulfilled promises. Moreover, the broad range of areas do not appear to provide a lot in the way of tangible policy acquisition or substantive African American policy as the majority of the efforts are largely symbolic and can be done without much support for the party organization.

It seems that in spite of its visibility and voice on certain issues, for more than 30 years the CBC has remained a largely symbolic, intensely partisan, political cadre that is viewed as a political outlier whose power, voice, and presence continues to be effectively neutralized by both the Democratic and Republican Party apparatus. Perhaps the CBC should rethink its motto and begin to develop some "permanent friends" on both sides so that the "vital currency" of the CBC as espoused by Katherine Tate can really "give voice and recognition to the interests of Blacks and poor Americans. In the marketplace of ideas and ideologies, this voice and recognition has vital currency" (Tate, 2003: 110). Still, the limited incorporation and political inclusion of the Congressional Black Caucus speaks to the limited perspectives of both the pluralist and coalition politics models in that it is extremely difficult and perhaps implausible to believe that 43 African American members of Congress (a figure which is still less than 1 percent of the 535 members of the United States House of Representatives and United States Senate) can effectively influence competing political parties and groups in an effort to sway political outcomes.

Moreover, the low numbers of African American federal level elected officials fail to provide the traditional win-win incentives that are a well-known feature of coalition politics models. Still, as Tate (2003) notes, the descriptive representation of African Americans in Congress, as well as some of the legislation these 43 men and women sponsor, even if seen as highly symbolic, is nonetheless politically significant as African American members of Congress are at least able to fight against some of the political, economic, and sociocultural marginalization that occurs in American society.

Black elected officials

As has been evidenced with the Congressional Black Caucus, one of the greatest benefits of political party activism and extension of benefits to African Americans has been a significant increase in the number of Black elected officials in the post-civil rights era. The rise in the number of Black elected officials has been aided by a host of significant judicial and legislative branch interventions including the Supreme Court's landmark ruling in Baker vs. Carr (369 U.S. 186 (1962)), the passage of the Civil Rights Act of 1964, and the passage of the Voting Rights Act of 1965 (Tate, 1993, 2003; Barker, Jones, and Tate, 1998; McClain and Stewart, 2005). As is widely documented, the policy enactments of the judicial and legislative branch were mitigated by the litigation and direct action stages of the civil rights movement which dramatically shifted the political and sociocultural landscape of America and forced the nation to extend and enforce basic civil liberties and civil rights to African Americans.

The extension and enforcement of African American civil and human rights impacted every area of governmental and institutional life in America – even that pertaining to "the mischief of factions" (Federalist #10). The resulting transformation in party politics in America was a subsequent increase and rise to power of Black elected officials on the local, state, and the national level of government. In this regard, there are more than 10,000 Black elected officials in both elected and appointed positions throughout the nation. These post-civil rights era politicians provide symbolic meaning, descriptive representation, and substantive policy enactment and service delivery to their diverse constituency bases. Moreover, these men and women have been able to shift the thinking and ideology of others in that some of these elected officials have been elected into office through the efforts of bi-racial and multi-racial coalitions as well as through the support of a significant cadre of White, Latino, and Asian voters (Browning, Marshall, and Tabb, 1984; McClain and Stewart, 2005).

In this regard, the number of African American mayors, county level commissioners, judges, sheriffs, city council representatives, and the like, especially, in the South, is incredible. Given the torrid history of Black political disenfranchisement, Jim Crow laws, segregation, and state's right political subterfuge, it is amazing to look at the data on Black elected officials (especially at the county level) in the South. Moreover, the states with the highest levels of African American elected officials are also impressive given the history of both Alabama and Georgia as members and strong supporters of the Confederacy in both historic and modern times.

Black mayoral leadership

Some of the most significant increases of Black electoral power have been in the realm of mayoral leadership. Since the historic election of Richard Hatcher as Mayor of Gary, Indiana in 1967, the number of African American mayors has continued to increase in both major metropolitan and progressive cities including Atlanta, Chicago, Detroit, and Los Angeles, as well as in smaller cities and towns including Richmond, Selma, and Savannah. The organization represents more than 500 African American mayors, many of whom are members of the National Council of Black Mayors, a private, non-partisan, 501(c)3 umbrella organization.

Founded in 1974, the National Council of Black Mayors' (NCBM) mission is to provide members with resources necessary to create vibrant and viable governing arenas. The NCBM focuses its energy on four distinct but complementary areas which include the following:

Table 8.3 States with the highest numbers of Black elected officials, 2001

Alabama	756
Arkansas	502
Georgia	611
Illinois	624
Louisiana	705
Michigan	346
Mississippi	892
North Carolina	491
South Carolina	534
Texas	460

Source: The Joint Center for Political and Economic Studies

- technical and management assistance;
- articulation of membership positions on national policy and legislation;
- serving as a municipal development clearinghouse;
- conducting educational forums for the exchange of ideas.

In doing these things the NCBM seeks to serve the African American mayor leaders that represent 27 states as well as the District of Columbia. Additionally, the NCBM serves as an umbrella organization and resource for its members, many of whom face similar challenges as they represent metropolitan areas with populations of over 50,000 people.

Black state legislators

The post-civil rights era has experienced an increase in Black state legislative power as some states have experienced significant rises in the number of African American state legislators. The primary umbrella organization that assists in the coordination and connection of these state-level officials is the National Black Caucus of State Legislators. The National Black Caucus of State Legislators engages in a four-prong agenda of interest articulation which is committed to the following:

- to serve as a national network and clearinghouse for the discussion, dissemination, and exchange of ideas and information among African American state legislators and their staff;
- to provide research, training, and educational services to African American state legislators and their staff;
- to improve the effectiveness and quality of African American state legislators;

Table 8.4 African American Mayors: populations over 100,000

John F. Street – Philadelphia (Pop. 1,517,550; 43.2% African American)
Kwame Kilpatrick – Detroit (Pop. 951,270; 81.6% African American)
Michael B. Coleman – Columbus, OH (Pop. 711,470; 24.5% African American)
Willie W. Herenton – Memphis (Pop. 650,100; 61.4% African American)
Sheila Dixon – Baltimore (Pop. 635,815; 64% African American)
Adrian M. Fenty – Washington, DC (Pop. 572,059; 60% African American)
C. Ray Nagin – New Orleans (Pop. 484,674; 67.3% African American)
Frank G. Jackson – Cleveland (Pop. 478,403; 51% African American)
Shirley Franklin – Atlanta (Pop. 416,474; 61.4% African American)
Ron Dellums – Oakland (Pop. 395,274; 37% African American)
Mark L. Mallory – Cincinnati (Pop. 331, 285; 42.9% African American)
Byron W. Brown – Buffalo (Pop. 292,648; 37.2% African American)
Cory A. Booker – Newark (Pop. 273,546; 53.5% African American)
Melvin "Kip" Holden – Baton Rouge (Pop. 227,818; 50% African American)
Samuel Jones – Mobile (Pop. 198,915; 46.3% African American)
Cedric B. Glover – Shreveport (Pop. 198,874; 51% African American)
L. Douglas Wilder – Richmond (Pop.197,790; 57.2% African American)
William V. Bell – Durham (Pop. 187,035; 43.8% African American)
Frank Melton – Jackson (Pop. 184,256; 70.6% African American)
Rhine McLin – Dayton (Pop. 166,179; 43.1% African American)
John Marks – Tallahassee (Pop. 150,624; 34.2% African American)
Otis S. Johnson – Savannah (Pop. 131,510; 57.1% African American)
William D. Euille – Alexandria (Pop. 128,283; 22.5% African American)
Roosevelt F. Dorn – Inglewood (Pop. 112,580; 47.1% African American)
Shirley Gibson – Miami Gardens (Pop. 105,414; 90% African American)
Kenneth E. Reeves – Cambridge (Pop. 101,355; 11.9% African American)
James W. Holley, III – Portsmouth (Pop. 100,565; 50.6% African American)

Source: National Council of Black Mayors

- to serve as a strong, united, and effective advocate for African American state legislators and their constituencies at the federal level.

Currently, there are 624 Black state legislators who are members of the National Black Caucus of State Legislators.

Black governors

In the history of the US, there have only been two African American governors elected to represent the interests of their states – L. Douglas Wilder and Deval L. Patrick. L. Douglas Wilder made history in 1990 as the first African American governor when the citizens of Virginia voted him into office. Prior to serving as governor, Wilder served the state of Virginia as Lieutenant Governor and won his gubernatorial race running as an economic and social conservative. It must be noted that Wilder won the race by such a small margin that a vote recount was issued to certify his victory. As governor of the state of Virginia, Wilder was known as a fiscal conservative who made some waves for his controversial decision to grant NBA superstar Allen Iverson clemency for a controversial case that many throughout the state of Virginia felt was racially motivated. Today, L. Douglas Wilder is mayor of Richmond, Virginia.

In 2006, Deval L. Patrick made history as the first African American to ever win a major political party's nomination for office as he won the Democratic Party primary for governor in the state of Massachusetts. Governor Patrick ran his campaign on a grassroots platform of hard work, hope, and community centeredness. No stranger to politics, Patrick served as the Assistant Attorney General for Civil Rights during the Clinton administration.

In Focus: African American Political Leadership in Georgia

The positive political gains of African Americans have been noted across America as increased political party access, beneficial Supreme Court rulings, and progressive Congressional legislation have translated into both symbolic and substantive electoral gains at the local, state, and national level. From Massachusetts to Mississippi, Black electoral leadership, especially in the South, is both noteworthy and impressive.

One state that has made incredible strides in its Black electoral leadership is Georgia. One of the primary strongholds of confederate control, the state of Georgia has come a long way since the race riots of 1906 which scared the city and caused it to subsequently reinvent itself as "The City Too Busy to Hate" under the mayoral leadership of Hartsfield (Stone, 1989).

Today, the state of Georgia has 50 African American legislators (39 members of the House and 11 members of the Senate); an African American Attorney General, Thurbert Baker; an African American Labor Commissioner, Michael Thurmond; and an African American Public Service Commissioner, David L. Burgess; an African American Mayor, Shirley Franklin (see "In Profile" section, p. 132); an African American City Council President, Lisa Borders; and a host of African American county commissioners, city council members, and law enforcement officials.

In spite of the positive electoral gains of African Americans, many critics argue that these men and women are highly symbolic political figureheads as they have not been able to effectively mobilize and lobby their fellow elected officials to engage in bi-racial and multi-racial economic and political

Table 8.5 2006 African American members of the Georgia General Assembly

House of Representatives	Senators
Rep. Roberta AbdulSalaam	Senator Robert Brown
Rep. Alberta Anderson	Senator Gloria Butler
Rep. Tyrone Brooks	Senator Vincent Fort
Rep. Roger Bruce	Senator Ed Harbison
Rep. Bob Bryant	Senator Emanuel Jones
Rep. Douglas Dean	Senator Steen Miles
Rep. Winfred Dukes	Senator Kasim Reed
Rep.Carl Epps	Senator Valencia Seay
Rep. Virgil Fludd	Senator Horacena Tate
Rep. Keith Heard	Senator Regina Thomas
Rep. Joe Heckstall	Senator Ed Tarver
Rep. Bob Holmes	
Rep. Earnestine Howard	
Rep. Carolyn Hugley	
Rep. Lester Jackson	
Rep. Lynmore James	
Rep. Sheila Jones	
Rep. Darryl Jordan	
Rep. David Lucas	
Rep. Randal Mangham	
Rep. JoAnn McClinton	
Rep. Billy Mitchell	
Rep. Alisha Morgan	
Rep. Howard Mosby	
Rep. Quincy Murphy	
Rep. Nikki Randall	
Rep. Freddie Powell Sims	
Rep. Ron Sailor	
Rep. Georganna Sinkfield	
Rep. Calvin Smyre	
Rep. LaNett Stanley-Turne	
Rep. Pam Stephenson	
Rep. Sharon Teague	
Rep. Able Mable Thomas	
Rep. Stan Watson	
Rep. Al Williams	
Rep. Earnest Williams	

Source: Georgia Legislative Black Caucus

Box 8.3 Cox vs. Taylor: Whose Line Was It?

The power and scope of African American political influence in the state of Georgia was tested in the hotly contested Democrat primary nomination for governor between Secretary of State Cathy Cox and Lieutenant Governor Mark Taylor. Both Cox and Taylor strongly courted the Black vote, making appearances at a variety of events including New Birth Missionary Baptist Church's Resurrection Sunday Service at the Georgia Dome (the event is the largest congregational gathering in the United States and makes national and international news annually). As the July 18, 2006 primary approached, both parties resorted to smear campaigns in an effort to show African American voter disloyalty.

The Cox campaign ran an old audio tape of the Lt. Governor inciting racial animosity by telling his White constituents that if they are "tired of paying for the sins of their forefathers" they should vote for him. The Taylor campaign slammed Cox for her failure to support Black civil rights organizations in their efforts to eliminate the state's voter ID law which requires voters to show photo identification before they vote. Both sides appealed to and used prominent African Americans including former mayor and Ambassador Andrew Young (Taylor supporter) and Atlanta City Council President Lisa Borders (Cox supporter) to gain the Black vote in Georgia.

In the end, Taylor defeated Cox and garnered the Georgia Democratic Party nomination for governor and unsuccessfully ran against incumbent Republican Governor Sonny Perdue who gained a slow but steadily increasing number of African American voters who said they voted for Purdue as a result of his faith-based views on same sex marriage, strong support of ethics in state government, and child safety and protection legislation.

In spite of the low blows and mudslinging that both the Cox and Taylor campaigns engaged in, two things are certain as it relates to the impact of the African American electorate in the state of Georgia. First, the partisanship of the African American community in the state of Georgia played a determining role in who ultimately gained the primary nomination in the state. As such, African American partisanship in the state of Georgia is a tangible political asset that has the power to sway elections. Second, the African American electorate in the state of Georgia is a conscious, attentive, and serious electorate that is not moved by mudslinging, empty rhetoric, and politicians that engage in smoke-and-mirror politics, especially on issues such as the Georgia voter ID law that have the potential to have a detrimental impact on Black voting rights.

coalitions. Additionally, the inability of African American elected officials to solidify voting blocs to curtail what many contend is the backwards public policy of the state which includes Georgia's infamous voter ID law has been troubling to many.

Seemingly, African American state legislators in Georgia are faced with the same challenge as African American members of Congress. Specifically, although they have been able to effectively utilize the democratization of the party organization to gain a voice via the party in the government, the number of African American Georgia state legislators, while significant, is not influential enough to sway legislation or develop a powerful voting bloc to compel a coalition politics model in the Georgia General Assembly. As such, African American state legislators in Georgia still have a considerable amount of work to do as it relates to transforming the seemingly racialized policy agenda of the state.

Where do we go from here?

The relationship between African Americans and the two political parties has come a long way since the first African American Congressman – Oscar de Priest – was elected to Congress during the Black Reconstruction Era. Although neither party proves to be the savior of the African American economic and political agenda, both parties have the potential to provide responsible party governance of the Black vote and African American constituents. The recent outreach efforts of the Republican Party – designed around the notion of African Americans giving the party a chance to help them become homeowners and entrepreneurs – speaks to the economic interests of African Americans. Similarly, the Democratic Party's emphasis on "change" is also geared towards both long-standing and potential new voters.

In Profile: Atlanta Mayor Shirley Franklin

In 2001, the Honorable Shirley Franklin made history and became the first African American and the first woman to be elected mayor of a major Southern city in the US. Franklin has a long and rich history of public service, having served the city of Atlanta during two other historic mayoral helms. She served the city's first African American mayor, the Honorable Maynard Jackson, as the Commissioner of Cultural Affairs and Executive Officer of Operations. Additionally, Franklin served as Chief Administrative Officer and City Manager under former Ambassador Andrew Young's tenure as mayor.

During her tenure in office, she introduced and has provided substantive policy delivery of the "Franklin Four" which focuses on (1) a safer, cleaner city; (2) a more responsive and effective government; (3) a better city for families; and (4) an open and honest city hall. Mayor Franklin's track record is stellar and her success has largely contributed to her ability to connect all aspects of the city to build winning coalitions to "usher in the Age of Atlanta" which encompasses an integrated regional transportation system, affordable housing, top performing schools, thriving businesses, and safe, beautiful, and thriving communities and parks. Some of the highlights of the Franklin Administration are:

- The $3.2 Billion Overhaul of the Water and Sewage System
- The Completion of the City's Fifth Airport Runway
- The Tax Allocation District (Beltway Project Funding)
- $100 Million Greenspace Bond
- The New Century Economic Development Plan

- Atlanta Reads . . . One Book, One Community
- The Gateway Center (a 24/7 Homeless Center that can serve 500 people a day)

In addition to these accomplishments, Mayor Shirley Franklin has also managed to lower crime rates, provide a balanced budget, provide 400 Atlanta public school students with college tuition assistance, and fill more than 3,000 potholes around the city. Most recently, the mayor has received national and international kudos for organizing a coalition of Atlanta business, entertainment, and community leaders to purchase the papers and scholarly writings of the city's native son, Dr Martin L. King, Jr, for $32 million dollars.

POINTS TO PONDER

1. What are political parties? Briefly detail some of the purposes of parties.
2. In what ways have the two major political parties evolved over time?
3. What impact has the increased number of Black elected officials had on African American public policy?
4. In what ways is the state of Georgia progressive in terms of its African American legislators? In what ways are African American state legislators in Georgia limited?

KEY PHRASES AND PEOPLE

Democratic Party	party in the government	Fannie Lou Hamer
Committee	party in the electorate	Patrick L. Duval
Republican Party	Congressional Black	Shirley Chisholm
Committee	Caucus	
party organization		

Part III

9

African Americans and Interest Groups

Whereas political parties seek to control politics by nominating and electing candidates to local, state, and national political office, interest groups seek to influence politics and public policy through a variety of group-focused activities, policy, personal agendas, and advocacy. In other words, the primary source of interest group interrelatedness is the issue or issues that motivate and inspire their activity. Interest groups are connected around a concentric self-interested agenda designed to improve their political standing and power by utilizing whatever means necessary to further their cause and/or passions (Truman, 1971; Wilcox, 1998). When operating at their optimal level, interest groups provide an alternative political voice and place external (information awareness campaigns and grassroots mobilization) and internal (lobbyists and PACs) pressure on the government to provide substantive policy for its members, and in some instances, society in general.

Many have argued that interest groups fit very neatly in the pluralist model of governance which argues that all individuals and groups have an equal opportunity to influence the political system. While in theory this may be true, in practice, especially as it relates to African American interests, the "heavenly hosts" of interest groups in America have been extremely biased towards those who have the financial acumen and political influence to pad the pockets of Congressional war chests, campaign fundraisers, and a host of other top-dollar events inside and outside the Beltway. Given the enormous financial and group-based resources interest groups require, as well as some of the biases which are inevitable components of group-based interest coalitions, the formation and development of African American interest groups has gone through a variety of highs and lows in terms of interest articulation, mobilization, and transformative policy action and implementation.

In this chapter, we will examine the purpose and function of interest groups in America. Also we will explore the history of African American interest groups as well as consider the long-term scope and influence of interest groups as a means of African American political empowerment in the American political system. Finally, we will examine social movement theory as a viable alternative for African American interest mobilization and look at non-traditional voices of African American interest articulation including the Black Church, African American media, and the hip-hop community in an effort to examine the ways in which traditional African American interest groups and alternative articulators of Black interests complement or confuse the African American political, economic, and sociocultural agenda in America.

Why interest groups?

Some political observers assert that interest groups are as American as apple pie. Dating back to the establishment of the institutional framework of the nation, various groups (the aristocrats, the wealthy, the educated, the land-owners, and the farmers) vied for power and organized and mobilized around complementary vested interests and activities. As James Madison commented in Federalist #10, "By a faction, I understand a number of citizens, whether amounting to a majority or a minority of the whole, who are united and actuated by some common impulse of passion, or of interest, adversed to the rights of other citizens, or to the permanent and aggregate interests of the community." Interest groups' "common impulse of passion" has been the glue which has held these clusters of individuals and groups together through their common cause and concern about a wide array of issues including agriculture, the environment, healthcare, transportation, and the like. In this regard, interest groups are an essential component of the democratic process as they perform a variety of functions including group mobilization, constituency representation, agenda setting, information dissemination, and political oversight as a means of galvanizing their members as well as the larger general public on a variety of issues.

As mentioned, one of the most important functions of interest groups is their ability to mobilize and organize large masses of people. Known as group mobilization, interest groups use a variety of tools including mass mailings, television, radio, and internet advertisements, and local mass meetings to inform and unite people around issue agendas. Additionally, interest groups use their large financial resources to provide information to members of Congress as well as to other key stakeholders including bureaucratic agencies, departments, and members of the White House staff to help government officials and agencies understand their policy preferences (Brooker and Schaefer, 2006). Finally, interest groups engage in agenda setting by working very closely with the media to disseminate their political and economic agendas as well as serving as government watchdogs (Barker, Jones, and Tate, 1998).

Primary functions of interest groups

Constituency service: Interest groups provide a host of services for members including representing the interests of members to key government leaders and stakeholders.

Group mobilization: Interest groups use a variety of methods and tactics to organize and inform group members including letter-writing campaigns, fundraising, and volunteerism.

Public education: Interest groups engage in a variety of initiatives including public awareness campaigns, town hall meetings, internet e-blasts, and blogs to inform group members and the general public.

Agenda setting: Interest groups set the public agenda by highlighting important issues through a variety of consumer media including television, radio, the internet, and billboards.

Government education/oversight: Interest groups also engage in a variety of strategies to provide elected officials and other government officials through the filing of amicus curiae (friend of the court) briefs, important information of Congressional legislation as well as serving as monitors (watchdogs) of government policy.

Types of interest groups

There are a variety of interest groups in America. Interest groups that focus on one specific interest are called single-issue interest groups. An example of a single-issue group is Mothers Against Drunk Driving (MADD). Interest groups that focus on protecting the financial interests of corporations and key stakeholders in the American political economy are classified as economic interest groups and usually represent business, organized labor, and the banking industry. An example is the Business Roundtable. Economic interest groups, arguably, are the most powerful and influential of all as they tend to use their vast resources to influence or as some contend buy political and economic access. Additionally, there are public interest groups such as Common Cause and Congress Watch (one of many powerful public interest groups founded by Ralph Nader), civil rights interest groups such as the Southern Christian Leadership Conference, the National Urban League, and the National Association for the Advancement of Colored People, religious interest groups such as the Christian Coalition and the National Council of Churches, and ideological interest groups such as the National Organization of Women (NOW) and the American Civil Liberties Union (ACLU).

Three kinds of benefits

Interest groups provide a variety of tangible and intangible benefits to their members. These benefits can be classified into three areas – material, purposive, and solidary benefits. In terms of material benefits, interest groups provide members with tangible benefits for being members. Material benefits usually provide group members with some type of financial/monetary advantage or discount that are not afforded to the mass public (Berry and Wilcox, 1977; Pinderhughes, 1987; Walton and Smith, 2007). Groups such as the American Association of Retired Persons (AARP), the Farm Bureau of America, and United Auto Workers (UAW) have been known to provide

> **Box 9.1 A partial list of interest groups**
> American Association of Retired Persons
> American Farm Bureau Federation
> Mothers Against Drunk Driving
> National Association for the Advancement of Colored People
> National Education Association
> National Association of Governors
> United Auto Workers
> US Chamber of Commerce

lucrative benefits to members. For example, the AARP provides members with discounts on their auto insurance premiums, prescription drugs, and vacation getaways.

Although material benefits can readily attract members to interest groups, given the deep-seated "passions" of people, interest groups also must provide some type of altruistic purpose or sense of connection that goes beyond an individual's immediate benefit in order to sustain long-term group affiliation and association. In this regard, both solidary and purposive benefits provide members with more substantive interest group membership. Solidary benefits provide interest group members with a sense of belonging. Similar to the feeling of inclusion and membership that joining a fraternity or sorority provides for college and university students, interest groups provide individuals with the same sense of belonging and commonality. Interest groups such as Emily's List and the National Association of Black Scientists and Engineers (NABSE) are two examples of groups that are able to provide their members with solidary benefits. It should be noted that a solidary benefit is more difficult to quantify because it is based on individual perception and feeling and may not provide the same type of quantifiable benefits to all group members.

The final type of benefit that interest groups provide to members are purposive benefits. A purposive benefit is rather self-descriptive in that it provides members with a sense of purpose and meaning. Interest groups that provide a sense of purpose usually rally around some type of universal issue or concern that has intersecting constituency group and policy implications. In effect, a purposive benefit provides members with a sense of being involved in a cause or movement that is greater than them. An excellent example of a purposive interest group is the Children's Defense Fund (CDF). The CDF was founded in 1972 by Marian Wright Edelman and has championed children's issues for more than 30 years.

Although, the benefits interest groups provide are great incentives for new recruits, it seems as if the common bond and success of long-standing interest groups is a focus on clear objectives, excellent group mobilization and public education tactics, and connection with key elected officials, bureaucrats, and institutions.

Lobbying

The most well-known function of interest groups is lobbying. Lobbying is the process whereby specific members of organized and registered interest groups (lobbyists) engage in a variety of relation-building techniques with members of Congress to educate, persuade, and inform members of both houses of Congress about the organization's issue agenda. In effect, lobbyists exercise the guarantee of the 1st Amendment of the US Constitution to "petition the government for redress of grievances." In so doing, lobbyists engage in a variety of activities to influence elected officials and bureaucratic leaders to shape policy in favor of their particular organized interest (Brooker and Schaefer, 2006; Kollman, 1998; Goldstein, 1999). Interest groups engage in both overt and subtle lobbying techniques in an effort to gain benefits for group members. Perhaps the most overt technique interest groups use is campaign finance and fundraising. In effect, interest groups use money to influence elected officials and candidates to adopt favorable policies. A more subtle use of lobbying is through the use of membership opinion polls and surveys that are distributed to key media and communications networks in an effort to keep an issue at the forefront of the American public (Herrnson, Shaiko, and Wilcox, 2004).

Although lobbying is a widely accepted form of interest group influence and participation in America, one of the strongest criticisms of the technique is that it is undemocratic. Many contend that lobbyists buy their influence and subsequent policy outcomes and thus aid in the corruption of the democratic process. Moreover, many contend that interest groups in general, and lobbying specifically, provide concrete evidence that the American political system is an elitist governing system where a small cadre of wealthy and powerful economic and business interests control government decision-making (Brooker and Schaefer, 2006). The proliferation of economic elite interest groups are also problematic for racial and ethnic minorities who traditionally have not occupied the top economic realms in American society and as such may not be able to effectively influence and shape public policy on behalf of their constituency bases.

The challenge of collective action

According to Mancur Olson (1971[1965]), it can be very difficult to sustain interest groups as large groups mobilized around specific causes can be difficult to manage and maintain over time. In his classic writing *The Logic of Collective Action*, Olson contended that groups with shared interests (ideologies) do not always automatically develop and engage in collective action around a particular issue or cause as has been widely championed through group politics models and pluralism. In his work on group behavior, Olson examined the challenges and limitations of group-oriented activity. In particular, he asserted that the challenges of group coordination, group consensus, and free riding (the benefits group members receive whether they engage in interest group activity or not) limit the ability of individuals to rally together and effectively lobby their interests to those who control the nation's governmental institutions.

African American interest group proliferation

In terms of African American interest group proliferation, it is important to understand the power of a "common impulse of passion or interest" as African American interest groups have had to hold fast to these passions as a means of overcoming the legal, extra-legal, and institutional mechanisms that were put in place to stifle and limit their political formation, participation, activity, and influence in the political system. In this regard, African Americans have also had to engage in and rely on non-traditional interest group strategies and tactics of group mobilization, agenda setting, public education, and government oversight as they have not always been granted access to or been included in traditional interest group paradigms (Polhmann, 1999).

The earliest recorded history of an African American interest group was the formation of the National Association for the Advancement of Colored People (NAACP) in 1909. The founding members of the NAACP organized around issues of injustice and violence related to African Americans. As African Americans pressed the United States' government for equal protection under the law, more interest groups concerned with the protection of rights developed. Although the issue agendas, mobilization strategies, and public awareness campaigns of these groups differed, all of the groups were interconnected as they concentrated their efforts on African American political, social, and economic empowerment and incorporation in America. In the next section, we will detail the history of a variety of African American interest groups that developed during the lobbying, litigation, and direct action phases of the civil rights movement.

Universal Negro Improvement Association

Founded in 1914 by Marcus Garvey, the Universal Negro Improvement Association (UNIA) was arguably one of the most controversial African American interest groups established in the US. Garvey, a native of Jamaica, started the interest group in an effort to unite people of African descent worldwide in the hopes of creating an autonomous Black nation and government. The motto of UNIA was "One God! One Aim! One Destiny!" At its height, the organization claimed more than 1,000 branches in 40 countries and worked toward establishing international trade agreements and colleges and universities focused on Afro-centric curriculums. The interest articulation of the UNIA was short-lived as Garvey's radical "Back to Africa" campaign was marred by federal mail fraud charges (Marable, 1998).

The NAACP

Founded in 1909 as an interracial organization designed to advance the interests of African Americans and other groups of color, the National Association for the Advancement of Colored People has been at the forefront of Black political and economic incorporation in the US. Using the legal acumen of its Legal Defense Fund, the NAACP has been instrumental in lobbying the Supreme Court to secure African American social and political equality through the 5th and 14th Amendments (www.naacp.org). The predominant strategy of the NAACP has been the tool of litigation. Prior to the successful use of litigation, the NAACP unsuccessfully engaged in direct action and lobbying campaigns. One of the organization's long-term interest group campaigns focused on lobbying Congress to pass anti-lynching legislation and anti-discrimination laws. Although the organization's anti-lynching campaigns did not produce substantive benefits for group members, the NAACP's anti-discrimination efforts have provided a variety of 5th and 14th Amendment benefits for African Americans. Some of the landmark cases of the NAACP include:

- Sweatt vs. Painter (1950)
- Brown vs. Board of Education (1954)
- Bolling et al. vs. Sharpe et al. (1954)
- Cooper vs. Aaron (1958)
- Baker vs. Carr (1962)

The Congressional Black Caucus Foundation

Established in 1971, the Congressional Black Caucus Foundation is the non-partisan and non-profit organizational umbrella of the Congressional Black Caucus and provides a number of services to its members. The Congressional Black Caucus Foundation works to ensure the political and economic empowerment of African Americans and other minorities by providing a variety of annual events including the Legislative Weekend which highlights the work of members of the caucus. Some of the topics covered at the annual Legislative Weekend include affirmative action, police brutality, hip-hop, political disenfranchisement, and the state of Black America.

The Children's Defense Fund

"The question is not whether we can afford to invest in every child; it is whether we can afford not to."

Marian Wright Edelman

Moved by the deplorable conditions of poverty and disempowerment of Blacks in the rural South, Marian Wright Edelman founded the Children's Defense Fund in 1972 as a tribute and continuation of the short-lived Poor People's

Campaign initiated by Dr Martin L. King, Jr. The CDF has evolved into a nationally known interest advocacy agency for children and women worldwide and continues to educate the masses of people about the issues of child poverty through its annual publication, *The State of America's Children Yearbook*. The Children's Defense Fund has also been instrumental in the passage of national legislation designed to protect the rights of children and families including the Juvenile Justice and Delinquency Prevention Act and the Family and Medical Leave Act (www.cdf.org).

The Joint Center for Political and Economic Studies

The Joint Center was established to provide a political bridge between the nontraditional protest strategies of the civil rights movement and the increasing use of traditional tools of political participation including voting, lobbying, and campaigning. The Joint Center has been labeled the "premier" African American think tank and has focused on a variety of interests including the development of Black elected officials, healthcare, faith-based initiatives, health policy, and economic empowerment.

The National Urban League

The Urban League was founded in 1910 by a group of New Yorkers concerned about the working conditions of African Americans. It is a non-profit and non-partisan community-based organization that fights against discrimination in a variety of economic, political, and social arenas. The National Urban League has more than 100 member organizations in over 30 states nationwide and serves more than 2 million people annually. Additionally, the League publishes *The State of Black America*, a 30-year-old annual report on the status of African Americans in a variety of areas including healthcare, education, employment, housing, and computer access and the ways in which the organization engages in interest articulation on behalf of its members.

The Southern Christian Leadership Conference

The SCLC was established in 1957 by a group of Southern ministers (Dr Martin L. King, Jr, Rev. Joseph Lowery, and Rev. Ralph D. Abernathy) who believed their mission was to "save the soul of America." Although most characterize the SCLC as a civil rights organization, many have failed to understand its organizational structure and direct connection to interest group development. The SCLC was established as a means of articulating and supporting the issues of Black enfranchisement and equality in America. Specifically, the leaders of the organization engaged in a nationwide campaign to lobby the United States government for the right to vote.

In his famous "Give Us the Ballot" speech which propelled him to the

> **Box 9.2 A partial list of African American interest groups**
>
> Blacks in Government (BIG)
> Jack and Jill of America
> National Association of Black Scientists and Engineers
> National Association of Black Psychologists
> TransAfrica
> United Negro College Fund
> Congressional Black Caucus Foundation
> The National Urban League
> The National Association for the Advancement of Colored People
> The National Council of Black Mayors
> The Joint Center of Economic and Political Studies

leadership forefront of the civil rights movement, Dr King called on all levels of government and lambasted them for the failure to grant African Americans their constitutional rights: "These men so often have a high blood pressure of words and an anemia of deeds" (Carson and Shepard, 2001: 49).

Although the government was slow to respond, African Americans did obtain the universal right to vote eight years later with the passage of the Voting Rights Act of 1965.

In the post-civil rights era, the number of African American interest groups has increased. Today, there are more groups that focus on individual and/or specialized interests and do not necessarily connect directly to the overarching issues of justice and equality that originally birthed African American interest group formation.

Moreover, African American interest group articulation in the post-civil rights era has focused on the implementation of coalition politics as African American interest groups have aligned with other interest groups to effectively implement or halt public policy, Supreme Court nominations, and bureaucratic legislation. An example of African American interest group use of the coalition politics model occurred in 2005 when the NAACP joined forces with a cadre of interest groups including NOW (National Organization of Women) to block the Supreme Court nomination of John Roberts. The NAACP has also joined forces with organized labor, education, and civil rights interests groups and filed *amicus curiae* briefs as a means of petitioning the Court on a variety of issues that directly impact African American interests. Still, the scope and influence of African American interest groups in America is extremely limited and has not had the same impact as better known, traditionally accepted interest groups such as the National Rifle Association (NRA), American Association of Retired Persons (AARP), and AFL-CIO.

Non-traditional African American interest articulators

There are many articulators of African American economic, political, and sociocultural interests that do not fit within the traditional framework of what constitutes an interest group. Many of these voices of empowerment are not officially classified as organized interest groups complete with registered lobbyists, political action committees (PACs), or access. Still, in some ways, these unorganized, push and pull, and oftentimes leaderless quasi-leadership entities and groups engage in interest articulation on, for, and on behalf of African Americans both domestically and globally. Given the ways these organizations utilize some of the methods of organized interest groups such as group mobilization, agenda setting, and public education to rally people, politicians, and the economic/business community around their cause(s), I believe it is important to include a review of them.

There are a host of African American institutions, cultural media, and individuals who use their entrepreneurial spirits to engage in critical and necessary interest articulation on behalf of the Black community. Many of these entities have been extremely successful as they are able to wield external, grassroots, community-based, and mobilized pressure on the government to support and pass policy beneficial to African American interests. A lot of these organizations are indigenous, non-partisan, and economically independent entities that are not beholden to government, philanthropic, or private contributions. As such, they are able to speak the truth about the nature of the relationship between the US and African Americans without fear of sanction, financial pull-outs, or other acts of neglect, ostracism, and financial alienation that has plagued organizations such as the SCLC since Dr King spoke out against the Vietnam War. In the next section, we will examine a host of African American interest articulators and assess whether the work they do on behalf of the African American political, economic, and sociocultural agenda is beneficial or harmful to the overall incorporation and empowerment of Blacks in the post-civil rights era.

The Black Church

The oldest indigenous African American organization in America, the Black Church, is an extremely powerful voice of Black interest articulation because of its independent financial resources, large membership, and independent voice. As Aldon Morris accurately details, "The black church filled a large part of the institutional void by providing support and direction for the diverse activities of an oppressed group . . . the church was also an arena where group interests could be articulated and defended collectively"(Morris, 1984: 5). Today, a large number of Black Churches have taken it upon their own congregational shoulders to speak out, inform, and even lobby elected officials and bureaucrats about a host of issues including improved educational opportunities, technological access, and healthcare. Moreover, many African American churches use their internal resources to provide an array of services to members and non-members alike, including financial and housing relief for victims of Hurricane Katrina, organizing letter-writing and petition campaigns to fight bans on teaching of abstinence in public schools, working to provide members with employment and home ownership opportunities, and meeting with key local, state, and national economic and political leaders to garner substantive benefits and policy for African Americans.

Black media

Another powerful source of African American interest articulation are the Black media. Dating back to Frederick Douglass's publication, *The North Star*, African Americans have a long and rich history of getting the word out (Walton and Smith, 2007; Pohlmann, 1999). There are a vast number of local African American weekly and bi-monthly newspapers that serve as forums of interest articulation on a variety of issues including education, health, politics, and economics (Walton and Smith, 2007; Barker, Jones, and Tate, 1998; Pohlmann, 1999). Many of these newspapers rely heavily on subscriptions and advertisements to sustain themselves. Nonetheless, they serve as a powerful source of non-traditional information dissemination, agenda setting, and public education as many African Americans rely on these media sources to tell the truth about what is really going on.

In spite of its proclivity to over-saturate the marketplace with song lists that exaggerate money, sex, and violence, there are also a growing number of African American radio personalities and disk jockeys that are making a substantial impact in the community. The cadre of independent leader radio personalities, such as Tom Joyner, Al Sharpton, Michael Baisden, Warren Ballentine, and Frank-Ski, have taken it upon themselves to sound the alarm of African American injustice and have used their media platforms to engage in public education campaigns, grassroots mobilization, and calls to action. These men and women are known personalities who do not represent a corporation, church, civil rights organization, or hold political office. They are independent entities predominantly focused in the entertainment arenas that have used their social capital and popularity to educate, uplift, and empower people about social, political, and economic ills and injustices that negatively impact the African American community.

The Tom Joyner morning show has been the most notable and successful media-based non-traditional articulator of Black interests and single-handedly worked to change the profiling policies of many corporations such as Eddie Bauer Clothing and Denny's. Given its more than two million listeners, the morning show DJ has spearheaded some of the most successful call-ins whereby he encourages listeners to call corporations and government agencies discovered to engage in discriminatory practices. These call-ins have been known to shut down major business for days on end because of jammed phone and internet lines.

More recently, Michael Baisden, host of "Grown Folks" radio – a nationally syndicated music and call-in show – used his platform to inform African

Americans of the injustices surround six African American teenage boys in Jena, LA. The efforts of Michael Baisden, Tom Joyner, Steve Harvey, and Warren Ballentine (all of whom have nationally syndicated African American radio programs), along with the efforts of thousands of local market radio personalities, launched the Jena Six Rally. In September of 2007, more than 30,000 African Americans marched through the small town to signal to the local authorities as well as the US Justice Department that racial injustice and biased sentencing will not be tolerated.

The hip-hop community

Known as the "CNN of Black America," the hip-hop community has also been an extremely important source of African American interest articulation. Dating back to "The Message," the hip-hop community has rhymed about the injustices of Black America for almost 30 years. Many of these "conscious" articulators of Black interests have shed light on the disparities in sentencing of African American criminals, racial profiling, driving while Black (DWB), police brutality, inadequate education, poor housing, modern-day political disenfranchisement, and a host of other issues including the war in Iraq, the bombing of the World Trade Center, and the gross mistreatment experienced by African Americans during Hurricane Katrina. Some of the most effective issue awareness and public education campaigns of the hip-hop community have been around the issue of HIV/AIDS in the Black community.

Black leaders and intellectuals

There are a host of Black leaders and intellectuals including Martin L. King, III, Maxine Waters, Al Sharpton, Jesse Jackson, Cornel West, Lani Guinier, Tavis Smiley, Jeff Johnson, and Michael Eric Dyson who have used their leadership and intellectual platforms to speak truth to power concerning a variety of issues pertinent to the long-term political and economic viability of Black interests in America. Most notably, Tavis Smiley's "State of Black America" annual town-hall style meeting has served as a source of Black interest articulation for more than ten years. Additionally, there are a host of events and forums that these African American political entrepreneurs spearhead or participate in as a means of informing, organizing, and galvanizing the Black community to action in order to ensure that African American faces and interests do not fade to Black in the traditional realm of organized interest group articulation and policy enactment in America.

While many will question and challenge the author's inclusion of the aforementioned groups as alternative voices of African American interest articulation, it is my belief that the inclusion and subsequent consideration of the brokering power of these groups must be considered as African Americans have not been able to make a sustainable impact in the American political

Plate 9.1 *Dr Cornel West, public intellectual*

landscape through traditional interest groups since the civil rights movement. Even then, the most effective African American interest group policy
came through the NAACP Legal Defense Fund's lobbying of the Supreme
Court through the use of *amicus curiae* briefs and appeals of constitutionality
via the 5th and 14th Amendments. As such, it is my belief that the activities
of African American interest articulators can only complement the work of
traditional interest groups – especially when these groups utilize the tools
of interest groups to inform and organize the public on behalf of issues that
have the potential to affect the entire Black community. Still, the African
American interest group trajectory remains limited by the absence of a singu-
lar interest group or multifaceted group that has a clear agenda, timetable,
and deliverables.

Where do we go from here?

As shared, one of the major challenges of Black interest group proliferation
is the absence of a clearly defined and articulated agenda that unifies the
diversity of interests, concerns, demographics, economic, educational, political, and social consciousness schisms of the African American community.

Whereas during the civil rights movement the agenda was unified, clear, and transparent, today the political and economic agenda is blurred by mixed agendas, countervailing issues, cynical political pundits, and economic and political priorities that seem to purposefully divide the collective action efforts of varying African American leaders, intellectuals, civil rights organizations, and interest groups. In this regard, perhaps the greatest failure of African American interest groups and interest articulators is that, unlike the Big Six leaders of the civil rights movement, many of the African American community's finest men and women are unwilling to leave their egos, entourages, partisanship, and private enterprise funding at the door in order to help those that truly need substantive governmental action and policy.

Moreover, it seems that African American interest group development, membership, and long-term sustainability has been limited by the post-civil rights generation's amnesia of whence they've come. The failure to consider the rich mobilization and organizational legacy which has been the bread and butter of the Black community is oftentimes dismissed as a thing of the past. Seemingly, many members of the new Black bourgeoisie distance themselves from African American interest groups while simultaneously reaping the free-rider benefits of their activities. Still, the new Black amnesiac middle class is not the only perpetrator of the free-rider syndrome (a phenomena wherein individuals benefit from the activities of others whether they participate or not), the majority of the hip-hop community (both artists and consumers) have fallen prey to an "amnesia of deeds" related to being dues-paying, card-carrying, educated, and active members of Black interest groups in America.

The sad reality of the current state of African American interest group proliferation is that all parties say the same thing about injustices such as Hurricane Katrina and Jena Six – namely that the government must do something. However, very few have been willing to be the first to roll the ball of collective action to bring about the modern-day change they seek. The future of African American interest group success requires a commitment to the past – in particular an examination of the height of Black interest group success – and an effective vision of the future to galvanize the diverse yet concentric economic, political, and sociocultural issues that still connect Dr Martin L. King, Jr to Mos Def and Mos Def to Marian Wright Edelman.

Points to ponder

1. What are interest groups? Briefly explain some of the functions and purposes of interest groups.
2. What role have African Americans played in the formation of interest groups in America?
3. Compare and contrast two African American single-interest groups.
4. What is the difference between an interest group and an interest articulator?

5. Do you believe groups like the Black Church, African American media, and the hip-hop community are helpful or harmful to African American interest group development and articulation?

KEY PHRASES AND PEOPLE

interest groups	agenda setting	material benefits
purposive benefits	Federalist #10	public education
Free Riders	collective action	Mancur Olson
interest articulators	Marian Wright Edelman	Black media

African Americans and the Civil Rights Movement

One of the most significant times in the political history of African Americans occurred during the modern civil rights movement of the 1950s and 1960s. The "movement" – a multidimensional approach to end racial discrimination and segregation in America – represented a significant turning point in the political aspirations, organization, and action of African Americans in the US. Armed with a broad array of non-traditional and traditional methods of political activism and engagement, African American leaders, organizations, and institutions echoed a unified clarion call for freedom, justice, and equality. Determined to no longer allow the racist, separatist, and staunch system of Jim Crow politics to ride their backs, African Americans pressed the United State government and its institutional pillars – most notably the executive, judicial, and legislative branches – to fully incorporate African Americans into the political, economic, and sociocultural arenas of America. In this regard, African American "movement" leaders and centers utilized the constitutional protections and guarantees of the 5th and 14th Amendments as a means of overcoming the ingrained second-class system of African American life that was widely enforced and accepted as the way things were in the nation.

Armed with a host of indigenous (internal), intra-community resources and strategies, the civil rights movement, particularly the direct action phase, represented a David and Goliath-like saga which gained momentum and victory through the use of non-traditional political and economic tools which included sit-ins, bank-ins, freedom rides, protests, marches, and boycotts. These tactics and strategies, which relied heavily on the principles and practices of nonviolence, revolutionized a nation content with the utilization of violence, fear, and intimidation tactics as a means of keeping "Negroes" in their place. Moreover, the adoption of the unconditional agape "love will conquer hate and violence" philosophy first utilized by Mohandas K. Gandhi of India opened the African American freedom struggle to an international community of sympathizers who witnessed first-hand the hypocritical, hateful, and xenophobic nature of America's policies and treatment of African Americans.

In this chapter, we will explore the evolution of the African American quest for civil rights and the leaders, institutions, and organizations that have been essential to the elimination of racial, political, economic, and sociocultural injustice in America. By civil rights, we are referring to a combination of constitutional guarantees, public policies, and legislation which ensure the equal treatment and protection of minorities regardless of race, gender, disability, religion, or other demographics. Additionally in this chapter, we will also examine the inroads of the direct action phase of the civil rights movement and the ways in which Black leaders and organizations placed it all on the line to ensure the freedom of future generations. Finally, the chapter will conclude with a discussion of what the future holds for African American civil rights leaders, organizations, and protest politics as a means of procuring rights and liberties in America.

The civil rights movement

If one were to trace the impetus of the African American civil rights movement in America, it probably would be quickly discovered that there is not necessarily a single event but a series of events that have shaped the ebbs and flows of African American freedom and liberty. Whether one places a historical marker in Jamestown, Virginia where the first African slaves arrived in 1619 (Franklin and Moss, 2000) or fast forward to 2007 and the controversy surrounding television and radio personality Don Imus's use of the "N" word, the procurement, protection, and enforcement of civil rights is a centrifugal component of modern-day discussions of African American political, economic, and social advancement and empowerment in the nation. As Dorothy Height shared in her autobiography, *Open Wide the Gates of Freedom*:

> There has always been within the black community a sense that this is our country. We haven't really been able to say, "My country cherishes me, and that this is why I do this for my country," but we still say, "This is my country." We have a heritage here. We are African American. We belong here just as any other Americans belong here. Negro Americans always have felt a strong sense of patriotism that calls us to fulfill our obligation to our country while we continue the fight for the right to be free. (Height, 2003: 143)

As such, although the chapter will examine the four phases of the civil rights movement – lobbying, litigation, direct action, and political incorporation – it is important to note that many of these phases are interconnected and interrelated.

In this regard, the Constitution of the United States must also be credited as it is the inspirational words of the founding fathers – specifically their espousal that "all men are created equal" – which have served as the cornerstone for all of the actions and activities that have led to the incorporation and empowerment of Black people in America. Although this chapter focuses on the four institutional phases of the civil rights movement, it is important to note that African Americans have always engaged in "movement" activity and policy.

Lobbying (1905–1929)

Most scholars agree that the first phase of the civil rights movement in America was characterized by the strategic use of "lobbying" as a means of gaining government protection and sanctions to curtail the violence, fear, intimidation, and Jim Crow practices that relegated Blacks to an inferior, colonial model of governance paradigm of oppression (Barker, Jones, and Tate, 1998; Marable, 2000; Franklin and Moss, 2000). According to Lester Milbrath, "lobbying is a communication by someone other than a citizen acting on his own behalf, directed to a governmental decision-maker with the hope of influencing his decision" (Milbrath, 1963: 7).

During the lobbying phase of the civil rights movement, a host of African American leaders and organizations petitioned the government to provide redress for the brutal treatment of Blacks. The lobbying phase of the civil rights movement was aimed at illuminating the unfavorable legal conditions of African Americans, especially the "extra-legal" use of fear and intimidation tactics such as lynching. One of the most ardent executors of the lobbying phase of the civil rights movement was the National Association for the Advancement of Colored People (NAACP). The NAACP understood the power and persuasion of lobbying and used the traditional political mechanism to heighten awareness about a variety of African American atrocities and injustices.

The most successful lobbying initiative of the NAACP was its anti-lynching legislation. Spearheaded by James Weldon Johnson, the organization was able to get the US House of Representatives to pass the Dyer Anti-Lynching Bill which imposed fines and penalties on people charged with lynching as well as municipalities which failed to protect citizens from such (Jonas, 2005; Hughes, 1962). The lobbying success of the NAACP in the House of Representatives was short-lived as the bill was killed through a Southern filibuster in the United States Senate in 1922. Ironically, in 2005, some members of the United States Senate apologized for not enacting anti-lynching laws.

The limited success of the lobbying phase of the civil rights movement can be attributed to the political climate of the United States in that during this phase of the movement, Blacks were still seen and treated as inferior in all areas of American life. Moreover, African Americans were subjected to two mutually restrictive governing models – elitism and colonialism. Absent both constitutional and institutional protections, African Americans were subject to the whims of riotous mobs, spineless leaders, and narrow-minded constituents who truly believed the Black race was an abomination that was unworthy of the full extension of rights and privileges guaranteed to American citizens (Franklin and Moss, 2000; Barker, Jones, and Tate, 1998).

Arguably, one of the most important cases of African American equal protection, Dred Scott vs. Sandford (1856) solidified the uphill journey of Black liberation in America. In this landmark decision, Chief Justice Roger B. Taney ruled that Blacks were not entitled to the rights of citizenship.

> The question before us is, whether the class of persons described in the plea in abatement compose a portion of this people, and are constituent members of this sovereignty? We think they are not, and that they are not included, and were not intended to be included,

under the word "citizens" in the Constitution, and can therefore claim none of the rights and privileges which that instrument provides for and secures to citizens of the United States. On the contrary, they were at that time considered as a subordinate and inferior class of beings, who had been subjugated by the dominant race, and whether emancipated or not, yet remained subject to their authority, and had no rights or privileges but such as those who held the power and the Government might choose to grant them. (Dred Scott vs. Sandford, 60 U.S. 393 (1857))

Justice Taney's definition of citizenship and subsequent ruling that Blacks did not constitute what was meant by the term was just one of many debilitating blows to African American political incorporation that limited the lobbying phase of the civil rights movement in America.

Litigation (1930–1950)

The Supreme Court of the United States of America has had a rather peculiar relationship with African Americans. Prior to the litigation phase of the civil rights movement, the majority of the Supreme Court expressed its hostility and indifference towards African Americans as the Court consistently ruled against the due process and equal protection of Black interests. Over time, however, the posture of the Court began to shift as the litigation efforts of the National Association for the Advancement of Colored People's Legal Defense Fund (NAACPLDF) substantially proved that the Jim Crow, separate but equal laws of the US were a violation of African Americans' 5th and 14th Amendment rights (Klarman, 2004).

The NAACPLDF was established in 1940 under the leadership of Thurgood Marshall. The early victories of the organization were the combined efforts of Marshall as well as NAACP Special Counsel Charles Hamilton who garnered seven out of eight Supreme Court rulings in his favor. One of Attorney Hamilton's most well-known early NAACPLDF victories was the case of Missouri ex rel Gaines vs. Canada (Jonas, 2005; Watson, 1993; Hughes, 1962). In the ruling, the Supreme Court ruled that it was unconstitutional for states to exclude African Americans from law school when there was no comparable school that existed under the separate but equal doctrine.

In 1957, the NAACPLDF, or LDF, became an independent entity which advocated on behalf of poor people. As the LDF details in its mission statement, the organization views itself as "America's legal counsel on issues of race." Throughout the years, the LDF has become best known for its four-prong litigation strategy in the areas of education, voter protection, economic justice, and criminal justice. Under Marshall's leadership, the LDF fought and won many landmark cases that represented clear and overt violations of the 5th, 14th, and 15th Amendments of the US Constitution. The most well-known LDF victory however was its landmark Supreme Court ruling in Brown vs. Board of Education, Topeka, KS (1954) (Jonas, 2005; Klarman, 2004).

In the case, Attorney Marshall and his legal team sought to admit an African

> ## Box 10.1 Supreme Court Ruling in Brown vs. Board of Education (May 17, 1954)
>
> Segregation of white and colored children in public schools has a detrimental effect upon the colored children. The impact is greater when it has the sanction of law, for the policy of separating the races is usually interpreted as denoting the inferiority of the Negro group. A sense of inferiority affects the motivation of a child to learn. Segregation with the sanction of law, therefore, has a tendency to retard the educational and mental development of Negro children and to deprive them of some of the benefits they would receive in a racially integrated school system. Whatever may have been the extent of psychological knowledge at the time of Plessy vs. Ferguson, this finding is amply supported by modern authority. Any language in Plessy vs. Ferguson contrary to this finding is rejected . . . We conclude that in the field of public education the doctrine of "separate but equal" has no place. Separate educational facilities are inherently unequal.

American student, Linda Brown, to one of the White public schools in the area. The strategy of the LDF was to have the Court consider the issue of equality that was circumvented in the Plessy vs. Ferguson (1896) case. Marshall, who later became the first African American appointed to the Supreme Court, argued that the notion of "separate but equal" was inherently unequal in that it placed an undue psychological and sociological burden on African Americans. In the landmark ruling, Supreme Court Chief Justice Warren sided with the argument presented by Marshall and his team of LDF lawyers.

The success of the LDF and NAACP

Undoubtedly, the success of the NAACP Legal Defense Fund was due, in part, to the leadership and structural inroads of its umbrella organization, the NAACP. Initially known as the "Niagara Movement" because of its initial meeting in Niagara Falls, Canada in 1905, the National Association for the Advancement of Colored People (NAACP) has been committed to providing preeminent leadership, strategy, and policy enactment for African Americans. Its mission of economic, political, social uplift and empowerment has continued to expand since its original 1909 charter (Jonas, 2005; Watson, 1993; Hughes, 1962). Using a two-prong strategy of lobbying and litigation to shed light on racial inequalities in the US, the NAACP has arguably remained the longest standing "go to" organization of African American interests. As stated in its charter, the NAACP's mission is:

> To promote equality of rights and to eradicate caste or race prejudice among the citizens of the United States; to advance the interest of colored citizens; to secure for them impartial suffrage; and to increase their opportunities for securing justice in the courts, education for the children, employment according to their ability and complete equality before the law.

The NAACP has over 500,000 members worldwide and is governed by a 64-member board. The current president of the organization is Benjamin

Todd Jealous and the chairman of the board is Julian Bond. The NAACP has headquarters in Baltimore, MD with regional satellite offices in California, Washington, DC, Georgia, Michigan, Missouri, New York, and Texas. The DC office also functions as the chief lobbying entity for the US government.

In addition to its work in the legal realm, the NAACP has also used its indigenous organizational resource mobilization skills and demographics to engage in strategic voting blocs of controversial political candidates, Supreme Court nominees, as well as to call for economic and social sanctions of those who engage in racist and discriminatory behavior (Jonas, 2005; Klarman, 2004). The organization is also involved in a variety of public awareness campaigns including the anti-confederate flag campaign, the "Get-Out-The-Vote" campaign, school vouchers, gun control vouchers and gun control law, and it recently filed an *amicus curiae* brief in the Supreme Court voter ID case (www.naacp.org).

One of the longest-standing civil rights institutions in the world, the NAACP has experienced its fair share of controversy and backlash. In more recent times, the organization experienced two harsh hits from the national government. First, in 2004, President George W. Bush declined an invitation by the NAACP to speak at its national convention, citing the "strained" relationship between the two parties. As President Bush remarked, "I would describe my relationship with the current leadership as basically nonexistent. You've heard the rhetoric and the names they've called me" (www.washingtonpost.com/wp-dyn/articles/A40255-2004Jul10.html). In declining the organization's invite, President Bush became the first sitting leader of the executive branch since Herbert Hoover (1929–1933) to decline an invitation to speak to the NAACP. Needless to say, President Bush's decline was not received well by organizational members and some allege that the second blow to the organization was in retaliation for its outspokenness related to the President Bush refusal. As such, the second blow to the NAACP occurred when the Internal Revenue Service (IRS) announced in 2004 that it was launching a full-fledged investigation into the tax-exempt status of the organization, claiming that the organization had misused funds.

The NAACP is still forging ahead and remains at the forefront of the African American civil rights movement. Most recently it has focused its efforts on an end to the digital divide, ensuring quality education and healthcare for African Americans, and engaged in a host of voter education and awareness campaigns.

Direct action (1950–1968)

The direct action phrase of the civil rights movement was one of the most prolific times in American political history. Fueled by more than 350 years of racial, economic, and political injustice, African Americans in the United States finally grew tired of men "riding their backs." Armed with the intermittent victories of the lobbying and litigation phases, the direct action campaign of the civil rights movement sparked a prairie fire of hope, endurance, long suffering, and overdue justice that propelled the collective action and interests of Black America forward (Morris, 1984; Kelley and Lewis, 2000; Levy, 1998).

Whereas the lobbying and litigation phases of the civil rights movement focused on legal integration and equality, the direct action phase of the movement focused on the obtainment of liberty and equality in every area of life. Additionally, the direct action phase of the civil rights movement allowed for and, in some respects, demanded a broader coalition of support, participation, and involvement of a wide array of African Americans as the livelihood of the maid and the medical doctor, the student and the scientist, and the minister and the musician was equally impacted.

On the move: from Baton Rouge to Montgomery

According to the historical record, the first nationally recognized direct action campaign of African American universal rights was the Baton Rouge bus boycott of 1953. The protest efforts of Rev. Jemison led to the first nonviolent bus boycott campaign and was used as a blueprint for the subsequent efforts in Montgomery in 1955. The Baton Rouge bus boycott was spearheaded by Reverend T. J. Jemison, the pastor of Mt Zion Baptist Church. Rev. Jemison called the boycott in protest at a fare increase that the Baton Rouge city-parish council approved (Eskew, 1997; Kelley and Lewis, 2000; Lincoln and Mamiya, 1990). The fare increase was seen as an affront to the city's Black residents, 80 percent of whom were public transportation users. Black passengers were upset because they had to pay the full fare and were also required by law to either sit or stand in the back of the bus even if the ten reserved seats for Whites were empty. Rev. Jemison's protest came after the council parish refused to enforce Ordinance 222 which initially abolished preferential seating.

For nearly three months, Ordinance 222 was merely symbolic with "White only" seating still being implemented throughout the parish. After a brief strike staged by White bus drivers protesting the council's substantive support of Ordinance 222, the attorney general of the state of Louisiana overruled the council parish's decision and declared the law unconstitutional. Rev. Jemison, Raymond Scott, and other Black residents formed the United Defense League (UDL) and launched the boycott on June 20, 1953 (Eskew, 1997; Kelley and Lewis, 2000). Four days later, the boycott ended when Black and White leaders compromised and supported the spirit of Ordinance 222 by reserving the first two rows of seats for Whites and the longer back seat for African Americans. It is both interesting and ironic that the Baton Rouge direct action campaign launched in Louisiana – the same state where the controversial Supreme Court Plessy vs. Ferguson (1896) "separate but equal" doctrine was birthed.

The beauty of the Baton Rouge bus boycott was that it utilized the internal resources of the African American community and in so doing began to shed light on the rich and plentiful indigenous leadership, financial, and organizational resources that have always been a key component of the Black community. These resources, according to Aldon Morris (1984), are the key components of successful direct action campaigns. In *The Origins of the Modern Civil Rights Movement*, Morris identifies seven characteristics that were at the core of successful movements. The seven characteristics are as follows:

1. A cadre of social change-oriented ministers and their congregations
2. Direct action organizations
3. Indigenous financing coordinated through the church
4. Weekly mass meetings that served as information sessions and forums
5. Implementation of nonviolent tactics
6. Infusion of rich Black Church culture
7. Indigenous grassroots support

Both the Baton Rouge direct action campaign as well as the subsequent Montgomery campaign had all seven of the characteristics in common. Moreover, the Baton Rouge bus boycott also served as a touchstone and blueprint of the power of coordinated mass mobilization and organizational efforts as a means of African American political, economic, and sociocultural incorporation in America.

Montgomery campaign

Similar to the Baton Rouge direct action campaign, the Montgomery bus boycott was precipitated by citywide Jim Crow laws and ordinances designed to maintain the White power structure of the city affectionately known as "the cradle of the Confederacy." The frustration of the Black citizens of Montgomery evolved around the ambiguous language of the city busing ordinance, the continued verbal and physical abuse of Black bus riders, and the arbitrary and seemingly harsh penalties and sentences of Blacks found guilty of violating the city's busing ordinance. Determined to stand up to the Jim Crow bus system in the city, a host of African American preachers, leaders, and organizers met and developed a strategic plan of action after the arrest of Mrs Rosa Parks – one of "Montgomery's finest citizens." It must be noted that the arrest of Mrs Parks was the final straw in a long series of arrests as well as test cases of busing integration that had been spearheaded by the local NAACP (King, 1958).

Nonetheless, the December 1, 1955 arrest of Mrs Rosa Parks for violation of the city's ordinance gave the Black citizens of Montgomery the courage and momentum needed to move forward. Led by a committee of several prominent African American men including E. D. Nixon, Ralph Abernathy, Rev. L. Roy Bennett, and Dr Martin L. King, Jr, the bus boycott proposal was slated to begin on December 5, 1955 and read as follows: "Don't ride the bus to work, to town, to school, or any place Monday, December 5th . . . Come to a mass meeting, Monday at 7:00 pm, at the Holt Street Baptist Church for further instruction" (Carson and Shepard, 2001: 52).

According to Dr Martin L. King, Jr, a miracle happened. In *The Autobiography of Martin Luther King, Jr*, he shared, "As I approached the front window Coretta pointed joyfully to a slowly moving bus: 'Darling, it's empty!'. . . A miracle had taken place. The once dormant and quiescent Negro community was now fully awake" (Carson and Shepard, 2001: 55). On the same day as the trial of Mrs Parks, Dr King was elected to head the Montgomery Improvement Association (MIA) – a local organization that provided the indigenous resources outlined by Aldon Morris as necessary components of a successful direct action campaign.

At 7:00 pm that evening, Dr King gave "the most decisive speech" of his life and began the process of love in action through nonviolent civil disobedience. In his "Montgomery Improvement Association" speech, Dr King did three things. First, King exposed the hypocrisy of some of the key tenets, institutions, and players of American democracy. Second, he reiterated the fact that the people of Montgomery engaged in the bus boycott were "a Christian people" whose only "weapon" was nonviolence through agape "unconditional love." Finally, he reminded his listening audience that the ultimate goal of the boycott was universal "freedom and justice and equality" for African American citizens of Montgomery, Alabama (Carson, 1998; Carson and Shepard, 2001). As King said in his opening comments at the launch of the Montgomery bus boycott, "We are here, we are here this evening because we are tired now. And I want to say that we are not advocating violence . . . I want it to be known throughout Montgomery and throughout this nation that we are a Christian people" (Carson and Shepard, 2001: 9).

The Montgomery bus boycott lasted more than a year – 381 days to be exact. The end result of the organized, collective action, indigenous protest was that the city of Montgomery conceded and the city ordinance that required Blacks to sit in the back of the bus and/or give up their seats to White patrons was repealed. In addition to the victory in Montgomery, the direct action phase of the civil rights movement also gained considerable national attention and support. In particular, on November 13, 1956, the Supreme Court declared bus segregation illegal (King, 1958).

The Montgomery bus boycott produced several substantive gains for the African American community, including nationwide and international visibility and articulation of the crisis of Black America, a distinct economic, political, and sociocultural protest vehicle which has been utilized in freedom struggles all around the world, and fundamental transformations in the structure, operation, and ideology of the United States government which led to the actualization of the tenets of democracy for Black people in America. In 2005, the city of Montgomery, Alabama celebrated the fiftieth anniversary of the Montgomery bus boycott and celebrated the legacy of many of the boycott's leaders including the late Mrs Rosa Parks and the Rev. Dr Martin L. King, Jr.

Southern Christian Leadership Conference

Utilizing the momentum garnered through the success of the Montgomery bus boycott, in 1957, Dr King, Ralph D. Abernathy, Joseph Lowery, and others formed the Southern Christian Leadership Conference (SCLC) to provide coordinated nonviolent mass direct action campaigns. The SCLC became the official nonviolence training and development clearinghouse of the civil rights movement and was strategic in mobilizing a nationwide cadre of followers and supporters (Peake, 1987; Eskew, 1997; Lincoln and Mamiya, 1990). In this regard, the development of the SCLC was critical in the maintenance of nonviolent civil disobedience as a means of strategically combating the unjust system of racism and oppression in the nation.

Birthed out of the Montgomery Improvement Association (MIA) which served as the institutional and logistical umbrella of the Montgomery bus boycott, the SCLC was instrumental in coordinating regional and nationwide efforts designed to promote and protect the civil rights of African Americans (King, 1958). Originally known as the Southern Leadership Conference on Transportation and Nonviolent Integration, at its first annual conference, members of the organization adopted the name "Christian" and agreed to a three-prong platform of nonviolence, local and regional intra-community networks, and racial inclusiveness and integration.

The first president of SCLC was Dr Martin L. King, Jr. King led the organization from 1957 until his untimely death in 1968. In 1968, Ralph D. Abernathy took over the leadership of the organization (1968–1977). Pastor and civil rights activist, Rev. Joseph E. Lowery presided over the organization for 20 years (1977–1997). In 1997, the SCLC made history as the son of Dr King, Martin L. King, III, took over the leadership helm of the organization (1997–2004). In more recent times, the SCLC has gone through both a leadership and organizational crisis. For a short while, former civil rights leader and foot soldier, Fred Shuttlesworth, ran the organization. Under the organization's current leadership, Charles Steele, Jr, the SCLC has focused on eradicating racial profiling and police brutality.

In the new millennium it seems as if the purpose, power, original intent, and transformational leadership of the SCLC's founder, Dr Martin L. King, Jr, has been lost and overshadowed by the politics of personality, leadership mismanagement, funding shortages, and short-sighted almost bandwagon-like economic and political strategies. If the SCLC, especially under its current leadership, is truly going to be representative of its mission "to save the soul of America," (www.sclc.org) it seems as if the organization is in need of an immediate conversion experience to rid itself of its personality and policy paralysis.

Congress of Racial Equality

The Congress of Racial Equality (CORE) was established in 1942 by an inter-racial group of students including founding organizational leaders – James Farmer and George Houser. The members of CORE (predominantly White college students from the Midwest) were very instrumental outside agitators who used sit-ins and freedom rides to bring attention to the racism and injustice in the United States (Kimbrough and Dagen, 2000; Klarman, 2004). CORE is most well known for its use of freedom rides. These crusades were used as a means of demanding federal government protection of interstate travel. As members traveled throughout the South, they were met with violence and angry mobs, and, in some instances, the buses they traveled on were bombed.

The national attention these nonviolent crusaders gained was extremely important in shedding light on the severity of the conditions of segregation in the US. The efforts of CORE were also instrumental in placing pressure on the federal government to respond with substantive legal protection as many state municipalities turned a blind eye and a deaf ear to the terror in their region.

Today, CORE is largely a paper organization that has been marred by financial constraints, limited vision, and a charismatic leadership deficit.

Student Nonviolent Coordinating Committee (SNCC)

The Student Nonviolent Coordinating Committee was established in April of 1960 by Ella Baker, a Shaw University student who coordinated the student lunch counter-protests in the Raleigh, Durham, and Greensboro areas. The primary purpose of SNCC was to "coordinate" the implementation and use of nonviolent direct action in response to segregation and other forms of racism and discrimination in America (Morris, 1984; Levy, 1998; Meyer, Whittier, Robnett, 2002).

In 1961, members of SNCC and CORE coordinated their efforts and engaged in freedom rides throughout the South. Some of the men and women who risked their lives and participated in the freedom rides were Hon. Congressman John Lewis (D-GA), former mayor of Washington, DC, Marion Barry, Diane Nash, SCLC nonviolence trainer, James Bevel, and Robert Moses. The significance of the two groups coming together is that they engaged in the coalition politics model of governance. The sight of a young, educated, bi-racial coalition based on decentralized leadership proved that the races could come together and engage in strategic planning for the greater good of the nation (Morris, 1984; McClain and Stewart, 2005).

SNCC also played an instrumental role in the historic 1963 March on Washington for Jobs and Freedom. Specifically, John Lewis, one of the organization's most outspoken student leaders, took the Kennedy administration to task and questioned its allegiance to substantive social change: "We march today for jobs and freedom, but we have nothing to be proud of, for hundreds and thousands of our brothers are not here – for they have no money for their transportation, for they are receiving starvation wages . . . or no wages at all. In good conscience, we cannot support the administration's civil rights bill" (Lewis and D'Orso, 1999). It must be noted that Lewis's comments were actually toned down as some members of the March on Washington committee and the Kennedy administration rejected his first draft fearing that it was too brash, offensive, and divisive.

Beyond the quest for jobs and freedom, SNCC was also very instrumental in organizing voter education and registration campaigns throughout the South. In the latter part of 1963, SNCC organized the Freedom Ballot – a mock election designed to show the willingness of Blacks to participate in electoral politics (Sales, 1994; Kelley and Lewis, 2000). The Freedom Ballot demonstration was significant because, although the 15th Amendment was ratified in 1865, in 1963 Blacks in America still did not have the substantive legislative and federal government support to enforce the constitutional provisions of the Amendment. Thus, the activities of SNCC illuminated the highly symbolic nature of the Civil War legislative Amendments. As such, SNCC's Freedom Ballot and Freedom School were an effort to put pressure on the federal government to provide more than "lip service" to African Americans, many of whom were still being denied the right to register and vote legally and extra-legally because of widely known and accepted fear and intimidation tactics throughout the South.

Along with CORE, SNCC was also instrumental in the Voter Education Project, targeted at increasing political consciousness and the registration of five million Black voters in the South. In 1965, SNCC attempted to help raise the pay wages of Black sharecroppers and formed the Mississippi Freedom Labor Union (Levy, 1992; Bloom, 2001; Eskew, 1997).

In 1966, the leadership as well as the political agenda of SNCC changed. Under the direction of Stokely Carmichael, SNCC embraced a more radical anti-integration and anti-nonviolence approach to race relations in America (Kelley and Lewis, 2000; Carson, 1998). SNCC even forced out its White staff, members, and volunteers under the guise that Blacks should work out their liberation without the interference of White people. The radical, 180-degree turn of the organization forced most mainstream civil rights organizations to denounce the tactics of SNCC, especially after Carmichael's embrace and incorporation of the term "Black Power" in 1966. As Dr King shared, after the rally where the term was first introduced and associated with civil rights, "Now, there is a kind of concrete, real black power that I believe in . . . certainly if black power means the amassing of political and economic power in order to gain our just and legitimate goals, then we all believe in that" (Carson and Shepard, 2001: 325).

Black Panther Party

The Black Panther Party for Self-Defense was formed in 1966 by Bobby Seale and Huey Newton. The organization was in direct opposition to the integrationist, nonviolent civil disobedience, and legalism approach of the NAACP, CORE, and SCLC. In many respects, the Black Panther Party solidified a new era of Black Nationalism (economic, political, and cultural self-determination). Some of the early voices of Black Nationalism included Marcus Garvey (the father of the Back to Africa movement) and the radical teaching and preaching of the Honorable Elijah Mohamed. Like Garvey and Mohamed, the members of the Black Panther Party (BPP) believed that the overall strategy of Black liberation in America was predicated on a strategy of self-defense and self-determination.

In this regard, BPP party members may be remembered for their 1967 march on the state capital of California where members entered the legislative chamber of the General Assembly bearing arms in protest at the state's attempt to ban public displays of loaded firearms. Additionally, the BPP instituted citizen patrols designed to monitor the behavior of local police.

Although the BPP did not believe in the White power structure, the organization worked with White organizations and even allowed White membership within its ranks. Further, the political ideology of the BPP was heavily influenced by the socialist, Marxist-Leninist party. In this regard, the party is most well known for its free breakfast program, the "Free Breakfast for Children" program, which aided thousands of low-income children in the San Francisco Bay Area.

In addition to its nationalistic leadership, one of the most radical components of the Black Panther Party was the organization's Ten Point Plan. The plan, a manifesto of Black liberation, was used to recruit new converts and educate the organization's membership (Jeffries, 2002; Berry and Blassingame, 1982). The Ten Point Plan provided a detailed list of the organization's demands for political, economic, and sociocultural uplift for oppressed, especially Black, people in the US.

Black Panther Party Ten Point Plan

1. We want freedom. We want power to determine the destiny of our Black Community.
2. We want full employment for our people.
3. We want an end to the robbery by the White man of our Black Community.
4. We want decent housing, fit for shelter of human beings.
5. We want education for our people that exposes the true nature of this decadent American society. We want education that teaches us our true history and our role in the present-day society.
6. We want all Black men to be exempt from military service.
7. We want an immediate end to police brutality and murder of Black people.
8. We want freedom for all Black men held in federal, state, county, and city prisons and jails.

9. We want all Black people when brought to trial to be tried in court by a jury of their peer group or people from their Black communities, as defined by the Constitution of the United States.
10. We want land, bread, housing, education, clothing, justice and peace.

The Black Panther Party's Ten Point Plan was never fully recognized as a substantive policy agenda because of the apparent biases and economic and political extremes the organization sought to mandate.

Overall, the success of the BPP was in its "free" programs. In addition to the "Free Breakfast for Children" program, the organization also provided free clothing, medical clinics, free economic and politics courses, and free self-defense/first-aid classes. The BPP's free medical clinics were responsible for testing over 500,000 African Americans for sickle-cell anemia. These tests were able to conclusively show that the disease is primarily a "Black" disease. The BPP was marred with internal leadership struggles, alleged drug abuse, government infiltration, and corruption. Although there has been a resurgence of the organization – the new Black Panther Party – it is not a widely acknowledged or utilized vehicle of Black political, economic, and sociocultural incorporation.

Malcolm X and the Nation of Islam

In order to properly understand the political and economic influence of Malcolm X and the Nation of Islam, a brief overview of Black Nationalism must be provided. The Black Nationalism or Black Power movement can be traced to the "Back to Africa" movement of Marcus Garvey. In 1914, Garvey founded the Universal Negro Improvement Association (UNIA). Under the economic and political leadership of Garvey, the UNIA boasted of one of the largest memberships and readerships via its Negro World newspaper (Skinner, 1992; Marable, 1998).

The objectives of the organization (which included a return of African people to their homeland in Africa) were as follows:

1. to promote the spirit of race, pride, and love;
2. to administer to and assist the needy;
3. to reclaim the fallen of the race;
4. to establish universities, colleges, and secondary schools for the further education and culture of the boys and girls of the race;
5. to conduct a worldwide commercial and industrial intercourse.

The organization promoted a race-conscious agenda aimed at the full economic, political, and sociocultural emancipation of Black people worldwide.

The belief that Blacks should develop and maintain autonomous economic and political institutions was not only a cornerstone tenet of Garveyism. It was also a foundational element of the rebirth of Black Nationalism in the 1950s, 1960s, and 1970s.

Malcolm X

As one of the most prominent leaders of the Nation of Islam (NOI), Malcolm X used his powerful and persuasive oratory skills to degrade and dismiss integration and nonviolent civil disobedience. In a speech aimed at the integrationist approach of Dr Martin L. King, Jr, he commented, "No sane black man really wants integration. No sane white man really wants integration . . . The honorable Elijah Muhammad teaches that for the black man in America the only solution is complete separation from the white man!" (Malcolm X and Haley, 1992: 250).

Known as a staunch race separatist, Malcolm X, a self-educated, disciplined, and reformed petty thief and hustler, embraced Islam while serving time in prison. Upon his release, Malcolm X became the prized pupil of Elijah Mohamed and traveled throughout the US spreading the Nation's beliefs on Liberation (Fisher, 2006; Davis, 1984; Malcolm X and Haley, 1992). At times, the brash and seemingly unapologetic arrogance of Malcolm X caused both Blacks and Whites to shudder. Perhaps the most well-known example was his response to the assassination of President John F. Kennedy. In an interview, X responded that such was the occurrence "when chicken heads come home to roost."

Pre-Mecca

Prior to his pilgrimage to Mecca in 1964, Malcolm X articulated an agenda of Black consciousness, Black separatism, and armed self-defense. Upon his return, he adopted a new Muslim name – El-Hajj Malik el-Shabazz – and formed a new political group – the Organization of Afro-American Unity (OAAU), an umbrella organization that worked with all people towards Black liberation (Fisher, 2006; Malcolm X and Haley, 1992). Perhaps most importantly, post-Mecca, Malcolm X denounced the Nation of Islam's "white devil" and "all Whites are evil" rhetoric in favor of a more worldwide humanistic approach to civil rights. In his speech detailing his experiences in Mecca, he wrote,

> Human rights are something you are born with. Human rights are your God-given rights. Human rights are the rights that are recognized by all nations of this earth. In the past, yes, I have made sweeping indictments of all white people. I will never be guilty of that again – as I know now that some white people are truly sincere, that some truly are capable of being brotherly toward a black man. The true Islam has shown me that a blanket indictment of all white people is as wrong as when whites make blanket indictments against blacks. (Malcolm X and Haley, 1992)

Malcolm X's new race consciousness, coupled with his public disagreement with the Nation of Islam and Elijah Muhammad, caused many within the Nation of Islam to dislike him. On February 21, 1965, while delivering a speech in honor of the first "Brotherhood Week," Malcolm X was shot and killed by three members of the Nation of Islam. Many argue that his radical pre-Mecca

Plate 10.1 *Malcolm X, minister and national spokesperson for the Nation of Islam*

armed self-defense ideologies were instrumental in the development of the more radical formation of SNCC in the late 1960s and in the creation of the Black Panther Party.

The Nation of Islam

The Nation of Islam was founded in the 1930s by Wallace Dodd Fard. Fard established the organization to "teach freedom, justice, and equality to his members." The organization also strives to develop the holistic needs (economic, psychological, social, and spiritual) of the Black community (www.noi.org; Marable, 1998). Two of the Nation's most prominent leaders were Elijah Muhammad and Malcolm X. The Nation of Islam (NOI) is currently led by Minister Louis Farrakhan. Farrakhan is most well known for his anti-semitism and the 1995 Million Man March. The Million Man March called for one million Black men to convene in Washington, DC to develop a strategic Black economic and social agenda. The march also encouraged Black men to "atone" for their sins as well as work toward strengthening the traditional, patriarchal family structure (Marable, 1996, 1998). In 2005, the NOI reconvened in Washington, DC in commemoration of the 10-year anniversary of the March.

The Millions More March, unlike the original march, called for "all people of color" to come together in protest.

In an open letter appeal, Minister Louis Farrakhan called for those of different beliefs and backgrounds to unite to create a better tomorrow for those yet unborn. The Millions More Movement is challenging all of us to rise above the things that have kept us divided in the past by focusing us on the agenda of the Millions More Movement to see how all of us, with all of our varied differences, can come together and direct our energy, not against each other, but at the condition of the reality of the suffering of our people, that we might use all of our skills, gifts, and talents to create a better world for ourselves, our children, grandchildren, and great grandchildren.

Collectively, the Million Man March and the Millions More March brought together the largest gathering of African Americans in the nation's history. The political and economic viability of these marches, however, has not been as easy to measure given the fact that unlike the 1963 March on Washington, these marches have not had concrete political and economic demands nor have they been endorsed by presidential administrations. For the most part, the Nation of Islam is seen as an extremist and separatist voice that is not widely accepted in traditional circles of American politics and is only superficially included in African American leadership and organizational arenas.

Political incorporation (1968–present)

By the end of the 1960s, the direct action strategies of the civil rights movement were rendered almost invisible. The assassinations of key leaders – Medgar Evers, Malcolm X, and Dr King – coupled with the rise in political partisanship and ideological divisiveness, flaky and tepid political leaders, Black Nationalism, and urban violence rendered most in the African American community leaderless, frustrated, and disgruntled with racial politics as usual in America (Marable, 1998; Barker, Jones, and Tate, 1998; Kelley and Lewis, 2000; Smiley, 2001; Walton and Smith, 2007). Interestingly, in the midst of all of the challenges faced by the African American community, the passage of the Voting Rights Act of 1965 was actually a ram in the bush in that, during the dark days of the late 1960s, African Americans began to walk through the Voting Rights Act of 1965-induced electoral politics door and entered political office in mass for the first time since the Black Reconstruction Era.

The immediate impact of the VRA was that the political landscape of the South changed as more than one million new Black voters emerged. As such, the move from lobbying, litigation, and direct action – non-traditional political mechanisms – to the utilization of traditional political mechanisms such as campaigning, fundraising, registering to vote, voting, and holding elected office introduced African Americans to the political incorporation phase of the civil rights movement. Additionally, the move from protest to electoral politics has been instrumental in producing the largest number of Black elected officials to date.

Today, there are over 10,000 Black elected officials that serve on the local, state, and national level of government. These numbers would not be possible absent African American political participation and voting which has dramatically increased in the 40-plus years since the passage of the Voting Rights Amendment. Additionally, there are a host of African American political appointees, advisors, political pundits, commentators, and analysts that also significantly contribute to the political process.

The political incorporation phase of the civil rights movement has also afforded the greatest number of African American college and university graduates, homeowners, White collar and federal government employees, members of the Armed Services, and entrepreneurs. Moreover, the number of African American CEOs, business owners, inventors, designers, PhDs, media moguls, doctors, lawyers, MBAs, and managers has also increased. In effect, the political incorporation phase of the civil rights movement has allowed for some of the greatest inroads and accomplishments of African Americans in every area of life. As such, arguably, these are some of the best times for African Americans to be in the land of the free and home of the brave.

Where do we go from here?

Undoubtedly, African Americans have come a long way since the insidious words of Justice Roger B. Taney. From lobbying to litigation to direct action to political incorporation, African Americans have made the nation and world respect both their personhood and dollar. Still, African Americans are on the frontline of a variety of ills that must be addressed internally. From the housing industry crash, which has caused an overwhelming number of African Americans to go into foreclosure, to the HIV/AIDS epidemic, which is disproportionately and unnecessarily ailing the Black community, to the increasing rates of youth incarceration and even mortality as a result of senseless machismo, nihilism, and violence, these are both the "best of times and the worst of times" for African Americans in the United States.

The future of African American political, economic, and sociocultural incorporation in America requires the continued expansion of rights, laws, and public policy designed to bring balance to, and hopefully eradicate the historical barriers that limited, Black interests to begin with.

POINTS TO PONDER

1. In what ways were the lobbying and litigation phrases of the civil rights movement instrumental to the "modern" tactic of direct action?
2. The NAACP used a traditional political strategy of lobbying in its early efforts. Do you believe this was an effective tool of African American politics? Please elaborate.

3. What role did Dr Martin L. King, Jr and the SCLC play in the evolution of the civil rights movement?
4. In what ways were SNCC and CORE complementary and where did the organizations differ?
5. Can Black Nationalism work as an alternative strategy of African American political incorporation?

KEY PHRASES AND PEOPLE

lobbying	direct action	Sweatt vs. Painter (1938)
James Farmer	Dr Martin L. King, Jr	CORE
John Lewis	litigation	The March on
Malcolm X	SNCC	Washington
		The NAACP

11

African Americans and the Black Church

We've come this far by faith

Without question, the most pivotal institution that spans the entire African American experience in America is the Black Church. Touted as the "it" institution of African American emancipation, salvation, and redemption, the Black Church both past and present has been the organizational center of all of Black life. As W. E. B. Du Bois commented, the Black Church and the birth of the charismatic leadership model produced "the most unique personality developed by the Negro on American soil" (Du Bois, 1903: 134). In this regard, according to Du Bois, a panoramic view of the Black Church experience details the interconnectedness, group consciousness, and linked fate of all who believe in the "Father, Son, and Holy Spirit." Moreover, the Black Church experience is the beginning and end of all of humanity as guided through the charismatic voice of the preacher who functions as "a leader, politician, an orator, a boss, an intriguer, and an idealist" (Du Bois, 2003: 134).

In addition to the Black Church providing a leadership model that has spanned generations, the "it" organizational center of the African American experience has also been strengthened by a multitude of faces and forces that make the Sunday morning worship experience both symbolic and substantive. Whether it is through the eyes of the church mother whose bright, colorful, and dignified Sunday hat tells the story of grace under pressure or the lifted hands of the Deacon board member who tirelessly gives of his time, talent, and resources to ensure that all the behind-the-scenes details, such as cleaning of the baptismal pool, are addressed, the Black Church is home to a wide array of African American political interests, economic diversifications, and socio-economic demographics.

When Sunday comes

There is a song by gospel recording artist Daryl Coley entitled "When Sunday Comes." The song is a beautifully rich, poetic, and melodic range that tells the story of the full gospel Sunday morning worship experience. According to Coley, no matter who you are – rich, poor, young, old, or in between, PhD or no degree, cum laude or as they say "thank you, lawdy," "When Sunday Comes" – none of the socio-economic status indicators of success matter as the sole purpose and function of the Sunday morning worship experience is designed to comfort, enrich, equip, encourage, and empower believers to continue to fight the good fight of faith and do the work of the Kingdom.

"When Sunday Comes" is also a time when the "preached" word – a word inspired by God and the Holy Bible – issues a clarion call of what the body of Christ is to do both collectively and individually. As such, "When Sunday Comes" is a time when the Black Church universal obtains its social gospel mandates to impact the economic, political, and sociocultural environments of the community, nation, and world.

During the civil rights movement, "When Sunday Comes" was a time when the Black Church – the undisputed center of all African American life – took to the streets demanding that the United States government honor what it put on paper as it related to the procurement of equal rights for African American men. Armed with the non-traditional political philosophy of nonviolent social change, the Black Church took the Judeo-Christian-inspired social gospel out of the four walls of the church and marched any- and everywhere necessary – the streets, the Supreme Court, the Lincoln Memorial, the White House, Selma, Albany, Chicago, Watts, and the Mississippi Delta – to demand the incorporation of the full rights and privileges as expressed in the Constitution of the United States of America.

Power, love, and a sound mind

In the New Testament, the Apostle Paul reminds his understudy, Timothy, of his assignment to preach the word of God boldly without taking into account the obvious disadvantages he faced as a young exhorter, corrector, and standard bearer. In his letter to Timothy, the Apostle Paul stated, "For God hath not given us the spirit of fear; but of power, and of love, and of a sound mind" (2 Timothy 1: 7). It seems that the apostle's reminder to Timothy experienced a new birth in the twentieth century through the political activism, ingenuity, and truth to power messages of the Black Church which used the pulpit to call America back to herself in terms of African American social, economic, and political equality. Moreover, it has been the continued activism of the Black Church and its leaders that has helped to ensure the equitable treatment of African Americans in the twentieth century through Paul's three-prong strategy of power, love, and stableness of thought. In this chapter, we will examine the role, purpose, and power of the Black Church as a complementary voice of African American political, economic, and sociocultural empowerment.

Additionally, we will examine the social gospel activism and ideology of the Black Church that many scholars credit to the prophet King – Dr Martin L. King, Jr – and his outspoken challenge to all Christian believers to do the right thing not only in America but globally as it related to injustice and suffering. In this chapter, we will also examine the rise of Black "Mega" Churches and the simultaneous impact and controversy that surround these high-tech,

Plate 11.1 *Bernice A. King (youngest daughter of Dr Martin L. and Mrs Coretta Scott King, Jr); one of 15 delegates selected to meet Pope Benedict XVI during his 2008 tour of the United States*

corporate-like, entities. Finally, we will conclude with a discussion of the future of the Black Church as it relates to a host of social issues including the HIV/AIDS epidemic, Hurricane Katrina, same-sex marriage, educational and economic equity, and other relevant issues.

In the beginning . . .

As shared, the Black Church is the oldest, longest-standing, independent, and financially self-sufficient institution in the African American community (Marable, 1983; Morris, 1984; Lincoln and Mamiya, 1990). In its capacity as an independent, "un-bossed and un-bought" institution, the Black Church has been put in a preferred political position as it utilizes its indigenous resources (large memberships, finances, communication networks, and trained experts and professionals) to organize, mobilize, and act as a means of placing demands on governmental institutions at the local, county, state, and national level to change the accepted political, economic, and social norms of American society.

One of the greatest strengths of the Black Church is its ability to get its membership to collectively move in the same direction. These memberships, which range from a low of 200 to a high of more than 25,000 members, have captured the attention of a host of economic, political, business, and international stakeholders who want to have access to the power, love, and sound mind housed in the Black Church experience. In this regard, especially over the past 50 years, the Black Church has not only been the go-to institution for social and political advice but it has also played a pivotal role as a swing voter as candidates understand the power of an appearance, acknowledgment, or waved hand at a Black Church.

In terms of some of the successful political inroads of the Black Church in the twentieth century, the Baton Rouge bus boycott, the Montgomery bus boycott, the Selma to Montgomery March for Voting Rights, the March on Washington, the Birmingham Campaign, the Chicago Campaign, and the Campaign Against the War in Vietnam can all be credited to the tripartite agenda of the Church which focused on the completeness of humanity in every area of life. Interestingly, and in line with the theological and historical credits of most scholars who have examined this political time period, Dr King and the Black Church were central figures in all of these efforts.

Still, as Dr King shared in his autobiography, his inspiration, motivation, and advocacy of a gospel that dealt with the holistic needs of humanity was inspired by his reading of Walter Rauschenbusch's *Christianity and the Social Crisis.*

> It has been my conviction ever since reading Rauschenbusch that any religion that professes concern for the souls of men and is not equally concerned about the slums that damn them, the economic conditions that strangle them, and the social conditions that cripple them is a spiritually moribund religion only waiting for the day to be buried. (Carson and Shepard, 2001: 18)

The leadership of Dr King and Black Church leaders, including Rev. Ralph David Abernathy, Rev. Joseph L. Lowery, Rev. Fred Shuttlesworth, Rev. C. L. Franklin, Rev. Dr Otis Moss, Jr, Hon. Andrew Young (also a licensed minister), Rev. L. Roy Bennett, and Rev. C. T. Vivian, was instrumental in the transformation and redemption of America from its ugly ways. As Rev. Dr Robert Franklin shared in a 2006 *Crisis Magazine* interview, "the Black Church led the movement to rehabilitate American democracy, which reached its height during the civil rights movement and the leadership of Dr King and church leaders who founded the Southern Christian Leadership Conference (SCLC). Without that Church-led movement, America might still be a nation marked by racial apartheid" (Smith, 2006). Thus, the mission of the SCLC, which was "to save the soul of America," was actualized through the strategic, unified, and non-traditional methodologies of the organization and its church-based membership.

In this regard, it can be argued that both historically and currently the Black Church has served as a thermostat of African American political behavior and social consciousness and as an adjuster of the static, separatist, and racist climate of the civil rights movement. Moreover, given the Black Church's rich historical legacy, it is hoped that the modern ecclesia will move towards repositioning itself to be at the forefront of America's twenty-first century economic, political, social, and cultural agenda.

Mega-churches

According to the Hartford Institute for Religion Research, a "Mega-church" is defined as a very large, mostly Protestant congregation that is characterized by the following organizational, demographic, and leadership criteria:

1. Massive numbers of persons in attendance
2. A charismatic, authoritative senior minister
3. A very active seven-day-a-week congregational community
4. A multitude of social and outreach ministries, and a complex differentiated organizational structure

These congregations that, on average, have about 2,000 members are distinguished by their faith-based beliefs which spill over into and shape their views and ideologies about politics, the economy, and social issues.

Usually led by a charismatic leader that wields influence both domestically and globally, Mega-churches have become multi-million dollar financial powerhouses that have even been recognized by *Forbes Magazine* for their corporate revenue-generating capacities. In more recent years the concept and definition of Mega-churches has expanded to include large African American ministries throughout the nation. Today, it is common nomenclature to ascribe the term Mega-church to large (2,000-plus) African American congregations (Lincoln and Mamiya, 1990; Tucker-Worgs, 2001/2). Similar to the definition of the Hartford Institute, large African American congregational churches that are now defined as Mega-churches also have been characterized by their corporate-like structures, charismatic leaders, multiple Sunday morning services (some averaging as many as four per week), wide array of in-house ministries and outreach services, and economic and entrepreneurial endeavors.

Although there are many critics of the Mega-church model, many African American pastors believe that it is their responsibility to create viable opportunities for their people. In a *Black Enterprise* magazine article, Rev. Charles Adams of Hartford Memorial Baptist Church defined and defended the economic positioning of faith-based institutions.

> The church needs to concentrate on the business of creating economic institutions . . . the issue is jobs. People being laid off through all this corporate downsizing is affecting every black community in this country. The church finds itself in a situation where it is the best continuing, organizing entity in the black community for the acquisition and redevelopment of land, the building of business enterprises and the employment of people. (Gite, 1993)

Unfortunately, however, the Black Church – in particular Mega-churches – focus on economic empowerment has come with its own cross to bear in that a large number of these independent entities have been dogmatically and notoriously labeled and attacked for their "prosperity" messages which are allegedly designed to trick congregants into giving money to finance the lavish and extravagant lifestyles of these charismatic men and women. The accusations and alleged concerns about the "get-rich quick" nature of these Mega-churches have even led to a Congressional investigation. US Senator Grassley has taken it upon himself to demand financial disclosure of what he alleges is over-the-top spending and living of several African American and White Mega-church ministries.

Sadly, what appears to be lost in all of the innuendo, accusation, and the current Congressional investigation is the fact that from slavery through political incorporation, the Black Church has always been the core institution of economic, political, social, and spiritual empowerment and uplift. In effect, all of the symbolism being thrown around about the validity, honesty, and integrity of Mega-churches fails to speak truth to power as it relates to the substantive inroads that have been a cornerstone of the Black Church, USA. As Rev. Dr Otis Moss, Jr observed in an *Ebony Magazine* article,

> One of the most remarkable and revolutionary contributions of the Black church in the 20th century is to be found in the areas of transformation and liberation. The Church literally played a transformational role in the whole of Christiandom in the 20th century, far beyond the borders of the United States of America, and the key figure in this transformation was Dr Martin L. King, Jr. I boldly state that the liberation movement could not have been what it was, or achieved what it did, without the dynamic leadership of the Black church. (Starling, 1999)

Moreover, the Black Church has been at the helm of a variety of community-based efforts including voter registration and education drives, blood drives, drug treatment and awareness programs, on-site job training seminars and job fairs, food and clothing drives, and HIV/AIDS awareness seminars. In an *Atlanta Journal-Constitution* newspaper article, Dr R. Drew Smith of Morehouse College's Leadership Center said it best: "Dating back to the 1700s, Black Churches have been innovators in independent institution-building in education, health, and politics in the black community." He added, "In present times, many African American Mega-churches are promoting community development by buying up entire city blocks to build social service centers and schools. On a less grandiose level, African American churches in the community are engaged in all sorts of entrepreneurial, community development, and educational activities." In effect, the substantive contributions of the Black Church span a broad array of industries while simultaneously remaining true to its social gospel foundation which calls it to make demands on as well as impact the governing and economic forces that determine the holistic prosperity of all people – including God's people.

The Black Church and same-sex marriage

One of the most controversial political issues at the close of the twentieth century was the issue of same-sex marriage in America. In certain regions of the United States, in particular, there were statewide marriage amendment referenda placed on the ballot which defined marriage as being that between one man and one woman. During the height of the 2004 presidential election, the debate over whether the United States should legalize same-sex marriage gained momentum in some of the highest political circles in the nation. As the conversation about same-sex marriage circled through the membership of the US Congress, the Congressional Black Caucus, and even the executive office, certain African American Mega-church pastors took a vocal and ardent stand against what they deemed was a direct affront to the political ideology and spiritual doctrine of their faith-based ministries. In this regard, several African American pastors and Mega-church leaders united and lobbied Congress to support a constitutional ban on same-sex marriages. Most notably, Pastor Keith Butler of Word of Faith International Christian Center directly appealed to the Black Congressional Caucus and asked members to recognize that "their support of the gay-lesbian agenda runs crosswise to the vast majority of the black clergy in the United States."

The "Stop the Silence" march

Perhaps the most controversial Mega-church stance surrounding the issue of same-sex marriage was the 2004 "Stop the Silence" march. The march was spearheaded by Bishop Eddie L. Long, pastor of New Birth Missionary Baptist Church. Concerned about the state of Black America as it related to the economic divide, the technological gap, the educational disparities, and the increased attack against the traditional African American family, Bishop Long called for the march as a means of the Church reasserting its commitment to the social gospel legacy of Dr Martin L. King, Jr. In many respects, the impetus and focus of the "Stop the Silence" march can be found in the words of the prophet King who years prior clearly articulated his beliefs about the role and responsibility of preachers of the social gospel.

> Above all, I see the preaching ministry as a dual process. On the one hand I must attempt to change the soul of individuals so that their societies may be changed. On the other I must attempt to change the societies so that the individual soul will have a change. Therefore, I must be concerned about unemployment, slums, and economic insecurity. I am a profound advocate of the social gospel. (Whittington, 2005: 7)

In many respects the "Stop the Silence" march revisited Dr King's clarion call in his sermon entitled "Rediscovering Lost Values" as Bishop Long, along with Elder Bernice A. King (the youngest daughter of the Dr Martin L. and Mrs Coretta Scott King), a host of pastors from around the nation and world, and more than 20,000 congregants drew a line in the sand of cultural and moral relativism. In effect, the "Stop the Silence" march did what the prophet King encouraged all people to do. As he exhorted in his sermon *Rediscovering Lost Values*,

> The thing that we need in the world today is a group of men and women who will stand up for right and be opposed to wrong, wherever it is. A group of people who have come

Plate 11.2 *Bishop Eddie L. Long, Elder Vanessa Long and Elder Bernice A. King during the "Stop the Silence" march in Atlanta, GA*

> to see that some things are wrong, whether they're never caught up with. Some things are right, whether nobody see you doing them or not.

The unequal nature of the educational systems in America, the digital divide, and the economic disparities that historically plagued the African American community were things that the conveners felt "wrong" and needed to be addressed from both a political and spiritual perspective.

The controversy surrounding the "Stop the Silence" march stemmed from what members of the media, political commentators, pundits, and the gay and lesbian community deemed to be inaccurate and inappropriate representations of Dr King's "Dream." Sadly, similar to the attacks waged on the "prosperity" gospel message, it seemed that the "Stop the Silence" march was subject to an agenda-setting snowball that misinterpreted and misrepresented the true purpose and mission of the call to action. Specifically, the involvement of Dr King and Mrs Coretta Scott King's youngest daughter set in motion a media frenzy aimed at dividing the family on the issue. Moreover, many outspoken critics of the march alleged that the younger King was a misdirected, ill-informed, political pawn of the evangelical right wing being used by Bishop Long to promote the Republican agenda. Both Bishop Long and Elder King were also accused of possessing a bigoted perspective of Christianity that was seen as detrimental and divisive to the overall African American agenda.

In public statements and media interviews, both Bishop Long and Elder King publicly responded to their critics and reasserted the true impetus, mission, and purpose of the "Stop the Silence" march as well as their individual and collective commitment to the full gospel of Jesus Christ and the teaching of nonviolence which surrounded the march. Moreover, both noted that the historical record will show that they embraced and walked in the fact that "nonviolence attacks issues not people" and as such the march was not an expression of hate but a genuine expression of love.

In an interview in the *New Birth Voice* magazine, Elder King shared her perspectives on the march, Bishop Long, and even critics of the march and reaffirmed her beliefs that the "Stop the Silence" march was in alignment with the gospel preached by her father, Dr Martin L. King, Jr:

> I believe our repositioning has striking similarities to what occurred during the campaign my father led in 1963 in Birmingham, Alabama. Before my dad and his followers took on segregation and the 68 bombings that occurred, there was a great deal of deception and acquiescence in the city, especially in the body of Christ . . . Prior to December 11th, there had been so many parallels between us and the church and clergy addressed in Birmingham. The fact of the matter is that we had allowed things to go unchallenged and unchecked in society. As my father said, instead of being a thermostat that transforms the standards of society, we had become a thermometer recording and emulating those things that have come out of society. (Burke, 2005: 11)

In terms of her perspective on Bishop Eddie L. Long, Elder Bernice A. King addressed the misrepresentation of Long as a prosperity preacher working in alignment with the Republican Party.

> The fact that we marched under the leadership of Bishop makes our display and declarations all the more powerful because Bishop has traveled the globe as an ambassador of the Kingdom of God in the earth. He is not the "pie in the sky" guy, the "prosperity" guy, or the "turn around three times and your trouble is gone" guy. Bishop Long is the "Kingdom of God" guy. (Burke, 2005: 33)

Finally as a means of clarifying the criticism directly waged against her for being a misguided follower of Long and others seeking to use her as pawn to usurp the all inclusive message of her father, Elder King encouraged critics to read Dr King holistically and in full context as first and foremost he was a minister of the Gospel of Jesus Christ, not a civil rights leader.

> I'd sincerely challenge and encourage the protestors to read, study, and ponder the entirety of my father's work, especially the Letter from Birmingham City Jail. I believe it is incumbent on anyone who professes to "know" King to go beyond the sanitized and pop culture aspects of "I Have a Dream." The speech in and of itself was a very controversial and radical speech addressing the mishandling and intentional misalignment of Blacks in America. Yet, just like many of us do with the Bible, the protestors took out of context the excerpts of my father's speeches that they believed supported their position. (Burke, 2005: 33)

In Profile – Select Black Mega-church Ministries

According to the Hartford Institute for Religion Research, Mega-churches provide full-scale services, ministries, and amenities for their parishioners. Beyond weekly Sunday school programs (95 percent of the Mega-churches surveyed provide weekly Sunday school), these ministries also engage a wide variety of self-help, spiritual growth and development, and community-building activities. Today, there are hundreds, if not thousands, of Black Mega-churches throughout the United States. The leaders of these full gospel ministries utilize the social gospel, along with their massive indigenous resources, as leverage to improve the overall economic and political access and empowerment of the Black community. As Dr Franklin asserted, the power of Black Mega-churches is that ". . . the black church . . . has a strong social-justice legacy that tugs harder at the black middle class and reminds them to engage Dr [Martin Luther] King's unfinished agenda in a way that many white churches simply don't have" (Smith, 2006). In this regard, Black Mega-churches have wed their legacy of strong social justice to the post-civil rights economic advancement and empowerment agenda of the Nixon administration. Moreover, as shared in a ReligionLink.com article, "black churches have always emphasized social services. Now, the growing number of predominantly African American Mega-churches is aggressively expanding outreach and economic development efforts in ways that are transforming entire communities." Arguably, it has been the union of social justice and economics that has been responsible for producing multi-million dollar quasi-business corporations that are able to effectively meet the needs of their diverse membership bases.

Mega-church profiles

Bishop T. D. Jakes – The Potter's House (Dallas, TX)

Bishop T. D. Jakes is the pastor of the Potter's House, a non-denominational, multi-racial, ministry with over 28,000 parishioners. Bishop Jakes pastors "one of America's fastest growing mega-churches," according to *Christianity Today*, and was named as "America's Best Preacher" by *Time Magazine* in 2001. The power of Jakes's Mega-ministry is that he is a "Shepard to the Shattered" and has built his ministry on redeveloping and revitalizing the lives of prisoners, drug addicts, single parents, and the abused through a holistic gospel that emphasized spiritual, financial, physical, and psychological wellness. Some of the outreach programs of the Potter's House include:

- The Guardians (homeless outreach ministry);
- Rahab International (an outreach to prostitutes and abused women);
- Transformation Treatment Program (drug and alcohol outreach ministry);
- AIDS Outreach;
- Prison Ministry Outreach.

The ministry also engages in a variety of family and leadership training and development conferences including Woman Thou Art Loosed, ManPower, and the very successful three-day family affair known as MegaFest. Bishop

Jakes also pastors a very economically and politically affluent congregation that consists of superstar athletes, entertainers, doctors, lawyers, business owners, and educators. Further, Bishop Jakes has been seen as a voice of clarity and consciousness in the nation and is a familiar voice and face during major American tragedies including September 11, 2001 and more recently Hurricane Katrina (2005).

Bishop Eddie L. Long – New Birth Missionary Baptist Church (Lithonia, GA)

Bishop Eddie L. Long has been the pastor of New Birth Missionary Baptist Church for 21 years. During this time, the Church has grown from 300 members to more than 25,000 members today. The mission of the Church is to "lead the world to worship God through serving, loving, evangelizing, and making disciples." In 2001, the New Birth Cathedral, a 10,000 seat multi-purpose facility, was opened to "accommodate the New Birth Staff Administrative Offices; Faith Academy, New Birth's Christian School of Excellence; and a variety of programs and activities such as conferences, concerts, theatrical productions, graduations, weddings, educational classes and more." New Birth has more than 40 in-house and outreach ministries designed to meet the needs of its members and the surrounding communities.

Some of New Birth's ministries include:

- Counseling Ministries;
- Family Violence Prevention Ministry;
- Kingdom Career Connections (employment network);
- Lay Institute for Empowerment (LIFE) Bible Institute;
- Next Generation Children's Ministry;
- Prison Ministry.

Additionally, the Church provides training and outreach to pastors around the globe through BELL ministries and initiatives which include The Urban Education and Family Initiative, The Father's House, Spirit and Truth, and Heart to Heart conferences.

Under the leadership of Bishop Long, New Birth Cathedral has been one of the most politically active and outspoken Mega-churches of modern times. Bishop Long has been an outspoken proponent of quality education, equal financial and technological access, and the political incorporation and empowerment of African Americans. Interestingly, Bishop Long has been able to produce effective, long-standing relationships with political, economic, and business leaders at both ends of the political spectrum. Most notably, he is one of the few Christian leaders who has been invited to the White House during both Democratic and Republican reigns. Further, in 2004, Bishop Long and the New Birth Cathedral extended the "right hand of fellowship" and hosted Tavis Smiley's "State of Black America" Summit which included Minister

Louis Farrakhan, Al Sharpton, and Cornel West. Although some panelists questioned whether Bishop Long was truly loyal to the Black community and its causes, given his "ties" to the Bush administration, in classic Long style he illuminated the substantive and transformative power of the gospel of Jesus Christ in that his ministry is able to visit the White House to discuss issues pertinent to the African American community regardless of whether a donkey or an elephant is in power.

Dr Creflo A. Dollar – World Changers Church International (College Park, GA)

Dr Creflo A. Dollar is the pastor of World Changers Church International, a 24,000-plus "global" ministry that has 60 in-house and outreach ministries designed to "change the world one person at a time." The vision of the church is to

> proclaim Jesus, the Christ, as head of the church and the manifested Word of God; our goal is to teach the Word of God with simplicity and understanding so that it may be applied to our everyday lives in a practical and effective manner; thereby being transformed into World Changers changing our immediate world and all those with whom we come into contact, ultimately making a mark that cannot be erased. (www.worldchangers.org)

The mission of the Church is fulfilled through its 60 in-house and outreach ministries that serve to meet the emotional, financial, physical, and spiritual needs of people. Some of the visionary programs that constitute the "social services" arm of World Changers include:

- WCM Career Center (employment ministry)
- A Food Distribution Center (60 tons of food is provided annually)
- The Joseph Project (male mentoring program)
- International Covenant Ministries (fellowship of affiliated ministries)

World Changers Church International rests on a sprawling campus that houses six buildings including "a state-of-the-art television studio; a computer graphic design suite; a publishing house; a high-tech music studio; a food distribution center; a large banquet facility; commercial cooking facilities; a daycare center; a Christian bookstore; an audio and video duplication center; and a professionally staffed fitness facility."

Dr Frederick K. C. Price – Crenshaw Christian Center (Los Angeles, CA)

Crenshaw Christian Center was established in 1973 by Dr Price and is one of the largest church sanctuaries in the United States of America. The center is housed on the former campus of Pepperdine University Los Angeles Campus. The more than 10,000-seat "Faith Dome" campus houses the ministry's

Table 11.1 African American Mega-churches (partial listing)

The Greater Allen AME Cathedral of New York – Bishop Floyd Flake
Faithful Central Bible Church – Bishop Kenneth Ulmer
Bethel Family Worship Center – Bishop George Bloomer
New Light Christian Center – Dr I. V. Hilliard
Greater St Stephens Full Gospel Baptist Church – Bishop Paul S. Morton
Word of Faith Ministries – Dr Leroy Thompson, Sr
West Angeles Church of God in Christ – Bishop Charles S. Blake
Inspiring Body of Christ Ministries – Pastor Rickie Rush
Bethel AME Church – Rev. Dr Frank Reid III
City of Refuge Church – Bishop Noel Jones
Temple of Deliverance Church of God in Christ – Bishop G. E. Patterson

preschool, elementary, middle, high school and correspondence school. Under the bold leadership of Dr Price, CCC has grown from 300 members to a congregation of more than 22,000 members. Dr Price's television broadcast – "Ever Increasing Faith" – reaches over 15 million households weekly. A successful author of books on faith, racism and religion, the Holy Spirit, and healing, Dr Price has sold over 2.1 million books since 1976.

The enormous influence of the Black Church, specifically Black Megachurches, has not gone unscathed. There are many, even in the body of Christ, who believe that these "superstar" pastors are nothing more than egotistical, flamboyant, money-hungry, false prophets capitalizing on the emotional and psychological weaknesses of hundreds of thousands of congregants throughout the United States.

Critics of the new Black "Mega-church" phenomena charge that these mega-ministers water down the social gospel (a Christian gospel designed to challenge political and social injustices) nationalized by the late Dr Martin L. King, Jr and turn a blind eye to the failures of the political system – particularly the Bush administration – to truly provide relief for African Americans. As Dr Franklin commented, "These leaders will stand on individuals becoming better people but will allow the president, Congress and Enron and other large institutions off the hook" (Smith, 2006). African American Mega-church leaders are also criticized for not being actively involved in a number of community concerns and issues such as HIV/AIDS awareness, voter registration and education drives, school choice, income equity, and healthcare. Still, the leadership role of the African American Mega-churches on a host of issues that directly impact their congregations is well documented. For example, the Mega-church ministries of the Potter's House, under the leadership of Bishop T. D. Jakes, is well known for its prison outreach ministries that reach over one million incarcerated men

> ## Box 11.1 Isaiah 61: 1–3
>
> The Spirit of the Lord God is upon Me, Because the Lord has anointed Me to preach good tidings to the poor; He has sent Me to heal the brokenhearted, To proclaim liberty to the captives, And the opening of prison to those who are bound; To proclaim the acceptable year of the Lord, And the day of vengeance of our God, to comfort all who mourn, To console those who mourn in Zion, to give them beauty for ashes, the oil of joy for mourning, the garment of praise for the spirit of heaviness, that they may be called trees of righteousness, the planting of the Lord, that He may be glorified.

and women. Moreover, blood drives, voter registration drives, HIV/AIDS awareness campaigns, and community outreach and benevolent efforts are documented. African American Mega-churches engage in a variety of social justice, healthcare, and economic empowerment initiatives.

An excellent example of the direct involvement of African American Mega-churches occurred during the 2005 Hurricane Katrina. More than a thousand African American churches were lost during the storm which caused both pastors and congregants to be relocated all around the nation. In an effort to help all those who were impacted by the floods, a host of African American Mega-churches took the lead to address what some deemed the first African American natural disaster.

One of the first African American Mega-church leaders to be called on was Bishop T. D. Jakes. President Bush, who had sought Bishop Jakes out before for advice, had the Mega-church leader travel with him to New Orleans after the floods. In response to the devastation of Hurricane Katrina, Bishop Jakes issued a pastoral statement to Hurricane Katrina survivors that were located in Baton Rouge and Houston. In the statement he shared his disappointment as well as commitment to ensure that assistance reached those who were in need:

> Like most Americans, I see the unfathomable suffering and it makes me angry. Help cannot come quickly enough. I go to Baton Rouge and Houston as a pastor and humanitarian to share God's love, and to be the eyes and ears of the Church. Suffering and pain are common denominators for people. They know no color or bias . . . We need to identify specific ways faith-based initiatives can serve people looking to us for help. We need to cut out the red tape and open communication for people who are suffering. (The Potter's House website, 2005)

Mega-church ministries around the county engaged in a variety of faith-based acts of kindness, including taking offerings specifically targeted at Hurricane Katrina survivors, holding clothing drives, and even providing meals and other types of assistance for those relocated as a result of the floods.

It seems that those who charge that Mega-churches must reclaim their social gospel ministry legacy fail to consider the fact that these ministries have never abandoned the mandate of Isaiah 61 and the diversified reality of the "When Sunday Comes" church community.

In response to critics, many Mega-church leaders have reasserted and in some instances clarified their commitment to the holistic development of their congregants. As Pastor Creflo A. Dollar shared, "Dr King stood for the freedom of all people, and I believe that deliverance from debt is an integral part of that freedom . . . When a man is out of debt, he is better able to accomplish God's divine purpose for his life by being a blessing to others." In effect, one could argue that this global ministry leader is taking the social gospel message of Dr King to the next logical place as it is well known that prior to Dr King's untimely assassination he was in the midst of launching the "Poor People's Campaign" which focused on the equitable distribution of income in America. In this regard, these global spiritual leaders have taken Dr King's message and philosophy of spiritual, economic, political, and social uplift and applied it to every area of life including business, home ownership, economic and community development, entrepreneurial training, healthcare, and politics.

Further, as has been claimed, these pastors are not tucking their tail or turning the other cheek as it relates to their mission and cause. Bishop Long clearly stated his economic and political position prior to his congregation's "Stop the Silence" march.

> We're not marching to the Capitol asking for a grant or a handout. We don't need [their] money 'cause it's already our money. We come to set things in order. We are not marching in search of a grant from President Bush's faith-based initiative. Like Joshua, we are foot soldiers, marching to bring down the walls of Jericho. We must understand that God works across generations. As the flame is being transferred over to us, we have a divine mandate to carry the flame, not to do the same things he [Dr King] did, but to take it to another dimension and another level, because God goes from glory to glory. (Whittington, 2005: 8)

At the conclusion of the December 11, 2004 march which commenced at The Martin Luther King, Jr Center for Nonviolent Social Change and ended at Turner Field (home of the Atlanta Braves baseball team), Bishop Long reminded the more-than-20,000 participants of the "great commission" that they embarked upon.

> As the body of Christ, Christians must leave the four walls of the church and become engaged in the conversations of the world. We must stop the silence and address the void in economic development. We must stop the silence and address unemployment. We must stop the silence and protect our values, morals, and what we Christians believe God has mandated. We must stop the silence. (Whittington, 2005: 8)

Where do we go from here?

In re-examining the title of Dr King's last book, *Where Do We Go from Here: Chaos or Community?*, it appears as if many of the Black Mega-church pastors have consciously and strategically leveraged their influence, finances, and large memberships to create holistic communities for the "least of these" as well as put pressure on long-standing economic and political institutions to extend to the Black community the same access and opportunity it has afforded other communities. In the spirit of the Black Church tradition, African American Mega-churches are exposing, protesting, and holding accountable leaders, politicians, organizations, and corporations that refuse to evenly distribute the bread of economic, political, and sociocultural life to their African American brothers and sisters.

In this regard, the role, influence, power, and prestige of the Black Church in America has been clearly established and continues to grow as the rise and proliferation of Mega-churches has attracted a new cadre of progressive, economically savvy, and socially conscious members whose holistic needs are neatly wed to the traditional, hard working, middle-class, blue-collar, and service industry-oriented base that has always filled the pews of the Black Church, USA. The large numbers, deep pockets, and extended political network of these mega-institutions undoubtedly position Black Mega-churches as some of the most pivotal social change agents in Black America. As such, it is critical that the political inroads and avenues that were paved by Dr Martin L. King, Jr develop into superhighways of African American holistic development and progress.

Still, it seems that there are major political, ideological, and theological divides as regards the Black Church vanguard and members of what has been dubbed the "new" Black Church (Mega-churches) – large congregations with charismatic leaders that allegedly preach a prosperity gospel while living extravagant lifestyles. Moreover, the politics of personality that appears to be rearing its ugly head is causing an unnecessary schism between the *new school* of African American ministers who have not been deemed "worthy" by the vanguard to carry the mantle of Black leadership in America.

Thus, some of the criticism and questioning of the ideology and theology of Black Mega-churches such as the Potter's House, World Changers, and New Birth is more personal and political than theological. That several of these church leaders have access to some of the highest officials of the land and have sometimes publicly gone against the traditional African American vanguard has seemingly motivated the bashing these entities receive. Whatever the flaws and faults of these leaders are in the eyes of their beholders, the fact still remains that they have tangible manifestations of their impact. As such, it seems that the African American civil rights machinery and vanguard ought to reach out to these leaders in an effort to engage in multi-prong agendas of progress and change. In doing so, perhaps a certain level of accountability, new direction, and a more aggressive social gospel movement can be fueled as a means of reminding these leaders that, of those to whom much is given, much is required.

Points to ponder

1. Why has the Black Church been able to sustain itself as an organizational leader and center of the African American community?

2. In what ways have Mega-churches added to the political acumen of the African American community?
3. Detail some of the key leadership roles of Black Mega-churches. Can they utilize this leadership in the political arena?
4. What are your thoughts on the "Stop the Silence" march?
5. In what ways is the economic empowerment message of the Black Church in line with the message of Dr Martin Luther King, Jr?

KEY PHRASES AND PEOPLE

The Black Church	Bishop Eddie L. Long	Bishop T. D. Jakes
Pastor Creflo A. Dollar	W. E. B. Du Bois	social justice
organizational centers	prosperity gospel	leadership
Mega-churches	"Stop the Silence" march	Elder Bernice A. King

African Americans and the Politics of Hip-Hop

Hip-hop is a multi-billion dollar music, video, clothing, film and lifestyle phenomenon. One of the most prolific genres of music – especially given its use of the beat box, scratching, sampling, and rhythmic lyrics – hip-hop and its first love, rap music, has taken both America and the world by storm. From Wall Street to Watts, hip-hop is ever-present in catch phrases, commercial industries, and even global awareness campaigns. In many respects, hip-hop is a way of life as it has permeated all things American and continues to leave its mark on every area of life.

Invisible people

The early foundation of hip-hop was rooted in the harsh realities of being young and Black in America in the post-civil rights era. Birthed in the Bronx, NY in the late 1970s as an expressive response, hip-hop sought to give voice to the voiceless by shedding light on the economic, political, and sociocultural inequalities that were common everyday experiences in the 'hood. Feeling unheard, ignored, and dejected, Black youth developed verbal hidden transcripts chronicling life in the "concrete jungles" of inner-city USA. Moreover, in an effort to sound the alarm of injustice that upwardly mobile, middle-class African Americans, the traditional civil rights community, and the government turned a deaf ear to, the early pioneers of hip-hop made visible what has prior to been invisible – realities of crime, poverty, police brutality, violence, drug use and abuse, unemployment, and the like.

Hip-hop, especially during its fundamental years, served as a megaphone of truth about the realities of urban life. In particular, the rise and development of conscious rap shed light on the uneven and disproportionate political and economic systems as well as inequalities in the realm of educational opportunities, police responsiveness, and community development. In this regard, the early pioneers of hip-hop were able to illuminate the inconsistencies in the watered-down, highly symbolic, racially unconscious legacy of the Carter administration and the blunt realities of "Reaganomics" wherein the former president sought to have ketchup count as a vegetable in the "free" school lunch program.

The politics of hip-hop

As America's political leadership and landscape evolved from Reagan to Bush, so too did the consciousness, story telling, and graphicness of hip-hop. In particular, hip-hop began to directly challenge the government and expose the racist nature of law enforcement, the criminal justice system, and the devastating impact of the crack cocaine epidemic. As icons and legends such as Too $hort, Ice-T, and N.W.A begin to shout out the police and tell them where they could go on the West Coast, on the East Coast, Chuck D and Public Enemy reiterated the sentiments of many in the 'hood when they declared that "911" is a joke.

As the 1990s came to a close and economic good times were ushered in through the election of William Jefferson Clinton, hip-hop once again shifted gear and began to embrace and promote all of the trappings of the worldwide global economy. As songs such as "Big Pimpin'," "Money, Power, and Respect," and "How Do You Want It?" emerged, so too did the seemingly senseless "beefs," turf wars, and personality politics between certain rappers which led to the untimely deaths of two of hip-hop's mega-stars – Tupac Shakur and the Notorious B.I.G. In more recent times, fans and critics of hip-hop alike contend that the content, creativity, and consciousness of hip-hop has gone on a downward spiral of decadency, debauchery, and degradation as the majority of artists rap about sex, the excessive misuse of money, and murder. Given hip-hop's torrid love affair with materialism, misogyny, promiscuity, thug life, and drugs, many wonder if the current direction of the genre will be able to effectively provide a credible voice for Black America. Moreover, many wonder whether or not hip-hop can turn its social and economic capital acumen into a transformative vehicle of political incorporation and empowerment. In this chapter, we will explore the political rise and prominence of hip-hop, its political significance, and the ways in which it can be leveraged as a political tool for African Americans, youth, and others not familiar with, disinterested and/or disenfranchised from traditional modes of political behavior and participation.

The message

Birthed in the late 1970s out of the South Bronx by DJ Kool Herc, hip-hop, particularly rap music, spoke to the oppressive conditions of poverty, neglect, isolationism, and abandonment of Black youth by core support foundations including the government, the civil rights vanguard, and in some instances even their parents. As the invisible "victims" of a presidential administration determined to prove itself as "distanced" from the African American community, many in the hip-hop community spoke to the dire lack of jobs, education, and housing that the Carter administration (in spite of its high number of visible African American appointments) was very much aware and informed about. Most notably, President Carter failed to provide substantive change in areas like the Bronx in spite of his development of the Department of Housing and Urban Development (Smith and Walters, 1996). In his work on Black political leadership in the post-civil rights era, Robert C. Smith details some of the schizophrenia of the Carter administration as it related to the Black community. The overt neglect of Black urban America which started with Carter continued on with the election of President Reagan in 1980. The policy of neglect became so pronounced that multiple voices of dissent developed an anti-establishment ethos in the ghettos and barrios of inner-city America. It was the rhythmic dialogues of every day life in the five boroughs of NYC that served as a megaphone of awareness and worldwide mass distribution education campaigns of "true life" in inner-city America which metaphorically was "like a jungle."

As Grandmaster Flash and the Furious 5 so powerfully reminded their listeners in "The Message," "Don't push me 'cause I'm close to the edge." In other words, the tough economic times and overall depressing conditions of his local environment was enough to make the artist want to give up. Further, "The Message" became the "voice" of the masses of voiceless brown and tan youth marginalized and criminalized by institutional systems that still viewed many of them as *urban guerillas* because of some of the radical stances and approaches taken during the civil rights movement by groups such as the Black Panther Party and SNCC (Student Nonviolence Coordinating Committee).

A voice for the voiceless

In spite of the phenomenal leadership, activism, and substantive social change birthed out of the civil rights movement of the 1950s and 1960s, the late 1970s proved to be shallow as many inner-city African Americans experienced economic, political, and sociocultural disenfranchisement (Wilson, 1987). The absence of a strong voice to counteract the prevailing thoughts of alleged deviance which characterized a large majority of the research on urban America in the 1970s, led to the creation of a counter-culture, i.e., rap and hip-hop culture, as a means of expressing the "truth" about life in the ghetto as well as exposing the depths of government, institutional, and law enforcement malfeasance and non-decision-making as it related to the treatment of Black youth (Bachrach and Baratz, 1970; Chang, 2005).

As Kaia Niambi Shivers explains about the origins of hip-hop, "this generational phenomenon emerged out of a lack of voice, out of frustration, out of neglected communities" (www.blackelectorate.com/11/22/2002). Feeling alienated and ignored, urban youth used the five elements of hip-hop – rap music, break-dancing, graffiti art, DJ-ing, and fashion – to chronicle police brutality, poor educational facilities, high rates of unemployment and joblessness, drug use and abuse, and myriad societal ills.

In many respects, the early pioneers of hip-hop served as frontline reporters keeping America aware of the story behind the story. As is often quoted, it was Chuck D of Public Enemy that referred to hip-hop as the CNN of Black America. In a personal interview, legendary rapper Too $hort corroborates this perspective, adding that early MCs were the Walter Cronkites and Barbara Walters of the 'hood.

> Rap music has really expressed, at times, what no one wanted to talk about. They criticize us and say we are not real artists . . . not true. Our canvas has been all of the experiences we've gone through. Our soul searching about why there are glocks and AK-47s in the hood. We were telling the real stories of what was happening in inner-city America when no one else would. (Too $hort, personal communication, 2006)

Rappers like Ice-T, Too $hort, and N. W. A. (Niggaz With Attitude) used gangsta rap to capture the hearts and minds of both Black and middle-class American White teens as well. Tales of drugs, violence, crime, sex, gangsta life and pimpin' were melodiously intermeshed with gripping first-hand accounts of poverty, high rates of unemployment, police brutality, crack cocaine, and unjust prison sentences for Black males which have historically characterized conscious aka political rap.

Whereas gangsta rappers injected the highs and lows of thug, also known as pimp life, into mainstream culture, Public Enemy, KRS One, and the X Clan infused Black consciousness and Black Nationalism into the psyches of Black youth seeking to make sense out of life in "the jungle." In "Black Nationalism and Rap Music," Errol Henderson details the impact of Black Nationalism, hip-hop culture, and Black self-determination.

> Shut Em Down moved the imagery of Black Nationalism beyond the simply caricaturing of Malcolm X. In this video, PE depicts some of the greatest heroes of the Black power movement over a pulsing bass line and Chuck D's hailing baritone invoking the Black masses to shut down those elements and institutions that do not provide for and promote Black community development. (Henderson, 1996: 329)

The power of such dynamic messages of grassroots activism is that, by the early 1980s, rappers were also able to utilize mass media, via music videos, to provide listeners with visual streams of consciousness concerning the state of Black America. Moreover, given the tumultuous political climate of the 1980s (including Reaganomics), disturbing racial conflicts such as Howard Beach, the unsuccessful presidential bids of Jesse Jackson in 1984 and 1988, the overall economic tension of the recession, federal government social service program cuts, gentrification, and the conservative assault on all things "civil rights," rap artists seemingly were provided with unlimited political canvases and backdrops to prick the consciousness of America's youth and "kept it real."

Keepin' it real?

One of the most well-known phrases to emerge out of the hip-hop community is "keepin' it real." To "keep it real" means to tell of one's real-life experiences in the ghetto or game (usually drug trafficking, crime, and/or pimping industry) without pretense or censorship. While the 1980s, Reaganomics, and the Bush I (George H. Bush) legacy came to a close, the 1980s era of Black nationalist, conscious, and overtly political hip-hop was slowly ending as well as artists began to usher in a new "realness" focused on materialism, sexuality, and misogyny. The 1990s birthed a new era of hip-hop, an era predominantly focused on me, myself, I, and my crew and not on the overall development of the Black community and Black nationalism as had been popularized in the prior decade.

The 1990s not only were host to the commercialization and subsequent cross-over success of hip-hop culture, the era also produced an overwhelming number of first generation, "new money" rappers and hip-hop artists who were in all respects 'hood rich. By this time, many artists were using their new-found fame and fortune to live lifestyles of the rich and famous without upgrading their environments, mentalities, and financial acumen. As a result, some of these artists have been the victims of all sorts of crimes because they have chosen to ride around their 'hoods driving luxury cars and donning hundreds of thousands of dollars in jewelry.

Overall, the 1990s era of hip-hop was dominated by artists on both coasts (East and West) glamorizing lives of luxury and hedonism while simultaneously demanding more money, power, and respect from those around them. Artists such as the Notorious B.I.G., Tupac, Mase, Jay-Z, Snoop Dogg, Dr Dre, and Puff Daddy flossed their post-civil rights limitless lifestyles in front of the entire world via extravagant lyrics, music videos, and DVDs chronicling their rise to fame and prominence. In spite of the 1995 Million Man March which challenged Black men to reclaim their rightful position as provider and protector of the Black family, many in the hip-hop community turned a deaf ear and continued down destructive paths of misogyny and nihilism that caused many to wonder if hip-hop could ever become a substantive vehicle of sociocultural and political change for the Black community.

As beefs (conflicts between two or more artists) escalated and spread across the nation (most notorious was the East Coast vs. West Coast conflict), lewd and profane lyrics became the main course of the day, and the South, through the slower, friendlier, and welcoming cadences of Outkast, Goodie Mob, and Arrested Development, began to make a name for itself. Arguably it was not until the senseless murders of two of raps most gifted sons – Tupac Shakur and the Notorious B.I.G. – that the hip-hop community began to wake up and realize the collective power and, more importantly, responsibility of their unique music genre. The deaths of hip-hop's favorite sons, in many respects, motivated many to join forces and proclaim an end to the violence of the East Coast vs. West Coast rivalry as well as to develop creative ways to fuel the power, force, and untapped economic, sociocultural, and political power of hip-hop.

In 1996, hip-hop mogul Russell Simmons hosted the first ever hip-hop summit. The gathering was significant because it marked the official end to the East Coast vs. West Coast rivalry as rappers from both coasts attended and engaged in a private truce and cease-fire. In 2001, Simmons organized a second summit. The second summit – "Taking Back Responsibility" – was a call to action for members of the hip-hop community to take personal responsibility and use their influence to promote transformative change in their communities. In an About.com 2001 interview with Ife Oshun, Simmons shared his vision of the gathering of hip-hop's elite.

> Our intention is to bring everybody together to first . . . feel how powerful we are . . . and to celebrate the success . . . but to make clear to everyone what responsibilities come with that power . . . Not many people in hip-hop realize that they are more powerful than the politicians, and they're more powerful than any other cultural influence and that they have the power to change the world in any way they decide.

Since Simmons's first call to action, there have been 40 subsequent gatherings over the years as well as several collaborations with key civil rights organizations including the NAACP, SCLC, and Urban League. Additionally, Simmons's organization, the Hip-Hop Summit Action Network (HSAN), developed a 15-point action plan designed to improve the overall state of Black America. Interestingly, some of the extremely broad tenets of HSAN's action plan were reminiscent of the Ten Point Plan of the Black Panther Party. The 15-point strategic action plan of HSAN (www.hiphopsummitactionnetwork.org) is detailed below.

1. We want freedom and the social, political and economic development and empowerment of our families and communities; and for all women, men and children throughout the world.
2. We want equal justice for all without discrimination based on race, color, ethnicity, nationality, gender, sexual orientation, age, creed or class.
3. We want the total elimination of poverty.
4. We want the highest quality public education equally for all.
5. We want the total elimination of racism and racial profiling, violence, hatred, and bigotry.
6. We want universal access and delivery of the highest quality healthcare for all.
7. We want the total elimination of police brutality and the unjust incarceration of people of color and all others.
8. We want the end and repeal of all repressive legislations, laws, regulations and ordinances such as "three strikes" laws; federal and state mandatory minimum sentencing; trying and sentencing juveniles as adults; sentencing disparities between crack and powdered cocaine use; capital punishment; the Media Marketing Accountability Act; and hip-hop censorship fines by the FCC.
9. We want reparations to help repair the lingering vestiges; damages and suffering of African Americans as a result of the brutal enslavement of generations of Africans in America.

10. We want the progressive transformation of American society into a Nu America as a result of organizing and mobilizing the energy, activism and resources of the hip-hop community at the grassroots level throughout the United States.

11. We want greater unity, mutual dialogue, program development and a prioritizing of national issues for collective action within the hip-hop community through summits, conferences, workshops, issue task force and joint projects.

12. We want advocacy of public policies that are in the interests of hip-hop before Congress, state legislatures, municipal governments, the media and the entertainment industry.

13. We want the recertification and restoration of voting rights for the 10 million persons who have lost their right to vote as a result of a felony conviction. Although these persons have served time in prison, their voting rights have not been restored in 40 states in the US.

14. We want to tremendously increase public awareness and education on the pandemic of HIV/AIDS.

15. We want a clean environment and an end to communities in which poor and minorities reside being deliberately targeted for toxic waste dumps, facilities and other environmental hazards.

Although according to Simmons, approximately 80 percent of hip-hop's listening audience is White, the issue agenda of HSAN is strategically aligned with increasing African American awareness and consciousness. In this regard, HSAN's mission, which is "dedicated to harnessing the cultural relevance of hip-hop music to serve as a catalyst for education advocacy and other societal concerns fundamental to the well-being of at-risk youth throughout the United States," is complementary to its action agenda.

Where did we go wrong?

Undoubtedly, the civil rights movement of the 1950s and 1960s produced concrete substantive benefits for the entire African American community. Many of these economic and political rights were obtained through the ultimate sacrifice of individuals laying down their lives. Tragically, it seems that today an entire generation of African Americans enjoys privileges such as the right to vote without a clear understanding that, as De La Soul stated in 1996, "stakes is high." In other words, there appears to be an entire generation of hip-hop heads that are oblivious to the fact that the "money, power, and respect" currently enjoyed and consumed by these "ballas" have come at a cost. Unfortunately, somewhere between the birth of hip-hop in the late 1970s and the consumerism and commercialism of hip-hop in the 1990s, a generation or two of hip-hop's finest failed miserably at developing a political agenda parallel to that of their young activist brothers and sisters of the civil rights movement.

Whereas during the movement teenagers were protesting and marching in the face of segregation, water hoses, and attack dogs, up until the 2000 election, seemingly, a majority of African American hip-hop youth were being lulled to sleep by the lures of "bling-bling" (diamond jewelry), "Benjamins" (money), and excessive braggadocio. The somewhat apparent disconnect of the hip-hop generation from anything socially conscious or political caused many in the civil rights community to question the generation's integrity and commitment to Black uplift and empowerment. The gap between the civil rights vanguard and the hip-hop community was further widened by the seeming disrespect these wannabe gangstas wielded for those who marched so that they could be "free at last." Additionally, three major rifts further widened the divide between these two intra-generational communities as the civil rights vanguard grew tired of (1) the refusal of many in the hip-hop community to be role models; (2) the refusal of many in the hip-hop community to take responsibility for the negative images of women in their songs and videos; and (3) the refusal of many in the hip-hop community to take responsibility for the promotion and proliferation of images of Black men as thugs, gangstas, super-predators, and pimps.

Clearly, these destructive behaviors have not only been perplexing to members of the civil rights vanguard but also to some members of the hip-hop community as well. Hip-hop feminist Joan Morgan detailed her plea to understand the self-destructive and nihilistic behavior of her hip-hop brothers in *When Chickenheads Come Home to Roost*. She wrote,

> My decision to expose myself to the sexism of Dr Dre, Ice Cube, Snoop Dogg, or the Notorious B.I.G. is really my plea to my brothers to tell me who they are. I need to know why they are so angry at me? Why is disrespecting me one of the few things that make them feel like men? What's the haps, what are you going through on the daily that's got you acting so foul? (Morgan, 2000: 115)

It seems as if Morgan and others were calling hip-hop artists to a higher plateau of existence and challenging them to wake up out of their sleep of apathy, self-hate, and destructive community behavior. On the flip side, members of the hip-hop community felt as if the civil rights vanguard and other African American leaders have and will continue to come down hard on them. In particular, some rappers feel like the civil rights community is clueless about the struggles of growing up in the 'hood, doing whatever is necessary to survive, and the use of the "N" word. As Nas shared in an October 2007 mtv.com interview,

> I'm a street disciple, I'm talking to the streets. Stay out of our business. You ain't got no business worrying about what the word "n***a" is or acting like you know what my album is about without talking to me. Whether you in the NAACP or you Jesse Jackson. I respect all of them . . . I just want them to know: Never fall victim to Fox. Never fall victim to the sh** they do. What they do is try to hurry up and get you on the phone and try to get you to talk about something you might not know about yet . . . to think that I'm gonna say something that's not intellectual is calling me a n***a, and to be called a n***a by Jesse Jackson and the NAACP is counterproductive, counter-revolutionary. (Reid, 2007)

Additionally, members of the hip-hop community feel like everyone is trying to blame them for the ills of society. As Jay-Z shared in a recent interview in *Stop Smiling*,

> Imus couldn't name three rappers; well, maybe he could, but he couldn't name their songs. Imus doesn't listen to rap, so he's not influenced by it. He didn't get that from us. I missed the point the discussion stopped being about Imus. If rappers stop cursing tomorrow, is that going to fix the ghetto or the fact that our schools are f-up and the living conditions are terrible? (www.stopsmilingonline.com, Issue 33).

Moreover, as one of Jay-Z's artists Beanie Sigel shared on a Rap City "Da Basement" show, "they say we violent but America is violent." Interestingly, Beanie Sigel remixed something that Dr Martin L. King, Jr said in 1967 when he declared in his "Beyond Vietnam" speech that he couldn't tell Black youth to stop engaging in violence because he had come to realize that "America is the greatest purveyor of violence in the world."

Vote or die?

The 2000 presidential election proved to be the wake-up call the hip-hop community needed to galvanize their economic and commercial success into grassroots political mobilization and activism. The 2000 election was one of the most controversial elections of the twenty-first century. To recap, the controversy surrounding the 2000 election initially focused on the state of Florida and the confusion over the ballot that state officials sanctioned (the infamous "butterfly" ballot vs. the "hanging chad" ballot). However, as the uncertainty as to who actually won the election moved beyond Florida, several other issues surfaced including:

- voter disenfranchisement as tens of thousands African American voters were denied the right to vote in spite of having proper identification;
- thousands of votes were not counted for a variety of reasons, including confusion over "butterfly ballots" and "hanging chads";
- in Ohio and other states hundreds of voters who stood in line for hours were turned away;
- fear and intimidation tactics, such as law enforcement vehicles being placed outside of polls, were used to deter "certain" voters.

Although the Supreme Court declared George W. Bush President of the United States of America, in the hearts and minds of many African Americans, especially those in the hip-hop community, there was a sense of disappointment and perhaps even betrayal, given all of the voter mobilization, registration, and increased turnout rates among African Americans. Until the concerted efforts of Russell Simmon's Hip-Hop Summit Action Network (HSAN) and P. Diddy's Vote or Die campaign, many in the hip-hop community believed that not voting was the politically correct thing to do. According to Adisa Banjoko, the feelings of apathy and non-participation in the hip-hop generation are normal. In a 2002 Jeff

Chang article on metroactive.com entitled "Impeach the President" he shared, "It's legitimate for hip-hop folks to be skeptical of the system. The 2000 elections broke a lot of spirits. It makes sense that people's hearts would be broken" (http://www.metroactive.com/papers/metro/10.27.04/hiphopolitics-0444.html). In the article, Chang substantiated these sentiments and contended that hip-hop's electoral non-participation is actually "hurt and anger masked as tough pragmatism." Whatever the rationale had been, it seems as if the 2000 election proved to many in the hip-hop community that in America money, power, respect, "bling-bling", Cristal, "Benjamins," and even "conscious" rap without political organization and mobilization does not translate into political equality and substantive public policy for the broader African American community.

We won't stop!

In spite of the disappointing outcome of the 2000 presidential election, the political resolve, grassroots activism, and community-based mobilization of the hip-hop community was stronger than ever before. In 2004, members of the hip-hop community engaged in a national media and organizational blitz targeted at capturing new voters as well as downloading the economic, educational, political, and sociocultural agenda of the community into the hard drive of its "head nodding" constituency base. Utilizing the commercial success and cross-marketing techniques of the industry that have made household names out of Jay-Z, Kanye West, Nelly, 50 Cent, and P. Diddy (now known as Diddy), members of the hip-hop community rallied together.

Some of the highlights of the hip-hop community's activism include more than 40 pre-election hip-hop summits around the nation, more than one million new registered voters through the efforts of HSAN's National Hip-Hop Civic Engagement Project, the Vote or Die, and Rock the Vote campaigns, and attendance at the Republican and Democratic conventions by members of the "we won't stop" generation.

Mission accomplished?

"Each generation must discover its mission, fulfill it, or betray it."

Frantz Fanon

Although the 2004 election may not have produced the tangible results some were hoping for as the nation (specifically the "red" states) supported four more years of "Dubya," many in the hip-hop community decided to "do something" and parlayed their cultural, economic, and cross-marketing power into substantive political power. As Congresswoman Maxine Waters stated, "I think hip-hop has captured the imagination of so many young people in our society, and this influence can be [used] to help make public policy decisions through the election of the kind of people that can change the direction of this country and pay attention to the issues and the concerns of young people."

As noted above, the influence of hip-hop translated into several collective collaborations and multiple "remixes" which produced more than one million new registered voters. Additionally, politicians on both sides of the aisle engaged in dialogue and photo-ops with hip-hop's new political leadership. Moreover, Detroit's own mayor, Kwame Kilpatrick, was dubbed the "Hip-Hop" Mayor. At present, it seems as if members of the hip-hop community are committed to fulfilling its mission to shed light on social ills, hold public officials accountable, and take responsibility for the uplift of their communities.

In preparation for the 2008 election it was suggested that members of the hip-hop community go from being politically visible to politically savvy. In this regard, the hip-hop community needed to continue to engage in grass-roots, local political mobilization efforts, and national electoral politics campaigns. Additionally, catchy marketing and campaign blitz were coupled with politically educated and aware artists, constituency groups, and a political blueprint of where to go from here. Moreover, hip-hop's core audience and potential constituency base needed to be as well versed in the political platforms of both parties as they are in the latest lyrics being "spit" by its franchise artists. Finally, the hip-hop community needed to leverage itself as a serious political cadre so as to become an "inside" player in the political arena and not merely another outside agitator subject to the whims of political thugs and "gangstas" that reside in both red and blue states.

"Bush don't like Black people"

On August 26, 2005 one of the worst natural catastrophes struck the United States. Hurricane Katrina bombarded the shores of Florida, Louisiana, Mississippi, and parts of Alabama. The aftermath of the hurricane produced many torrid images of an overwhelming number of African Americans left behind to survive by any means possible as basic necessities such as water took three days to be shipped into the flood-torn areas. In the aftermath of the storm, many fingers were pointed at elected officials. Members of the clergy, entertainers, artists, and everyday citizens demanded answers as to why tens of thousands of African Americans were left to die without any federal government intervention. In an effort to "save ourselves," many hip-hop artists used their own money to fill up 18-wheeler trucks and chartered buses to go down to New Orleans and help their African American brothers and sisters.

Controversy over who dropped the ball – Mayor Nagin, Governor Blanco, President Bush, FEMA (or all of the aforementioned) – was the breaking news of every hour until Friday, September 3, 2005. On this evening, the NBC television network hosted one of many "live" television events to raise relief funds for the victims of Hurricane Katrina. Multi-platinum Grammy award winning artist Kanye West decided to break away from the written script and gave an impromptu, heartfelt interpretation of his perspective on the natural disaster. Kanye West's unexpected and therefore uncensored remarks about the

Plate 12.1 *Kanye West, hip-hop artist and trendsetter*

tragedies of Hurricane Katrina split the nation and poured even more salt into the infected wound of racism and racial tensions in America.

In his remarks, West accused the media of being irresponsible. In particular, West spoke of his disgust with the way the media portrayed African Americans during the crisis situation. He said, "I hate the way they portray us in the media. You see a black family and they say we are looting, you see a White family and they say they are looking for food." Interestingly, what West spoke about had already been a point of contention and disdain as many in the African American community took offense at the differentiation in use of the terms "looters" and "those looking for food." According to Herbert Gans (1996), author of *The War Against the Poor*, the attempt by some in the media to negatively stereotype one group or person can be purposive. One of the strategies to keep poor and/or deviant people in their place is to label and stereotype them. Gans contended that the role of the media is to reinforce and legitimate the labels created to stigmatize the undesirable group of people. Thus, the media's use of the terms "looters" and "refugees" to characterize the behavior of some of New Orleans African American residents may have been done to cause racial division and contempt.

Another claim West made was that America was set up to "help the poor, the Black people, the less well off as slow as possible." This comment was not met with much criticism as arguably it was lost in the shuffle of the most controversial charge Kanye West made that evening. Most notably, he said, "We already realize a lot of the people that could help are at war right now, fighting another way. And now they've given them permission to go down and shoot us . . . George Bush doesn't care about Black people." (http://www.washingtonpost.com/wpdyn/content/article/2005/09/03/AR2005090300165.html). The truth of the matter is that once he said "George Bush doesn't care about Black people," everything else was dismissed. In the aftermath of West's comments, the network, political pundits, and some members of the African American community went on the firing lines, either refuting or defending Mr West.

First, in an effort to not offend those watching the live television fundraiser, NBC ran a statement throughout the rest of the broadcast distancing the network from West's comments. Second, every political pundit and cable news personality took the story and ran with it – usually attempting to discredit the perspectives of Mr West. Third, many in the African American community supported West's perspectives both publicly and privately. One of the reasons why so many Blacks supported him is that they felt as if the president should have done more to help the majority of the victims of the hurricane that were stranded on highways, at the Superdome, and left for dead throughout the streets of New Orleans. The belief that the government should do more is in line with the basic tenets of democracy which state that the government should ensure the domestic tranquility of its people.

Consciousness revived

To this day, no one knows for sure who the then president liked or disliked. It would seem as if President Bush was fond of some African Americans as he appointed several to high-ranking cabinet positions. Nonetheless, all of the media's negative spin on the "who, what, and when" of Kanye West's comments missed the significance of the rebirth of "consciousness" in hip-hop that occurred that evening. Whether he knew it or not, West invoked that same sense of "questioning" and "anti-establishment" thought that made songs like "The Message" so powerful and transformative. West's impassioned plea was not one of absolution as he first condemned himself. "And even for me to complain, I would be a hypocrite because I would turn away from the TV because it's too hard to watch. I've even been shopping before even giving a donation, so now I'm calling my business manager right now to see what is the biggest amount I can give."(http://www.washingtonpost.com/wpdyn/content/article/2005/09/03/AR2005090300165.html)

In being transparent about even his own failings, West critiqued his own efforts within the context of the initiatives of others. Further, whether West knew it or not, in speaking out, he actually revised the "conscious" spirit of hip-hop that had been almost completely wiped out by the lusts of commercialism and capitalism. Moreover, as Errol Henderson contends, West was able to speak of "Afrocentric" uplift which connects to a communal duty to "educate our youth and to demand of our youth an appropriate respect for their true heritage, legacy, and the responsibility that accompanies both" (Henderson, 1996). In the final analysis, perhaps Hurricane Katrina was the "Why?" the hip-hop community needed to organize and help clean up the mess of economic, political, and sociocultural disenfranchisement and disdain in the African American community.

The "N" word

One of the most unsettled debates in all of hip-hop is the use of the "N" word. From the perspectives of many artists, when African American members of the hip-hop community use the word it is meant to connote affection, brotherhood, and close association. In this regard, it is argued that the hip-hop community's use of the word is not offensive as it seeks to take the sting and power out of the word and remix and reuse it. On the other side of the coin, prominent African Americans including Oprah Winfrey contend that the use of the word by anyone – especially African Americans – is offensive and counterproductive, as a consequence of the horrible historical roots of the word and the effects of the word on the psyche of the Black community given its original intent to intimidate, scare, and literally scar its victims.

Seemingly the debate over the use of the "N" word came to a climax in 2007 as two prominent White Americans – Michael Richards and Don Imus – both used an "N" word to insult African Americans. In the first case, Richards, who starred in the sitcom *Seinfeld*, shouted the slur repeatedly and even reminded the two African American males he was arguing with about how back in the day (of slavery and segregation) the two of them would have been hanged from trees. In the other incident, shock-jock Imus referred to the members of a women's basketball team as "nappy-headed hoes." In an attempt to justify his comments, Imus said he felt it was OK to use such language because rappers like Snoop Dogg did.

In response to the Imus incident, Oprah dedicated two days of her syndicated television show to the use of the "N" word in the African American community. On the show, hip-hop mogul Russell Simmons defended the use of the word while the majority of the panel contended that it was time to raise the bar in the hip-hop community and eliminate the word from dialogue. When the dust cleared, the "N" word was still in heavy rotation. Moreover, hip-hop icon street disciple Nas is slated to release an album entitled N***A. As Nas explained,

> We're taking power [away] from the word. No disrespect to none of them who were a part of the Civil Rights movement, but some of my n***as in the streets don't know who Medgar Evers was. I love Medgar Evers, but some of the n***as in the streets don't know Medgar Evers, they know who Nas is. And to my older people who don't know who Nas is and who don't know what a street disciple is, stay outta this mutha f**** conversation. We'll talk to

you when we're ready. Right now, we're on a whole new movement. We're taking power [away] from that word. (www.mtv.com/news/articles/1572287/20071018/nas.jhtml)

Civil rights activists including the Rev. Al Sharpton strongly disagree with the street disciples' use of the word and contend that they are actually helping racists when they continue to use the word in the marketplace.

One rapper who did have a change of heart is Chamillionaire. The platinum-selling artist decided not to use the "N" word or any other profanity on his most recent CD release. On his BET.com blog, Chamillionaire detailed why he decided to stop using certain language:

> To me, the whole cursing thing is a moral issue and I think people do it based on their morals. I made the decision not to curse way before the Don Imus controversy . . . more white kids are showing up to the shows than black kids. I got 20,000 white kids at my show. My DJ would try to be funny and stop the music right when I was about to say the "n" word just so we could hear the audience say it. So I felt like I'm standing on the show teaching white kids how to use the "n" word. (http://blogs.bet.com/music/hhvsa/chamillionaire-blogs/)

Chamillionaire's decision to stop using profane language is definitely a step in the right direction. However, the hip-hop community has a long way to go before it truly understands the ways in which they may have misused and abused their 1st Amendment right to freedom of speech as a whole new generation of young people use the "N" word with reckless abandon and no regard for the sacrifices that were made in order for them to stay "so fresh and so clean."

Stop snitchin'

The other controversial issue in the hip-hop community evolves around the popularization of snitchin'. In particular, a host of hip-hop artists, DJs, and faithful listeners/followers have made it known that anyone who is an eye witness to a crime or has information about the perpetrators of a crime and reports such to the police is a snitch. The sad reality is that until its remix in the hip-hop community, an eye witness to a crime was seen as a hero, a Good Samaritan, a witness even. Today, however, the "stop snitchin'" movement has gone nationwide and has been accompanied by a variety of hip-hop songs, DVDs, and clothing, some of which even has stop signs riddled with bullet holes to symbolize what happens to snitches.

The problem with the "stop snitchin'" movement is that it is extremely detrimental to law enforcement investigations. One of the most well-known examples of the refusal of members of the hip-hop community to share information with the police occurred on the set of a Busta Rhymes video shoot in Brooklyn, New York. On February 5, 2006, one of Busta's bodyguards – Israel Ramirez – was shot and killed in front of the hip-hop star. To this day, Busta has refused to cooperate with law enforcement officials as he seemingly is honoring the street code of silence by "not snitchin'."

In an effort to offer an explanation about why artists don't snitch, hip-hop artist Cam'ron contended that telling on people is not good for business. Cam'ron, who was shot in both arms in an attempted robbery in 2005, explained to CNN host Anderson Cooper the methodology of remaining silent. "Because with the type of business I'm in, it would definitely hurt my business. And the way that I was raised, I just don't do that. I was raised differently, not to tell . . . it's about business but it's still also a code of ethics . . . there's nothing really to talk about with the police, I mean for what?" Cam'ron later retracted his comments and issued an apology as he received a great deal of criticism for contending that he would not help the police find a serial killer. Still, Cam'ron has gone on record and even made a video where he bashes hip-hop mega-star Curtis "50 Cent" Jackson for being a snitch.

Where do we go from here?

What do you do with a thirty-year-old child that has not had the proper instruction, nurture, and guidance of its elders yet has tremendous charisma, charm, social capital, global reach, and wealth? Do you put the child on punishment and demand that it change its ugly ways or do you celebrate the slow growth and revitalization of consciousness that occurs in ebbs and flows? Such is the dilemma of hip-hop in America. Clearly, the influence, impact, and infectious nature of hip-hop as a global art form and canvass is without question. From Seoul to South Africa, young heads are noddin' to the jazz infused riffs of Jigga, the old school break beats of 50 Cent, and the forever James Brown sounds of Kanye and Diddy. Still, the social and economic acumen of hip-hop has yet to be transformed into lucrative political influence and power.

In terms of where we go from here, it seems as if the hip-hop community must make a decision as to who it wants to be. In other words, in order to become effective political stakeholders that have the potential to swing elections, the hip-hop community must grow up, accept responsibility, and develop an action agenda that speaks to the needs of its forgotten constituency – African American youth. In this regard, hip-hop can no longer go on unchecked, uncensored, and unprotected escapades of nihilism, misogyny, violence, and disrespect. In this regard, if hip-hop is going to step into the political arena, it must pull up its pants and become educated about the two-party system, institutional politics, the history and effectiveness of the civil rights movement, and electoral politics.

Moreover, if the hip-hop community is going to become the major political force it has the potential to become, the genre must diversify and reinvent itself as an educated, responsible, and socially conscious adult. As such, hip-hop must invest in the political process the same drive, determination, skill set, and creative ingenuity it does in creating lyrics, videos, clothing lines, and even lifestyle brands that have made it a multi-billionaire industry in the first place.

Points to ponder

1. Briefly detail the early development of hip-hop and its connection to political events and leaders.
2. In what ways is hip-hop a voice for the voiceless? Can this voice be translated into political power?
3. In what ways are political organization and mobilization strategies such as the Rap the Vote and Vote or Die campaigns effective tools?
4. Is hip-hop a mirror of American society politically, economically, and/or socioculturally? Please explain.

Key phrases and people

The Bronx	Chuck D	globalization
hip-hop	Black Nationalism	Hip-Hop Action Network
The Carter Administration	The Message	Black consciousness
War on Poverty	Gangsta Rap	Russell Simmons
Nas	Jay-Z	Kanye West
Vote or Die Campaign	snitchin'	the "N" word

Part IV

13

Where Do We Go From Here?

A little more than 40 years ago, Dr Martin L. King, Jr addressed the annual meeting of the Southern Christian Leadership Conference. In celebration of the ten-year anniversary of the faith-based civil rights organization, Dr King shared his thoughts on the future of the organization as a champion of African American incorporation and empowerment in an address entitled "Where Do We Go from Here?" In his address, Dr King shared a detailed framework of the state of affairs of Negroes in America prior to the leadership activism of SCLC, discussed some of the most significant victories of the organization, and concluded with a prophetic mandate of the future which linked economic, political, and social uplift and advancement with a clearly defined commitment to a "revolution of values" which would cause America to be "born again." Held in Atlanta, GA which up until recently was known as "The City Too Busy to Hate," Dr King shared his blueprint of success. At the top of the list was the nationalization of "Operation Breadbasket," the organization's economic empowerment campaign designed to return opportunities and investments to the Black community.

In his discussion of the success of "Operation Breadbasket," Dr King shared the significance of the SCLC's motto which boldly told corporate American industries like Sealtest "If you respect my dollar, you must respect my person." In effect, the African American community demanded substantive community reinvestment from all industries that profited off it by demanding that these corporations hire African Americans, deposit funds in African American banks, and advertise in African American medial entities. As Dr King stated, "The most dramatic success in Chicago has been Operation Breadbasket. Through Operation Breadbasket we have now achieved for the Negro community of Chicago more than 2,200 new jobs with an income of approximately 18 million dollars a year" (Carson and Shepard, 2001: 176). In effect, Operation Breadbasket was a strategic economic initiative that provided complementary assistance to the newly gained sociocultural and political incorporation and empowerment garnered by the Black community through the passage of the Civil Rights Act of 1964 and the Voting Rights Act of 1965.

In spite of the new liberation of the Black community, Dr King felt compelled to tell his listening audience that there still was more work to be done in order for the collective consciousness of America to rise above its ugly past. In essence, Dr King argued that the collective strength and power of traditional

American leaders, institutions, organizations, and even the government must rally around the united struggles of its people. In effect, if America were to accept the mandate by the prophet King to be "born again," it would have to accept responsibility for all of its "dastardly acts of cowardice" that caused the hem of its red, white, and blue garments to tear in the first place.

Where do we go from here?

> "In short, over the last ten years the Negro decided to straighten his back up, realizing that a man cannot ride your back unless it is bent. We made our government write new laws to alter some of the cruelest injustices that affected us . . . For this we can feel a legitimate pride. But in spite of a decade of significant progress, the problem is far from solved."
>
> Dr Martin Luther King, Jr (1967)

In 1967, Dr Martin L. King, Jr reflected on how the Negro community straightened up its back and began to walk out the promises guaranteed to it through the 5th and 14th Amendments, a host of Congressional Acts, presidential executive orders, and landmark Supreme Court decisions. In spite of these tremendously paradigmatic shifts in the structure, scope, and sensibility of the nation, African Americans still lagged significantly behind their White counterparts in a variety of socio-economic indicators of success and attainment of the "American dream." In particular, as Dr King shared in his SCLC 10th Anniversary address, "Now in order to answer the question, 'Where do we go from here?' which is our theme, we must first honestly recognize where we are now . . . Of the good things in life, the Negro has approximately one half those of whites. Of the bad things of life, he has twice those of whites" (Carson and Shepard, 2001: 172).

Interestingly, as Senator Ted Kennedy (D-MA) shared in his commentary about the speech, "Change a few words in the speech – replace "Negro" with "African American" – and the readers will think they're reading the work of one of the best and brightest of today's social commentators. His great speech touches on many specific issues that are especially important today, such as economic opportunity, community reinvestment, affordable housing and home ownership, and education." More profound, seemingly, is the fact that more than 40 years after this address, African Americans in the United States are still contending with these basic issues, some of which are federal and state entitlements. To be clear, some of the most pressing needs of Black and Brown communities across the country revolve around issues of economic opportunity and empowerment, educational equity and technological access, unequal and uneven distributions of justice, home ownership as well as protections against predatory and sub-prime lenders, and governmental extension and protections of rights such as affirmative action. As King warned,

> With all the struggle and the achievements, we must face the fact, however, that the Negro still lives in the basement of the Great Society. He is still at the bottom, despite the

few who have penetrated to slightly higher levels. Even when the door has been forced partially open, mobility for the Negro is still sharply restricted . . . and the Negro did not do this himself; it was done to him. (King, 1967)

As such, in addressing the question of where we go from here, King re-articulated the fundamental responsibility of the Negro community to do three complementary things. First, the Negro had to reassert his dignity and worth. Second, the Negro had to acquire political and economic power. Finally, the Negro had to recommit to nonviolence. In many respects, African Americans have loosely embraced the three tenets promoted by King as is evidenced by the progress of the Black community in a variety of economic, political, and sociocultural areas of American society.

Others argue that the blueprint issued by Dr King was more of a spiritually imbued, esoterically conceived, doctrine of faith, hope, and love and not a practical, pragmatic, or precise political tool of implementation for the twentieth century. Today, there are tens of thousands of African American elected officials that serve on the local, state, and national levels in a variety of capacities. Additionally, the number of African American millionaires has skyrocketed in a host of business, technology, law, and multimedia industries. Still, where the collective African American community may need to revisit the prophet King is in the areas of reasserting one's dignity and worth and recommitment to nonviolence as, while the political and economic success of the African American community is at an all-time high, so too are the pathologies and problematic behaviors of this "fleecy locked" family.

How do we grow from here?

Throughout *African American Politics*, I have sought to bring balance to what tend to be one-sided, blame-game explanations of African American economic, political, and sociocultural advancement and success. Clearly, not an easy task, especially for one who is undeniably a part of the hip-hop community, I have gained strength, voice, and balance from what I believe is the beautifully interwoven experiences of my exposure to the writing and prophetic underpinnings of Dr Martin L. King, Jr. I was first introduced to Dr King and his "I Have a Dream" speech as a first grader. I was reintroduced to his seminal and unfortunately last book – *"Where Do We Go from Here: Chaos or Community?"* – as a graduate student in a Black Studies course at The Ohio State University. What I admire most about Dr King was his ability to tell the truth in love while simultaneously shedding light on the ills and misfortunes of the nation, all the while providing direction, guidance, and pragmatic solutions as a means of healing the "land of the free and the home of the brave." As such, in answering the question, "How do we grow from here?" I will seek to utilize my mentor's mantra of God-given grace, dignity, and collective consciousness to share how it is that I believe African Americans who are engaged in the political process, as well as in what Dr King characterized as "the three dimensions of

Plate 13.1 *Hurricane Katrina survivors*

a complete life," can grow, develop, and take their rightful place in American society in the twenty-first century.

Our dignity and worth

As shared, Dr King contended that, in order for the collective community of Black interests to grow, the Negro community which is now politically identi-fied as the African American community must "massively assert our dignity and worth." In so doing, Dr King contended that the Black community had to develop a "majestic sense of values" that transcended the shell of Blackness that we were temporarily assigned by God. Moreover, he shared that we could no longer be ashamed to be Black even though it seemed as if "semantics have conspired to make that which is black seem ugly and degrading." Continuing he said,

> In *Roget's Thesaurus* there are some 120 synonyms for blackness and at least sixty of them are offensive, such words as blot, soot, grim, devil, and foul . . . the tendency to ignore the Negro's contribution to American life and strip him of his personhood is as old as the earliest history books and as contemporary as the morning's newspaper. (Carson and Shepard, 2001: 183)

In effect, Dr King suggested that the first step in the growth process of Africans in America was through self-purification and love that detoxified the soul of all of the governmental, institutional, psychological, and sociocultural mechanisms that were purposively put in place to make the Negro, then Black, and now African American community think, believe, and embrace a colonial model ideology of inferiority that made Asians and not African Americans the "model" minority.

Today, as in 1967, I believe that the African American community must "massively assert our dignity and worth" as the overall community is still marred by the divisiveness of the War Against the Poor wherein social scientists, K-12 and academic institutions, government agencies, and the media engage in "labeling" as a means of distinguishing desirable and undesirable elements and behaviors. An excellent example of this occurred after Hurricane Katrina when media entities sought to distinguish African American and White people who were all breaking the law in the aftermath of the storm.

In asserting our collective dignity and worth, African Americans will be able to reside above what Dr King contended was "cultural homicide" and boldly proclaim "I'm black, but I'm black and beautiful." Still, the question remains, what does this have to do with African American politics? Simply put, as the argument is made and beautifully articulated by Dr King, what holds the African American community back from exponential growth is our inward grasp of freedom, liberty, and equality. As he acknowledged, "No Lincolnian Emancipation Proclamation, no Johnsonian civil rights bill can totally bring this kind of freedom" (Carson and Shepard, 2001: 184).

Clearly, there is a humungous portion of the African American community that has done exactly as the prophet King instructed. Still, there is a large portion of the community that has refused to take off the shackles of nihilism, misogyny, self-sabotage, and anger (most notably some members of the youth and hip-hop communities). Labeled as "super-predators" who have no regard or respect for morality, authority, adults, and the law are some of the hat-to-the-back thugs that make civil rights leaders like Jesse Jackson relieved to discover that when he is walking down the street at night that it is a group of White males behind him.

In this regard, I believe that the African American community will holistically grow and develop effective action-agendas that engage the disengaged, discouraged, and perhaps even disturbed generation of young people who have been neglected by a host of adults – oftentimes including their parents. Although some have suggested that the best avenue of growth for this cadre of the African American community is the church, I believe that the entire community plays a role – especially those in the hip-hop community who seemingly glorify dying over anything, including "respect." Whereas during the "movement," there were organizational centers, leadership circles, and hands-on training and development, today the psychosis of "me, myself, and I-ism" seems to have made the village devoid of genuine leaders, mentors, and advisors to guide this technologically and unfortunately Tek-9 savvy generation.

In this regard, it is my humble position that in the next 50 years the gains of the civil rights movement and subsequent African American economic, political, and sociocultural inroads may very well vanish into thin air. Why? It seems as if a new generation of privileged African Americans has irresponsibly remixed Dr King's contention in *Where Do We Go from Here?* that the Negro community must assert its dignity and worth into a never-ending soundtrack of self-absorption, over-consumption, and excessiveness which equates "money, power, and respect" to large entourages, the latest Escalade, and evenings with a rainbow of delicatessens and divas.

By no means am I solely pointing the finger at the hip-hop community. As a member of the community, such narrow focus is self-incriminating. I do, however, wish to issue a challenge to my brothers and sisters of "The Message," "Edutainment," "How Do You Want It?" "The Blueprint," "Ready to Die," "What U Know 'Bout Me," and "I Get Money" generation to utilize our collective bling (cultural, economic, intellectual, political, social, and spiritual capital) and inherited power for more productive and premeditatedly prosperous purposes. In this regard, I hope that today's "Leaders of the New School" embrace the fact that "power properly understood is nothing but the ability to achieve purpose. It is the strength required to bring about social, political, and economic change." Furthermore, as previously shared, I also hope that my fellow hip-hoppers – some of whom are willing to do anything including kill or be killed for something as elusive as "respect" – will quickly understand that, as Dr King said, "we have got to get this thing right. What is needed is a realization that power without love is reckless and abusive, and that love without power is sentimental and anemic. Power at its best is love implementing the demands of justice, and justice at its best is love correcting everything that stands against love" (Carson and Shepard, 2001: 186).

The power of growth in the new millennium

In spite of the efforts of many with counter-agendas to render Dr Martin L. King, Jr static, mythical, time-bound, and limited to the overly misrepresented and watered down "I Have a Dream" speech, the depth and breadth of this philosopher, theologian, social commentator, critic, and prophet is undeniable. Clearly, Dr King was able to tap into the pulse of America and issue the necessary prescriptions vital to its long-term recovery and rebirth. As such, it is my sincere belief that the ability of the African American community to experience growth in the new millennium is directly correlated to King's three-prong action plan of economic, political, and sociocultural success wherein the Negro community first looks within and reasserts its dignity, value, and worth as a viable and contributing member of the American political landscape. Still, to be certain, there are several problems that restrict the development of a three-prong strategy of holistic empowerment and advancement in the African American community.

First, the African American community is sharply divided, and in some instances at odds, on a variety of value-based issues such as abortion, homosexuality, out-of-wedlock births, the death penalty, and "three strikes and you're out" laws. Second, the African American community has yet to deal with the elephant in the room as it relates to the ugly schism between what can be characterized as the *Old School* leadership civil rights vanguard and the *New School* leadership social sophisticates that include a cross-section of members of the hip-hop, Mega-church, academic, private, public, and non-profit communities. Finally, there is no longer a monolithic voice or agenda of African American interest which further complicates the divisions in the community. In this regard, the question of "who" should be at the leadership table of African American growth in the new millennium is always complicated by the seemingly double-mindedness of members of both the hip-hop and Black Mega-church communities. The largest criticism of the hip-hop community is its embrace of self-destructive behavior and language, including the use of the "N" word, while the greatest criticism of the Black Mega-church community is its embrace of the Republican Party and conservative values.

Economic and political power

Undoubtedly, African American procurement of the vote provided broad institutional and legal acumen to fight against the "extra" legal mechanisms such as the grandfather clause, the poll tax, literacy tests, and other intimidation tactics that were used to circumvent and usurp the Black vote in America. In spite of the fact that there are a limited number of African American interest groups, PACs, and economic and political advocacy groups, African American office-holding on the local, state, and national level continues to grow and expand. Moreover, the 2004 presidential election and the 2006 midterm election produced two of the most significant rates of African American voter registration and turnout nationwide. In Georgia, Virginia, and Ohio, African American voter turnout was credited with giving the Democrats majority control in both the US House of Representatives and the US Senate. Clearly, 2008 proved to be a record year as Barack H. Obama was elected as the first Black president of the United States of America. Finally, the efforts of the NAACP Legal Defense Fund, coupled with the loud dissent of many African American leaders and political figures, was temporarily successful in restricting the implementation of Georgia's voter ID law, a Republican Party legislative initiative which many fear is nothing more than a modernized and sophisticated voter dilution tactic designed to frustrate and suppress votes in states with large African American demographic representation.

Still, the question remains as to whether the vote, alone, is enough, as seemingly once African Americans laid to rest the non-traditional mechanisms of protest politics, something in the political atmosphere shifted. In particular, it seems that the African American community, in distancing itself from the combined strategies of protest and traditional politics, has lost ground as we still grapple over and negotiate for rights, privileges, access, and respect that should have long been established.

In terms of economics, the future growth of the African American community seems to be predicated on the decisions of the United States government and its willingness to provide a "living wage" for its citizenry. As detailed in chapter 3 – "African Americans and Dollars and Sense" – similar to the harsh realities of 40 years ago, the African American community still lags behind its White counterpart in terms of employment opportunities, dollar per dollar earnings, home ownership, investments, and inheritance in most cities through the nation. Moreover, the penalty many African Americans pay in terms of the per capita rate of denied bank loans, lines of credit, higher interest rates, and joblessness further reinforces the slow psychological, political, and economic growth of the community.

In Profile: Bridges of Hope – Mrs Rosa Parks and Mrs Coretta Scott King

The close of 2005 and the beginning of 2006 were extremely significant in the history of the African American freedom struggle. The loss of two of the greatest matriarchs and martyrs of the modern civil rights movement was certainly a blow to the African American community as their symbolic and substantive acts of civil disobedience, social change, and social justice have served as touchstones and reminders of the power of one individual to make a difference. Nonetheless, the individual and collective accomplishments of these two great women have undeniably served and remain a bridge of hope for future generations.

Rosa Parks (1913–2005)

Rosa Parks, a Montgomery, Alabama resident, has been described as a wife, seamstress, servant of God, and secretary of the local chapter of the NAACP. Mrs Parks's triumphant act of courage in 1955 set in motion the modern civil rights movement as she refused to comply with the city's busing ordinance which was economically unbiased, in that all riders paid the same fare, yet racially discriminatory as all Black passengers had to sit at the back of the bus as well as give up their seat to a White rider if the bus became full. As she detailed, "December 5, 1955, was one of the memorable and inspiring days of my life. History records this day as the beginning of the modern civil rights movement that transformed America and influenced freedom revolutions around the world" (Carson and Shepard, 2001: 3).

For 381 days African Americans proved that both their money and

Plate 13.2 *Mrs Rosa Parks, one of the catalysts of the Montgomery Bus Boycott*

personhood were to be respected as they refused to ride the city buses of Montgomery. More than a year after Mrs Parks's initial act of courage, the Supreme Court of the United States of America ruled in favor of the African American citizens of Montgomery, Alabama and declared the city busing ordinance unconstitutional. Mrs Parks's willingness to lay down her life provided the bridge of African American equality and justice needed to produce federal government protection and privileges that the African American community still benefits from today. Moreover, the development of a new generation of Rosa Parks-like men and women who possess the courage, fortitude, strength, and sacrifice to tackle systems, institutions, ideologies, and individuals that are counterproductive, harmful, and destructive to the growth of the African American community in the new millennium is essential.

Mrs Coretta Scott King (1927–2006)

Another bridge-builder and trailblazer of the modern civil rights movement was Mrs Coretta Scott King. Born in Marion, Alabama, Coretta Scott attended Antioch College in Yellow Springs, Ohio where she majored in music. Upon graduation, she attended the prestigious New England Conservatory of Music in Boston where she met her husband, Dr Martin L. King, Jr. The two intellects and serious advocates of social justice made a conscious decision to return to the segregated South upon completion of their degrees as they felt they had a commitment to serve the Black community. During the civil rights movement, Mrs King helped raise funds through Freedom Concerts. She was also very instrumental in capturing some of her husband's now famous speeches including that given to the Montgomery Improvement Association.

Throughout the 13 years of Dr King's leadership in the movement, Mrs King was a loyal, faithful, and courageous support system for her husband. She even remained by his side after their home was bombed during the beginning of the Montgomery Bus Boycott of 1955. Mrs King is also credited with being one of the voices that ultimately led to Dr King's stance against the Vietnam War as she was the first in their household to publicly go on record against the war. Upon the untimely assassination of her husband, it was Mrs King who returned to Memphis in April of 1968 to lead the march he was unable to complete. Most importantly, in an effort to build a living memorial to her husband, it was Mrs Coretta Scott King who was instrumental in raising the funds to build the Dr Martin Luther King, Jr Center for Nonviolent Social Change in Atlanta, Georgia.

In her role as the founder and CEO of the Dr Martin Luther King, Jr Center for Nonviolent Social Change, Mrs King worked diligently to gain passage of the first national holiday in honor of an African American. In 1982, President Ronald Reagan signed the federal Dr Martin L. King, Jr Holiday legislation which is commemorated on the third Monday of January. In addition to her King Holiday efforts, Mrs King lent her voice, wisdom, and credibility to a variety of democratic causes including peace studies, women's rights, and African American civil rights. Keenly aware that she was birthed to fulfill a greater purpose, Mrs King is often remembered for sharing that she did not just marry the man (Dr King), but that she also "married the movement." The impact of Mrs King's international, non-partisan, and collective bridge building was evidenced during her funeral where she made history twice over as four living presidents of the United States of America – Jimmy Carter, George H. W. Bush, Bill Clinton, and George W. Bush – attended her home-going celebration and she became the first African American to lie in state at the Georgia State Capitol.

Although there will never be another Mrs Rosa Parks or Mrs Coretta Scott King, I believe that the African American community should glean from these two great leaders the fact that the struggle for African American liberation is bigger than an individual cause or person. Moreover, I believe that the life and legacy of these two women speak to the power of selflessness and genuine leadership which does not seek to be a "searcher of consensus but a molder of consensus."

In closing: "An audacious faith in the future"

The future of African American politics awaits a politically educated, savvy, non-partisan, and purposive cadre of voices that is willing to not count it

Plate 13.3 *Mrs Coretta Scott King, wife of Dr Martin L. King, Jr, founder of the Martin Luther King, Jr Center for Nonviolent Social Change, and humanitarian campaigner*

robbery to evaluate and reconsider its present state of affairs in an effort to make room and better choices for up-and-coming leaders. In this regard, as the African American community forges forth ahead in an "audacious faith in the future," it is critical that three action agenda items of growth be considered and incorporated to ensure that the bridges built on the backs of civil rights leaders of the past do not subside, slow down, or succumb to laissez-faire politics, economics, and sociocultural systems.

The first action agenda item of growth that the African American community must consider is the power of multi-racial and multi-ethnic coalitions, joint partnerships, and creative collaborations which are conjoined around complementary interests, ideologies, valence issues, and beliefs. The second action agenda item that the African American community must consider is the development of substantive bridges of partnership, leadership, politics, economics, and community building between the civil rights vanguard and the hip-hop community. An excellent example of the two communities coming together for the collective good occurred during BETs (Black Entertainment Television) Saving Our Selves Hurricane Katrina Relief Telethon. Finally, the African American community must examine effective ways to utilize the economic, political, and social conscious and justice legacy of the Black Church as leverage in local, state, and national arena to impact change. As Aldon Morris (1984) accurately detailed, the Black Church remains the single most autonomous institution of the African American community. As such, the Black Church – especially Mega-churches – can provide a triple threat of demographics (the average Mega-church has a base membership of 7,000 people), financial coffers, and voice to speak truth to power and reformulate and reshape policy, procedures, norms, and ideologies related to African American political, economic, cultural, and social perceptions and realities in America.

History has become *Ourstory*

Without a doubt, the election of Barack Obama is one of the most historic political event to happen since the founding of the great United States of America. The historic nature of America's first African American president is multifold and speaks to a variety of theoretical as well as articled principles of the nation. As such, from a theoretical standpoint, the election of Barack Obama is an actualization of the democratic ideals of our nation. In particular, the willingness, commitment, and follow-through of more than 50 percent of America's voting population to elect a "Black" man into office beautifully syncs and harmonizes the democratic ideals of individual dignity, equality before the law, widespread participation in public decisions, and public decisions by majority rule with one person having one vote.

Beyond the actualization of our democratic ideals, the 2008 election is also historic in that the true potential of the 15th Amendment (extension of the right to vote to African American men), the 19th Amendment (extension of the right to vote to women), and the Voting Rights Act of 1965 and its extensions (the elimination of voting restrictions used to discriminate against African Americans and other minorities) have finally been realized. Moreover, the pernicious, narrow, and deftly discriminatory comments of former Supreme Court Chief Justice Roger B. Taney were laid to rest in that in 2008 the Black man has many gifts – economically, politically, spiritually, and socially conscious – that "the white man is bound to respect." Perhaps, more telling have been the personal narratives of many "card-carrying" members of the Republican Party who for the first time in their lives were split-ticket voters and cast their presidential ballot for the Kenyan-descended, Hawaiian-raised native son.

Moreover, forty years after Dr Martin L. King, Jr delivered his prophetic "I've Been to the Mountaintop" speech where he declared "we, as a people, will get to the Promised Land," the election of Barack Obama is historic in that our nation will realize Dr King's powerful vision of the "World House" where all people add value and make significant contributions to the foundational and futuristic fibers of our nation. In this regard, the election of Barack Obama brings to an end more than 400 years of "dreams deferred" and speaks to the hope, promise, and future of "other-centered" executive level decision-making that hopefully will set a new precedent of global leadership, reconciliation, and rediscovery of "lost values."

On a similar yet different note, the election of Barack Obama also has served to reignite the passion, perspectives, and political voice of an entire generation and genre of young people in America. As such, the 2008 election is historic in that for the first time in the history of our nation, there is a voluminous number of young people who recognize that as hip-hop legends De La Soul said, "Stakes is High," and who did all they could do (registering to vote, participating in a variety of canvassing, fundraising, blogging, using MySpace, YouTube, and Facebook political forums, early voting, and most importantly voting) to make their economic, sociocultural, and political preferences known to "make this land a better land for you and me." Most notable were the efforts of hip-hop and R&B icons Jay-Z, Beyoncé, Sean "P. Diddy" Combs, Mary J. Blige, Usher, Lil Wayne, John Legend, Kanye West, Will.I.Am of the Black Eyed Peas, and others to "Barack the Vote." These culture, fashion, and music icons used their social capital to parlay political acumen and votes for their presidential candidate and created avenues and anthems of support and change including Jeezy's "My President is Black" featuring Naz, the Jay-Z and Wyclef's "Last Chance for Change" concert, and Jim Jones's new-found commitment to eliminate the "N" word with the saying "What's up, My Obama?" The efforts and acumen of this generation of Social Rights activists is well understood by the president. As President Obama shared in a Black Entertainment Television (BET) interview, "The potential for [rappers] to deliver a message of extraordinary power that gets people thinking [is there]. The thing about hip-hop today is it's smart, it's insightful. The way they can communicate a complex message in a very short space is remarkable."

The potential of an Obama White House

In reflecting on the potentiality of the Obama White House, it seems that our president has been afforded a wonderful opportunity to usher in a new beginning of twenty-first century leadership. In this regard, President Obama *does not* have to create a new tone or style. He merely has to walk in the paradigmatic atmosphere of "hope," "change," and "Yes We Can" that has captured, renewed, and revitalized the faith of an intergenerational remix of people both across the nation and around the world. In this regard, it seems that our president will be a very pragmatic centrist focused on uniting the country to help move us forward. Clearly, his initial Cabinet appointments and presidential inauguration choices speak to his commitment to honor one of his campaign promises of making executive level leadership fair, balanced, well thought out, and representative of the wealth of intellectual, racial, gender, and ideological diversity of our nation. Moreover, President Obama's decisions speak to a cross-section of interests (women, minorities, intellectuals, and even pragmatists) as does his ability to capture the attention, respect, and political realignment of those who did not support his 2008 candidacy.

Finally, in terms of the African American community, I believe this historic

Plate 13.4 *President Barack Obama, the 44th president of the United States of America*

election was the necessary shift the Black community needed and serves as the *beginning* of the fulfillment of Dr Martin L. King, Jr's prophetic mandate. Along with President Obama, the African American community has been blessed with many known and unknown leaders of the New School who I've termed the "Faithful Ones" who are willing and able to carry the torches of freedom, liberty, equality, and justice first set ablaze by African American leaders from 1619 to the present. These "New School" leaders, armed with boldness, determination, strength, and courage will do the right thing as, like Dr Martin L. King, Jr, they *too* will understand "that the road ahead will not always be smooth. There will still be rocky places of frustration and meandering points of bewilderment. There will be inevitable setbacks here and there . . . but difficult and painful as it is, we must walk on in the days ahead with an audacious faith in the future" (Carson and Shepard, 2001: 197).

Glossary

Abraham Lincoln   The sixteenth president of the United States. President Lincoln was responsible for the passage of the Emancipation Proclamation which ended slavery.

affirmative action   Based on Executive Order 11246, this executive office policy mandate seeks to eliminate past racial discrimination barriers by ensuring that individuals will be given positive consideration in a host of arenas including employment, government contracts, college and university admissions, and the like.

agenda setting   The ability of different groups of people (usually the media and/or members of interest groups) to set the public agenda.

Baker vs. Carr (1962)   A landmark Supreme Court case that legalized the "one person, one vote" ruling in the US.

Black Church   The oldest and most independent institution in all of Black America; a place (congregation) where the word of God is preached; also associated with Mega-church ministries and Black liberation theology.

Black Codes   State laws and procedures incorporated throughout the South to obstruct and limit the political, economic, and social advancement of African Americans. The Black Codes later evolved into Jim Crow laws designed to modernize the limitations of African American freedom in America.

Black Congressional Caucus (CBC)   Formed in 1971, the CBC is the umbrella organization of the 43 African American members of Congress. The CBC defines itself as a policy-specific, interest, and advocacy entity of African Americans.

Black Nationalism   Theoretical model that advocates Black pride, racial uplift, and economic, social, and political separatism.

Black Reconstruction Era   Short-lived period of African American political incorporation and empowerment that began after the passage of the 13th Amendment in 1865. During this era, African American state legislators were elected from North Carolina, South Carolina, Georgia, Louisiana, and Mississippi, and Virginia.

Black utility heuristic   Theoretical model that examines the collective action, group consciousness, and linked fate of African Americans from a political and economic standpoint.

Brown vs. Board of Education (1954)   A landmark Supreme Court case which reversed the decision of Plessy vs. Ferguson and declared that "in the field of public education the doctrine of 'separate but equal' has no place."

Civil Rights Act of 1964 Landmark Congressional legislation outlawing segregation and discrimination in schools, public places, and in the realm of employment.

Civil War Amendments   The 13th, 14th, and 15th Amendments to the United States Constitution which were ratified between 1865 and 1870; they are sometimes referred to as the Reconstruction Amendments.

coalitions   Groups of individuals who join together and coalesce around common issues, interests, and/or agenda.

collective action   The ability of groups to coalesce around a common agenda.

colonialism   System of governance wherein a dominant group exerts power and control over a subordinate group of people.

Congressional Black Caucus   An umbrella organization of political activism and policy implementation for the 43 African American members of Congress.

conservatism   A political ideology that believes in free market enterprise, limited government, individualism combined with tradition, law, and morality in social affairs.

Coretta Scott King (1927–2006)   Founder of the Dr Martin L. King, Jr Center for Nonviolent Social Change; civil and social rights activist; wife of Dr Martin L. King, Jr; mother of Yolanda D. King (1955–2007), Martin L. King, III, Dexter Scott King, and Bernice Albertine King.

delegate   An elected official who makes political decisions based on the desires of his/her constituents.

democracy   System of government that established rule by the people, for the people.

direct action   The third phase of the civil rights movement which utilized non-traditional political participation methods such as sit-ins, boycotts, marches, and nonviolent civil disobedience.

Dred Scott vs. Sanford (1857)   A controversial Supreme Court ruling which denied African American citizenship, prohibited Congress's authority to abolish slavery, and denied slaves the ability to sue in a court of law.

elitism   System of governance wherein a small group of powerful, wealthy, and influential stakeholders determine government decision-making and policy outcomes.

Emancipation Proclamation   Written by Abraham Lincoln in 1862, this political document established the freedom of slaves in Confederate states.

Equal Employment Opportunity Commission (EEOC)   US federal government agency that enforces anti-discrimination laws and policies.

Fannie Lou Hamer   Civil rights and voter rights activist who was a founding member of the Mississippi Freedom Democratic Party (MFDP) and who was instrumental in getting members of the MFDP seated at the 1964 Democratic Convention in Atlantic City, NJ.

Federalist #10   Historical essay written by James Madison (one of the nation's founding fathers) which warned against the development of factions also known as interest groups.

felony re-enfranchisement   The process whereby convicted felons can have their voting rights restored.

Frederick Douglass (1818–1895)   African American abolitionist; publisher of one of the first African American newspapers, *The North Star.*

free rider   An individual or member of a group who receives the benefits of collective action and/or government intervention without contributing to the costs associated with such action.

Freedmen's Bureau   A government organization designed to assist newly emancipated slaves in a host of areas including education, employment, and healthcare.

gangsta rap   A term popularized by mainstream media to describe a certain genre of rap music which glorifies drugs, violence, and crime; also known as a genre of rap made famous by its commitment to "keep it real," i.e., tell the truth.

gerrymandering   The illegal manipulation of a US Congressional District as a means of providing an unfair electoral advantage to a political candidate or political party.

Hon. Barack Obama   Current US president, elected 2008. Previously Senator, Illinois, 1997–2004. Senator Obama made history as the first African American to win the presidential nomination of a major political party, and – momentously – the first to be elected as president.

Hon. Cynthia Mckinney   Former US Representative of Georgia's racially gerrymandered 11th district.

Hon. Harold Ford   Former Tennessee Congressman elected at age 26. Congressman Ford served the 9th District of Tennessee for five consecutive terms before losing a senatorial bid in 2006.

Hon. John Lewis   A 12-term Congressman representing the 5th District of Georgia; civil rights activist who was mentored by Dr Martin L. King, Jr and is the only living civil rights leader to have spoken at the 1963 March on Washington.

Hon. Jesse Jackson, Jr   Congressman Jackson has represented the 2nd District of Illinois for five consecutive terms and is the fifth-ranking Democrat on the US House of Representatives Appropriations Committee.

interest group   An organized group of people who seek to influence governmental policy-making.

James Farmer (1920–1999)   One of the founding members of the Congress of Racial Equality (CORE).

Jim Crow Laws   System of governance whereby African Americans were conferred second-class citizenship status which was enforced through the use of "separate but equal" laws.

labor force participation   The rate at which certain racial/ethnic groups participate in the civil workplace.

litigation   The second phase of the civil rights movement wherein groups, most notably the NAACP Legal Defense Fund, used the 5th and 14th Amendments to gain equal rights in the educational arena.

lobbying   The first phase of the civil rights movement whereby groups such as the NAACP lobbied Congress for the passage of anti-lynching legislation and other laws to protect African Americans. Lobbying is also a political instrument used by organizations and groups to petition members of Congress to pass legislation favorable towards their collective interests.

Lyndon B. Johnson   The 36th president of the United States of America. President Johnson was a very instrumental figure during the direct action phase of the civil rights movement and is most known for his War on Poverty program.

Malcolm X (1925–1965)   Radical leader of the Nation of Islam, outspoken critic of integration, and an advocate of Black separatism prior to his radical enlightenment via his 1964 trip to Mecca, Saudi Arabia.

March on Washington   Landmark civil rights demonstration in August of 1963 where more than 250,000 people participated in a day-long protest for jobs and freedom.

Dr Martin L. King, Jr (1929–1968)   One of the most prolific leaders of the modern civil rights movement in America. His nonviolent philosophy of Christ-like agape love revolutionized the African American freedom struggle and was instrumental in the procurement of civil and voting rights.

Marian Wright Edelman   A civil rights and child rights advocate; founder of the Children's Defense Fund which advocates on behalf of children and the poor.

material benefits   Usually a monetary or tangible benefit that interest groups give to members as an incentive for joining.

median income   Average household income of a particular area or group of people. It usually consists of one half of the households above and one half of the households below the average family income.

movement centers   The mobilization, organization, and collective action entities, usually the church, during the civil rights movement.

National Association for the Advancement of Colored People (NAACP)   The oldest civil rights organization in the United States, the NAACP works to ensure the equal rights and protection of racial and ethnic minorities.

National Association for the Advancement of Colored People Legal Defense Fund (NAACPLDF)   Former Supreme Court Justice Thurgood Marshall founded the LDF in 1940 as a means of providing legal assistance to African Americans unable to afford counsel. The LDF has been an instrumental entity in African American legal recourse and is most well known for its historic victory in Brown vs. Board of Education (1954).

nonviolent direct action   One of a variety of methodologies used during the African American freedom struggle that utilized the Judeo-Christian beliefs of loving your enemies and turning the other cheek.

organizational centers   African American institutions such as the Black Church that coordinated all aspects of the civil disobedience and protest activities during the civil rights movement.

packing   A redistricting initiative whereby potential voters are saturated in a single district which in effect equates to a wasted vote.

party in the electorate   American voters who identify with the political parties.

party in the government   Elected members of the political party on the local, state, and national level.

party organization   Leaders and members of the state and national party organization including state party officials, convention delegates, committee members, and the like.

Plessy vs. Ferguson (1896)   A landmark Supreme Court case that ruled against the equal protection clause of the Constitution and upheld racial segregation on the state level.

pluralism   A political ideology initially introduced by political scientist Robert

Dahl which contends that democracy can be achieved through competition and group politics.

political behavior   The study of the rational actions and decisions of individuals and groups to determine their beliefs and opinions about politics.

political culture   Widely shared beliefs and views about government and public policy.

political ideology   The study of the way people think about government and politics.

political parties   Organizations that seek to influence government through elective office.

poll taxes   One of the extra-legal barriers designed to limit the ability of African Americans to vote.

Poor People's Movement   The last campaign of Dr Martin L. King, Jr designed to address the second phase of the civil rights movement. The large-scale massive resistance demonstration sought to bring more than 1,000 demonstrators to Washington, DC to lobby Congress for an economic bill of rights.

poverty   A state of insufficient income to provide a sustainable living for individuals and their dependents.

poverty rate   The percentage of people who are in poverty (in the US, as defined by the US Census Bureau).

prosperity gospel   Theological teaching that advances the holistic development of the individual; a controversial component of some Mega-churches that is misinterpreted as a gospel based on acquiring riches and wealth.

purposive benefits   The ability of interest groups to provide members with a sense of purpose in joining a particular organization.

reapportionment   The redrawing of US Congressional districts based on 10-year demographic (shift) apportionment data of the US Census.

redistricting   The redrawing of legislative boundary lines based on data provided every ten years by the US Census Bureau.

Republicans   Card-carrying or issue-oriented voters who identify with the values of the Republican Party.

Republican Party   One of the major political parties in America which favors economic liberalism, social conservatism, and traditional family values.

Rosa Parks (1913–2005)   Civil rights activist whose refusal to give up her seat sparked the Montgomery bus boycott of 1955; affectionately referred to as the "mother" of the modern civil rights struggle in America.

Separate But Equal   Ruling of the Supreme Court in Plessy vs. Ferguson (1986) which legalized racial segregation under the stipulation that the facilities were equal.

Shirley Chisholm (1924–2005)   A seven-term Congresswoman who represented New York's 12th district who made history as the first African American candidate for president of the United States of America.

snitchin'   Controversial philosophy in the hip-hop community which advocates the ostracism and even harm of individuals who inform law enforcement officials of criminal activity and/or crime.

social justice   A theoretical model that seeks to achieve justice in all areas of life in society.

stacking   A racial gerrymandering technique used to minimize the African American voting base in representational districts.

Student Nonviolent Coordinating Committee (SNCC)   Student-formed and -led organization responsible for the integration of interstate travel; most well known for its participation in freedom rides throughout the South.

substantive politics   Political representation wherein non-descriptive indicators of electoral achievement are championed over descriptive characteristics such as race and gender.

symbolic politics   Political representation characterized by descriptive traits such as race, gender, geographical region.

trustees   Elected officials who in making decisions consider the desires of their constituencies but ultimately engage in decision-making based on what they believe to be in the best interests of their district/state.

US Congress   The bicameral legislature of the United States consisting of the 435 members of the US House of Representatives and the 100 members of the US Senate. These 535 men and women are responsible for creating legislation, providing oversight, and a check and balance on the executive and judicial branches of government.

War on Poverty   A short-lived government aid program developed by former president Lyndon B. Johnson to provide assistance to the poor during the civil rights movement.

W. E. B. Du Bois (1868–1963)   African American scholar, sociologist, theorist, and civil rights leader. One of the founding members of the NAACP, he is most well known for his classic book *The Souls of Black Folk*.

Vote or Die Campaign   An electoral registration and participation campaign developed by rap mogul Sean P. "Diddy" Combs which has been responsible for registering more than 100,000 new voters between the ages of 18 and 24.

References

Bachrach, Peter, and Baratz, Morton S. 1970. *Power and Poverty: Theory and Practice.* New York: Oxford University Press.

Barker, Lucius, Jones, Mack H., and Tate, Katherine. 1998. *African Americans and the American Political System.* Upper Saddle River, NJ: Prentice Hall.

Belknap, Michael R. 2005. *The Supreme Court under Earl Warren, 1953–1969.* Columbia, NC: University of South Carolina Press.

Berry, Jeffrey M. and Wilcox, Clyde. 1977. *The Interest Group Society.* 3rd ed. Princeton, NJ: Princeton University Press.

Berry, Marion Frances, and Blassingame, John W. 1982. *Long Memory: The Black Experience in America.* New York: Oxford University Press.

Bloom, Alexander. 2001. *Long Time Gone: Sixties America Then and Now.* New York: Oxford University Press.

Brooker, Russell and Schaefer, Todd. 2006. *Public Opinion in the 21st Century: Let the People Speak.* Boston, MA: Houghton Mifflin.

Browning, Rufus P., Marshall, Rogers, Dale, and Tabb, David H. 1984. *Protest Is Not Enough.* Berkeley, CA: University of California Press.

Burke, Edmund. 1907 (1774). Speech to the electors of Bristol on being elected, in *The Works of Edmund Burke.* Vol. II. New York: Oxford University Press.

Burke, Vanessa. 2005. "A King Perspective: The March, Its Impact and Repercussions," in *The New Birth Voice*, January/February.

Cannon, David. 1999. *Race, Redistricting, and Representation.* Chicago, IL: University of Chicago Press.

Carmichael, Stokely, and Hamilton, James. 1967. *Black Power: The Politics of Liberation.* New York: Vintage Books.

Carson, Clayborne (ed.). 1998. *The Autobiography of Martin Luther King, Jr.* New York: Warner Books.

Carson, Clayborne and Shepard, Kris (eds). 2001. *A Call to Conscience: The Landmark Speeches of Dr Martin Luther King, Jr.* New York: Time Warner.

Chang, Jeff. 2005. *Can't Stop, Won't Stop: A History of the Hip Hop Generation.* New York: St Martin's Press.

Cimbala, Paul A., and Miller, Randall M. 1999. *The Freedman's Bureau and Reconstruction.* Philadelphia, PA: Fordham University Press.

Dahl, Robert A. 2000. *Who Governs?: Democracy and Power in an American City.* New Haven, CT: Yale University Press.

Davis, Lenwood G. 1984. *Malcolm X: A Selected Bibliography.* Westport, CT: Greenwood Press.

Dawson, Michael C. 1995. *Behind the Mule: Race and Class in African-American Politics*. Princeton, NJ: Princeton University Press.

Denton, John C. 1972. *Warren Court and the Constitution: A Critical View of Judicial Activism*. Boston, MA: Pelican Publishing Company.

Du Bois, W. E. B. 1903. *The Souls of Black Folk*. Chicago, IL: McClurg.

Easton, David. 1953. *The Political System: An Inquiry into the State of Political Science*. New York: Knopf.

Epstein, Lee, and Walker, Thomas G. 1998. *Constitutional Law for a Changing America* (3rd edn). Washington, DC: CQ Press.

Eskew, Glenn T. 1997. *But for Birmingham: The Local and National Movements in the Civil Rights Struggle*. Charlotte, NC: University of North Carolina Press.

Fenno, Richard F. 1978. *Home Style: House Members in Their Districts*. Boston and Toronto: Little, Brown, and Company.

Fisher, Klaus P. 2006. *America in White, Black, and Gray: The Stormy 1960s*. New York: Continuum.

Fluker, Walter, E. *The Stones that the Builders Rejected: The Development of Ethical Leadership from the Black Church Tradition*. 1998. Harrisburg, Pennsylvania: Trinity Press International.

Foner, Eric. 1995. *Free Soil, Free Labor, Free Men: The Ideology of the Republican Party before the Civil War*. New York: Oxford University Press.

Foner, Eric. 2002. *Reconstruction: America's Unfinished Revolution, 1863–1877*. New York: Harper Collins Publishers.

Franklin, John Hope, and Moss, Alfred P. 2000. *From Slavery to Freedom: A History of African-Americans* (7th edn). New York: Alfred A. Knopf.

Gans, Herbert. 1996. *The War against the Poor*. New York: Basic Books.

Gaventa, John. 1980. *Power and Powerlessness: Quiescence and Rebellion in an Appalachian Valley*. Urbana, IL: University of Chicago Press.

Gilbert, Jonas. 2005. *Freedom's Sword: The NAACP and the Struggle against Racism in America, 1909–1969*. New York: Routledge.

Gilliam, Franklin D., Jr. 2001. *Farther to Go: Readings and Cases in African-American Politics*. New York: Harcourt Brace.

Gite, Lloyd. 1993. "The New Agenda of the Black Church: Economic Development for Black America," *Black Enterprise Magazine*, http://findarticles.com/p/articles/mi_m1365/is_n5_v24/ai_14680366/

Goldstein, Kenneth M. 1999. *Interest Groups, Lobbying, and Participation in America*. New York: Cambridge University Press.

Gomes, Ralph and Linda Faye Williams (eds). 1992. "Coalition Politics: Past, Present, and Future" in *From Exclusion to Inclusion: The Long Struggle for African American Political Power*. Westport, CT: Praeger Press.

Guinier, Lani. 1994. *The Tyranny of the Majority*. New York: Free Press.

Gurin, Patricia, Hatchett, Shirley and Jackson, James. 1991. *Hope and Independence: Black Response to Electoral and Party Politics*. New York: Russell Sage.

Hacker, Andrew. 1992. *Two Nations: Separate and Unequal*. New York: Scribner.

Hammond, Scott J., Hardwick, Kevin R., Lubert, Howard L. (eds.). 2007. *Classics of American Constitutional and Political Thought: Origins Through the Civil War*. Vol. 2. Indianapolis, IN: Hackett Publishing.

Harding, Vincent. 1981. *There is a River: The Black Struggle for Freedom in America*. New York: Harcourt, Brace, Jovanovich.

Height, Dorothy. 2003. *Open Wide the Freedom Gates: A Memoir*. New York: Public Affairs – Perseus Books Group.

Henderson, Errol. 1996. "Black Nationalism and Rap Music." *Journal of Black Studies* (January) 26(3): 308–39.

Herrnson, Paul S., Shaiko, Ronald G., and Wilcox, Clyde. 2004. *The Interest Group Connection: Electioneering, Lobbying, and Policymaking in Washington* (American Politics Series). Washington, DC: CQ Press.

Hughes, Langston. 1962. *Fight for Freedom: The Story of the NAACP*. New York: W. W. Norton.

Jeffries, Judson L. 2002. *Huey P. Newton: The Radical Theorist*. Oxford, MS: The University of Mississippi Press.

Johnson, Lyndon Baines. 1965. Public Papers of the Presidents of the United States: *Lyndon B. Johnson, 1963–1964*. Vol. II, entry 446. Washington, DC: Government Printing Office.

Jonas, Gilbert. 2005. *The NAACP and the Struggle Against Racism in America, 1909-1969*. New York: Routledge.

Judd, Dennis R., and Swanstrom, Todd. 1994. *City Politics: Private Power and Public Policy*. New York: Harper Collins.

Judd, Dennis R., and Swanstrom, Todd. 2005. *City Politics: The Political Economy of Urban America* (5th edn). New York: Harper Collins.

Kelley, Robin D. G., and Lewis, Earl. 2000. *To Make Our World Anew: A History of African-Americans*. New York: Oxford University Press.

Kellogg, Frederic R. 2006. *Oliver Wendell Holmes, Jr., Legal Theory, and Judicial Restraint*. New York: Cambridge University Press.

Kimbrough, Mary, and Margaret W. Dagen. 2000. *Victory without Violence: The First Ten Years of the St. Louis Committee of Racial Equality (CORE)*. St Louis, MO: University of St Louis Press.

Kinder, Donald R., and Lynn M. Sanders. 1996. *Divided by Color: Racial Politics and Democratic Ideals*. Chicago, IL: University of Chicago Press.

King, Martin Luther. 1958. *Stride Toward Freedom: The Montgomery Story*. New York: Harper and Row.

King, Martin Luther. 1967. *Where Do We Go from Here: Chaos or Community?* New York: Harper and Row.

Klarman, Michael. 2004. *From Jim Crow to Civil Rights: The Supreme Court and the Struggle for Racial Equality*. New York: Oxford University Press.

Kluger, Richard. 1977. *Simple Justice: The History of Brown vs. Board of Education and Black America's Struggle for Racial Equality*. New York: Vintage Books.

Kollman, Ken. 1998. *Outside Lobbying: Public Opinion and Interest Group Strategies*. Princeton, NJ: Princeton University Press.

Leighley, Jan E., and Vedlitz, Arnold. 1999. "Race, Ethnicity, and Political Participation: Competing Models of Contrasting Explanations" in *The Journal of Politics*, 61(Nov. 4): 1092–114.

Levy, Peter B. 1992. *Let Freedom Ring: A Documentary History of the Modern Civil Rights Movement*. New York: Praeger Press.

Levy, Peter B. 1998. *The Civil Rights Movement*. Westport, CN: Greenwood Press.

Lewis, Anthony. 2006. *Gideon's Trumpet.* New York: Knopf Doubleday.

Lewis, Fredrick P. 1999. *The Context of Judicial Activism: The Endurance of the Warren Court Legacy in a Conservative Age.* New York: Rowman and Littlefield.

Lewis, John, with D'Orso, Michael. 1999. *Walking With the Wind: A Memoir of the Movement.* San Diego, CA: Harcourt Brace.

Lincoln, Abraham. 1862. "Letter to Horace Greeley," in *Collected Works of Abraham Lincoln,* Vol. 5. Rutgers, NJ: Rutgers University Press.

Lincoln, Abraham, 1865. Second Inaugural Address. www.bartleby.com/124/pres32.html

Lincoln, C. Eric, and Mamiya, Lawrence H. 1990. *The Black Church and the African-American Experience.* Durham, NC: Duke University Press.

Lublin, David. 1997. *The Paradox of Representation: Racial Gerrymandering and Minority Interests.* Princeton, NJ: Princeton University Press.

Malcolm X, and Haley, Alex. 1992. *The Autobiography of Malcolm X.* New York: Ballantine Books.

Marable, Manning. 1983. *How Capitalism Underdeveloped Black America.* Boston, MA: South End Press.

Marable, Manning. 1996. *Speaking Truth to Power: Essays on Race, Resistance, and Radicalism.* Boulder, CO: Westview Press.

Marable, Manning. 1998. *Black Leadership.* New York: Columbia University Press.

Marable, Manning. 2000. *Dispatches from the Ebony Tower: Intellectuals Confront the African American Experience.* New York: Columbia University Press.

Markovitz, Irving. 1987. *Studies in Power and Class in Africa.* New York: Oxford University Press.

Mauer, Marc. 2006. *The Race to Incarcerate.* Washington, DC: The Sentencing Project.

McAdam, Doug. 1982. *Political Process and the Development of Black Insurgency.* Chicago, IL: University of Chicago Press.

McClain, Paula D., and Stewart, Joseph, Jr. 2005. *"Can We All Get Along?": Racial and Ethnic Minorities in American Politics.* 4th ed. Boulder, CO: Westview Press.

McPherson, Edward. 1865. *The Political History of the United States of America during the Great Rebellion.* Washington, DC: Philp and Solomons.

Meyer, David S., Whittier, Nancy, and Robnett, Belinda. 2002. *Social Movements: Identity, Culture, and the State.* New York: Oxford University Press.

Milbrath, Lester. 1963. *The Washington Lobbyists.* Chicago, IL: Rand McNally.

Mills, C. Wright. 1956. *The Power Elite.* New York: Oxford University Press.

Morgan, Joan. 2000. *When Chickenheads Come Home to Roost.* New York: Simon and Schuster.

Morris, Aldon D. 1984. *The Origins of the Civil Rights Movement: Black Communities Organizing for Change.* New York: Free Press.

Myrdal, Gunnar. 1944. *An American Dilemma: The Negro Problem and Modern Democracy.* New York: Harper Row Publishers.

Newton, Leon. 2006. *The Role of Black Neo-Conservatives during President Ronald Reagan's Administration.* Washington, DC: White House Studies.

Olson, Mancur. 1971. *The Logic of Collective Action: Public Goods and the Theory of Groups.* 2nd ed. Cambridge, MA: Harvard University Press.

Parenti, Michael. 1995. *Democracy for the Few.* New York: St Martin's Press.

Peake, Thomas R. 1987. *Keeping the Dream Alive: A History of the Southern Christian Leadership Conference from King to the Nineteen Eighties*. New York: Peter Lang Publishing Company.

Pinderhughes, Diane. 1987. *Race and Ethnicity in Chicago Politics: A Reexamination of Pluralist Theory*. Urbana, IL: University of Illinois Press.

Pitkin, Hanna. 1972. *The Concept of Representation*. Berkeley, CA: The University of California Press.

Piven, Frances F., and Cloward, Richard. 1977. *Poor People's Movement: Why They Succeed, How They Fail*. New York: Pantheon Books.

Pohlmann, Marcus D. 1999. *Black Politics in Conservative America*. New York: Addison Wesley Longman Press.

Reid, Shaheem. 2007. www.mtv.com/news/articles/1572287/20071018/nas.jhtml?rsspartner=rssMozilla. Accessed 22.5.2009.

Sabin, Arthur J. 1999. *In Calmer Times: The Supreme Court and Red Monday*. Philadelphia, PA: University of Pennsylvania Press.

Sales, William W. 1994. *From Civil Rights to Black Liberation: Malcolm X and the Organization of Afro-American Unity*. Boston, MA: South End Press.

Schattschneider, E. E. 1975. *The Semisovereign People: A Realist's View of Democracy in America*. Florence, KS: Cenage Learning.

Schwartz, Bernard. 1998. *The Burger Court: Counter-Revolution or Confirmation*. New York: Oxford University Press.

Shapiro, Thomas. 2004. *The Hidden Cost of Being African American: How Wealth Perpetuates Inequality*. New York: Oxford University Press.

Singh, Robert. 1998. *The Congressional Black Caucus: Racial Politics in the US Congress*. London: Sage Publications.

Skinner, Elliot P. 1992. *African Americans and US Policy Toward Africa 1850–1924: In Defense of Black Nationality*. Washington, DC: Howard University Press.

Smiley, Tavis. 2001. *How To Make Black America Better*. New York: Doubleday Publishing.

Smith, R. Drew, 2001. Interview. *Atlanta Journal Constitution*, April 20.

Smith, Vern E. 2006. "The Politics of the Pulpit." *Crisis Magazine*, http://www.the crisismagazine.com/issues/2006/06_07-08.htm

Smith, Robert C., and Seltzer, Richard. 2000. *Contemporary Controversies and the American Racial Divide*. Lanham, MD: Rowman and Littlefield.

Smith, Robert C., and Walters, Ronald W. 1996. *We Have No Leaders: African Americans in the Post-Civil Rights Era*. Albany, NY: State University of New York Press.

Sniderman, Paul M., and Piazza, Thomas. 1993. *The Scar of Race*. Boston, MA: The President and Fellows of Harvard College.

Sonenshein, Raphael J. 1990. "Biracial Coalitional Politics in Los Angeles," in *Racial Politics in American Cities*, Rufus P. Browning, Dale Rogers Marshall, and David H. Tabb (eds). New York: Longman, pp. 33–48.

Starling, Kelly. 1999. "Stand the Storm: The Black Church and the Triumph of the Black Spirit". *Ebony Magazine*.

Stone, Clarence. 1989. *Regime Politics: Governing Atlanta, 1946–1988*. Lawrence, KA: University of Kansas Press.

Swain, Carol. 1993. *Black Faces, Black Interests: The Representation of African Americans in Congress*. Cambridge, MA: Harvard University Press.

Tate, Katherine. 1993. *From Protest to Politics: The New Black Voter in American Elections.* Cambridge, MA: Cambridge University Press.

Tate, Katherine. 2003. *Black Faces in the Mirror: African Americans and Their Representatives in the US Congress.* Princeton, NJ: Princeton University Press.

Truman, David B. 1993 [1971]. *The Governmental Process: Political Interests and Public Opinion.* 2nd ed. Berkeley, CA: Institute of Governmental Studies.

Tucker-Worgs, T. 2001/2. "Get on Board, Little Children, There's Room for Many More: The Black Megachurch Phenomenon." *Journal of the Interdenominational Theological Center* 29(1/2): 177–203.

Verba, Sidney, and Nie, Norman. 1972. *Participation in America: Political Democracy and Social Equality.* New York: Harper and Row Publishers.

Walters, Ron. 1998. *Black Presidential Politics: A Strategic Approach.* Albany: SUNY Press.

Walton, Hanes. 1985. *Invisible Politics: Black Political Behavior.* Albany, NY: State University of New York Press.

Walton, Hanes. 1994. *Black Politics and Black Political Behavior.* Westport, CT: Praeger Press.

Walton, Hanes, and Smith, Robert C. 2007. *American Politics and the African American Quest for Universal Freedom.* Upper Saddle River, NJ: Longman Publishing Group.

Watson, Denton L. 1993. "Assessing the Role of the NAACP in the Civil Rights Movement." *The Historian,* Vol. 55.

Weiss, Nancy. 1983. *Farewell to the Party of Lincoln: Black Politics in the Age of FDR.* Princeton, NJ: Princeton University Press.

Whittington, Lisa Love. 2005. "Reigniting the Legacy," *The New Birth Voice* (January/ February).

Wicker, Tom. 2002. *Dwight D. Eisenhower.* The American President Series, Arthur M. Schlesinger (ed.). New York: Henry Holt and Company.

Wickham, Dewayne. 2002. *Bill Clinton and Black America.* New York: Ballantine Books.

Wilcox, Clyde. 1998. "PACs and Pluralism: Interest Group Formation and Partisanship." *Polity* 21(1) (Autumn): 155–66.

Williams, Juan. 1998. *Thurgood Marshall: An American Revolutionary.* New York, NY: Three Rivers Press.

Wilson, William J. 1987. *The Truly Disadvantaged: The Inner City, the Underclass, and Public Policy.* Chicago: University of Chicago Press.

Woodson, Carter G. 1933. *The MIS-Education of the Negro.* Washington: Associated Publishers.

WEBSITES

Barack Obama – www.barackobama.com

The Black Commentator – www.blackcommentator.com

The Black Electorate – www.blackelectorate.com

Black Entertainment Television – www.bet.com

Cable News Network – www.cnn.com

The Children's Defense Fund – www.cdf.com

Congressional Black Caucus – www.congressionalblackcaucus.net

Cynthia McKinney – www.cynthiaforcongress.org

Fannie Mae National Housing Survey. 2003 – www.fanniemae.com/global/pdf/
 media/survey/index.jhtml

Harold Ford, Jr – www.haroldfordjr.com

The Hartford Institute for Religion Research – www.hartsem.edu

Hillary Clinton – www.hillaryforpresident.com

Jesse Jackson, Jr – www.jessejacksonjr.org

Metroactive online – www.metroactive.com

Music Television – mtv.com

New Birth Missionary Baptist Church – www.newbirth.org

The Potter's House – www.pottershouse.org

Religion Link – www.religionlink.org

Stop Smiling Online Magazine – www.stopsmilingonline.com

US Census Bureau – www.census.gov

World Changers International Church – www.worldchangers.org

Index

CPSIA information can be obtained
at www.ICGtesting.com
Printed in the USA
BVHW011814051020
590332BV00007B/182

9 780745 632810

The Goal/Question/Metric Method:
a practical guide for quality improvement of software development

The Goal/Question/Metric Method:
a practical guide for quality improvement of software development

Rini van Solingen

and

Egon Berghout

THE McGRAW-HILL COMPANIES

London · Chicago · New York · St Louis · San Francisco · Auckland
Bogotá · Caracas · Lisbon · Madrid · Mexico · Milan
Montreal · New Delhi · Panama · Paris · San Juan · São Paulo
Singapore · Sydney · Tokyo · Toronto

Published by
McGraw-Hill Publishing Company
SHOPPENHANGERS ROAD, MAIDENHEAD, BERKSHIRE, SL6 2QL, ENGLAND
Telephone +44 (0) 1628 502500
Fax: +44 (0) 1628 770224 Web site: http://www.mcgraw-hill.co.uk

---

British Library Cataloguing in Publication Data

A catalogue record for this book is available from the British Library

ISBN 007 709553 7

Library of Congress Cataloguing-in-Publication Data

The LOC data for this book has been applied for and may be obtained from the Library of
Congress, Washington, D.C.

Further information on this and other McGraw-Hill titles is to be found at
http://www.mcgraw-hill.co.uk
Authors Website address: http://www.mcgraw-hill.co.uk/vansolingen

While having complete faith in the methods explained in this book when they are properly
applied, neither the authors nor the publisher can accept any responsibility for the outcome
of the application of these methods by users.

Publishing Director: Alfred Waller
Publisher: David Hatter
Typeset by: The Authors
Produced by: Steven Gardiner Ltd
Cover by: Hybert Design

1 2 3 4 5 CUP 3 2 1 0 9

Printed in Great Britain at the University Press, Cambridge

Table of contents

Acknowledgements

This book is based on many experiences we had in GQM measurement programmes. These experiences were gained in cooperation with so many other people. We like to emphasise that this book could not have been written without the help of all these people.

First of all, we want to thank the Schlumberger/Tokheim project teams that participated in the GQM measurement programmes. Their positive experiences and enthusiasm motivated us to continue the enhancement of the GQM method. It is not possible to include everyone personally, however, special thanks to Wim van der Bijl, Henry van den Boogaert, Erik Rodenbach, Erich Sigrist, Frank Simons, and Anita Verwegen.

The (inter) national research projects ESSI/CEMP, PROFES and SPIRITS certainly also contributed to the development of the GQM method presented in this book. Through the cooperation with all the organisations involved in these research projects, practical application of GQM was realised, evaluated and improved. Again, for these projects it is also impossible to name everyone involved, however, special thanks to Andreas Birk, Janne Järvinen, Rob Kusters, Frank van Latum, Markku Oivo, Dieter Rombach, Günther Ruhe, Jos Trienekens, and Erik van Veenendaal.

Several Master of Science students contributed to the research through supporting the application in practice and through adding many suggestions for improvements of the GQM method. Many thanks to Erik Kooiman, Hans Leliveld, Shyam Soerjoesing, Paul Stalenhoef, Arnim van Uijtregt, and Cees de Zeeuw. A special thanks goes to Hans Leliveld for his contribution to an elementary version of this book. Marieke van Santen for her contributions to the web pages. Finally, we thank Rina Abbriata, Conny van Driel and Karin Nuijten for decoding our handwriting.

Rini van Solingen,   Egon Berghout,
Eindhoven   Rotterdam

                                                              The Netherlands
                                                              March, 1999

Foreword

The original ideas for the Goal Question Metric Paradigm came from the need to solve a practical problem back in the late 1970s. How do you decide what you need to measure in order to achieve your goals? We (Dr. David Weiss and I) faced the problem when trying to understand the types of changes (modifications and defects) being made to a set of flight dynamics projects at NASA Goddard Space Flight Center. Was there a pattern to the changes? If we understood them could we anticipate them and possibly improve the development processes to deal with them? At the same time, we were trying to use change data to evaluate the effects of applying the Software Cost Reduction methodology on the A-7 project requirements document at the Naval Research Laboratory.

Writing goals allowed us to focus on the important issues. Defining questions allowed us to make the goals more specific and suggested the metrics that were relevant to the goals. The resulting GQM lattice allowed us to see the full relationship between goals and metrics, determine what goals and metrics were missing or inconsistent, and provide a context for interpreting the data after it was collected. It permitted us to maximize the set of goals for a particular data set and minimize the data required by recognizing where one metric could be substituted for another.

The process established the way we did measurement in the Software Engineering Laboratory at Goddard Space Flight Center, and has evolved over time, based upon use. Expansion involved the application to other areas of measurement (such as effort, schedule, process conformance), the development of the goal templates, the development of support processes, the formalization of the questions into models, and the embedding of measurement in an evolutionary feedback loop, the Quality Improvement Process and the Experience Factory Organization. Professor Dieter Rombach was a major contributor to this expansion.

The GQM paradigm represents a practical approach for bounding the measurement problem. It provides an organization with a great deal of flexibility, allowing it to focus its measurement program on its own particular needs and culture. It is based upon two basic assumptions (1) that a measurement program should not be 'metrics-based' but 'goal-based' and (2) that the definition of goals and measures need to be tailored to the individual organization. However, these assumptions make the process more difficult than just offering people a "collection of metrics" or a standard predefined set of goals and metrics. It requires that the organization make explicit its own goals and processes.

In this book, Rini van Solingen and Egon Berghout provide the reader with an excellent and comprehensive synthesis of the GQM concepts, packaged with the support necessary for building an effective measurement program. It provides more than the GQM, but describes it in the philosophy of the Quality Improvement Paradigm and the Experience Factory Organization. Based upon experience, they have organized the approach in a step-by-step set of procedures, offering experience-based heuristics that I recognize as effective. They have captured the best ideas and offer them in a straightforward manner. In reading this book, I found myself constantly nodding in agreement, finding many ideas I had not articulated as well. They offer several examples that can be used as templates for those who wish to have a standard set of goals and metrics as an initial iteration.

If you work on a measurement program, you should keep this book with you as the definitive reference for ideas and procedures.

Professor Victor R. Basili
University of Maryland
and
Fraunhofer Center for Experimental Software Engineering, Maryland

'Its not enough to do your best;
you must know what to do, and then do your best'
W. Edwards Demming

1   Introduction

1.1   Objectives

In the past few years we gained many experiences of organising software quality improvement programmes in industry. Although there are many textbooks available on quality improvement, we were surprised by the gap between theory and practice. Most literature on software quality is quite comprehensive, however, it often lacks the goal-driven nature of business. Business is not just looking for ultimate quality, but for the best quality to be given to other goals, such as timeliness, product features, complexity, or cost.

The Goal/Question/Metric method (GQM) supports such a business driven quality improvement approach very well, however, this method is merely published in scientific journals. This motivated us to write a practical GQM guide. We hope this book will inspire you during your quality improvement work in practice, and sincerely hope the practical material in this book prevents you making some of the mistakes we did.

This book has been written to support people that are working on quality improvement in the area of software development. It will focus on GQM and will provide:

- motives to start goal-oriented measurement;
- detailed steps to take for GQM application;
- examples of possible support for GQM;
- our lessons learned to prevent others making the same mistakes;
- templates of the necessary deliverables for GQM application;
- results from practice regarding goals we actually pursued and attained;
- suggestions for feedback material in which data is presented from projects we worked on.

This book is intended for:

- project managers setting up measurements towards a project or product goal;
- quality assurance personnel aligning the quality measures with the goals of their company and business;
- software engineers that want to structure their personal metrics;
- consultants that support companies in their process improvement and measurement programmes;
- teachers that want to explain to their students how to practically apply software measurement;
- last but not least, any other people interested in working actively towards a certain measurable objective.

1.2   Organisational setting

Our experience with GQM application has been developed in cooperation with many other companies and people mainly by participating in (inter)national projects. Three important projects are described below together with links to detailed information.

ESSI/CEMP: Customised establishment of measurement programmes.

The ESSI/CEMP project aimed at evaluation of the GQM-approach in the industry. The ESSI/CEMP project consisted of three practical case studies that investigated the introduction of GQM-based measurement in industry. The goals of the ESSI/CEMP project were:

- to provide cost/benefit data from three industrial case studies performed within ESSI/CEMP;
- to develop a set of guidelines and heuristics for the introduction of GQM-based measurement.

The ESSI/CEMP internet home-page contains free publications and deliverables of the ESSI/CEMP project: http:/www.iese.fhg.de/Services/Projects/Public-Projects/Cemp.html.

PROFES: Product focused improvement of embedded software processes.

The PROFES project particularly focuses at organisations developing embedded software systems, in sectors such as telecommunications, medical systems, retailing systems and avionics. The PROFES methodology provides support to an integrated use of process assessment, product and process modelling, GQM measurement and experience factory. More information can be found on: http://www.ele.vtt.fi/profes/.

SPIRITS: Software process improvement in embedded IT environments.

SPIRITS was a research project of Schlumberger Retail Petroleum Systems (RPS) which was executed in cooperation with the Eindhoven University of Technology, The Netherlands. SPIRITS developed concepts and methods for process improvement to accomplish high and quantifiable reliability of embedded products. The main objectives were the design of:

- methods for process improvement in embedded systems development;
- methods for measurement and evaluation of the effectiveness of process improvement activities on the reliability of embedded products.

The practical application of the concepts and methods was validated in several case studies within Schlumberger RPS. The set of instruments was based on practical experiences and validated by a number of pilot projects.

1.3   Schlumberger/Tokheim

Schlumberger Retail Petroleum Systems (RPS) has been working for many years on developing and producing high quality products for petrol stations. As with most electronic products, the amount and importance of the software included in products is getting more and more important. Because of this trend, Schlumberger RPS extensively worked with software quality initiatives to manage the quality of their software. This book provides an overview of the experiences gained during these initiatives. It was written, because particularly in the area of GQM, there was little documentation available. This book is intended as a guide for GQM application in practice.

This book is based on many quality initiatives within Schlumberger RPS over the past few years, such as:

- ISO9001 certification;
- TickIT certification;
- CMM assessments;
- Goal-oriented measurement by the GQM paradigm.

Initially, Schlumberger RPS worked with software measurement based on ISO procedures and CMM. However, this way of working was considered unsatisfactory. Not all collected data were actually used and other data were missing. In other words, the measurement programme lacked a clear goal and was experienced as being inefficient itself (Latum et al, 1998).

This observation led to the conclusion that software metrics should be defined in such a way that the collected data is relevant, and that it helps in achieving goals of business quality, such as product reliability which is not an isolated business goal. Because of this observation, the Goal/Question/Metrics paradigm was adopted to structure the measurements. During the several years of GQM application it appeared that there was little or no documentation on 'how' these measurement programmes should actually be carried out. At many events we met people from several industries or academics who all supported the power of the GQM paradigm, but none of them could point us to practical procedures, templates, or detailed examples from practice. Based on this notion we decided to capture our expertise in GQM application and write it down in this book.

September 1998, the RPS division of Schlumberger was sold to Tokheim, a company dedicated to fuel dispenser production. This sale created the largest system and service supplier in the retail petroleum market. Currently, Tokheim employs 5,000 people world wide, and has a yearly revenue of almost 1 billion US dollars.

1.4   Origin of GQM

The GQM method was originally developed by V. Basili and D. Weiss, and expanded with many other concepts by D. Rombach. GQM is a result of many years of practical experience and academic research. With this book we aim at contributing to their original work. Our contribution is the detailed analysis of the method and the addition of several techniques. An example of such an addition is cost/benefit analysis. Also included are many practical examples and suggestions to realise successful measurement programmes.

1.5 Outline

This book intends to be a practical guide to the GQM method. It, therefore, includes many examples, checklists and document templates. The book is divided into three parts. The more knowledge you already possess of GQM, the later you are advised to start in the book.

- Part 1: General description of software quality improvement and GQM measurement. This part provides a background on the theory behind this book, contains motives to apply GQM measurement in practice, and reports cost/benefit information from GQM application in practice.

- Part 2: GQM method stepwise. This part describes the phases of the GQM method and guidance to apply GQM in practice. This includes procedures, documents and checklists.

- Part 3: Cases on application of GQM's four practical measurement goals. This part describes four measurement goals from Schlumberger/Tokheim programmes. Many details are described such as, the results of the GQM phases, lessons learned, and measurement results presented in graphs and tables. Each case also contains the GQM documentation that might serve as an example whenever you would like to measure a similar measurement goal. This documentation includes: GQM plan. measurement plan, data collection forms and feedback session reports.

We hope that this book will support you during measurement programmes in practice. Our aim was to capture our own experience of GQM application, and to present it in such a way that it will help you as much as possible and prevent you from making some of the mistakes we made. We wish you good luck in applying the GQM method and are looking forward to your results and experiences.

PART 1

Software quality improvement
and
goal-oriented measurement

2 Software process improvement

2.1 Introduction

Today's software development is still error prone. For instance, projects are completed too late, exceed their budgets, or require substantially more resources than planned. Often developers are working in an unstructured and stressful way. Resulting in a poor or unknown level of product quality. These problems are often addressed as the 'software crisis' (Gibbs, 1994), and by applying various software process improvement (SPI) approaches, organisations developing software try to resolve this crisis.

In this chapter, first the main improvement areas of software development are described, being, software products, software processes and software quality itself. Subsequently, the most common improvement goals encountered in practice are discussed: decrease of costs or risks; shortening of project cycle time; and improvement of product quality. Finally, the main approaches to improve software processes are introduced.

2.2 Improvement areas of software development

In this section a brief general introduction is given to the current status of software products, software development processes and software quality.

2.2.1 Software products

A software product is defined as the complete set of computer programmes, procedures, and associated documentation and data, designated for delivery to a user (IEEE, 1994). Software products often struggle with quality problems. Due to the enormous size and complexity of many software products, software developers are often not capable of providing reliable information on the quality of their products. As a result, many high-tech software projects eventually turn out to be disastrous.

Furthermore, today's software should comply with many implicit demands from a variety of users. Even if the software functions correctly, the functionality should also be logical for the users, clearly documented and supported by training of the users on how to use the software.

Another problem for the software community is the fact that software is not a static product, but a product that needs to be adapted all the time because of a changing environment. Flexibility is, therefore, considered to be one of the most important strengths of software. This flexibility is most apparent during the maintenance of software: as the requirements of a software product often change over time, the product should be easily maintainable. Flexibility is, however, also the largest weakness of software, as this flexibility makes it possible to change a product so completely that it's original architecture is put under a lot of pressure.

Finally, software products tend to become larger and more complex every day: the size of software in mobile phones, for example, increases 10 times every 1000 days (Karjalainen et al, 1996). Philips has noted that 70% of product development is spent nowadays on software development and has become the critical path in product development (Rooijmans et al, 1996). As a result of all these effects the quality of the product will often be at stake.

2.2.2 Software processes

Two major phases can be discerned in the software product life-cycle: the development phase; during which the product is initially created, and the exploitation phase; during which the product is used in practice and changes to the product are implemented in order to maintain the software. This book addresses the development of software only. This does not imply that the book is unusable for maintenance activities, however, it will not particularly address this phase. Software processes, therefore, refers to the development phase of a software product.

A software development process is defined as all activities necessary to translate user needs into a software product (based on ISO9000-3, 1991 and IEEE, 1994). Pfleeger states that such a process consists of a Requirements Analysis and Definition phase, a System

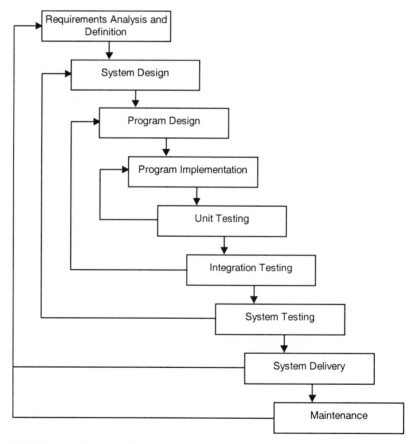

Figure 2-1: Phases within a software development process (Pfleeger, 1991).

Design phase, a Program Design phase, a Program Implementation phase, a Unit Testing phase, an Integration Testing phase, a System Testing phase, a System Delivery phase, and finally, a Maintenance phase (Pfleeger, 1991). This is illustrated in Figure 2-1.

Software processes are considered to be the main area for quality improvement, because they contain the activities during which the product is actually created. The earlier quality problems are detected, the easier and cheaper they can be resolved. Three typical problems exist regarding software processes:

- software processes are often not defined;
- software development is highly dependent on individual craftsmanship;
- Software development is difficult to manage.

Methods like the CMM focus on making software development manageable as a first step to continuous improvement (Paulk et al, 1993).

Software processes are often not well-defined. Although many methods are available, few are actually used in practice. Due to this lack of clearly defined processes, software development depends to a large extent on the individual skills and craftsmanship of the developers. Software development is still a very creative process (Glass, 1995), and individual developers maintain a significant influence on the end result (Bemelmans, 1991).

The Software Engineering Institute (SEI) has defined a five level model to describe the 'maturity' of the way in which the organisation addresses the importance of people: the 'People-CMM (P-CMM)' (Curtis, 1995). Humphrey, also the originator of CMM, has described an approach for the individual improvement of software engineers: the Personal Software Process (PSP) (Humphrey, 1995).

The dependence on individuals makes software development difficult to manage. It is often problematic to switch tasks between developers. Due to unclear or undocumented development processes it will be problematic to predict delivery times. A lot of research is still going on to enable organisations to improve their software development process, and, for instance, move to higher CMM levels (Humphrey, 1989).

2.2.3   Software quality

Software quality is defined as all characteristics of a product that bear on its ability to satisfy explicit and implicit needs of the user (ISO9126, 1991). An example of such characteristics is shown in Figure 2-2. Other subdivisions of quality in attributes have been described by, for example, Boehm, McCall and Cavano (Boehm, 1978; McCall et al, 1977; Cavano et al, 1978).

Quality is an important aspect of attracting customers. However, it is certainly not the only aspect. Other examples of important product characteristics would be price and delivery date. Also, the perception of quality will be different for many individuals. The software market itself is a typical example of a market where you may have a very successful product that is of poor quality, due to for example, missing functionality or software failures.

Several problems exist regarding software quality that are all related to two basic problems:

- It is difficult to specify software quality in measurable terms.
- It is difficult to select the most efficient and effective development process that produces a product with the specified level of quality.

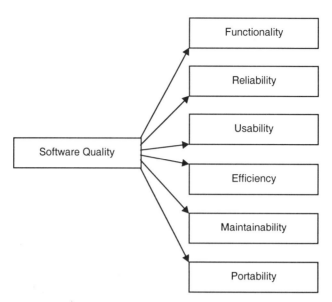

Figure 2-2: ISO 9126 software quality characteristics (ISO9126, 1992).

These two basic problems are also related to each other. Quality involves many aspects and these aspects often require subjective judgments. An example of an aspect that is often subjectively measured is: *usability*. An aspect such as *reliability* is probably more suitable for objective measurement. *Reliability* can, for example, be measured by means of particular failure rates. Even though a characteristic like reliability is also interpreted differently by different users.

In practice most quality requirements for software are not made explicit during the definition phase of software development. In such a case, it will be quite difficult for developers to create quality. Most development methods only specify functional requirements, leaving the fulfilling of other quality characteristics to the experience, craftsmanship and personal interest of the developers.

Even if quality is adequately specified, software quality is still difficult to build. Many software engineering methods, techniques, and tools, are used in the software industry, yet their effectiveness remains mostly unknown. As a result, it is very difficult to select the most appropriate development process. Furthermore, during the development process, insufficient measurement is often applied in order to create the possibility to take corrective action.

The quality of today's complex software systems should be achieved by combining experience and knowledge of many different disciplines. Integrating disciplines means cooperation of experts from particular disciplines, probably causing communication problems. Human failures then become more likely and can easily lead to lower product quality.

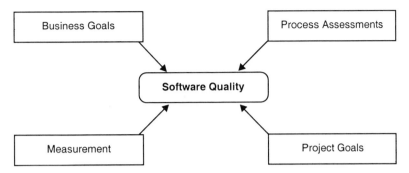

Figure 2-3: Identification of improvement goals.

2.3   Software process improvement goals

To improve their software development, organisations need a definition of clear improvement goals, otherwise the improvement activities will turn out to be as chaotic as the development process itself. These improvement goals should support business objectives in the best possible way. For example, it is not recommended to base improvements on a method that prescribes the installation of a software configuration management system, while most projects in the organisation fail because of bad requirements management.

Improvement goals can be defined in different ways. First of all, corporate management can prescribe quality objectives, from which improvement goals can be derived. Secondly, organisations can conduct software process assessments, in order to identify main areas suitable for improvement. Based on the identification of such areas, improvement goals can again be defined.

Refining high level business goals into specific goals for software development will always be difficult. It is recommended to use the Software Engineering Institutes (SEI) *Goal-Driven Software Measurement: A Guidebook*, for such a purpose. This report is publicly available and can be downloaded from the SEI home page on the internet.

Measurement also provides means to identify improvement goals. By applying measurement to a specific part of the process, problems within the process can be identified on which improvement goals can be defined. Finally, improvement goals may be defined with respect to particular project needs.

The next paragraphs describe four main areas to which software process improvement activities usually focus: the decrease of project costs, the decrease of project risk, the shortening of project cycle time, and the increase of product quality.

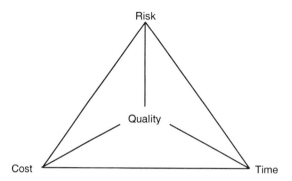

Figure 2-4: Process improvement focus.

2.3.1   Increase quality

If an organisation intends to improve the quality of its products, improvement goals in the area of product quality attributes should be defined, and thus the need for clearly specified requirements on functionality, reliability or other quality attributes arises.

By focusing on quality increase as an improvement goal, the software development process will eventually need to be fully defined, as having a quality improvement goal without an established development process seems unfeasible. The responsibility for the product quality lies with the people that create the product. By adopting quality improvement goals in an organisation, developers become aware of the need for high quality. Therefore, software process improvement supports the creation of a 'quality culture' within organisations very well.

When introducing quality increasing improvements in an organisation it is possible that project teams will ask whether that is really necessary. They might state that they already develop high quality products. Therefore, make sure you can show that a quality increase is indeed necessary, probably not because it is bad, but because business almost always looks for higher quality. And, it is always possible to improve.

Improvement goals in the area of quality often start with some kind of software defect measurement or detection topic. Both product and process failures will then be registered in order to identify the areas in the development process that have the highest need for improvement. Also initial defect detection improvements will be the implementation of Fagan inspection or other review techniques. However, more subjective approaches on quality improvement, such as focusing on customer satisfaction or keeping documentation up-to-date, can also be defined within a quality improvement goal.

2.3.2   Shorten project cycle time

Shortening time-to-market is an improvement goal which is frequently heard of in practice. Marketing and competition requirements make market introduction one of the most stringent requirements for product development. Especially in the embedded product area where cycle-time is currently most relevant. The project life-cycle or development time can be decreased by, for example, increasing productivity, parallel development, prototyping or reuse of already existing software. Productivity can be increased through, for example, specialisation of software design. Parallel development will be encouraged through a modular design of the software.

Cycle-time reduction is often one of the reasons to define an improvement goal with respect to developer productivity. However, one should be careful choosing this approach. Measuring individual performance is difficult and if not fully supported by the software developers, it might very well destroy the improvement initiative.

Software process improvement is an excellent method to evaluate whether new tools or techniques that are pushed into the market are really decreasing the development cycle. Many 'silver bullet' stories are available on successful applications in organisations, though they never seem to fulfil all promises. We recommend to guide any method or tool introduction with measurement in order to evaluate whether such a change is actually an improvement.

2.3.3   Decrease costs

Decreasing the costs of software development is primarily realised by decreasing the software development labour, and therefore cost reduction will mostly aim at executing software development processes more efficiently. A first step to this is identifying current effort and expenditure. Examples from practice in which costs are expressed are costs per source line, costs per function point, costs per life-cycle phase, or costs per product (sub-system). Software measurement is an excellent tool to start improving on this type of data. The focus will not only be on 'doing things better' but also on 'doing the right-things', because eliminating unnecessary activities will be one of the most interesting cost cutting activities.

Embedded software products, however, should be examined more carefully with respect to costs: the cost of the product is not only related to the development cost of the software and to the development of the accompanying hardware. Often the product cost of an embedded system is largely determined by hardware, especially because eventually the production cost of hardware is higher than software, as production costs of software are negligible. Development of software is expensive and production is almost free (copy *.*).

Decrease of cost can also be established by reusing hardware designs, software components or documentation. Finally, an obvious reason to focus on cost reduction in an improvement programme is the fact that corporate management will often be interested in financial figures.

2.3.4   Decrease risks

In order to decrease risks that are involved in executing a project, project management has to be able to manage risk factors that are relevant for specific projects. This can be accomplished by identifying possible risk areas and applying measurements to those particular areas in order to track status and identify the need for corrective actions (Heemstra et al, 1998).

By increasing process maturity, the risks involved in executing the relevant process will decrease, because problem areas in the development process will be tackled by the software process improvement activities. Furthermore, explicit risk reduction makes projects more manageable, and is therefore a suitable and obvious way of improving software processes.

2.4   Approaches to software process improvement

Currently, many software development practitioners and researchers are involved in Software Process Improvement (SPI). Several improvement models, methods and techniques are available, divided over two major streams.

- Top-down approaches, such as CMM (Paulk et al, 1993), SPICE (SPICE, 1997) and BOOTSTRAP (Kuvaja, 1994). These approaches are mainly based on assessments and benchmarking.
- Bottom-up approaches, such as GQM (Basili et al, 1994a), QIP (Basili et al, 1994b) and AMI (Pulford et al, 1995), which mainly apply measurement as their basic guide for improvement.

The top-down improvement stream applies a normative model that is assumed to be the best way of developing software. By assessing an organisation, using this model, it becomes possible to identify the 'maturity' of that organisation, and propose relevant improvements (Humphrey, 1989). The bottom-up improvement stream measures software development to increase understanding within a specific context. Both streams are successfully applied in practice.

2.4.1   Assessment

A popular top-down approach to software process improvement that is based on assessments, is the Capability Maturity Model (CMM) of Figure 2-5 (Paulk et al, 1993). The CMM helps organisations improve the maturity of their software processes through an evolutionary path from ad hoc and chaotic to mature and disciplined. A low level of maturity incorporates a high level of risk in performing a process. As organisations become more capable, risks decrease and productivity and quality are expected to increase.

Each maturity level progressively adds further enhancements that software organisations typically master as they improve. Because of its progressive nature, the CMM can be used to determine the most important areas for immediate improvement. For this purpose, the

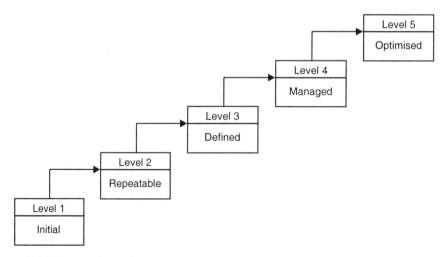

Figure 2-5: CMM maturity levels (Paulk et al, 1993).

CMM provides an assessment method to objectively and consistently assess the capability of software organisations and place them on one of CMM's five maturity levels. A software process assessment is a review of a software organisation to provide a clear and factual understanding of the organisation's state of software practice, to identify its major problems, and to initiate actions to make these improvements (based on Humphrey, 1989). After executing these actions, organisations can then return to re-assessing the established process, as process improvement is a continuous cycle.

Another well-known top-down approach to process quality is the ISO9000 approach. The theory behind the ISO9000 standards is that a well-managed organisation with a defined engineering process is more likely to produce products that consistently meet the purchaser's requirements, within schedule and budget, than a poorly managed organisation that lacks an engineering process. Within the ISO9000 family, ISO9001 is the most complete set of quality system requirements and consists of twenty clauses that represent requirements for quality assurance in design, development, production, installation and servicing, that define which aspects of a quality system have to be available within an organisation. ISO9001 does not, however, provide details on how those aspects should be implemented and institutionalised. ISO9000-3 provides guidelines for applying ISO9001 to the specification, development, supply and maintenance of software (ISO9000-3, 1991).

The ISO9000 family has the following structure (ISO9001, 1994; ISO9000-3, 1991, Looijen, 1998):

- ISO9000 Quality management and quality assurance standards, consisting of:
    - ISO9000-1 Guidelines for selection and use;
    - ISO9000-2 Generic guidelines for application of ISO9001, ISO9002 and ISO9003;
    - ISO9000-3 Guideline to apply ISO9001 to software development and maintenance.
- ISO9001 Quality systems: a model for quality assurance in development, production, installation and servicing.
- ISO9002 Quality systems: a model for quality assurance in production, installation and servicing.
- ISO9003 Quality systems: a model for quality assurance in final inspections and testing.
- ISO9004 Quality management and quality system elements guideline.
- ISO9004-2 Quality management and quality system elements part 2: guideline for services.

Receiving ISO9000 certification from an independent certification body enables purchasers of software products and services to demonstrate engineering and management capability. ISO9000 certification assures customers that an audited company has all its processes and work instructions documented to conform to the ISO9000 requirements, and that these processes and work instructions are being followed on a continuous basis. Frequent follow-up audits by the certification body will ensure that the certified company continues to comply with the prescribed quality requirements. However, ISO9000 certification does not give any guarantee for product quality, nor that the described process is actually executed. Even though some negative sounds are heard on ISO certified quality systems, many companies still claim success by ISO certification.

Many other top-down approaches have been developed during the past few years, most of which are based on the principles of CMM and ISO9000. Examples of such methods are

BOOTSTRAP, SPICE, and Trilium. The Bootstrap method (Kuvaja et al, 1994), which is the result of a European Esprit project, provides an alternative for organisations that are interested in improving their software development process and in attaining ISO9001 certification. It combines and enhances the methods provided by the CMM and the ISO9000 quality standards. ISO12207 describes a software product life cycle by defining a number of activities that should be performed in any organisation (ISO12207, 1995). ISO15504 adds metrics to identify how well practices are performed (Spice, 97).

The basis of the Bootstrap methodology is similar to CMM. Like the CMM, an assessment is based on five maturity levels, but the Bootstrap method uses another scale to measure an organisations' or projects' overall strengths and weaknesses. The ISO9000 quality standards (ISO9001 and ISO9000-3) are incorporated in the methodology because they provide guidelines for a company-wide quality system. The CMM does not include such guidelines. Furthermore, many European companies use ISO9000 as a primary quality standard. Bootstrap can be used by organisations to determine readiness for ISO9001 certification.

2.4.2 Measurement

The other stream contains the bottom-up approaches, which are based on applying measurement on the current software practices within an organisation. Bottom-up approaches are based on careful analysis of applied software practices, on selection of improvement goals derived from these analyses, and on management of improvement activities supported by measurement. Examples of such approaches are the quality improvement paradigm (QIP) as a framework for process improvement, and the Goal/Question/Metric paradigm to support measurement on the goals that were defined in QIP. These two paradigms will be discussed in detail in the next chapter that deals with goal-oriented measurement.

2.5 Conclusions

Many approaches are available to improve software processes, in order to solve problems that occur during software development. The two main streams are *assessment based* and *measurement based*. In practice, both streams are rarely applied together, although they complement each other very well. It is recommended that assessment approaches are used to create a first overview on the status of a software organisation.

Based on the results of this assessment, improvement goals should be identified that suit the organisation in the best possible way. Guidance of the improvement activities toward these goals should be done by applying some form of measurement to these activities, since measurement provides an overview and the opportunity to evaluate whether implemented changes are actual 'improvements'. Because measurement supports the execution of improvement activities towards clearly defined goals, a so-called 'goal-oriented measurement' method should be selected to implement measurement. The subject of goal-oriented measurement is described in the next chapter.

For embedded software development an improvement methodology is developed that combines both assessments and goal-oriented measurement. This method is made in the PROFES project. More information can be obtained from the internet address: http://www.ele.vtt.fi/profes/.

2.6   Questions and assignments

2.6.1   Questions

1. Which are the six ISO 9126 characteristics of software product quality?
2. Which improvement goals typically exist for software development?
3. From which sources can software process improvement (SPI) goals be derived?
4. Which are the five levels of the Capability Maturity Model (CMM)?
5. What is the difference between *development cost* and *production cost* of software?
6. Which two particular approaches are discerned for SPI approaches? What are their main differences?
7. Consider the statement that software quality improvement should always be based on a particular business goal, such as market share, or increasing profit margins. Do you agree with this statement and if so, do you find adequate support in the particular approaches to operationalise this linkage?

2.6.2   Assignments

A small company develops a very innovative mobile phone. It is expected to outclass all existing phones by providing revolutionary special features. The competition is working on such a product as well. However, the company has a lead of at least one calendar year. The product is developed within a team of 20 highly creative people, of which 15 have less than 2 years experience in software development. You are assigned as SPI co-ordinator.

1. Prioritise the four improvement focuses in Figure 2-4.
2. Describe four possible SPI goals for the two most important improvement focuses.

3   Goal-oriented software measurement

3.1   Introduction

In this chapter goal-oriented measurement is described. Its relation with general quality improvement initiatives is explained and the GQM-method is positioned. The GQM-method itself will be elaborated upon in Chapter 5 and beyond.

3.2   What is software measurement?

In general, 'measurement' is the process by which numbers or symbols are assigned to attributes of entities in the real world in such a way as to describe them according to clearly defined rules (Fenton and Pfleeger, 1996). The numerical outcome is called a 'measurement'. This can be applied to both a software development process and a software product.

Software measurement is the continuous process of defining, collecting, and analysing data on the software development process and its products in order to understand and control the process and its products, and to supply meaningful information to improve that process and its products.

3.3   Software metrics

Measurement on a software development process and its products is performed by applying particular software 'metrics'. Measuring will normally comprise several metrics, again resulting in several measurements per metric.

A lot of categorisations and examples of metrics can be found in literature, some examples are (Pfleeger, 1991; Fenton and Pfleeger, 1996; Grady, 1992):

- product and process metrics;
- objective and subjective metrics;
- direct and indirect metrics;
- explicit and derived metrics;
- absolute and relative metrics;
- dynamic and static metrics;
- predictive and explanatory metrics.

The most common types of metrics are described below.

Product and process metrics

First of all, measurement is applied to a process and/or a product, which results in process and/or product metrics.

A *product metric* is a measurement of an intermediate or final product of software development, and therefore addresses the output of a software development activity. Examples of such metrics are a size metric for the number of requirements, a complexity metric for the software code, etc.

Process metrics measure the characteristics of the overall development process, such as the number of defects found throughout the process during different kinds of reviews, etc.

Objective and subjective metrics

Objective metrics are absolute measures taken of the process or product, and count attributes or characteristics in an objective way (Humphrey, 1989), such as number of lines of code, number of faults discovered. These metrics have a fundamental starting point, a natural zero.

Subjective metrics are measurements of a process or product that involve human, subjective judgement. Examples of subjective metrics are expected complexity and degree of conformance to coding standards. These measurements are classifications of observations.

Direct and indirect metrics

A *direct metric* is a measurement of a process or product characteristic that does not depend on the measurement of any other characteristic. Examples are the number of faults in a product, number of hours spent during certain process, etc. An *indirect metric*, on the other hand, is a measurement of a process or product characteristic that involves the measurement of one or more other characteristics, such as productivity, fault density, etc. An indirect metric always contains a calculation of at least two other metrics.

3.4   Software measurement goals

Measurement provides a valuable tool for understanding the effects of actions that are implemented to improve a software development process. Examples of results are (Möller and Paulisch, 1993; Pfleeger, 1991):

- increased understanding of the software development process;
- increased control of the software development process;
- increased capacity to improve the software development process;
- more accurate estimates of software project costs and schedule;
- more objective evaluations of changes in technique, tool, or methods;
- more accurate estimates of the effects of changes on project cost and schedule;
- decreased development costs due to increased productivity and efficiency;
- decrease of project cycle time due to increased productivity and efficiency;
- improved customer satisfaction and confidence due to higher product quality.

Software measurement data is interpreted by people to provide information that can be applied for three different purposes (Figure 3-1). In the first place, the data provide visibility of the current development process and the characteristics of the software products. This visibility is required to reduce complexity and increase *understanding* of the process and products. Understanding means determining the different variables that exist during execution of a process. Once basic understanding has been established (the variables

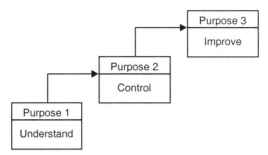

Figure 3-1: Applying measurement for three purposes.

are known), the collected and analysed data can be used to *control* the process and the products, by defining corrective and preventive actions. This means that the relationships between the process variables have to be determined. Once these relationships are known, they can be used to control the process. Furthermore, based on analysis, the collected measurement data can be used to assess the process, and therefore, act as an indicator of development process problem areas, from which *improvement* actions can be identified. Improvements can be made by influencing or changing process variables and their relationships. This hierarchy of measurement is illustrated in figure 3-1.

3.5   Management commitment

Attainment of business goals will be a result of several activities. Measurement by itself will of course not result in attainment of business goals. Specific actions are needed in an organisation to give such results. However, successful implementation of a measurement programme will facilitate continuous improvement and makes benefits more visible. One important prerequisite for successful implementation of a measurement programme is the level of support provided by the management of the company. Many of the positive effects are based on a positive change of attitudes in a project team towards quality improvement. Management should, therefore, actively support a measurement programme to influence these corporate culture changes. Business goals should be clearly defined and the measurement programme goals should reflect and support those business goals.

In order to facilitate a successful measurement programme, management needs to be sufficiently involved to support the entire initiative and operationalise business goals. However, at the same time they should also keep a certain distance to leave some privacy and encourage the personal responsibility of the software developers. Talking about quality, is also talking about mistakes and problems.

Implemented successfully, the measurement programme and the related software development process improvement activities will, in time, become an integral part of the software project management culture, and metrics will become an ongoing practice adopted and used by all project personnel (Möller and Paulisch, 1993).

3.6   Concepts of goal-oriented software measurement

Software measurement should only be performed towards an explicitly stated purpose. This so-called 'goal-oriented measurement' is especially used for improvement programmes as described in this book. The method applied in this book, is the GQM method (Basili and

Weiss, 1984). The following sub-sections introduce the basic phases and concepts of the GQM method. In Part 2 of this book, the GQM method will be described in detail.

The GQM method contains four phases:

1. The Planning phase, during which a project for measurement application is selected, defined, characterised, and planned, resulting in a project plan.
2. The Definition phase, during which the measurement programme is defined (goal, questions, metrics, and hypotheses are defined) and documented.
3. The Data Collection phase, during which actual data collection takes place, resulting in collected data.
4. The Interpretation phase, during which collected data is processed with respect to the defined metrics into *measurement* results, that provide *answers* to the defined questions, after which *goal attainment* can be evaluated.

The four phases of the GQM method are illustrated in Figure 3-2. The planning phase is performed to fulfil all basic requirements to make a GQM measurement programme a success, including training, management involvement and project planning. During the definition phase all GQM deliverables are developed, mainly based on structured interviews or other knowledge acquisition techniques. The definition phase identifies a goal, all questions, related metrics and expectations (hypotheses) of the measurements. When all definition activities are completed, actual measurement can start. During this data collection phase the data collection forms are defined, filled-in and stored in a measurement database. Then the 'real work' can start: using the measurement data. During the interpretation phase, the measurements are used to answer the stated questions, and these answers are again used to see whether the stated goals have been attained.

Activities such as packaging measurement results to be used in other parts of the organisation are not considered to be part of the GQM method, but of a wider perspective, such as a company wide improvement programme.

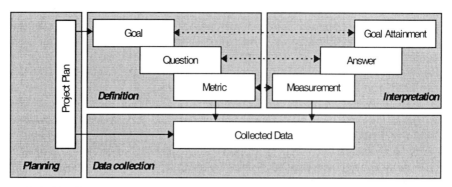

Figure 3-2: The four phases of the Goal/Question/Metric method.

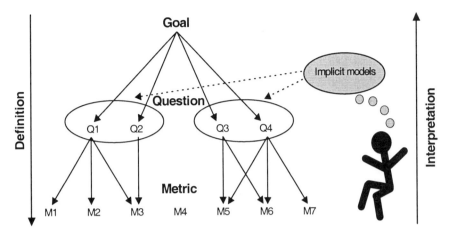

Figure 3-3: The GQM Paradigm (Basili and Weiss, 1984).

3.6.1   The measurement concept: the GQM paradigm

GQM represents a systematic approach for tailoring and integrating goals to models of the software processes, products and quality perspectives of interest, based upon the specific needs of the project and the organisation (Basili et al, 1994a). The result of the application of the GQM method is the specification of a measurement programme targeting a particular set of issues and a set of rules for the interpretation of the measurement data.

The principle behind the GQM method is that measurement should be goal-oriented. Therefore, in order to improve a process, organisations have to define their measurement goals based upon corporate goals and transform these goals into activities that can be measured during the execution of the project.

GQM defines a certain goal, refines this goal into questions, and defines metrics that should provide the information to answer these questions. By answering the questions, the measured data defines the goals operationally, and can be analysed to identify whether or not the goals are attained. Thus, GQM defines metrics from a top-down perspective and analyses and interprets the measurement data bottom-up, as shown in Figure 3-3.

The GQM model starts top-down with the definition of an explicit measurement goal. This goal is refined into several questions that break down the issue into its major components. Each question is then refined into metrics that should provide information to answer those questions. Measurement data is interpreted bottom-up. As the metrics were defined with an explicit goal in mind, the information provided by the metrics should be interpreted and analysed with respect to this goal, to conclude whether or not it is attained.

GQM trees of goals, questions and metrics should be built on knowledge of the experts in the organisation: the developers. Therefore, knowledge acquisition techniques are also applied to capture the implicit models of the developers built during years of experience. Those implicit models give valuable input into the measurement programme and will often be more important than the available explicit process models.

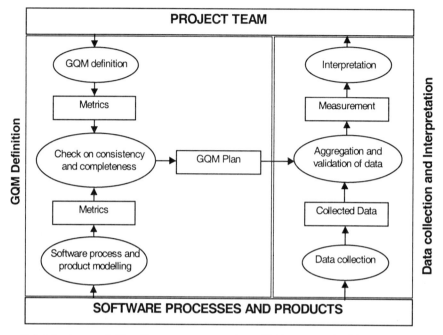

Figure 3-4: Metrics modelling from two perspectives (Solingen et al, 1995).

Over the years, GQM has evolved to include models of software processes and products, resulting in a model-based GQM approach (Solingen et al, 1995), that defines metrics from two different perspectives, as shown in Figure 3-4:

- Metrics definition by members of the project team, using GQM techniques.
- Metrics definition based on models of software processes and products.

By modelling both perspectives, two sets of metrics are identified that can be mutually checked for consistency and completeness. This will identify subjects that are missing, or badly defined. After the models of these two perspectives have been checked and enhanced, a GQM plan is developed. The GQM plan is the documented description of all the information that the measurement programme is based on. This document represents the measurement goals, related questions and identified metrics. Based on the GQM plan, a measurement plan is developed that defines procedures for collecting data.

When the plans are approved, measurement can start. Data are collected on the software development process and products, aggregated and validated. Finally, the measurement results are returned to the project members for analysis, interpretation and evaluation on the basis of the GQM plan (Solingen, 1995).

Figure 3-4 illustrates that GQM modelling can be checked for consistency and completeness on the basis of software process and product models. The following activities are required:

1. Check on the presence of all GQM based direct metrics in the software development process model.
2. Adjust the software development process model, adding the missing direct metrics.

3. Check the GQM definition on missing metrics that are defined in the software development process model and identify their relevance.
4. Adjust GQM definition, adding the missing direct (or indirect) metrics.
5. Decide on accepting the set of direct metrics.

The consistency and completeness check between the software development process models and GQM means that all metrics defined in a measurement programme, also need to be defined in the software development process model. If a certain direct metric is not defined in the software development process model, however, as required in your GQM model, the software development process model should be enhanced, adding the specific metric. In this way GQM also supports improving your software development process models.

3.6.2   The improvement concept: QIP

The quality improvement paradigm (QIP) is a quality approach that emphasises continuous improvement by learning from experience both in a project and in an organisation (Basili et al, 1994a). This learning from experience is built on experimentation and application of measurement. Each new development project is regarded as an experiment and available results of every foregoing and ongoing experiments should be packaged and reused, too. This reuse is applicable to experience on, for example, processes, products, problems, methods and resources. All the available information should therefore be packaged and reused on both project and corporate level to improve current and future performance.

QIP identifies a six step cyclic approach, which is based on the plan-do-check-act approach of Shewart/Demming (Basili et al, 1994). The QIP cycle consists of the following six steps (Figure 3-5):
1. *Characterise*. Understand the environment based upon available models, data, intuition, etc. Establish baselines with the existing business processes in the organisation and characterise their criticality.
2. *Set Goals*. On the basis of the initial characterisation and the capabilities that have a

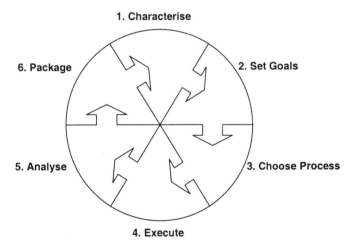

Figure 3-5: QIP cyclic approach (Basili et al, 1994a).

strategic relevance to the organisation, set quantifiable goals for successful project and organisation performance and improvement. The reasonable expectations are defined based upon the baseline provided by the characterisation step.

3. *Choose Process.* On the basis of the characterisation of the environment and of the goals that have been set, choose the appropriate processes for improvement and supporting methods and tools, making sure that they are consistent with the goals that have been set.

4. *Execute.* Perform the processes constructing the products and providing project feedback upon the data on goal achievement that are being collected.

5. *Analyse.* At the end of each specific project, analyse the data and the information gathered to evaluate the current practices, determine problems, record findings, and make recommendations for future project improvements.

6. *Package.* Consolidate the experience gained in the form of new, or updated and refined models and other forms of structured knowledge gained from this and prior projects and save it in an experience base to be reused on future projects.

Once the experience has been packaged during the last step, a new cycle is initiated toward further improvements and additional experience and knowledge. This emphasises the continuous character of QIP. The quality improvement paradigm implements two feedback cycles:

• *Project feedback cycle.* This control cycle provides the project with feedback during project execution. Resources should be used as effectively and efficiently as possible by the project and quantitative information is used to prevent and correct problems.

• *Corporate feedback cycle.* The corporate feedback cycle provides knowledge to the complete organisation, by comparing the project data with the nominal ranges in the organisation and analysing concordance and discrepancy. This experience is accumulated and, based on analysis, can be reused to improve performance of future projects.

Within QIP, software measurement is considered an indispensable component to capture experiences and retrieve knowledge on development activities. To collect the information on software development in an organisation, software measurement should be integrated in the software development process. A feedback process should exist in order to establish a continuous learning process in the organisation.

QIP suggests the GQM method as the measurement mechanism to define and evaluate the improvement goals of QIP. The organisational concept for such improvement programmes is described in the next section.

3.6.3   The organisational concept: experience factory

An experience factory consists of the *GQM definition* and *GQM analysis team* and is defined as: 'The experience factory is a logical and/or physical organisation that supports project developments by analysing and synthesising all kinds of experience, acting as a repository for such experience, and supplying that experience to various projects on demand' (Basili et al, 1994b). It packages experience by building informal, formal or schematised and productised models of measures of various software processes, products, and other forms of knowledge via people, documents, and automated support'.

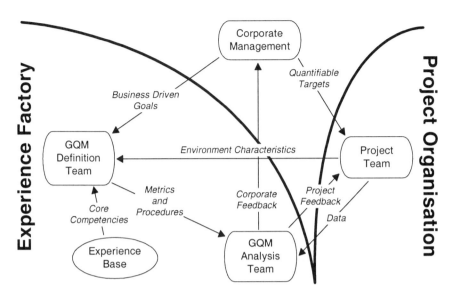

Figure 3-6: The Experience Factory (Basili et al, 1994b).

The stakeholders that are distinguished in a measurement programme are corporate management, GQM definition team, GQM analysis team and project team (Basili et al, 1994b). The experience factory is illustrated in Figure 3-6.

Corporate management provides a project team with project objectives for software development, and a GQM definition team with business-driven goals. The *GQM definition team* translates these goals into measurement goals and refines these measurement goals into related metrics and procedures, based on environmental characteristics provided by the project team and previous experience that is packaged in the *experience base*. The *project team* provides the *GQM analysis team* with measurement data. The GQM Analysis Team processes these data and presents results to corporate management and the project team.

In the experience factory an GQM analysis team processes gathered data and provides feedback to projects. A GQM definition team maintains the information, makes it efficiently retrievable and controls and monitors access to it.

In this book we do not make such a distinction between two GQM teams. We will use the term 'GQM team' for all those activities that should not necessarily be carried out by the software development team (project team). We think this is a more practical approach which encourages learning by the GQM team and minimises overhead.

A GQM team and project team principally have overlapping tasks. Two extremes are conceivable. First, all support is provided by a GQM team and merely the results are presented to a project team. In this case a feedback process is limited to the presentation of conclusions. The GQM team interprets these data and decides upon improvements, resulting in a new model of the development process. In this case the role of the project team is limited to the execution of improvements. On the other hand, the entire improvement process could be carried out by the project team itself, without support from a GQM team. This will result in substantially more commitment towards the results. However, other priorities may lead to a lack of effort spent on the measurement programme: when deadlines are approaching, the project team will focus on finishing their core activities and forget about the measurement programme.

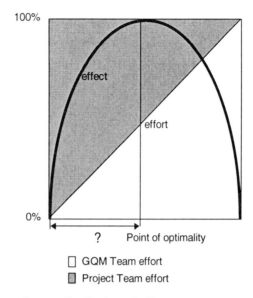

Figure 3-7: Effect depending on distribution of effort.

In our opinion, ideally, the entire quality effort should be executed by the software developers themselves, being most knowledgeable in their field. However, practice shows that in these cases most quality programmes stop when project deadlines emerge. A separate GQM team that safeguards the quality effort is therefore indispensable. However, if such a GQM team also interprets the measurement data and establishes the conclusions (the suggested improvement actions), the quality effort may well loose the commitment of a project team. A kind of balancing of effort is therefore required. This balancing of effort of a GQM team and project team is illustrated in Figure 3-7.

Our experience is that a good balance is often found when a project team carries out 30% of the overall effort of a GQM measurement programme and 70% of all work is done by a GQM team (see also Birk et al, 1998).

3.7   Questions and assignments

3.7.1   Questions

1. Which are the four phases of the GQM method?
2. What is the difference between:
    a. A product and a process metric?
    b. An absolute and a relative metric?
    c. A direct and an indirect metric?
    d. An objective and a subjective metric?
3. Which three purposes of measurement exist? What are the differences between them?
4. Explain the paradox in management commitment and involvement of management.

5. Which phase of the four phases of the GQM method is considered to be the most important one?
6. The GQM paradigm has a top-down and a bottom-up process. Where do these two processes interconnect?
7. What is the most important benefit of linking GQM metrics to the software development process?
8. Which are the six steps of the quality improvement paradigm (QIP)?
9. What is the difference between a project team and a GQM team?
10. Explain the advantages and disadvantages of having most of the effort of the measurement programme put in by either members of the project team or GQM team.

3.7.2   Assignments

1. Write down two typical measurement goals that have an improvement purpose (purpose 3 in Figure 3-1).
2. Derive from each of these goals, pre-conditions that should be under control (purpose 2 in Figure 3-1). Rewrite these pre-conditions to measurement goals with a control purpose.
3. Derive from the control type measurement goals, the underlying topics that must be understood (purpose 1 in Figure 3-1) before control can be striven for. Formulate these understanding pre-conditions as measurement goals too.

4 Costs and benefits of GQM measurement programmes

4.1 Introduction

The cost/benefit analysis of this chapter will illustrate that setting up a measurement programme where benefits exceed costs is not as straightforward as may be expected. Our hypothesis is that in practice many measurement programmes are abandoned, because management perceives them as unbeneficial. When a cost/benefit analysis is included in a measurement programme such perceptions are made more explicit and open to discussion. Including this type of analysis is, therefore, regarded as an essential element of a successful measurement programme. First, costs of measurement programmes will be discussed and secondly benefits.

4.2 Cost of GQM measurement

The operational cost model of GQM measurement programmes which is presented in this section has been derived from six GQM measurement programmes (Birk et al, 1998). Almost all costs are costs of labour eg effort of personnel for the particular activities of a measurement programme. The operational cost model will be described for two particular situations, being:

- initial application of GQM measurement in an organisation (first time usage); and
- routine application of GQM measurement (any other usage than first time).

This distinction is made because a first measurement programme requires substantially more effort than any subsequent one. The two variants of the cost model are described in the two following sections. For each variant first, the underlying assumptions are stated. Second, the effort figures are provided for each process step and role involved in the measurement process. Third, the cost structure is explained, and fourth, typical variations of the scenario are discussed. In both costs models the following typical activities are discerned:

1. *GQM programme planning.* This includes the identification of available input, preconditions and constraints, the set up of an infrastructure, the selection of an improvement area, the selection of a project, initial planning of the measurement programme, and the preparation and training of the Project team.
2. *Identify and define GQM goals.* This includes the characterisation of the project and organisation, identification and selection of improvement goals, definition of the measurement and GQM goals, modelling of the relevant software processes involved in the measurement programme, and the identification of artefacts to be reused.

3. *Conduct GQM interviews.* This includes studying documentation, defining, scheduling and inviting interviewees, briefing of a project team, conducting GQM interviews and reporting them.

4. *Develop GQM deliverables.* This includes definition, reviewing, and refining of a GQM plan, the definition of a measurement plan, identification and definition of data collection procedures, reviewing and refinement of a measurement plan, and development of an analysis plan.

5. *Data collection.* This includes a data collection trial to test data collection procedures and forms, briefing the project team and kick-off of the measurement programme, collection, validation, coding and storage of measurement data.

6. *Data analysis and interpretation.* This includes analyses of the measurement data, preparation of the presentation material, planning, conducting and reporting of the feedback sessions.

The operational cost model for routine application of GQM measurement programmes is addressed first, because it refers to the standard situation once GQM is introduced. This model is also less complex. In section 4.2.2 the cost model for first application will be described.

4.2.1   Effort model for routine application of GQM

In this section a cost model for routine application of GQM is described. First, a typical project for which the total effort will be calculated is introduced. Second, the model itself will be stated. Third, the model will be explained.

The cost model is applied on a typical GQM measurement programme containing the following characteristics:

- *Participants.* The cost model is based on a typical software project where four engineers and one project manager need to be interviewed. The GQM team consists of one person.

- *GQM goals.* The measurement programme contains one (major) GQM goal, however, three different viewpoints (i.e., management, quality assurance, and software engineer) are possible.

- *Size of project team.* The project team consists of ten software engineers.

- *Support infrastructure.* There is an existing tool infrastructure for supporting a GQM measurement programme (including computer tools and paper forms).

- *Training and briefings.* There is no special need for training and briefing, because the participants of the measurement programme are familiar with GQM measurement.

- *Feedback session.* As feedback sessions are both the most valuable and costly part of a measurement programme, it is assumed that five feedback sessions are sufficient to attain the specified goal.

Task	GQM team	Manager	*Single engineer*	For 10 engineers	Total
GQM programme planning	4	2	*-*	-	6
Identify and define GQM goals	8	1	*1*	10	19
Conduct GQM interviews	40	2	*2*	8	50
Develop GQM plan	40	1	*1*	6	47
Data collection	24	1	*1.5*	15	40
Data analysis and interpretation per feedback session[1]	*48[1]*	*2[1]*	*2[1]*	*20[1]*	*70[1]*
Data analysis and interpretation (5 feedback sessions)	240	10	*10*	100	350
Total	356	17	*15.5*	139	512

Figure 4-1: Effort model of routine application of GQM (effort in person hours).

Figure 4-1 shows the operational cost model for routine application of GQM. Required effort is given in hours. Please note that the total effort is, of course, based on the project description stated before. The cost model, however, contains sufficient information to calculate other project settings. The cost model is referred to as an 'effort model' here, because we will focus on required effort only. In order to calculate costs, the required effort needs to be multiplied by the appropriate labour costs of an organisation.

The following cost structure is typical for routine application of GQM:

- Roughly 30% of the effort is spent on defining the measurement programme, while 70% is spent on continuation of the measurement programme, which is almost completely spent on the feedback sessions.
- 70% of the effort on the measurement programme is spent by the GQM team, and only 30% of the total effort is spent by the project team.
- The effort spent by the project team is less than 1% of their total working time.
- A total three person-months of effort is required for a typical GQM measurement programme, distributed over one calendar year

Planning and definition normally requires a period of 4 to 6 weeks. Availability of the interviewees is critical for the duration of the definition. Duration of data collection and feedback depends on the frequency of feedback sessions and on quickness of goal attainment. Experience shows that an elapse time of a year is normal to attain a measurement goal.

---

[1] The cost data for data analysis and interpretation apply for one data collection cycle lasting 2 months and being concluded by one single feedback-session. However, experiences showed that for goal attainment 3-7 feedback sessions are normally needed. So, the table contains data under the assumption that 5 feedback sessions are held within the measurement programme.

GQM definition phase

All activities for setting up the measurement programme from preparation to start of data collection, take on average 11½ working days (92 hours) for the GQM team. The effort needed for the project manager and the engineers is relatively little for all measurement definition tasks, respectively 6 hours, and 4 hours. Clearly, in this stage most effort is performed by the GQM.

Data collection phase

An opening briefing is held with an effort of half an hour per participant. The effort of the GQM team is spent on a full day for the briefing and another two days for data validation.

GQM interpretation phase

The GQM team typically needs five days to prepare a feedback session. Feedback sessions take approximately two hours per participant, and another six hours for a GQM team member are needed to report the feedback session. After goal attainment, the experiences of the measurement programme should be documented to capture gained expertise.

There are many factors that influence the required effort of a GQM measurement programme. Three important ones are:

- *Number of GQM goals.* An increasing number of GQM goals also increases the required effort of all activities. Furthermore, the complexity of a measurement programme increases rapidly as more goals are included. Practice shows that three goals are really a maximum and even that is already difficult.
- *Size of a project team.* The increasing size of a project team also increases the required effort, both absolutely and relatively. More project team members need to be interviewed, and feedback sessions will require more time.
- *Number of feedback sessions.* As feedback sessions are the most important and also the most time consuming part of a measurement programme, the number of feedback sessions is an important factor. It is, however, advised not to save on feedback sessions, because a measurement programme without appropriate analyses will loose all its benefits. Benefits are derived only from feedback sessions.

4.2.2   Effort model for initial introduction of GQM

In this section the cost of a first GQM measurement programme is described. The cost categories are identical to the previous model of routine application, however, required effort per category is significantly higher. A typical first GQM measurement programme has the following characteristics:

- An *external GQM expert* is a member of the GQM team and acts as a coach to the project team and the other members of the GQM team.
- The project team contains *less engineers*. The subsequent example mentions eight engineers and this is even quite large for initial GQM introduction. A first project with five engineers is more than sufficient.
- There is *no measurement infrastructure*, such as tool support for data collection or measurement forms. Usually data collection support is developed gradually, starting with paper-based data collection forms and is later moving towards on-line data collection.

Activity	GQM expert	GQM member	Manager	*For single engineer*	For 10 engineers	Total
GQM programme planning	24	32	4	*4*	40	**100**
Identify and define GQM goals	18	8	2	*1*	10	**38**
Conduct GQM Interviews	35	35	2	*1*	4	**76**
Develop GQM deliverables	196	138	2	*1*	10	**346**
Data collection	-	16	-	*3*	30	**46**
Data analysis & interpretation per feedback session	*12*	*48*	*8*	*4*	*40*	*108*
Data analysis and interpretation (5 feedback sessions)	60	240	40	*20*	200	**540**
Total	**333**	**469**	**50**	*30*	**294**	**1146**

Figure 4-2: Effort model for initial introduction of GQM (effort in person hours).

Figure 4-2 shows the cost model for initial introduction of GQM. The effort is again stated in person hours. In order to calculate costs, these hours again need to be multiplied with the appropriate labour costs per hour.

The following cost structure is typical for initial introduction of GQM measurement:

- An initial GQM measurement programme needs approximately eight person-months of effort. This is significantly more than the three months mentioned for routine application. A first project requires a lot of initial work. An example is the initial training of the GQM team.
- Approximately 50% of the total effort is spent on defining the measurement programme. This differs significantly from the 30% in routine application. Especially the definition of the GQM and measurement plan requires more effort.
- 70% of the total effort on the measurement programme is spent by the GQM team (including expert), and 30% by the project team, which is identical to routine application.
- The effort spent by the project team is less than 2% of their total working time, which still is double the amount compared to routine application of GQM measurement.

Planning and definition requires approximately three months (compared to four to six weeks in a routine application). The additional time is primarily spent on training and learning. For data collection and feedback the same rules of thumb apply as for routine application. Effort depends on the frequency of feedback sessions and on speed of goal attainment. Experience shows that approximately one year should be sufficient to attain a measurement goal. However, first feedback sessions proved to be difficult for some project teams. The interactive, open and learning character of feedback sessions might be quite new for engineers. Therefore, it is not unlikely that a first measurement programme takes even longer.

Other differences compared to routine application of GQM measurement are:

- *GQM programme planning.* Contains significantly more effort for the GQM team. The effort is three days for the external GQM expert and four days for the other members of the GQM team.
- *Identify and define GQM goals.* The GQM team again needs additional to allow training and clarification by the GQM expert.
- *Develop GQM deliverables.* Again significantly more effort is needed, because the GQM team needs to be instructed how to set up such a plan. Furthermore, a measurement infrastructure needs to be developed for the first time. This type of effort, containing for example the set-up of data collection procedures, documents, tools and forms, requires a lot of effort.
- *Data collection.* The additional effort is one day for coaching, validation and "trouble shooting" of the measurement database and data collection forms. Some additional effort is also required to motivate the project team during the start of data collection.
- *Data analysis and interpretation.* Interpretation is the most important part of a measurement programme. The project team will have to learn how to analyse measurement data. It will be especially difficult to learn that the performance of individuals should not be evaluated, but that a development process needs to be improved. Interpretations should focus on improvement actions and answering of GQM questions.

Again there are many factors that influence the required effort of a GQM measurement programme. The most important ones are:

- *Resistance to change.* There will always be resistance to change. This can be overcome by focusing on process aspects, showing the need for the change and make sure that the project team receives sufficient training in order to be prepared. Including the goals and questions of a project team is also an important element in overcoming resistance.
- *Size of project team.* If one is less experienced the size of a project team becomes more important. All phases will require more time and overall it will take considerably more time until the measurement programme will produce any results. This increases the chance that people loose their interest. It is, therefore, recommended to start with a project team of approximately five engineers.

4.3   Benefits of GQM measurement programmes

Measurement programmes may have various kinds of benefits. The most desirable benefit is achievement of the explicitly stated improvement goals. Such improvement goals can be product- or process-related (e.g., product reliability or process effectiveness). In addition, measurement can have numerous other effects such as improving communication within a project team, attitude of personnel, process definition, and process execution.

Eventually, benefits should result in financial gains. However, it will often be difficult to make a financial appraisal of quality improvement, because many indirect links are involved. For example, the improved software development process, will lead to better embedded software, increasing product characteristics, increasing sales and ultimately profits. However, many other elements will also change in the mean time and it will therefore be quite complicated to link the additional profits to the process improvements. In this type of situation it is advised not to calculate the exact financial benefits and to remain with a quantitative description. Management should then evaluate whether the costs can be expected to be worthwhile. Knowledge of how customers will value a better quality is essential here.

However, it may also be relatively easy to quantify financial benefits. For instance, in one of the measurement programmes (Chapter 11), how developers were interrupted during their work was investigated. Based on the findings, work and communication practices in the team were improved, and the number of interrupts was decreased significantly. The improvements had a measurable impact on productivity and the associated cost reduction could be calculated.

In any case every software measurement or improvement programme has a set of goals to be achieved. These goals are made explicit and measurement will play an effective role in achieving them. These goals can address product and process aspects. Based on the measurement results, the developers can (re-)focus their development activities towards achieving these goals. Team members will identify process changes themselves. This ensures that improvement actions are very well supported and therefore implemented successfully. This is experienced as a significant benefit from measurement and GQM feedback sessions in particular.

As stated before, many other benefits will result from measurement that are not directly related to the achievement of explicit goals. Typically, they are related to communication and interaction in a project team, attitude and knowledge of the team members, and the degree to which quality assurance and improvement actions are integrated with software development.

A general impression from the measurement and improvement programmes is that GQM measurement makes improvement initiatives solid and successful. The project teams use GQM as a change agent for improving their work practices and the products they produce. Furthermore, the goal-orientation of GQM helps to keep improvement programmes focused: it helps limiting the scope of an improvement programme to what is feasible in a given situation, and it helps to identify the necessary improvement actions in a well-informed and appropriate manner.

4.4   Questions and assignments

4.4.1   Questions

1. Which two typical applications are there for the GQM method in an organisation?
2. What is the typical effort distribution in percentages, for GQM measurement programmes, looking at:
    2.1.   Distribution over project team and GQM team, in a routine situation?
    2.2.   Distribution over defining and continuation of the measurement programme, in a routine situation?
    2.3.   Distribution over project team and GQM team, in an initial situation?
    2.4.   Distribution over defining and continuation of the measurement programme, in an initial situation?
3. How long (in calendar time) does the typical set-up of a measurement programme take in a routine situation? And in an initial situation?
4. Why should benefits of GQM measurement programmes not only be evaluated financially?

4.4.2 Assignments

A project team consisting of ten engineers and a manager, that have already been involved in two measurement programmes, are working on the definition of a new measurement programme. The objective is to identify product features that need most customer support during the first six months after release. Based on these findings improvements will be made regarding, for example, documentation, help-files, and customer support desk manuals.

Develop a time plan in which the participation of the project team members is listed. Use the effort table in Figure 4-1, to estimate the required effort. Please, do not forget to include work that has to be done by GQM team members. Also note that during the period in which this measurement programme is defined, the project team is preparing a release of new software. They therefore work under pressure and appointments with the GQM team have the chance of being changed at the last moment.

PART 2

The GQM method stepwise

5 · GQM planning phase

Checklist GQM planning phase		
------	---	✔
No.	**Checklist item**	
5.1	Separate GQM-team is assigned and installed	
5.2	GQM-team has sufficient resources available	
5.3	Corporate improvement objectives are formulated and approved	
5.4	Project team is established and supports improvement objectives	
5.5	Project team has at least 2% resources reserved for GQM programme	
5.6	Project plan is available	
5.7	Communication and reporting procedures are defined	
5.8	Training and promotion is planned and described	
5.9	Management is committed and regularly informed	
5.10	Management has approved the project plan	

5.1 Introduction

In Chapter 2 the four main phases of the GQM method were introduced, being *planning*, *definition*, *data collection* and *interpretation*. In this chapter the first phase is described. In this phase a framework is given to introduce a measurement programme. The position of a planning phase in the GQM method is illustrated in Figure 5-1.

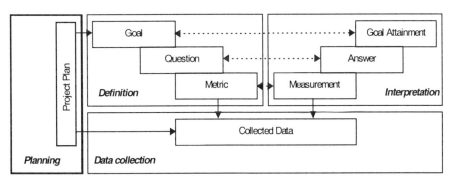

Figure 5-1: The planning phase of the GQM method.

5.2   Planning procedures

The primary objectives of the planning phase are to collect all required information for a successful introduction, and to prepare and motivate members of an organisation for a measurement programme. A *project plan* is an important deliverable of a planning phase. Such a project plan documents procedures, schedules and objectives of a measurement programme and provides a basis for promotion to and acceptance by management. A project plan should also contain a planning for training of the developers involved. The planning phase consists of five steps which are illustrated in Figure 5-2. In the following sections these particular steps will subsequently be described.

5.2.1   Step 1: Establish GQM team

Practice shows that without a separate independent team responsible for the continuity of a measurement programme, measurement activities tend to fail. When deadlines emerge, measurement activities often receive less attention, unless an independent GQM team is established (Basili et al, 1994b). Although this team should be independent, it is of course

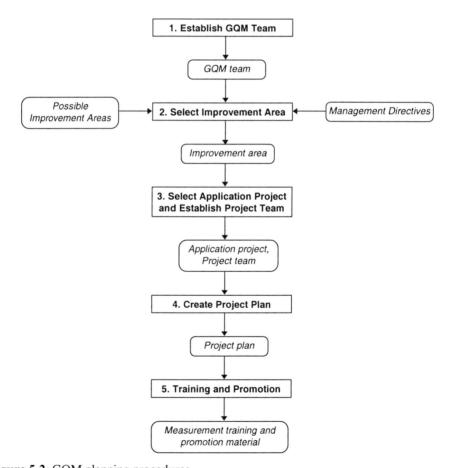

Figure 5-2: GQM planning procedures.

possible to incorporate its activities in for example a Quality Assurance department, Software Engineering Process Group, or SPI department. A GQM team should:

a. Be independent from project teams, and have no interest in measurement results.
b. Possess sufficient background knowledge on the objects of measurement.
c. Keep in mind that the project team 'owns' the improvement programme, because a project team is most knowledgeable on a project.
d. Be improvement oriented, which includes that it is willing to improve itself too.
e. Be enthusiastic, in order to motivate the project team.

An important requirement for the success of a measurement programme, is the level of mutual trust and cooperation between the GQM team and the project team (Solingen et al, 1997). Therefore, it is important that the GQM team has no interest in the data that the project team gathers. In order to be able to guide and support a measurement programme, the GQM team needs to have a certain level of background knowledge regarding the development processes and products the measurement programme focuses on. This is an important prerequisite, as the GQM team should be able to discuss interpretations with the project team.

Furthermore, the GQM team should regard itself as a facilitator of learning (Solingen et al, 1997) and have an improvement-oriented mind. The GQM team should show respect to the project team regarding the execution of the development tasks, as not always pre-defined procedures will, or can, be followed. The GQM team should have an open mind toward such issues, as in the end, the developers have all the knowledge on the processes and products and are eventually responsible for their project and its measurements.

The roles of the GQM team are 'manager' (responsible for continuation of the measurement programme), 'coach' (expert on GQM), and 'support engineer' (to support measurement activities). The main activities of the GQM team are:

- *Plan* measurement programmes within development projects.
- Carry out measurement *definition* activities and develop GQM deliverables.
- Check *data collection* by the project team and process available data.
- Prepare *interpretation* of the measurement data by organising feedback sessions.
- Moderate feedback sessions.
- Report progress to project team and management, and disseminate and package results.

Personal skills of GQM team members play a crucial role in the success of a measurement programme, particularly their ability to motivate others. When a GQM team lacks this ability, the whole measurement programme stands little success. A GQM team should therefore include reputable staff.

5.2.2   Step 2: Select improvement area

After initiation of a GQM team, the next step is the identification and selection of suitable product or process improvement areas. Examples are:

- Apparent problems that the organisation struggles with.
- Process improvement areas identified by means of an assessment.
- Product improvement areas based on high-level business goals.

The improvement areas should be operational refinements of corporate improvement objectives and business goals. Particularly corporate improvement objectives together with the four basic aspects: *cost*, *time*, *risk* and *quality*, should give an idea of improvement goals. Examples of such goals are 'increase customer satisfaction', and 'expand market share', however, they can also be derived from governmental directives, such as, safety or environmental issues.

Guidance during the refinement of high level business goals into improvement and measurement goals is difficult. However, SEI has issued a report which contains some steps to support this refinement. This report is publicly available and can be downloaded free of charge from the SEI home-page. The title is 'Goal-Driven Software Measurement: a Guidebook'. This report primarily focuses on the *definition* of software measurement.

Apparent process or product problems are usually indicated by departmental management or the developers themselves. Information on such issues can be retrieved during interview sessions with representatives that are directly involved, or responsible for handling those problems. Because these problems are usually straightforward, the people involved are normally well motivated to solve them and to apply measurement in doing so. If members of an organisation are unable to give a clear description of their problem, however, brainstorming sessions with departmental and group representatives can be held in order to create a better understanding of the issues. Such sessions typically start with defining the purpose of the organisation on a company-wide level, followed by focusing on a specific department, group, or team, and ending with describing particular problems or improvement areas (Solingen et al, 1995).

Another method to identify improvement areas is to conduct an assessment. An assessment is a review of a software development organisation to provide a clear and fact-based understanding of the organisation's development practice, to identify its major problems, and to initiate actions to make improvements (based on Humphrey, 1989).

Once suitable improvement areas have been identified, the following details have to be described:

- problem or improvement area;
- processes or products involved;
- environmental, legislative, organisational, and technological influences
- people involved;
- previous experience of these people with measurement and GQM.

These characterisations will be used as input for a subsequent phase of the GQM method. To support these characterisations, questionnaires can be used. However, questionnaires always have to be tailored to a specific organisation or project.

5.2.3   Step 3: Select application project and establish a project team

A project team consists of all the people that work on a particular software development project. Since the project team members are the people that will actually perform measurement activities and in the end may need to adopt their work processes, the success of a measurement programme heavily depends on their willingness, motivation, and enthusiasm. Therefore, effort should be spent to align measurement objectives and improvement ideas of a project team. This is a responsibility of a GQM team. They will continuously monitor and stimulate the dedication of a project team regarding the measurement activities.

Because an improvement area is selected first, even before a project team, a GQM team has a significant influence on the measurement area. However, a GQM team should never be made fully responsible for a measurement programme, since all measurements should be related to specific goals of a project team. The project team becomes the owner of a measurement programme and responsible for the results. If the project team decides to stop specific measurements, or to change the scope of measurements, this needs to be done. The GQM team is, of course, allowed to challenge a project team and to discuss their proposed changes. Possibly, the GQM team can convince the project team that their proposed changes are not appropriate. However, it is emphasised that an improvement initiative is the responsibility of the actual developers and not of a GQM team.

5.2.4   Step 4: Create project plan

Once a GQM team and project team have been established and improvement areas selected, a proposal for a measurement programme should be developed on which the measurement programme will be based. This proposal, ie the project plan, is primarily created by the GQM team based on input (and approach) from the project team, and should contain the following items:

- *Management abstract*, which presents the measurement programme in approximately 20 lines.
- *Introduction*, which presents the scope of the measurement programme, and the relation of the improvement objectives to the software development project goals.
- *Characterisation*, which describes the outcomes of the characterisations that were held within the programme on the organisational, project, project team and GQM team levels.
- *Schedule*, which presents the managerial issues for the measurement programme, such as a timeline, list of deliverables, resource allocation and a cost-benefit analysis.
- *Organisation*, which describes the relevant organisational, project team and GQM team structures of the measurement programme.
- *Management process*, which presents priorities, management reporting procedures and risk control activities.
- *Training and promotion*, which presents the activities planned for training the project team and for promotion and dissemination of the results over the organisation.

As indicated, the main part of the project plan is based on the information gathered in the first steps of the planning phase. However, the project plan should contain at least two sections that will contribute to the acceptance of the project by corporate management.

In the first place, the project plan should contain an *initial cost-benefit analysis* of the project. This analysis is based on the proposed effort of the GQM team and project team necessary to completely execute the measurement programme, and the expected benefits the improvement goals will offer once they have been achieved.

Furthermore, the GQM team should also make a *realistic planning* of the measurement programme, in which all steps to be taken in the subsequent procedures of the GQM definition, data collection, and interpretation phase of the project are scheduled in time. This planning should also indicate to what extent members of a project team will be involved in the particular steps of the project. Project milestones and deadlines, together with a list of the deliverables at each point, also need to be specified in a project plan.

A project plan will primarily serve as a proposal to management in order to receive management approval of, and commitment to, a project. Once a proposal is accepted, a project plan will be maintained by the GQM team. During a project additional information will become available and a project plan will probably evolve over time.

5.2.5   Step 5: Training and promotion

Crucial for the success of a measurement programme is that all people participating in the project are enthusiastic and motivated, and remain committed to the objectives of the project. To accomplish this, the GQM team should organise regular training and promotion sessions during which:

- a clear definition of proposed improvement goals are presented;
- benefits of the measurement programmes are explained;
- the impact of measurement on daily development activities is indicated;
- experiences from other organisations/projects are discussed.

If possible, all people participating in a measurement programme should be present during these sessions. Particularly important is that persons responsible for managing the project team are present at those sessions, as well as representatives from higher-level management.

An indication of the investment and the expected benefits needs to be given up-front. This should be done for two reasons. One, because the project manager needs to assign his people to the programme, so he should plan their effort. Two, because the effort spent by the project team is considered as an investment, which should not be undertaken if the expected revenues would not exceed the investment.

Once a project is approved, the project team members have to be trained according to their roles within the project. To accomplish this, the GQM team should organise training sessions during which:

- principles of measurement are explained;
- the GQM paradigm is explained;
- the GQM method is explained.

The main focus of the training sessions should be on the last point: explaining the GQM method. The GQM team should explain the particular process steps within a measurement programme to the project team members, and should indicate to them to what extent they will be involved in these steps. Next to the explanation of the method, the project time table should be presented to the project team members, so they know at what point in time effort is required from them. During such training sessions, the GQM team should be aware that not too much emphasis is put on the theoretical background of GQM. Rather, the project team is interested in hearing practical issues regarding the method, as it wants answers to questions such as:

- What measurement tasks should I perform?
- Why should I perform those tasks?
- How and when should I perform those tasks?
- How much effort is required by me to perform those tasks?
- Do the tasks influence my daily activities?
- What do I get back from this? What will I learn?

Minimally, one training session should be organised during which the above points are discussed. If necessary, more should be added. All people involved in the project should be trained before the actual project activities start.

5.3   Questions and assignments

5.3.1   Questions

1. Which are the five steps of the GQM planning phase?
2. Which items should be included in a project plan of a measurement programme?
3. Which typical practical questions of a project team should be addressed during briefing or training of the project team?
4. Which percentage of project effort should a project team plan for a GQM measurement programme?
5. Who selects the improvement areas? How can this be supported?

5.3.2   Assignments

1. Design a table of contents for a project plan for the GQM measurement programme of which you have defined goals in the assignment of Section 4.4.2.
2. Download the characterisation questionnaire for a GQM programme from 'http://www.iese.fhg.de/Services/Projects/Public-Projects/Cemp/GQM-Process-Model/pm_76.html'. Complete such a characterisation for one of your recent projects and try to derive improvement areas from this characterisation.

'The truth is that you always know the right thing to do.
The hard part is really doing it'
H. Norman Schwarzkopf

6 GQM definition phase

Checklist GQM definition phase		
No.	**Checklist item**	✔
6.1	GQM goals are defined	
6.2	Project team adopts GQM goals	
6.3	Process models that identify measurements are available	
6.4	GQM question definitions are available and consistent with the goals	
6.5	GQM metric definitions are available and consistent with the questions	
6.6	GQM metrics are checked on consistency with process model	
6.7	GQM plan is available	
6.8	Measurement plan is available	
6.9	Analysis plan is available	

6.1   Introduction

This chapter describes the definition phase of a GQM measurement programme. The definition phase is the second phase of the GQM process (see Figure 6-1), and concerns all activities that should be performed to formally define a measurement programme. During this phase three documents are produced:

- GQM plan;
- measurement plan;
- analysis plan.

These three plans contain all pertinent information regarding the measurement programme.

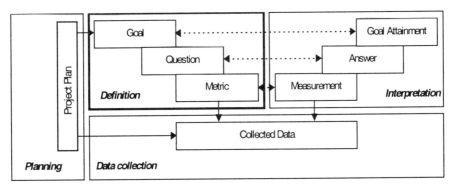

Figure 6-1: The definition phase of the GQM method.

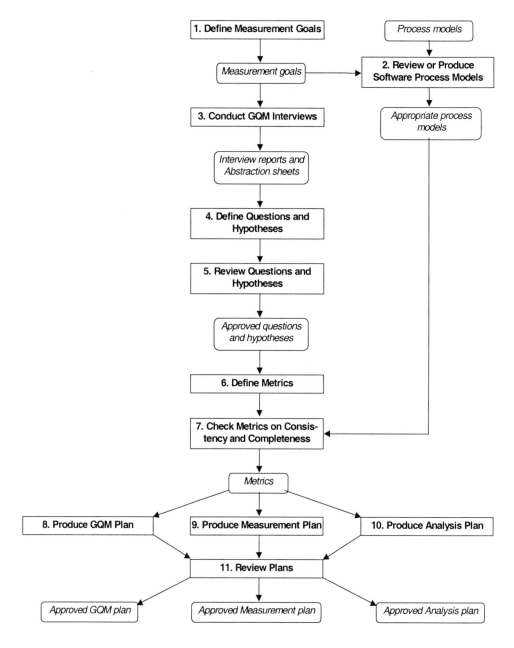

Figure 6-2: GQM Definition procedures.

6.2   Definition of procedures

To complete the definition phase, an eleven-step procedure is proposed, of which the flowchart is shown in Figure 6-2. The next sections describe in more detail the eleven steps of a GQM definition phase:

1. Define measurement goals
2. Review or produce software process models
3. Conduct GQM interviews
4. Define questions and hypotheses
5. Review questions and hypotheses
6. Define metrics
7. Check metrics on consistency and completeness
8. Produce GQM plan
9. Produce measurement plan
10. Produce analysis plan
11. Review plans

6.2.1   Step 1: Define measurement goals

The first step in the definition process is the definition of formal measurement goals. These measurement goals are derived from the improvement goals which were already identified in the preceding planning phase and are described in the project plan. All people participating in the measurement programme should be involved in the definition of measurement goals. Without this involvement, people's commitment to the measurement programme is at risk, as it may no longer be clear to them why measurement is applied. As already described in Chapter 3, the people participating in the measurement programme are the project team members, their manager and the GQM team members.

Measurement goals should be defined in an understandable way and should be clearly structured. For this purpose, templates are available that support the definition of measurement goals by specifying *purpose* (what object and why), *perspective* (what aspect and who), and *context* characteristics (Basili et al, 1994). This template is illustrated in Figure 6-3.

If a project team has little experience in GQM goal definition, the GQM team can refine the global improvement goals into GQM measurement goals, and have these goal definitions evaluated during a review session in which all project members participate. If a project team already has some experience with GQM goal definition, the GQM team should preferably define GQM goals in cooperation with all project members during a session. At the end of this session, all people should fully understand and agree upon the defined GQM

Analyse	the object under measurement
For the purpose of	understanding, controlling, or improving the object
With respect to	the quality focus of the object that the measurement focuses on
From the viewpoint of	the people that measure the object
In the context of	the environment in which measurement takes place

Figure 6-3: GQM goal definition template (Basili et al, 1994a).

measurement goals.

Within such a brainstorming session it is always possible to define many goals. However, these should be relevant to the business, represent strategic goals from management, and support high priority processes of the organisation. Sometimes it will be obvious what the measurement goals should be, for example an urgent problem that needs attention. However, often it will be difficult to select or prioritise measurement goals. In this case, multicriteria analyses are a possibility. A mechanism to support goal definition and selection in a meeting, is by asking the 'seven questions' stated below:

1.   What are the strategic goals of your organisation?
2.   What forces have an impact on your strategic goals?
3.   How can you improve your performance?
4.   What are your major concerns (problems)?
5.   What are your improvement goals?
6.   How can you reach your improvement goals?
7.   What are possible measurement goals, and what are their priorities?

All members of a project team should be involved in the definition of the goals in order to establish their commitment. If they have selected the goals themselves, they will also be motivated to work on the measurement programme. Management involvement is also a critical success factor. Management should be able to show how measurement goals relate to business goals and support business improvement.

Deliverable 6.1: *List of GQM measurement goal specifications*

6.2.2   Step 2: Review or produce software process models

Models of the software development process are used to support the definition of a measurement programme by checking the set of metrics of forthcoming step 7 on completeness and consistency. Examples of software process models are given in section 6.3 on page 59.

If process models are already available in the organisation, they have to be reviewed, and, if necessary, improved to support definition of measurements. Possible review methods include formal reviews, brainstorming sessions, structured interviews, or presentations. There should be an agreement on the models by all people involved in the measurement programme. Make sure the process models describe in which way the work is really done and not the ideal way in which it should be done. As measurement is done during the actual work of the project, the process models must give a real picture of that actual way of working.

If no process or product models relevant to the defined measurement goals exist, the GQM team should develop them. As these models are supposed to support the definition of measurements, the application of a modelling technique that identifies measurements on the basis of processes is preferred. Once the GQM team has modelled all relevant processes, the project team should agree upon these newly defined process models.

For a more comprehensive description of suitable process modelling techniques, this chapter contains a section at the end on process modelling (Section 6.3).

Deliverable(s) 6.2: *Approved process models, suitable to identify measurements.*

6.2.3   Step 3: Conduct GQM interviews

The project team should always be closely involved in the development of the measurement programme, however, during the definition of goals, questions, metrics, and hypotheses, the input of the project team is of crucial importance. The team members are the experts with respect to the object under measurement. Therefore, this knowledge can only be extracted from them.

To extract the knowledge from the project team with respect to the defined measurement goals, the GQM team should conduct structured interviews with the individual members. The interviews aim at capturing the definitions, assumptions and models of the project team related to the measurement goals, and therefore, the main purpose of these interviews is to make the implicit knowledge of the project members explicit.

Though it may seem more efficient to interview more than one team member in one interview, it is recommended to conduct individual interviews. As the purpose of the interview is knowledge acquisition, it is important to extract the knowledge from the people without the presence of factors that may influence their opinion. If more than one person is being interviewed during a single session, these people may influence each other's opinion, and not all available knowledge or honest opinions may be extracted from them. Also, the interviewer should not push the interviewee in any direction. The information acquired from different people during interviews will be combined in subsequent steps.

Using abstraction sheets

To support the communication between a GQM team and a project team during interviews, a GQM team uses so-called 'abstraction sheets' (Latum et al, 1998). The use of abstraction sheets during interviews provides a structured approach to focus on relevant issues regarding the goal, and prevents issues being overlooked. An abstraction sheet summarises the main issues and dependencies of a goal as described in a GQM plan and is discerned in four sections. The four sections of an abstraction sheet are (see Figure 6-4):

- *Quality focus*: what are possible metrics to measure an object of a goal, according to the project members?
- *Baseline hypothesis*: what is the project member's current knowledge with respect to these metrics? His or her expectations are documented as 'baseline hypotheses' of the metrics.
- *Variation factors*: which (environmental) factors does a project member expect to be of influence on the metrics?
- *Impact on baseline hypothesis*: how could these variation factors influence the actual measurements? What kind of dependencies between the metrics and influencing factors are assumed?

An example of an abstraction sheet is given in Figure 6-4. Hypotheses are grouped in two sections of the abstraction sheet, and are associated to the corresponding questions in the other sections. The four sections can be checked for consistency and completeness, because mutual relations between the sections exist. For example: for every Quality focus, there should be at least on Baseline hypothesis, and possibly some Variation factors. Also, for every Variation factor there should be at least on Impact on the hypothesis. The GQM team can use abstraction sheets in several ways:

- Fill in the abstraction sheet together with the project member, starting with discussing quality focus and baseline hypothesis, and after that variation factors and the corresponding impact. When all sections are filled in, one should follow this approach iteratively until the abstraction sheet is satisfactory completed.
- Train the project team in using abstraction sheets, and when they are familiar with the concept, let them fill in an abstraction sheet themselves. This approach requires some investment, since it is not easy to train people on the abstraction sheet concept.
- Fill in the abstraction sheet in advance before the interview. In this way the GQM team prepares the interview, and a kind of draft version becomes available. This approach must be handled carefully, since the interviewer is in fact representing his or her implicit models on the abstraction sheet. The interview is then some kind of validation of the draft version. To follow this approach, knowledge of the context and subject of the measurement goal is needed.
- Use the abstraction sheets as a guidance for analysis and interpretation of results during feedback sessions.

Abstraction sheets are a powerful tool that can be used during the set-up of the measurement programme: information from interviews can be organised in a structured way and copied from the abstraction sheets into the GQM plan. However, abstraction sheets can also be used for structuring the presentation and interpretation of measurement data during feedback sessions. In fact, an abstraction sheet is a one-page summary of a GQM plan. Not all direct measurements defined in a GQM plan are represented on abstraction sheets, only the basic ones that reflect the most important metrics. An example of an abstraction sheet is shown in Figure 6-4.

Deliverable(s) 6.3: *Set of interview reports and abstraction sheets.*

Object	**Purpose**	**Quality Focus**	**Viewpoint**
Delivered Product	Understanding	Reliability and its causes	Project Team

Quality Focus	**Variation Factors**
Number of failures: • by severity • by detection group • number of faults • by module	Level of reviewing

Baseline Hypotheses (estimates)	**Impact of Variation Factors**

Distribution of failures:
• By severity:
    • Minor 60%
    • Major 30%
    • Fatal 10%
	The higher the level of reviewing, the less minor failures will be detected after release

Figure 6-4: Example of an abstraction sheet.

6.2.4   Step 4: Define questions and hypotheses

With respect to the measurement goals, questions should be defined to support data interpretation towards a measurement goal. As goals are defined on an abstract level, questions are refinements of goals to a more operational level, which is more suitable for interpretation. By answering the questions, one should be able to conclude whether a goal is reached. Therefore, during question definition, checks should be performed as to whether the defined questions have the ability to support conclusion of the goal in a satisfactory way.

If the questions are defined on a level that is still too abstract, data interpretation towards answering the questions provides difficulties as the relationship between the questions and the data is difficult to understand (see Figure 6-5). If, on the other hand, the questions are defined at too detailed a level, clear interpretation from the questions toward the goal will also not be possible. To support an optimal interpretation from collected data to answering questions to concluding on the goal, the questions should be defined at an intermediate level of abstraction between the metrics and the goals.

In order to come to the right level of abstraction for GQM questions, it is useful to document the questions formulated by the project team members in the interviews explicitly. Such interview questions will mostly be on the 'too detailed' level of abstraction, but they might also be too abstract. By grouping similar questions together it will normally be clear what the appropriate GQM question should be. Examples of working towards adequate GQM questions are give in the case studies of Part 3.

Subsequently, for each question, *expected* answers are formulated as *hypotheses*. Formulating hypotheses triggers the project team to think about the current situation and therefore stimulates a better understanding of the process and/or product. Furthermore, after measurement, during data interpretation, these hypotheses of measurement results will be compared with the actual measurement results. The purpose of this comparison should not be to evaluate a possible correctness of the hypotheses, but to encourage the project team to identify and analyse the underlying reasons that caused the actual results to deviate, or conform, from their expectations.

In other words, hypotheses are formulated to increase the learning effect from measure-

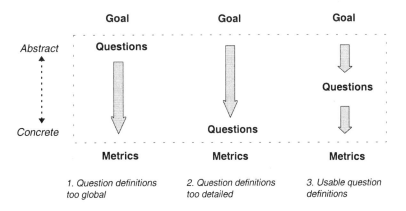

Figure 6-5: GQM question definition (Solingen, 1995).

ment. By formulating hypotheses, current knowledge of the project team is made explicit. Learning theory has shown that adults always learn against an existing frame of reference (Senge, 1990). People already have much knowledge and experience gathered throughout their lives, and learning requires that new knowledge is related to existing knowledge. Therefore, it is important to make knowledge people already possess explicit, before absorbing new information. This way, links can be created between new and existing knowledge, allowing the unfamiliar to be interpreted by the familiar. The previous knowledge of the project team with regard to the measured process, is captured by building the measurement programme on their knowledge of a development process, through close co-operation, structured interviews, and hypotheses formulation. Formulation of hypotheses also prevents ending up in a situation where people mistakenly think they knew the outcome along.

Deliverable(s) 6.4: *List of measurement questions and hypotheses, defined with respect to the measurement goals.*

6.2.5   Step 5: Review questions and hypotheses

To make sure that the right questions and hypotheses have been captured and correctly formulated, they should be reviewed. The questions are the basic translation from goals to metrics. When the actual data will be collected and presented to a project team, it should help in answering the questions of the project team. So, the questions take a central role, not only during definition, but also during interpretation. Therefore, it is important to make sure that these questions are correct. Also, that the questions have been reformulated from the input of the project team during the interviews. During that translation it is possible that mistakes are made or that the GQM team makes misinterpretations.

The hypotheses should be reviewed as well, because together with the questions, the hypotheses are used to define the metrics that will be established for data collection.

Deliverable(s) 6.5: *List of approved measurement questions and hypotheses.*

6.2.6   Step 6: Define metrics

Once goals are refined into a list of questions, *metrics* should be defined that provide all the quantitative information to answer the questions in a satisfactory way. Therefore, metrics are a refinement of questions into a quantitative process and/or product measurements. After all these metrics have been measured, sufficient information should be available to answer the questions.

Furthermore, *factors* that could possibly be of influence to the outcome of the metrics should also be identified. After all, factors that directly influence metrics, also influence the answers to the questions that the metrics are related to. If the influencing factors were not to be considered during definition of a measurement programme, some conclusions or interpretations of the collected data may not be correct. These influencing factors are usually also defined as metrics.

Deliverable(s) 6.6: *List of metrics suitable for supplying information to answer the questions.*

6.2.7 Step 7: Check on metric consistency and completeness

The defined goals, questions, and metrics must be consistent and complete with respect to models of the object under measurement (see Figure 6-6). To safeguard this, consistency and completeness checks have to be performed throughout the entire definition phase. Whenever, during these checks, definitions appear to be missing, incomplete, or inconsistent, either the definitions have to be adjusted to comply with the process models, or the process models have to be adjusted to comply with the goal, question, and metrics definitions.

If product metrics are defined these should be checked as to whether they are in fact possible and whether they can actually be measured at a specific moment in the development process.

Deliverable(s) 7.7: *Consistent and complete definitions of questions and metrics related to the measurement goals. Process models that are consistent and complete with the measurement goals, questions, and metrics.*

6.2.8 Step 8: Produce a GQM plan

A GQM plan is a document that contains the goals, questions, metrics and hypotheses for a measurement programme as defined in the previous steps. The GQM plan serves as a guideline for data interpretation, and provides the basis for the subsequently developed *measurement plan* and the *analysis plan*.

The GQM plan describes the refinement from the measurement goals into questions and subsequently from questions into metrics. As some of these metrics may be indirect metrics, it also describes all direct measurements that should be collected for each indirect metric. The GQM plan is used for the following purposes:

- Explicit description of goals, questions, metrics and hypotheses. This way, the GQM plan represents the formal documentation of the measurement programme.
- Guideline for interpretation of collected data. As the refinement from goals into questions and subsequently questions into metrics is described in the GQM plan, the

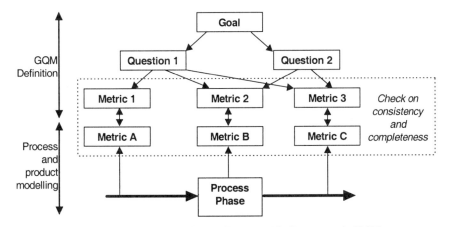

Figure 6-6: Checking on consistency and completeness (Solingen et al, 1995).

plan should also be used as a guideline for the interpretation of the measurement results by the project team. The measurement results should provide answers to the questions defined in the GQM plan, and once these questions have been answered, one should be able to draw conclusions regarding the GQM goals.

- Basis for definition of data collection procedures. As the GQM plan defines the metrics to be collected, it serves as the basis for the measurement plan, in which the data collection procedures are described.
- Basis for an analysis plan, that simulates and proposes data interpretation using graphics and tables before actual data has been collected.
- Basis for the measurement support system. The measurement support system that is described in the next chapter supports the GQM team in storing, maintaining, analysing and presenting measurement data. The GQM plan serves as the basis for the development of the part of the support system that analyses the collected data.

Deleverable 6.8: *Preliminary GQM plan*

6.2.9   Step 9: Produce measurement plan

A measurement plan describes the following aspects of each direct measurement that was identified in a GQM plan:

- It provides formal definitions of direct measurements.
- It provides textual descriptions of direct measurements.
- It defines all possible outcomes (values) of the direct measurements.
- It identifies a person that collects a particular direct measurement, ie a programmer, engineer, project manager, tester etc.
- It defines the particular moment in time when the person should collect the direct measurement.
- It defines by which medium (tool or form) that person should collect the direct measurement.

Furthermore, a measurement plan defines and describes both manual data collection forms and automated data collection tools. These forms and tools are described in more detail in Chapter 7 on page 65.

Deliverable 6.9: *Preliminary measurement plan.*

6.2.10   Step 10: Produce analysis plan

An analysis plan is a document that simulates data interpretation according to the GQM plan before actual measuring starts. Simulated outcomes of the metrics, graphs and tables are presented in this document that are related to the questions and goals as defined in the GQM plan. The analysis plan already gives an indication to the project team which charts they can expect to receive. Valuable adjustments in this material, but also in the GQM plan, can be expected from delivering such an analysis plan.

The main purpose of an analysis plan is to describe how the relevant measurement information is processed in such a way that it can be easily interpreted by the project team. An important starting point are the baseline hypotheses of the project team members which can be compared with the actual data. The analysis plan contains graphs and tables, which validate the hypotheses and, furthermore, contains descriptions of how the corresponding numbers of the variation factors are going to be used in the results. The illustrations are developed according to the questions in the GQM plans.

The analysis of the data will consist of an analysis of the hypothetical data, the actual data and the data of the variation factors, which possibly could influence the metrics. In this way it can be analysed if the estimated impact of a variation factor is a major, minor, or insignificant factor for the goal under investigation. Furthermore, hypothetical and actual data can be compared, which preferably should be interpreted and explained by the persons who provided the hypotheses and the data for the metrics (top-down refinement and bottom-up interpretation).

Again it is emphasised that the data should be presented in such a way that interpretation by the project team is facilitated. It is important that the interpretations regarding the data, are only guided by the GQM team. By developing an analysis plan, a starting point for the development of feedback material is established, that can be presented to a project team to motivate them with respect to commitment to the measurement programme.

Deliverable 6.10: *Preliminary analysis plan.*

6.2.11 Step 11: Review plans

As the GQM plan, measurement plan and analysis plan represent the formal definitions of a measurement programme and describe all related data collection procedures, they should be reviewed and approved by a project team before data collection can actually begin. The review session should focus on:

- Do project members agree upon the defined goals, questions and metrics?
- Do project members identify any missing or unnecessary definitions?
- Do project members agree with the proposed definition of feedback material?

This means that review sessions focus more on the contents of the GQM plan and analysis plan, than on the measurement plan. The most important part of the measurement plan to be reviewed, is the part that describes the measurement tools and forms, because all project members should understand how to use these tools and forms. Preferably this is done, however, during the instruction sessions before the data collection and the trial data collection period (see Chapter 7). Once the three plans are approved by the project team and the GQM team the next phase can start: *the data collection phase.*

Deliverable(s) 6.11: *Approved GQM plan, measurement plan, and analysis plan.*

6.3   Modelling the software processes

6.3.1   Why model the development process?

The software development process is modelled to provide a more formal definition of the development of software. Such a model is essential to enable a structured development process and can also be used to identify and validate metrics. The development of a reference model is also emphasised in the quality improvement paradigm (Basili et al, 1994b).

A *task* in a software development process is defined as the lowest level of sub-processes in a software development process that creates a certain output. Even though a software development process is never the same, particular tasks are frequently executed, and often in the similar way. The software development process has the following characteristics:

1. The overall software development process consists of several sub-processes that each can be described as a software development process itself (recursion principle).
2. The lowest level of the software development process is a single task.
3. The order in which tasks are executed is not prescribed, and can not be defined beforehand.
4. Single tasks possess input and output products.
5. Single tasks in the software development process have certain properties.
6. Input and output products also have properties.
7. Properties of tasks, and input and output products, relate to certain metrics.

Through modelling the software development process to a level of many single tasks, a set of tasks becomes available with associated input and output products. These input and output products all possess particular measurable properties. Metrics can be associated with the input and output products. After modelling the entire software development process and all (intermediate) products, a comprehensive set of metrics is available for measuring the development of software.

Suitable techniques for modelling a software development process to a level suitable for measurement is the ETXM (Entrance criteria-Tasks-eXit criteria-Metrics) modelling technique (Humphrey, 1989), which is a refinement of the ETVX modelling technique.

6.3.2   The ETVX modelling technique

The ETVX model is used for modelling the phases and sub-phases of a software development process, and identifies four aspects in modelling an activity (Radice et al, 1985):

- A list of entrance criteria (E) that should be met before starting the activity.
- A set of tasks (T) that should be executed to perform the activity.
- A set of verification (V) tasks to ensure quality of the output of the tasks.
- A list of exit (X) criteria that should be met before the activity can be considered complete.

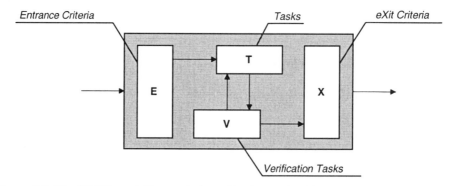

Figure 6-7: The ETVX modelling technique (Radice et al, 1985).

The ETVX modelling technique is illustrated in Figure 6-7. The principle idea is that a type of activity is defined by its entrance criteria, a task description and validation, and the exit criteria. The way the process is exactly executed cannot be defined beforehand, but the criteria that should be met can be defined. Input and output products of the development phase or activity are defined implicitly in the entrance and exit criteria. The sequential order of the tasks is not defined within the model. Changes in the process due to iterations, rework, work ahead, prototyping etc, can also be constructed with the ETVX modelling technique.

The ETVX model can be refined into any required level. A model can be made for the overall software development process, but also for phases, tasks, or sub-activities.

6.3.3   The ETXM modelling technique

At the lowest level of modelling a software development process, the ETXM model (instead of ETVX model) is used, because the verifications in ETVX are implied in the tasks that should be executed and measurements over the model are defined.

The ETXM modelling technique, based on the work of Humphrey, is used to model a single task (T) in an activity. It identifies entrance criteria (E) that have to be met before executing the task and exit (X) criteria that have to be met after execution of the task. Furthermore, ETXM identifies measurements on the entrance criteria, the exit criteria, and the task. This identification of measurements makes the modelling technique suitable for creating models to support the definition process of GQM-based measurement programmes. An example of applying ETXM to software development is shown in Figure 6-9.

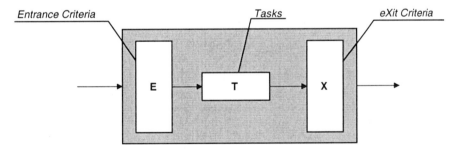

Figure 6-8: The ETXM modelling technique (based on Humphrey, 1989).

Software Program Implementation

Entrance criteria:
- Required detailed designs are available and approved
- Technical specification document is available and approved
- High level design document is available and approved.

Exit criteria:
- Code is available
- Code is written according to coding standards
- Code is written according to the procedures in the coding guidelines

Tasks:
- Coding
- Debugging
- Documenting code

Measurements:
- Size of Code (kB, LOC, number of Pages)
- Schedule time from start to finish (days, hours, start-date, finish-date)
- Resource time for coding (person-hours)
- Resource time for documenting code (person-hours)
- Number of revisions in the code
- Number of compile times
- Fault fixing data (time to locate a fault, time to fix a fault, cause of a fault, ...)
- Review data (person-hours, number of faults found, severity of faults found, amount of rework caused by review, number of people involved in review)
- (Part of) code reused (yes/no)
- (Part of) documentation reused (yes/no)

Figure 6-9: Example of ETXM modelling.

6.4   Questions and assignments

6.4.1   Questions

1. What are the 11 steps of a GQM definition phase?
2. What are the three deliverables of the GQM definition phase?
3. What are the five dimensions of a GQM goal template?
4. GQM measurement goals can be identified by answering 'the seven questions'. Which are the seven questions? Are they always applicable?
5. What are the four sections of an abstraction sheet? How are they related?
6. What are the characteristics of a good GQM question?
7. What is the purpose of hypotheses?
8. What types of inconsistencies can be detected in step 7 of the GQM definitions phase? Also propose specific follow-up actions for each inconsistency type.
9. What can be used as a summary of a GQM plan?
10. What should be described for each metric in a GQM measurement plan?
11. In which case is the development of an analysis plan not necessary?
12. What is the purpose of reviewing a GQM measurement and analysis plan?

6.4.2 Assignments

Select one of the cases below. Take the one that suits your ideas best.

Case A: The objective of a GQM measurement programme is to identify a product's reliability before it is released on the market. In this case a payment terminal which is currently under development. The payment terminal contains 10 sub-systems which are concurrently developed in a period of one year.

Case B: The objective is to identify how you can save $3000 in one year. This will allow you to purchase a personal computer. However, it is not possible to earn additional money. Your income will be exactly the same as last year. You will have to find cost savings. Sources of data are, for example, your agenda, bank notes and salary receipts.

1. Define the GQM goal for this measurement programme according to the GQM goal template.
2. Define a set of GQM questions related to the measurement goal (maximum of 6 questions).
3. Check and improve these questions according to the criteria of good GQM questions given in step 4.
4. Refine your GQM Questions into metrics. Make a distinction between direct and indirect metrics.
5. If possible list your hypotheses regarding your questions (or metrics) and carry out some trial measurements from historical data to test the GQM tree you have established.

7   GQM data collection phase

Checklist GQM data collection phase		
No.	**Checklist item**	✓
7.1	Tools and forms are available	
7.2	Trial measurement period is held	
7.3	Tools and forms are updated	
7.4	Measurement kick-off session is held	
7.5	MSS metrics base is available	
7.6	MSS analysis sheets comply with GQM plan and analysis plan	
7.7	MSS presentation slides are created	
7.8	Data collection forms are completely and correctly filled in	
7.9	Validated measurement data are stored in MSS metrics base	

7.1   Introduction

This chapter describes the basic ideas of the data collection phase of a GQM measurement programme. It starts with data collection procedures and corresponding tools to perform the registration. Subsequently, a section is included at the actual start of collecting data which consists of a kick-off session, a trial period and training. The final section of this chapter contains details on the functionality and development of a measurement support system (MSS), which is required to efficiently run a measurement programme.

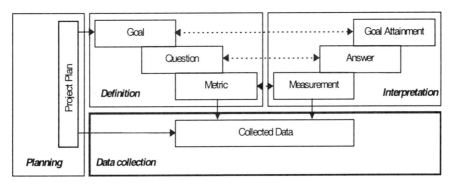

Figure 7-1: The data collection phase of the GQM method.

7.2 Data collection procedures

This section describes all details with respect to the data collection procedures of a GQM measurement programme. This includes the way in which procedures are defined, the way in which data collection forms are applied, and the way in which tools can support the data collection process. Examples of data collection procedures and form are given in the case studies of Chapter 9 to 12.

7.2.1 The need for data collection procedures

Data collection procedures define all the aspects that are necessary to carry out the data collection tasks. They are described in a measurement plan and concern the following aspects with respect to data collection:

- For a certain metric, which person should collect the data?
- When should the data be collected?
- How can the data be collected most efficiently and effectively?
- To whom should the collected data be delivered?

Based on the identification of these aspects for each measurement and the definition of corresponding procedures, tools such as paper forms or database applications are developed to support data collection.

7.2.2 Manual forms of data collection

Manual data collection forms are an easy, flexible and often applied tool in collecting GQM measurement data. This paragraph describes a number of prerequisites for developing such forms, and describes a way in which these forms can be used.

Manual data collection forms usually consist of a single page form on which data can be entered corresponding to the metrics defined in the GQM and measurement plan. To enable verification, a manual data collection form should always contain an entry field which identifies the originator of the measurement data. Furthermore, the form should be organised in such a way that they can be filled in sequentially, it should express all possible values of a measurement explicitly and it should contain a section in which the values are explained. Usually, a form also contains a section in which project team members can write down additional remarks, for instance, with respect to ease of use of a form.

The data collection forms should be filled in each time a particular event occurs that is being considered within the measurement programme. Frequently, preferably each day, the project team members submit their completed manual data collection forms to the GQM team, which enters the data into the measurement database.

Data collection forms are by no means static, but will evolve during the course of a measurement programme. Changes to a form, however, should always be supported by the project team. Changes should, of course, not only be processed on a form, but also in the GQM plan and the measurement plan.

7.2.3   Electronic forms of data collection

An efficient way of collecting data is by using electronic data collection forms which automatically handle the data entry activity. Several possibilities exist for electronic data collection forms of which we will discuss e-mails, web-pages and database applications.

Electronic forms require the same effort for project team members as manual forms, however, their advantage is that the data do not have to be re-typed into the measurement database. When on-line data collection is used, there is also the benefit that the measurement database is always up-to-date.

Electronic forms are an improvement over manual forms, because manual forms should be continuously available, distributed, updated, etc. While electronic forms can be centrally maintained, accessed by all members of the project team and transferred to the database more easily, project teams are often also used to sending e-mails and not to filling out forms.

E-mail data collection is normally easy to implement. An empty e-mail form should be created which can be filled in and be sent back to the GQM team. By having the data available in e-mail format there is the advantage for the GQM team that:

- tracking and checking of data collection are included in their daily process, since they will normally read their e-mail anyway;
- data do not have to be manually entered into the measurement database, because it can be entered using cut-and-paste functionality;
- implementation is not very time consuming, if the e-mail infrastructure is already available.

It is also possible to use spreadsheet forms for data collection, which can again be attached to e-mail. Transporting the data to the measurement database will then require even less effort than copying data from e-mail.

Another possibility is database driven data collection. This has as main benefit that the project team members store their data directly in the database which will be used for interpretation purposes. In this case, the GQM team spends less time in storing data. There is also the opportunity to provide on-line feedback material to the project team, because the data in the database are always up-to-date. However, there might be some problems with using a database tool, because in most cases it means that such a tool needs to be installed. Since this might include installing it on all computers the project team works with, this might be quite time consuming and will be more expensive. The time that project team members spend on data collection should also be limited.

Web-page data collection seems to combine the best of both e-mail and database data collection. On the one hand data collection is performed using an existing infrastructure that can be accessed by all members of the project team with already installed tools. On the other hand, data are stored directly into the database, which creates the benefits mentioned before. We advise you to set-up your data-collection based on this technology, which will also be quite beneficial within a distributed organisation. However, changes to electronic data collection forms are more time consuming than changes to manual data collection forms. Therefore it is advised to start with manual versions, or to use flexible database tools that can be changed easily.

7.2.4   Automated data collection tools

It is also possible to get support during the measurement programme from automated data collection tools, which calculate specific metrics according to some predefined algorithms. Examples are:

- Static analysers that can be used as automated data collection tools.
- Specific software metrics calculators. These tools calculate source-code metrics such as the number of code-lines, number of statements and possible paths in the structure of a programme.
- Other automated data collection tools, for example, CASE-tools, word processors, readability calculators, configuration management systems, workflow tools, or other automated calculators.

7.2.5   Restrictions to data collection tools

Use of automated data collection tools may be efficient, however, be careful and do not limit data collection to these tools. The most valuable information generally comes from people and not from tools. It is quite possible that project team members dislike data collection. They will then emphasise that only automated data collection tools should be used. Remember that goal attainment is the main purpose of each measurement programme, so whenever manual data collection is sufficient to answer a specific question, convince a project team that automatic data collection is unnecessary.

All data collection procedures, tools and forms should be defined and documented, and all people involved in the measurement programme should know how to apply them. Before data collection can actually start, people need to be instructed. This is done during the phase of data collection start-up and training, which is described in the next section.

7.3   Data collection start up and training

In this section the steps that need to be taken during the start-up of data collection and the associated training that needs to be organised, will be described. These steps are illustrated in Figure 7-2.

Before the actual data collection starts, a certain trial period should be held. After the improvements of the trial have been included in the data collection procedures, a kick-off session is organised in which both project-team and GQM-team start data collection. If necessary, additional training is organised on how to use the data collection forms or tools. In parallel with the actual data collection, the GQM team develops a Measurement Support System (MSS), which will become the basis of the interpretation phase. In the following sections our experiences regarding these activities will be described in more detail.

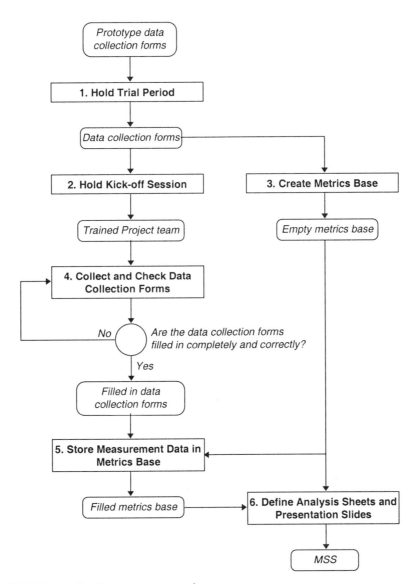

Figure 7-2: Data collection start-up procedures.

7.3.1   Trial period

Preceding the actual data collection period, a trial measurement period should be held during which the defined data collection procedures, tools and forms are tested. During this trial period, data collection is performed by only one or two people for only one or two days. It is advised to include at least one of the senior engineers, because a senior engineer can give more valuable suggestions and because the other engineers will be more confident of the procedure if they know that one of their seniors has approved it. Based on these trial experiences, improvements will normally be necessary on the procedures, tools or forms.

Deliverable(s) 7.1: *Data collection forms.*

7.3.2   Kick-off session

Once all procedures, tools and forms are up-to-date, the GQM team organises a so-called 'kick-off session', during which all people participating in the measurement programme should be present. The main objective of this session is to get an agreement with the project team, that data collection will indeed start. During this session, once again the goals of the measurement programme are explained, and the project team members are instructed with respect to the data collection procedures, tools, and forms. At the end of the session, everybody has to agree that data collection can actually start.

Only if a large number of people participate in a project team, or if the procedures, tools, and forms seem complicated to the project team, may the GQM team decide to organise separate sessions with individual team members or small groups These smaller groups will then focus on training particular skills with respect to data collection.

Even when data collection has started, the GQM team should monitor the project team's use of the procedures, tools and forms. If any unfamiliarity's with, deviations from, or wrong usage of the procedures, tools and forms are observed, the GQM team should provide immediate additional support and training regarding those issues. Small problems tend to escalate during data collection.

Deliverable(s) 7.2: *Trained and motivated project team.*

7.3.3   Data collection activities

During the data collection period, filled-in data collection forms are gathered by, or delivered to, the GQM team on a frequent basis, preferably daily. The GQM team then checks the forms on correctness and consistently. If any mistakes are observed, corrective actions should immediately be taken. Completed and corrected forms are stored by the GQM team in a metrics base, that is created when the measurements start. As shown in Figure 7-2, the definition of a metrics base is the first step in the establishment of a measurement support system. The next section describes in detail how such a measurement support system (MSS) is built.

Deliverable(s) 7.3: *Completely filled in data collection forms.*

7.4   Building a measurement support system (MSS)

This section describes the development of a measurement support system. To enable the interpretation of the gathered data the measurement support system is an essential element in the measurement programme. It is advised to set up a proprietary MSS for every measurement programme[2]. Basis of an MSS will often be generic tools such as spreadsheets, statistical tools, database applications, and presentation tools. These tools

---

[2] One commercial GQM measurement tool is available. It is called 'MetriFlame', and information can be obtained from the internet page: http://www.ele.vtt.fi/docs/soh/metriflame/index.html.

normally provide sufficient flexibility to change measurement forms, charts, or tables. And that they will change during the course of a measurement programme is absolutely certain.

7.4.1 The need for an MSS

The measurement support system (MSS) supports all measurement activities. These activities are:

- Collecting measurement data, which means registration of the data by a project team.
- Storing measurement data, which means entering data into the measurement database.
- Maintaining measurement data, which means, for example, performing corrective changes.
- Processing measurement data, which means for example, combining, sorting, and dividing data to provide the required metrics.
- Presenting measurement data, which means the visualisation of metric data in an interpretable format, such as tables or charts.
- Packaging measurement data, which means the storage of data for expected presentation in the future. This can be during presentations, seminars, or conferences, but also for application in other measurement programmes with a similar measurement goal.

Particularly, flexibility and accessibility are important features of an MSS. Flexibility is required to adapt the MSS to the changing demands of the measurement programme without loosing earlier captured data. Accessibility will be crucial during the review sessions of the measurement data that will be organised later on in the measurement programme. The MSS will enable the project team members to 'play' with the measurement data and receive answers to any type of question regarding the measurement data.

In the next section the functionality of the MSS with respect to supporting these activities is described.

7.4.2 Development of an MSS

An MSS should preferably be built in parallel with the development of the measurement programme. However, as the basis of the MSS is provided by the GQM plan, the MSS will, in most cases, not be built earlier than data collection starts. The MSS is built by the GQM team because the resources spent by the project team on the measurement programme should be limited.

We always use a spreadsheet tool and a presentation tool. The spreadsheet tool is used to store, maintain and process the collected measurement data. The presentation tool is then used to prepare the presentation of the measurement results.

The reason for using a spreadsheet tool is its flexibility. Measurement programmes evolve over time, as measurement goals may be adjusted, added or removed. Spreadsheet tools provide the flexibility necessary to support these kinds of adjustments. The presentation tool should support both preparation of overhead slides and preparation of fully automated presentations using a data projector. Such an on-line data projector is essential to enable 'going into the data' during future feedback sessions.

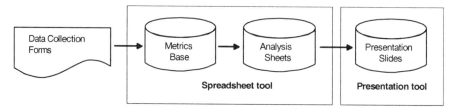

Figure 7-3: Building blocks of a measurement support system (based on Kooiman, 1996).

The MSS consists of three basic parts: a database for storage (metrics base), a data analysis part for abstracting data (analysis sheets), and a data presentation part for expressing information in charts and tables (presentation slides). These building blocks are illustrated in Figure 7-3 and will subsequently be described.

MSS metrics base

The metrics base can be implemented in a spreadsheet tool and contains all raw data as collected from the data collection forms. The data are entered into the metrics base by the GQM team. Checks need to be performed on correctness and completeness of the data. The hypotheses that were defined by the project team and described in the GQM plan, should also be incorporated in the metrics base. The metrics base should be established as soon as possible to support immediate processing of the first data by the GQM team.

MSS analysis sheets

The data in the metrics base are aggregated in analysis sheets. An analysis sheet is built in three layers with different levels of abstraction (Kooiman, 1996).
 The lowest level of abstraction is found in the *raw data layer*, as it only contains raw data copied from the metrics base. In the *processed data layer,* data from the raw data layer is processed to a level of abstraction suitable for creating graphs and tables. For this purpose, processing data includes selecting relevant data, calculating data and sorting data. The results of processing the data are stored in the processed data layer and provide the basis for

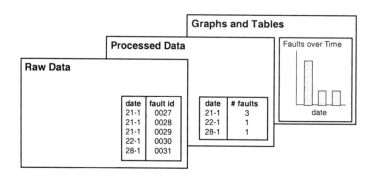

Figure 7-4: Three abstraction levels in an analysis sheet (Kooiman, 1996).

the *graphs and tables layer*. This graphs and tables layer transforms the results from the processed data layer into graphs and tables, suitable for presentation and interpretation.

The analysis sheets are created preceding the first feedback session. The basis for the implementation of analysis sheets is provided by the measurement programme's GQM plan. As a GQM plan defines the relationships between goals, questions and metrics, it also defines the framework for analysing the measurement data. To support data processing towards analysis and interpretation of measurement data, the analysis sheets should be structured according to the relationships defined in the GQM plan.

For each measurement goal, a separate spreadsheet-file is used to create an analysis sheet. It is not recommended to use one single spreadsheet file for processing data with respect to all the measurement goals, as processing time increases significantly if large amounts of data are concerned. By using single files for single goals, processing time will normally be within acceptable limits.

Each analysis sheet consists of the following worksheets:

- A *goal sheet* that describes the goal and the related questions, as stated in the GQM plan.
- A *data sheet*, that contains all data relevant to answering the questions with respect to the goal, including the hypotheses. These data are all copied directly from the metrics base into the analysis sheet.
- Several *question sheets*. For each question relevant to the goal, a separate question sheet is created. On the question sheets, the raw data is processed and transformed into graphs and tables. Therefore, the questions sheets represent the implementation of the processed data layer and the graphs and tables layer.

MSS analysis slides

After the analysis described in the previous section, the graphs and tables from the graphs and tables layer of the analysis sheets need to be copied to a presentation tool. In this file, the graphs and tables are prepared for subsequent presentation.

Consistency between the presentation tool and the graphs and tables in the analysis sheets can be maintained with automated links between the different files. This way, any change in the analysis sheets will automatically result in updating the presentation slides.

Data distribution

Data distribution concerns the distribution of interpreted material to all people involved in the measurement programme. As will be explained in the next chapter, we particularly encourage interactive sessions to discuss measurement results. However, it might be necessary to provide specific measurement information to be used in daily decision making to specific persons, for example, a project manager or a test engineer. On-line feedback of measurement data will then be necessary. Examples of questions that are supported by such a system are:

- Which sub-system should be tested first?
- What is the project progress if expressed in percentage inspected?

All parts of an MSS can be developed on different quality levels. It is advised to build it in an iterative way, allowing a low cost start and continuous improvement.

7.5   Questions and assignments

7.5.1   Questions

1. What are the six steps of the data collection start-up?
2. Which two types of data collection forms exist? What are their differences?
3. What is the purpose of the data collection trial period?
4. What is the purpose of a Measurement Support Systems (MSS)?
5. Which three typical levels exist in an analysis sheet of an MSS?
6. Which measurement activities are supported by an MSS?

7.5.2   Assignments

1. Design a data collection form of the GQM tree defined in your assignment of section 6.4.2.
2. Does your assignment contain possibilities for electronic data collection? If so, indicate how.
3. Make a list of advantages and disadvantages of collecting data electronically in general, and in your particular case.

8   GQM interpretation phase

Checklist GQM interpretation phase		✔
No.	**Checklist item**	
8.1	Feedback material is consistent with GQM plan	
8.2	Presentation slides are correct and up-to-date	
8.3	Presentation handouts are distributed among project team	
8.4	All GQM and project team members are invited for feedback session	
8.5	Accommodation and equipment has been reserved	
8.6	Feedback session reports are distributed among participants	
8.7	Measurement results are reported	

8.1   Introduction

In this chapter the data interpretation phase is described. An essential phase, because in this phase we will try to find answers to the questions underlying the measurement programme. It is still remarkable for us to see how companies sometimes invest large amounts of money into a measurement programme without ever using the collected data.

In the previous chapter, the data collection phase was described. This phase included all activities required to actually gather, store and process the measurement data. In the data interpretation phase we will focus on drawing conclusions regarding the measurement programme. Of course, these conclusions will be specific for every measurement programme, however, the process and conditions that enable a productive interpretation process will be very similar. Therefore, we will focus on these issues in this chapter.

Results of a measurement programme are discussed in so called *feedback sessions*. It is our experience that the success of a measurement programme is primarily determined by the quality of these feedback sessions. Particularly, maintaining a constructive and goal driven attitude by all participants is a delicate element.

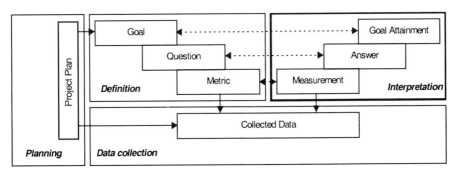

Figure 8-1: The interpretation phase of the GQM method.

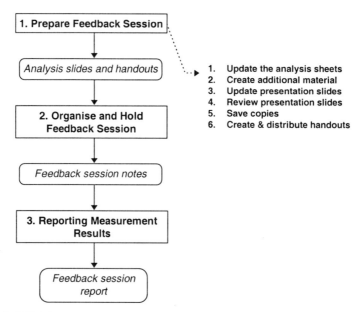

Figure 8-2: GQM interpretation procedures.

In the following sections, our suggestions for organising feedback are described. First, the activities for preparing a feedback session are described. Then, the activities for organising and holding feedback sessions are discussed. The last section in this chapter concerns reporting results of the measurement interpretations. This outline is illustrated in Figure 8-2.

8.2   Preparation of a feedback session

Preparing feedback sessions concerns processing the collected data into presentable and interpretable material. The GQM plan provides the basis for preparing feedback sessions: feedback material should support answering the questions as defined in the GQM plan, and based on these answers, one should be able to conclude whether the defined measurement goals are attained. The analysis should also be supported by the measurement support system (MSS).

The GQM team primarily does the preparation of feedback sessions. However, some involvement of (representatives of) the project team will often be beneficial. A guide to the first set-up of the MSS can be the analysis plan of the definition phase in which a first set-up of the data interpretation is documented.

A six step procedure, which is pretty straightforward, is used for the preparation of feedback sessions:

1.   Update the analysis sheets in the MSS
2.   Create additional feedback material
3.   Update presentation slides
4.   Review presentation slides
5.   Save copies of slides and metrics base
6.   Create and distribute handouts

These steps will subsequently be discussed.

8.2.1   Step 1: Update the analysis sheets of the MSS

Preceding the first feedback session in a measurement programme, usually a large number of feedback material has to be created, requiring a lot of effort from the GQM team. To minimise the effort necessary for preparing following feedback sessions, the analysis sheets in the measurement support system should support automatic updating of the feedback material. One should consider excluding measurements that significantly deviate from all other data. If possible, include the original GQM question in the slide that the particular chart purports to answer.

Deliverable(s) 8.1: *Updated analysis sheets.*

8.2.2   Step 2: Create additional feedback material

Feedback material should, of course, answer the GQM questions of the project, and address relevant issues. As questions and needs may change during a measurement programme, additional feedback material should sometimes be created. Creation of additional feedback material should, of course, never lead to abandoning the original goals and questions.

Deliverable(s) 8.2: *Additional analysis slides.*

8.2.3   Step 3: Update presentation slides

The graphs and tables of the presentation that have a link to the analysis sheet of the MSS can be updated automatically.

Deliverable(s) 8.3: *Updated analysis slides.*

8.2.4   Step 4: Review presentation slides

It is advised to present 15 to 20 slides at most in a single feedback session. Therefore, the selection of slides will often require significant effort. The slides that are selected should of course be free of errors to avoid incorrect interpretations. It is therefore advised to have the presentation reviewed by another GQM team member and a project team member.

Deliverable(s) 8.4: *Approved analysis slides.*

8.2.5   Step 5: Save copies of slides and metrics base

It is advised to store the measurement data and related feedback material for future use (not only those selected for interpretation). To prevent automatic updating, these copies should not contain any link to the analysis sheets.

Deliverable(s) 8.5: *Copy of metrics base and copy of analysis slides.*

8.2.6   Step 6: Create and distribute handouts

Handouts and large tables containing measurement data are hard-copied and distributed several days before a feedback session. This way, the people participating in the session can study the material before the actual session, resulting in a more effective and efficient feedback session.

Deliverable(s) 8.6: *Hard-copies of support material and hard-copies of feedback material.*

8.3   Holding a feedback session

Feedback sessions are meetings of all project team and GQM team members in which the measurement results are discussed. Feedback sessions are held approximately every six to eight weeks. They typically last about 1.5 to 2 hours, with a maximum of 3 hours. Any longer is normally experienced as counter-productive. This time is sufficient to discuss some 15 to 20 slides (containing graphs and tables).

Organising the session includes arranging a meeting room suitable for group sessions and all the required facilities necessary for presenting the feedback material, such as a computer, data projector and/or overhead projector. Furthermore, all people participating in the measurement programme have to be invited to the feedback session, and, if more than five people participate in the session, a moderator has to be appointed within the GQM team in advance, who will present the material and lead the group discussion. As well as the role of the moderator, there is a clear distinction between the role of the GQM team and the role of the project team during the feedback session.

In principal, a project team should run a feedback session alone. They analyse, interpret and draw conclusions regarding the measurements, and translate their conclusions into action points. After all, they are the experts with respect to the object under measurement. The project team should focus on:

- evaluating action points from earlier sessions;
- interpreting measurement data with respect to the questions and goals as defined in the GQM plan;
- translating interpretations into conclusions and action points.

The GQM team should avoid interpreting the data themselves, as they are not the experts. Their role is to challenge a project team, for example, by offering alternative interpretations (Solingen et al, 1997). Furthermore, the GQM team will make notes of the feedback sessions. These notes provide the basis for the meeting report that is created afterwards.

The moderator presents the slides to the project team using automated tools (computer with data projector) or an overhead projector, and leads the group discussions. During this discussion, the moderator should keep the attention focused on discussing the group's performance, and not the performance of individual group members. The moderator should also make sure that a common language is used during the feedback session, so the different attendants of the sessions all understand the issues involved. Feedback sessions generally have the following outline:

1. Opening by a member of the GQM team.
2. Overview of the GQM paradigm: a short presentation on the principles of GQM.
3. Detailed overview of the measurement object: the process or product under measurement and the related measurement goals are described.

4. Presentation of graphs and tables: graphs and tables relevant to answering the questions defined for the goals are presented to the project team for interpretation.
5. Evaluation: not only is it evaluated whether the project team can act upon the measurement results, ie formulation of action point, the measurement programme is itself evaluated for the purpose of improving all measurement related activities.

Deliverable(s) 8.7: *Session notes containing observations, interpretations, conclusions, and action points.*

Feedback sessions are a delicate phase in a measurement programme. Mutual trust among all participants is, for example, an essential element of a feedback session. Through focusing on identified goals, questions and metrics, the discussion will start on the basis of facts. It is the role of the moderator, and if necessary of the whole GQM team, to make sure that the discussion remains focused on facts and improvement actions. Make sure that measurement analysis does not become focused on individual performances. For more tips on data analysis we refer you to (Goodman, 1993).

8.4   Reporting interpretations of measurement results

After the feedback session, the GQM team writes a meeting report containing all relevant observations, interpretations, conclusions and action points that were formulated during the session. This report should, of course, be distributed to the project team. Be careful with submitting all measurement details or feedback session reports to higher management, because they often misinterpret data. It is advised to stay with the rule that the project team 'owns' the measurement data and therefore decides on distribution of both data and reports to management. When the GQM team wants to inform higher management, the GQM team only uses particular, often aggregated, results and asks permission to do so.

In order to reuse measurement results and experiences in future measurement programmes, the results of a measurement programme should be documented in such a way that they are easily accessible and understandable. It is difficult to perform effective packaging, because future needs for measurement information are usually not known in advance. However, some suggestions can be made on how organisations can deal with packaging measurement results.

Furthermore, the most important results of the measurement programmes should preferably be disseminated to the entire organisation to create awareness. This can be achieved by presenting the results of the measurement programmes on bulletin boards or posters in the organisation. Another approach is to make the measurement results available in an electronic way, such as an intranet.

Deliverable(s) 8.8: *Feedback session report and measurement programme packages.*

8.5   Cost and benefits analysis of a measurement programme

Goal attainment is, of course, an essential element of the success of a measurement programme, however, an analysis of costs and benefits should also be included in the final report of a measurement programme. In such a cost/benefit analysis, it should be evaluated whether the estimated benefits exceed overall costs.

Typical costs of a measurement programme are:

- time spent to prepare a measurement programme by GQM team (salary and overhead);
- time spent in meetings by project team;
- time spent to fill in data forms by project team;
- time spent to develop MSS;
- purchase of additional hardware and software to support measurement programme;
- time spent to process measurement data and prepare feedback sessions by GQM team.

Typical benefits are:

- additional sales because of improved quality;
- avoidance of a decrease in sales because of improved quality;
- time savings of software development effort because of a better understanding of development process;
- cost savings through better resource management;
- cost avoidance through better resource management.

A cost/benefit analysis is often experienced as difficult to perform, however, the contrary is true. The objective of a cost/benefit analysis is not to calculate the exact 'return on investment' of a measurement programme, but to identify whether the project was worthwhile from an economical perspective. Many people will claim that you can not value quality against cost. We strongly oppose this view. In most organisations, for example, the marketing department knows exactly how sensitive customers are to quality and what increases in turnover may be expected given additional ore improved product features.

Not including a cost/benefit analysis means that management and project team members will make their own implicit cost/benefit analyses. These analyses will often be based on less detailed information and your measurement programme might be abandoned because people think it is no longer worthwhile. Making a cost/benefit analysis is a responsibility of the GQM team.

Deliverable(s) 8.9: Cost/benefit analysis report.

8.6   Questions and assignments

8.6.1   Questions

1. Which six steps are discerned to prepare a feedback session?
2. Why is the interpretation phase the most important phase of a measurement programme?
3. What are the objectives of a feedback session?
4. What is a typical agenda of a feedback session?
5. Which typical cost and benefits should be considered for the cost/benefit analysis of a measurement programme?

8.6.2   Assignments

Feedback sessions are considered to be the most crucial part of a measurement programme. They are also the most expensive part (see Chapter 4). Try to identify alternatives for a feedback session that have the same effect, yet require less effort. An example of an alternative would be to place posters in your organisation. Do so by:

1. Identifying the effects that will occur during a feedback session in which measurement results are openly discussed.
2. Identifying alternative ways to communicate feedback material.
3. Plot effects and ways to communicate in a two-by-two matrix and evaluate the effects of particular ways to communicate.

PART 3

Cases

9 Case A: reliability measurement

9.1 Description of project A

This chapter describes a project during which product reliability was measured. The impact of reuse on product reliability was also taken into account. This project, referred to as 'project A', was the first GQM based measurement programme for the particular organisation.

Project A aimed at developing both software and hardware for a real-time low-end cashing system. It's final product was designed for service station personnel and their managers giving access to site control and management information. This project was a second (incremental) release of the system and a considerable part of the software was reused from an earlier release as well as from other projects. At the end of the project, product A contained over 70,000 source lines of C-code. The project team consisted of a project leader, two hardware engineers and two software engineers. This project had a duration of 2 years.

The results presented in this chapter are based on the whole measurement programme. Therefore, results consist of measurement data, conclusions drawn by the project team during feedback sessions, and actions taken which were based on the measurements. In this chapter the four GQM phases of project A will subsequently be described, being, planning, definition, data collection, and interpretation.

This chapter also includes documentation of the particular measurement programme, such as GQM plan, data collection forms and feedback charts. This documentation can be reapplied to other measurement programmes with a similar goal.

9.2 Planning

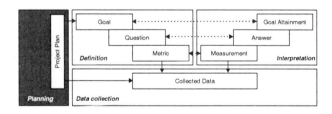

This particular measurement programme started with the establishment of a GQM team. Head of the team was the Quality Assurance manager, assisted by a quality engineer. Their objective was to start project measurement in a structured way, to support projects with information to manage product quality. Goal-oriented measurement had to be used, because earlier measurement experiences had failed, probably caused by a lack of clear goals.

Based on the current status of product quality in the organisation, it was decided to focus on reliability measurement. This was done for several reasons:

- 'Reliability' was the most important quality requirement for that system.
- Practical relevance of reliability measurement was clear to the project team.
- Comparison of results with other projects was possible because of the international setting of this measurement programme.
- This project was also a try-out of GQM measurement. The GQM team also had to learn about such programmes, therefore the improvement area selected was not the most ambitious one. Success of this initial programme was therefore more likely to be achieved, which supports in spreading measurement further through the company.

This particular measurement programme was introduced by applying the QIP paradigm, because the GQM method presented in part II of this book did not yet exist at that time. A project plan was established that consisted of the six steps of QIP, starting with 'characterisation' up to 'packaging'. Both GQM team and project team received training on GQM concepts. Corporate management was frequently informed and formulated the initial objective to start with measurement in a goal-oriented way.

Both the organisation and the project were characterised by filling out a characterisation questionnaire. This questionnaire included both quantitative and qualitative questions. The results of the characterisation were used to create a project plan for this measurement programme. The characterisation questionnaire was also applied during the selection of improvement areas and measurement goals.

9.3   Definition

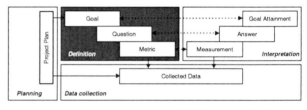

Based on the Project plan, the measurement programme was officially started. During several meetings with the Project manager a selection was made from the possible measurement goals based on the project objectives and the results of the characterisation. The definition process of the reliability measurements is presented in this section. Two measurement goals were defined for this programme.

Reliability:

Analyse the:	delivered product and development process
for the purpose of:	understanding
with respect to:	reliability and its causes
from the viewpoint of:	the project team
in the following context:	project A

Reuse:

Analyse the:	delivered product
for the purpose of:	understanding
with respect to:	effectiveness of reuse
from the viewpoint of:	the project team
in the following context:	project A

Achieving those measurement goals would yield a better understanding of reliability and reuse. All members of the project team were consulted for definition of these goals and they were highly interested in reaching them. Management was involved as well and illustrated the relation of the measurement goals to the business goals.

The most important activity of the definition phase was the refinement of the selected goals into questions and metrics. This refinement was divided into two parts. First, a knowledge acquisition part, aimed at understanding the current knowledge within the project team and representing this knowledge in quantitative or qualitative models. Second, a measurement planning part, which involved documenting the Goal/Question/Metric refinement and corresponding measurement procedures.

Knowledge was acquired through structured interviews as was advised in Chapter 5. The main purpose of these interviews was to make knowledge of the project members explicit. During the definition phase of this measurement programme interviews were held with all project team members. A report was written of every interview and returned to the interviewee for review. This interview report already contained a first abstraction sheet. As the project team was familiar with the abstraction sheet concept, this made it easier for them to review the interview report.

The interviews were also intended to motivate project team members for the measurement programme. The team members gave valuable input and realised that the data to be collected was related to issues raised by themselves. The result of the definition phase was a well-defined measurement programme, documented in the following three deliverables:

- The GQM plan which defined in a top-down way what would be measured. It defined the goals and the refinement into questions and metrics. The GQM plan of this measurement programme is attached in Section 9.6.
- The measurement plan which described how the measurements should be done. It described metrics and procedures and media to report, collect and validate the data.
- The analysis plan that defined how to close the feedback-loop by providing verified and validated measurement results to the project team on a proper abstraction level. Being a basic guideline to support feedback of measurement information to the project team.

The GQM team, based on input from the project team, wrote all three plans. The plans were reviewed by members of the project team, mostly by the project manager or a senior engineer. The GQM plan was reviewed thoroughly to obtain a standard terminology and to eliminate obscurities and ambiguities in the plan. We used several short follow-up interviews, and the entire team pursued an extensive review. It was essential to communicate that the GQM plan was going to be *the* basis for analysis and interpretation: insufficiencies here would lead to problems with drawing conclusions from the data.

9.4   Data collection

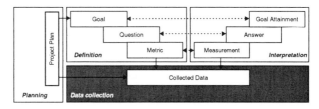

Data collection started with a 'kick-off session' in which the data collection forms were explained. The metrics defined in the measurement plan were largely covered by an existing defect tracking tool that the project team already used. A manual paper form was designed to record several additional metrics on fault handling.

The measurement data was collected according to the procedures defined in the measurement plan. Before measurement data could be stored in the measurement support system, it has to be thoroughly verified and validated (see Section 7.4 on page 70 for details of an MSS). In this measurement programme the GQM team performed the following checks (in cooperation with the project team):

- completeness of the data;
- timeliness of the data;
- accuracy of the data;
- whether the data is within range;
- correctness of classifications.

No procedures were defined for the further handling of the data by the GQM team. In practice, this handling was supported by the MSS. This tool was used by the GQM team for saving, maintaining and processing data of measurement programmes. The MSS was implemented in a spreadsheet tool, because of its flexibility. Experience had shown that measurement programmes evolve over time and analyses were not static. A flexible MSS appeared to be an important requirement, which caused spreadsheets to be highly applicable.

For this measurement programme a customised MSS was implemented. The implementation is divided over several files. Consistency between the files is accomplished by using automatic links between the different files. Two files were created for this measurement programme: a metrics base and analysis base (Figure 9-1). The analysis sheets that are stored in the analysis base were printed and photocopied onto transparencies for presentation on an overhead projector.

Data collected by the project team was entered into a database, the 'metrics base', by the GQM team. While entering the data into the metrics base a manual check on correctness and completeness was performed. Hypotheses were also included in the metrics base (stated in the GQM plan). The metrics base was created before actual measurement started. This way, the gathered data could be stored in the metrics base as soon as measuring started. The analysis sheets of the data were implemented in a separate analysis base. The analysis sheets were created preceding the first feedback session.

Two analysis databases were created in association with the two identified measurement goals. The analysis sheets were linked to the metrics base to assure consistency between the files (changes in the metrics base are automatically updated in the analysis sheets). One analysis sheet consisted of different worksheets for the questions that relate to the goal of

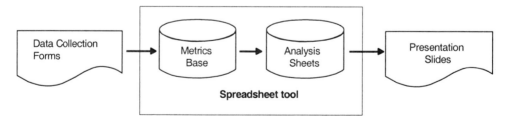

Figure 9-1: Processing data collection into presentation slides via the metrics base and analysis sheets.

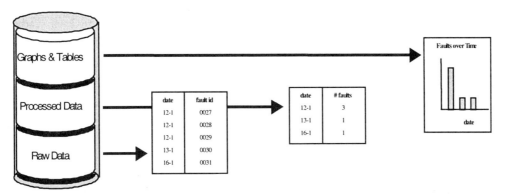

Figure 9-2:Three layers within an analysis sheet.

the analysis sheet (question worksheets). Within an analysis sheet, three different levels of abstraction for the data were distinguished. These levels of abstraction were called layers. Each analysis sheet was built up from three layers (Figure 9-2):

- raw data layer;
- processed data layer;
- graphs & tables layer.

The raw data layer contained links to the metrics base and, therefore, like the metrics base itself, contained raw data only. To be able to create graphs and tables it was often necessary to process the data in one way or another to get a suitable result. Processing data included, for instance, selecting particular data, calculating data and sorting data. The results of processing the raw data was kept in the processed data layer. Finally, the last layer contained the data as they were presented. These graphs & tables data layer also contained the questions from the GQM plan, which the project team members intended to answer.

Through connecting the processed data layer with the graphs & tables layer, this layer was updated automatically. Processing raw data into graphs and tables was carried out with the GQM plan as a guideline: the graphs and tables should support answering the GQM questions. This was already partially described in the analysis plan, however, additional analysis sheets appeared to be necessary during the course of the measurement programme.

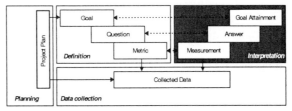

9.5   Interpretation

In this section the measurement results of project A are presented. During project A's measurement programme more than 4000 data points were collected. In total, eleven feedback sessions were held. The final feedback session for this measurement programme took place two years after starting the measurement programme. In the final meeting few new results were presented. However, the original measurement goals were officially attained by the project team during this final feedback session.

The two goals of the measurement activities were to *understand* product and process reliability, and to *understand* the effects of reuse. The results of the measurements were not only presentations of empirical data regarding these subjects, but also conclusions drawn or actions taken by project team members based on measurement information.

A selection of conclusions drawn and action taken by the project members based on the measurement results is presented here:

- Modules with high user interaction were expected to produce much more failures whenever a single fault was detected and were, therefore, reviewed quite intensively.
- Novice-user-tests appeared to be very effective and should be held more often. Novice-user-tests were also immediately introduced in another project.
- Complexity of a module appeared to be a cause of faults. This conclusion was based on the correlation between fault density of modules and cyclomatic complexity (McCabe's complexity metric). The measurement programme also showed a relation between fault density of modules and length of a module.
- Engineers found 55% of all failures. This percentage was expected to decrease when more field releases were done and engineers stopped testing.
- The test group found 25% of all failures and half of all minor failures. The project team concluded that the test group was stricter while testing and that this promoted continuing independent testing. Engineers appeared not to test on minor bugs.
- The project team identified that most fatal failures detected during testing were not likely to be found in a structured review. This is in contrast with literature on this subject that claims that approximately 60% of all faults can be found during reviews (Humphrey, 1989). Identifying the effectiveness of reviews was however NOT a measurement goal, so one should be really careful in drawing such conclusions. The opinion might be caused by an unclear view on that topic.
- Paper proposals for enhancement request appeared to cause most requirement faults, so this was not the right communication medium. No empirical results of the measurements reflected that this was based on the communication medium. Therefore, the possibility remained that the enhancement request had simply not been correctly written down. The project team already had the opinion that enhancement requests were often not clear, and repeated their statement supported by the measurements.
- Availability of the right test equipment increased detection of faults before delivery. This conclusion was based on an identification by the project team that most failures found after release were caused by a different configuration than available during test. Whether it was possible to create a test installation that covered all possible field configurations needed further investigation.

At the end of project A, conclusions towards the goal were drawn. The project team reached understanding on the reliability of the product, but since this understanding was required all the time, measurement was continued. However, the goal could be changed from 'understanding reliability' to 'control reliability'. The contribution of GQM in this measurement result was significant, because the focused measurements provided specific information that could easily be translated into practical improvements.

GQM was introduced by strict application of the QIP, which caused some minor problems because particularities of the development process of project A were not taken into account during the definition phase. If software development models would have been used as a reference (as illustrated in Figure 3-4), the measurement programme could have been even more beneficial. Now the testing phase was initially not taken into account and the impact of testing on the reliability goal was not considered. Afterwards it was concluded that, therefore, the causes of fault detection could not be analysed fully.

The remainder of this chapter presents feedback material which supported answering questions, and goal attainment.

9.5.1   Product overview

In presenting the measurement results, the first two slides served an introductory purpose. This first slide in the feedback session offered a detailed overview of the modules in which faults were detected (Figure 9-3). A slide like this gives an overview of the entire product on unit level: the most important attributes for the stated goals were presented in one table. It answers several questions from the GQM plan like:

- Q.1: What is the composition of the product?
- Q.3: What is the complexity of the delivered software
- Q.9: What is the distribution of faults after delivery
- Q.13: What percentage of the delivered code was covered by peer reviews?
- Q.21: What is the distribution of modules among reuse modification classes?

It was found to be an important aid in tracking measurement data back to their cause: trends and distributions in graphs and tables can often be explained by considering other metrics. The overview acts as a reference in this consideration.

Module	# Faults	Fault ranking	Modification faults	Original faults	Reuse	Review	Size (KSLOC)	Complexity
Module 1	17	1	10	7	More than 20%	yes	4.56	624
Module 2	13	2	8	5	More than 20%	yes	3.10	560
Module 3	12	3	4	8	More than 20%	yes	4.10	624
Module 4	8	4		8	No reuse	no	2.10	207
Module 5	8	4		8	No reuse	no	0.68	210
Module 6	7	6		7	No reuse	yes	2.10	245
Module 7	6	7		6	No reuse	yes	0.50	70
Module 8	5	8	3	2	More than 20%	yes	4.68	420
Module 9	4	9		4	No reuse	yes	0.46	55
Module 10	4	9		4	No reuse	yes	0.45	8
Module 11	4	9		4	Less than 20%	no	0.39	39
Module 12	3	12	1	2	Less than 20%	yes	1.80	303
Module 13	3	12		3	No reuse	no	2.24	309
Module 14	3	12		3	No reuse	no	1.20	150
Module 15	3	12		3	No reuse	yes	1.20	132

Figure 9-3: First feedback slide with an overview on all data.

Total product size = 60.9 KSLOC
System fault density = 1.9 faults/ksloc

Data collection was carried out during 22 months

Trouble reports	Number	Real	Hypothesis
Failures	133	81%	50%
Change requests	31	19%	50%
Total	164	100%	100%

Number of detected failures = 133

Number of repaired faults = 118

Total effort for locating faults = 183 hours
Total effort for fixing faults = 138.4 hours
Effort per fault = 2.7 hours

Figure 9-4: Second slide in feedback session: global overview.

9.5.2   Overview on data collection

The next step in presenting the measurement data, was to give an overall impression of the product under measurement. The slide in Figure 9-4 presented a global overview of the product, including total product size, system fault density and number of analysed trouble reports. Often, project members have so much inside knowledge of the project that it becomes difficult for them to maintain a general overview of the product. A slide like this offered an overview.

9.5.3   Q.6: What is the distribution of failures after delivery?

Figure 9-5 illustrates the amount of failures reported by project A. The number of failure reports on the product approached zero. This chart did not only reflect reliability of the product, but also detection events that were executed during the development, for example in April of the first year a Novice User Test had been executed and therefore the number of failure reports was much higher. Another increase was visible in November, where the first field release was done. During the integration phase several failures were detected. The relatively low number of failures during July and August of year 1 reflect the summer holidays during which no detection activities were executed. Please note that this emphasised the need to let the project team interpret measurement data, because an outsider might have concluded that the product was becoming reliable.

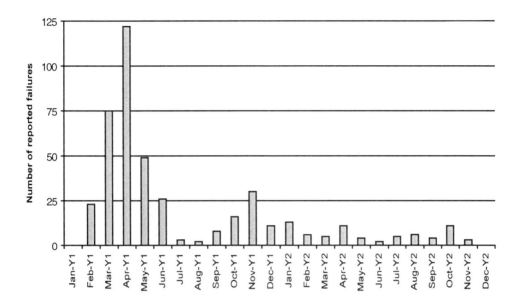

Figure 9-5: Number of failure reports on product under development.

Drawing conclusions on the current reliability of the product only based on Figure 9-5 was not possible, because no information was included on the amount of effort spent on finding failures. Because this major aspect of reliability was not identified during the definition process of the GQM plan, conclusions regarding this issue could not be drawn. This again illustrated the need for process models as references during the definition phase. The version of the GQM approach which was applied for this project did not include process models as described in Section 6.3. Otherwise, the absence of measurements on testing were certainly detected, because testing (detection) is one of the major techniques to detect failures.

9.5.4   Q.7: What is the distribution of failures over severity classes?

Severity of a failure was considered an important aspect of reliability. For example, after release of a system to the field it is not acceptable to find Fatal failures, while some minor failures were acceptable (for project A). Therefore, the GQM plan contained a 'severity' metric which defined three classes for severity of a failure:

- Fatal failures. For example, system failed, system executed wrong transactions, system lost transactions.
- Major failures. For example, system refused legitimate transactions, or system produced redundant outputs with small impact on performance.
- Minor failures. For example, aesthetic problems such as misspelling or output formatting problems.

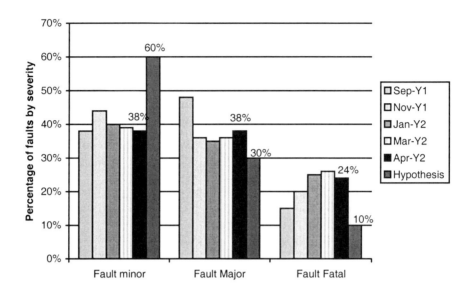

Figure 9-6: Number of faults per severity category.

Figure 9-6 illustrates the distribution of faults found over time per severity category. The hypotheses as the project team stated them in February year 1, are also presented in this chart.

The percentage of fatal failures was stabilising at around 25% while the expected number of fatal failures was 10%. The project team had now learned how failures were distributed by severity, and this knowledge could be used in future projects. These numbers could also be used in future projects to plan failure repair.

9.5.5 Q.9: What is the distribution of faults after delivery?

Historic overviews were popular in feedback sessions. A successful presentation of historic data was found at module level: the slide in Figure 9-7 presents the top 8 of fault-containing modules, and the accumulated number of faults detected over time. In this slide, both a graph and a table were presented. Experience showed that different people have different preferences when analysing data: some people preferred graphs, others preferred tables. Therefore, in most cases, both graphs and tables should be presented together. Although this might not always be possible.

9.5.6 Q.22: What was the relation between module reuse and reliability?

One of the measurement goals was to understand the effects of reusing software in project A. Please note that productivity increase was *not* taken into account during this measurement programme, because the project team decided to reuse software for reliability reasons only, not for productivity reasons. The software that was developed in this project contained a large amount of reuse. Figure 9-8, shows that the fault density (number of faults

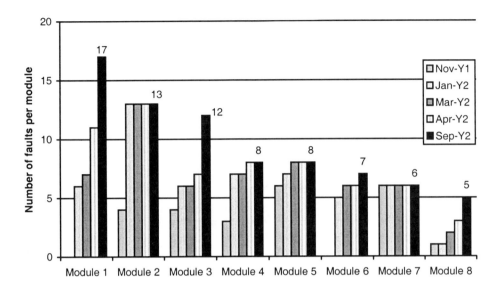

Figure 9-7: Project A top 8 fault containing modules.

per thousand source lines of code) was linearly decreasing as the amount of reuse increases. Also the amount of newly introduced faults decreased when the amount of reuse increases. When more than 20% of the code was reused this resulted in five time fewer new faults compared to complete new development. In all modules that were completely reused in the product, no faults were identified. The project team learned that it was beneficial to reuse (parts of) modules during development.

When reusing modules it was also possible to reuse faults that were already present in the code, so reuse could also be a cause for faults (whether this is negative was not clear, because it was also beneficial to identify faults in code that was already installed in the field). The project team concluded that reuse was not only a development approach, it was also a fault detection method! The relation between fault density and amount of reuse was almost linear in our measurement programme. However, there was also a relation between functionality and reuse, but this will be described in the next section.

The project team defined action to increase the amount of reuse in new development, and when a module was developed from scratch it was developed in such a way that it was more easily reusable. A concrete example that showed that the project team actually learnt from the measurements was that the project manager recently provided another department with certain modules they could reuse during their own new development. In the opinion of the project manager he would not have done that without the knowledge obtained in the measurement programme.

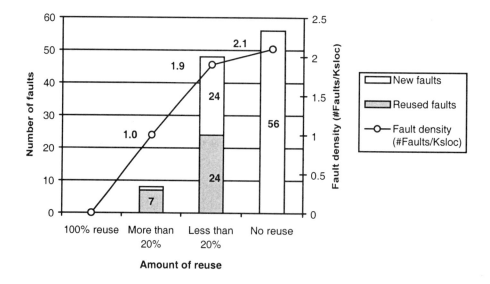

Figure 9-8: Fault densities of modules categorised by the amount of reuse.

Conclusions on reuse drawn by the project team:

- Reuse was a useably method for fault prevention, and detection.
- Most of the faults in partially reused modules were detected before release, which was caused by a lower confidence of engineers in partially reused modules than in personally developed modules.
- Reuse resulted in lower fault density.

These empirical results can be used to convince managers and engineers of the effectiveness of reuse, and can also be used to promote the reusability of code in the organisation. A new measurement programme could consider the productivity increase that is caused by reuse. The decrease of fault density caused by reuse was already identified in this measurement programme.

9.5.7 Q.12: What is the relation between module complexity and reliability?

Figure 9-9 is a complex chart. It shows at the x-axis the functionality categories of the product (as they are defined by the project team). The left vertical axis shows the size of the according software in SLOC (*Source* Lines Of Code). The amount of code is in the bars and also visualised by amount of change (reflecting in reverse the amount of reuse). For example the largest amount of 100% reused code (Unchanged) is in the console.

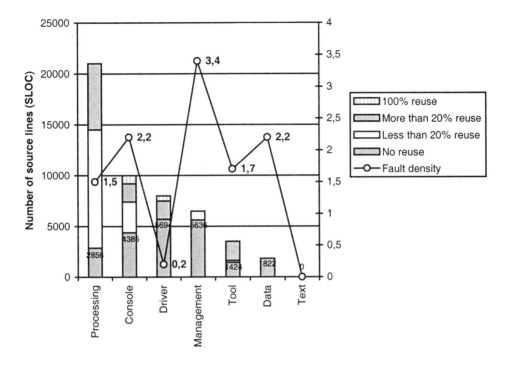

Figure 9-9: Software size per functionality and according fault density.

The right vertical axis reflects the fault density (in number of faults per KSLOC). The fault density appears to be related to the amount of new developed code (no reuse), looking at the processing, console and management functionality's. Those categories reflect the three major parts of the product. The drivers are different from this trend, because drivers are very well documented and therefore contain far fewer faults than average. The white numbers in the bars are the exact number of KSLOC for the no-reused modules.

Often, results are presented that seem to have important implications. It is important not to draw conclusions too easily. Such a premature conclusion may be drawn when considering Figure 9-10: this slide presents a number of metrics grouped by functionality. The code of the management functionality seems to be very prone to errors when considering the fault density in the last column. A closer look reveals the true cause of its high fault density: the relatively small size of the functionality causes the fault density to grow rapidly with every fault found. Also, the management functionality has a high user interaction, which causes a failure to be much more visible, and to be reported sooner. Closely analysing data and underlying data appears to be important in gaining valid interpretations. And again: this interpretation can only be done fully by the members of the project team.

Functionality	# Faults	% Faults	Size (KSLOC)	% Size	Fault Density (Faults/KSLOC)
Processing	47	43%	26.7	44%	1.8
Management	24	22%	7	11%	3.4
Console	18	16%	10.1	17%	1.8
Tool	8	7%	3.8	6%	2.1
Driver	8	7%	11.3	19%	0.7
Data	5	5%	1.9	3%	2.6
Text	0	0%	0	0%	0.0
TOTAL	110	100%	60.8	100%	
Average	16		8.7		1.8

Figure 9-10: Faults found classified according to functionality.

9.5.8   Q.8: What is the distribution of failures over detection mechanism?

Figure 9-11 reflects the percentage of failures detected by each detection mechanism. The hypotheses as they were put to the project team in February of the first year are also presented in this chart, creating the possibility for the project team to learn from fault detection.

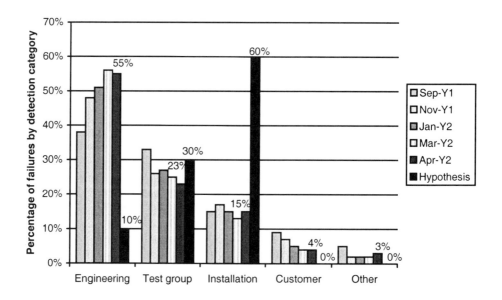

Figure 9-11: Detection efficiency of detection mechanisms (percentage of failures per category).

As visible in Figure 9-11 the amount of failures found by the installation department is still much lower than expected. The project team expects this number to increase when more systems are being installed. Most of the expected failures will be change requests. Conclusions and observations from the project team:

- Engineers find 55% of all failures.
- Test group finds 25% of all failures, but 45% of all minor failures (test group is more strict while testing).
- External testing is much more efficient than testing by engineers.
- Most fatal errors that were detected during testing were not likely to be detected in a review.

9.5.9   Types of severity by detection mechanism

Figure 9-12 reflects the percentage of types of severity of failures. For each detection mechanism it was presented how many of their detected failures were fatal, major or minor failures. As visualised, the test group found most minor failures. This was very positive since it reflected that the test group were more critical testers. Customer and other appeared to find only major failures and fatal failures, but as was already visualised in Figure 9-11 the amount of failures found was low. Note that customers tend to report only fatal and majors failures.

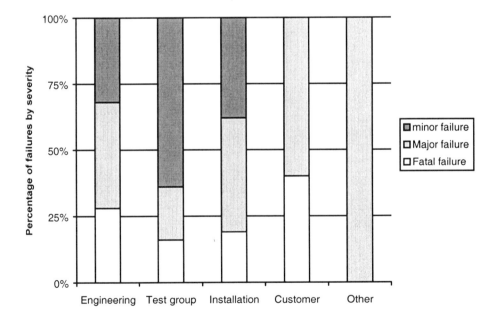

Figure 9-12: Percentage of failure severity found by detection mechanism.

9.5.10   Q.17: What is the distribution of failure handling effort?

Figure 9-13 shows the average effort for failure repair per development phase of introduction of the fault. It appeared that faults that were introduced in the requirement phase costed three times the average time to repair, while faults introduced during detailed design and implementation required 0.6 of average time to repair. No faults were introduced during evaluation and release. Better formulation of requirements and early customer involvement was concluded to be valuable with to respect to repair costs.

As Figure 9-13 shows, the effort needed to repair requirement faults is more than nine hours per fault. This number was used to promote the introduction of inspections during the requirements phase, since only two faults needed to be detected in an inspection of four hours with four people, in order to be beneficial. Additional research on the severity of faults during development phases, and effectiveness of inspections was also necessary, however, results in literature already identified high potential for increasing the efficiency of the development process by introduction of inspections.

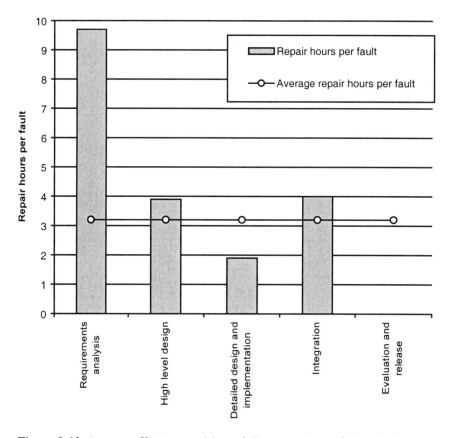

Figure 9-13: Average effort on repairing a failure, per phase of introduction.

Conclusions drawn and action taken by the project team with respect to repair effort:

- Requirement faults were expensive. This was caused by the fact that several requirements were not available in the original requirements document, and therefore had to be included later, when problems occurred.
- Early detection of requirement faults would pay itself back (requirements should be intensively reviewed). This was already concluded by the project team, identifying their readiness for detection methods on, for example, requirements and specification documents.
- Customers should be involved earlier during development. This conclusion of the project team was based on the fact that the marketing department was currently formulating the requirements. Early involvement of customers might cause other problems like unrealistic or non-profitable requirements. Further research should identify which approach could best solve these problems. A possible approach might be developing a prototype in order to identify missing, or incorrect requirements.
- The marketing department should be involved more frequently during development. This conclusion was related to the previous one. A project team was not always able to identify the requirements of customers.
- Finding requirement and high level design faults took less time than repairing them afterwards. This was a clear observation on the measurements, caused by the fact that missing functionality, or wrong interpreted specifications were directly clear as soon as the failure was reported, while implementation errors really needed to be recovered.
- Total effort spent on repairing requirement faults was equal to total effort spent on repairing implementation faults, however, there were six times more implementation faults.

Based on these numbers the project team decided to take several actions. They concluded that requirement faults took too much time, which caused planning delays. Therefore, the decision was made that all requirement faults would be considered to be 'change requests', which needed to be included in the planning of a next release. A major benefit from this was also that marketing was then responsible for the planning, so only those requirement faults would be repaired that had commercial impact.

9.5.11 Correlation of complexity versus size

When metrics showed a clear relation, the analysis could be limited to one of both metrics. In the case of project A, many metrics were related to size and cyclomatic complexity (see for example Figure 9-14). By showing that there was a relation between the two, analysis could be limited relative to either size or complexity.

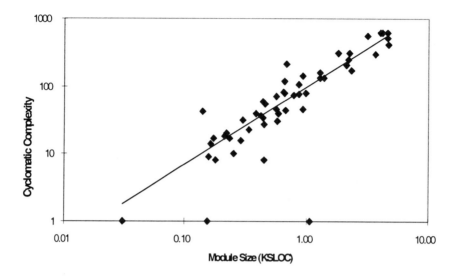

Figure 9-14: Relation between module size and cyclomatic complexity in project A: opportunity to limit the analysis.

9.6   Documentation of project A

This section contains a number of essential documents of the project A measurement programme. Examples are the GQM plan and a feedback session report. These documents are given as an example. Please note that project A was the first measurement programme undertaken. Therefore, the documentation also includes mistakes, that resulted in some recommendations included in part II of this book.

The feedback session report presented in this section presents the results of the final feedback session of the project A measurement programme.

9.6.1   Project A GQM plan

Introduction

Background

The *M*easurement *I*nformation *SYS*tem (MISYS) is a partly automated system, that contains a metric base, a database, historical base and procedures for data processing. The metrics, the data and the procedures for reporting, collecting and verifying data were defined according to the GQM paradigm. This section describes the GQM plans and the metric plan for the pilot project for measurement, project A.

Selected application project

To set up a GQM plan, the members of the project team of project A were interviewed as well as the software development leader of a project which was going to reuse some of the software developed by project A. Note that the hardware development leader and the SW development leader also worked as engineers.

Measurement goals

It was defined that two GQM goals would be incorporated: one for analysing the reliability of products and one for analysing the development processes with respect to reuse.

Goal 'reliability':
Analyse the	delivered product and development process
for the purpose of	better understanding
with respect to	reliability and its causes
from the viewpoint(s) of	the software development team (SW project leader and software engineer)
in the following context:	project A

Goal 'reuse':
Analyse the	delivered product
for the purpose of	understanding
with respect to	effectiveness of reuse
from the viewpoint(s) of	the software development team (SW project leader of a project developing for reuse and SW engineer of another project reusing software)
in the following context:	project A

Goal 'reliability'

GQM abstraction sheets

With respect to the 'reliability' goal, two interviews were made, one with the software development leader of project A and one with the software engineer of the project.

First, the summarised information was presented in a GQM plan abstraction sheet, which was derived from the abstraction sheets, which represented the two interviews. In the interviews the implicit knowledge of engineers and managers was made explicit. Therefore, questions were asked regarding their definitions of the quality focus, and the classifications within those definitions. Then questions about quantification of the expectations regarding those definitions were asked, the baseline hypothesis. Followed by questions regarding factors concerning the process and the product itself, that could influence the expected numbers from the baseline hypotheses, the variation factors. And the way those factors could impact the baseline hypotheses. The abstraction sheet is given in Figure 9-15.

Object: product and process	Purpose: better understan-ding	Quality focus reliability and its causes	Viewpoint: SW development team	Environment Project A	External GQM plan Represen-tation

Quality Focus
# of Failures
- Overall
- By Severity (Minor, Major, Fatal, Other)
- By Detection (Engineer, Test Group...)
# of Faults
- Overall
- By Life-Cycle Phase
- By Modules
Cost: Effort in Hours
- Overall
- Cost By Module
- Cost By Activity
- Locating vs. Fixing

Variation Factors
Process Conformance:
- Are the reviews done as prescribed in the process model:
Code Reviews - 100%,
Code Inspection <100%
- Deadlines
Domain Conformance:
- Experience Level Engineers
Attributes:
- Adherence to Coding Standards
- Complexity
- Consistency of Documents

Baseline Hypothesis
Distribution of Failures by Severity:

Minor:	30%
Major:	15%
Fatal:	5%
Change Request:	50%

By Detection (Pre, After release, Customer)

Engineer	80%	10%	10%
Test Group	20%	30%	nap
Installation	nap	60%	30%
Customer	nap	nap	60%

Top 6 fault containing modules (ranked):
- Module 1, module 2, module 3, module 4, module 5, ...
Modules with most effort for fixing failures (ranked):
- Module A, module B, module C, module D, ...
Distribution of effort for fixing faults after delivery per introduced activities:

	# of faults	effort
Req's analysis and spec:	10%	35%
High level design:	5%	6%
Design and implementation	60%	35%
Integration	10%	6%
Evaluation and release:	15%	18%

Distribution of Effort between Locating and Fixing a Fault:
- Locating 60%, Fixing 40%

Impact on Baseline Hypothesis
- Better Process Control results in:
  - fewer failures,
  - less faults slipped through code review,
  - % of coding faults is reduced
- Too severe deadlines will increase the # of failures
- Higher Experience SW Engineers results in less faults introduced
- Better adherence to coding standards results in:
  - less faults in general
  - less effort for locating and fixing faults
- Complex modules have more faults
- Not updated documents could result in more errors in a later phase of the project

Figure 9-15: Example of abstraction sheet project A.

GQM plan for product goal

The following goal was established regarding the particular software product:

Goal 'reliability product':

Analyse the	delivered product and development process
for the purpose of	characterising
with respect to	reliability and its causes
from the viewpoint(s) of	the software development team (SW project leader and software engineer)
in the following context:	project A

In the subsequent paragraphs this goal will be decomposed into measurement questions and metrics.

Product definition

Attributes measured here were the composition of the product, the consistency of documents with the delivered product, adherence to the coding standards, and the size of the software.

Q.1   What is the composition of the product?

         M.1.1   List of life cycle documents.

         M.1.1   List of subsystems.

         M.1.1   List of modules.

         A module is a part of a subsystem (SW system) with a defined functionality.

Q.2   Is the source code in accordance with the coding standards?

         M.2.1   Adherence to coding standards per module (high, low).

Q.3   What is the complexity of the delivered software?

         M.3.1   Overall size of software (KSLOC).

         M.3.2   Size of software per module (KSLOC).

         M.3.3   McCabe's cyclomatic complexity per module.

         M.3.4   Level of user interaction per module (high, medium, low).

         M.3.5   Change rate of the module (categories or numbers)?

         M.3.6   Personal assessment of the overall complexity per module (high, medium, low)?

         M.3.7   Combined complexity based on the individual complexity metrics per module.

         We may later define a combined complexity metrics based on the relative importance of the individual complexity metrics.

         M.3.8   Combined complexity per functionality of the system (eg, dispenser).

Quality model 'failures after delivery'

Reliability of a product was modelled on the number and severity of failures detected after delivery, ie after installation of a pilot release. In the case of project A, a release implied:

- shipment of all up to date modules to the customisation group(s), which added the country specific software modules;
- delivery to Installation;
- commercial release of complete product to customer;
- delivery to customer.

To get more insight, and to identify improvement opportunities, a distinction was made between, faults, failures and defects. Defects was the most general term that was used to denote anything that went wrong. According to the IEEE standard definition, *errors* were defects in the human thought process made while trying to understand given information, to solve problems, or to use methods and tools. *Faults* were concrete manifestations of errors within the software, ie one error might cause several faults and various errors might cause identical faults. *Failures* were departures of the operational software system behaviour from user expected requirements. Thus a particular failure might be caused by several faults and some faults might never cause a failure.

To investigate failures further, numbers from the trouble reports were used, reported failures were separated from change requests, and each failure was tracked back to faults. Failures were classified according to severity and according to the detection mechanism. Faults were classified according to the life-cycle phase where the fault was introduced, according to subsystems where they were found, and according to the type of fault. Costs were broken down into costs per module, costs per activity (documents that were updated), and costs for fault locating versus costs for fault fixing. Model definition:

Q.4   How long did data collection take place?
      M.4.1   Number of months after delivery was used for trouble data collection.
Q.5   What was the percentage of failures reported in the trouble reports?
      M.5.1   Number of trouble reports after delivery.
      M.5.2   Percentage of trouble reports, not being change requests.
      It was assumed that trouble reports addressed both failures and change requests. With respect to reliability the change requests were to be ignored.
      Hypothesis: 50% of trouble reports addressed change requests.
Q.6   What was the distribution of failures after delivery?
      M.6.1   Overall number of detected failures for software system after delivery.
Q.7   What was the distribution of failures after delivery over severity classes?
      M.7.1   For each detected failure: classification by severity (minor, major, fatal, other).
Q.8   What was the distribution of failures after delivery, over detection mechanisms?
      M.8.1   For each detected failure: classification by detection mechanism (engineer (provide name), test group (provide name), acceptance test group (provide name), Installation (provide country), customer (provide name), other).
Q.9   What was the distribution of faults after delivery?
      M.9.1   Overall number of software system faults detected after delivery.
      M.9.2   For each fault detected after delivery of the software system: life-cycle phase the fault was introduced (requirements analysis, specification/high level design, detailed design/implementation, integration, evaluation/ release.
Note that the information with respect to life-cycle phases had to be treated carefully. Since the document frequently was not updated when requirements changed during the development process, all changes were implemented in the software code. Therefore, it happened that, for example, design faults were perceived as code faults.
Hypothesis: see abstraction sheet.

M.9.3   For each fault detected after delivery of the software system: name of the module the fault was located in.

Hypothesis: top 6 modules containing faults were module 1, module 2, module 3, module 4, module 5, module 6.

M.9.4   For each fault detected after delivery of the software system: name of the functionality the fault was located in.

Q.10   What was the distribution of failure handling effort after delivery?

M.10.1   Total effort for handling failures after delivery (locating faults and fixing them) in staff-hours.

M.10.2   For each failure detected in the software system after delivery: effort in hours for locating and fixing the fault(s) by module.

M.10.3   For each failure detected in the software system after delivery: effort in hours spent on activities related to various life-cycle phases (FEASIB, REQANAL, SPEC,. HLDES, DDES, IMPL, INTEGR, UDOC, EVALREL).

The idea was that if, for example, the high-level design document was to be updated because the failure was due to a design fault, effort was spent on an activity associated to the phase HLDES (high level design).

Q.11   What was the effort spent on fault locating vs. the effort spent on fault fixing?

M.11.1   For each fault detected in the software system after delivery: effort in hours for locating the fault.

M.11.2   For each fault detected in the software system after delivery: effort in hours for fixing the fault.

Q.12   What was the relationship between module complexity and reliability?

M.12.1   For all modules: what were the average complexity metrics.

M.12.2   For top faulty modules: what were the complexity metrics.

M.12.3   For top non-faulty modules: what were the complexity metrics.

M.12.4   For all modules: what was the fault density.

M.12.5   For top simple modules: what was the fault density.

M.12.6   For top complex modules: what was the fault density.

The complexity metrics included all the complexity metrics defined earlier in the product definition. The fault density could be replaced with another metric defining reliability if some other metrics was more descriptive for project A.

Process definition

Process conformance:

Q.13   What percentage of the delivered code was covered by peer reviews and inspections (with respect to number of modules and KSLOC)?

This question also applied to updates of the product, then the amount of modified source lines of code was taken into account (ΔKSLOC).

M.13.1   Total number of modules in operational software system.

M.13.2   Size of operational SW system (KSLOC).

M.13.3   Number of modules in the operational SW system whose code was peer-reviewed.

M.13.4   Aggregated size of peer reviewed modules in the SW (KSLOC).

M.13.5   Number of modules in the operational SW system whose code was inspected.

M.13.6   Aggregated size of inspected modules in the SW (KSLOC).

Q.14   What is the relationship between code reviews and reliability?

M.14.1   For all modules: what is the fault density.

M.14.2   For code reviewed modules: what is the fault density.

M.14.3   For non-reviewed modules: what is the fault density.

M.14.4   For all modules: what is the percentage that has been reviewed.

M.14.5   For top faulty modules: what is the percentage that has been reviewed.

M.14.6   For top non-faulty modules: what is the percentage that has been reviewed.

Domain conformance:

Q.15   What is the experience of the SW development team? (percentage of SW team members for each of the experience classes)

M.15.1   SW development team: classification of experience with application domain (high, average, low).

M.15.2   For each SW development team member: classification of experience with earlier phases of the same project (participation in directly preceding phase, participation in earlier phase but not the directly preceding one, participation in all preceding phases, no participation in earlier phases, no earlier phases of project existing). These are assumed to be variation factors. Hypothesis: higher experience results in fewer faults and failures.

Quality model 'failures during development'

To understand the causes for reliability the failures that are detected during development, ie in the life-cycle phases up to and including Evaluation and Release are investigated and tracked down to faults.

   The issues addressed by the questions are the roughly the same as in the GQM for goal 'reliability1.product'. The difference is that here the failures detected during development are considered, and not the failures that are detected after delivery of the system.

Model definition:

Q.16   What is the distribution of detected failures before delivery?

M.16.1   Overall number of SW system failures detected before delivery.

M.16.2   For each detected failure before delivery: classification by severity (minor, major, fatal, other).

M.16.3   For each detected failure before delivery: classification by detection mechanism (engineer (provide name), test group, acceptance test group, other).

Q.17   What is the distribution of failure handling effort?

M.17.1   Total effort for handling failures detected (locating faults and fixing them) in staff-hours.

M.17.2   For each failure detected in the SW system: effort in hours for locating and fixing the fault(s) by module.

M.17.3   For each failure detected in the SW system: effort in hours spent on activities related to various life-cycle phases (FEASIB, REQANAL, SPEC,. HLDES, DDES, IMPL, INTEGR, UDOC, EVALREL).

The idea is that if, for example, the high-level design document is to be updated because the failure was due to a design fault, effort is spent on an activity associated to the phase HLDES.

Q.18   What is the effort spent on fault locating vs. the effort spent on fault fixing?

M.18.1   For each fault detected in the SW system before delivery: effort in hours for locating the fault.

M.18.2   For each fault detected in the SW system before delivery: effort in hours for fixing the fault.

Goal 'Reuse'

GQM abstraction sheets

With respect to the 'reuse' goal, two interviews were made, one with the software development leader of project A (who works as an software engineer as well) and one with the software development leader of a related project which is to reuse software developed by project A.

First, the summarised information is presented in a GQM plan abstraction sheet, which is derived from the abstraction sheets, which represented the two interviews. Note that the abstraction sheet in Figure 9-15 was filled out only partially, because the project team had no experience with reuse to provide sound expectations (hypotheses).

Object: delivered product	Purpose: understanding	Quality focus effectiveness of reuse	Viewpoint: software development team	Environment Project A	External GQM plan represen- tation

Quality Focus	**Variation Factors**

Reuse of Software, any kind of document or code (core development only)
 • Degree of modification: (unchanged, part of document deleted, part of document changed (up to 20%), part of document changed (more than 20%) which should be an exception)
 • Reused artefacts: Life Cycle documents or code
 • Defects and reuse:
     - Faults in reused artefact vs. faults introduced when modifying artefact
     - Faults in reused modules vs. faults in non-reused modules
 • Cost of reuse: Overall, per component, vs. cost for new development
	Process Conformance:
	 • 1st or later phase of a project (if the project is phased)
	
	 Domain Conformance:
	 • Experience of the development team with reuse or the reused software
	 • Is developing for reuse done, for example appropriate structures, coupling and object oriented techniques

Figure 9-16: Summarised GQM plan abstraction sheet project A.

GQM plan for 'reuse goal'

The following goal was formulated regarding reuse of code:

Goal 'reuse':
Analyse the	delivered product
for the purpose of	understanding
with respect to	effectiveness of reuse
from the viewpoint(s) of	the software development team (SW project leader of a project developing for reuse and SW engineer of another project reusing software)
in the following context:	project A

In the subsequent paragraphs this goal will be broken down into measurement questions and metrics.

Quality model 'software reuse'

Here the reuse of software for core development is investigated; The questions are related to the following issues: document types that are reused (code or documents) and their origin, amount of reuse overall and for certain subsystems of the developed system, degree of modification when reusing components, defects in reused components, cost of reuse.

Model definition:

Q.19   What is the percentage of modules that were not developed from scratch, ie some kind of document or code is reused (overall and per subsystem)?

      M.19.1 For each software module: developed from scratch (Yes, No). Hypothesis: 70 %.

      M.19.2 For each software module: name of subsystem the module belongs to.

Q.20   What is the percentage of reused code (overall and per subsystem)?

      M.20.1 For each SW module: code reused (Yes, No).

      Hypothesis: 70 % of modules some degree of reuse

      M.20.2 For each SW module: name of subsystem the module belongs to.

Q.21   For SW modules where code is reused: What is the distribution of modules among reuse modification classes (overall and per subsystem)?

      M.21.1 For each SW module where code was reused: degree of code modification (code is unchanged, mainly deletions, less 20% of lines changed, more than 20% of lines changed).

      Hypothesis: 30% of reused modules are unchanged, 10% of reused modules require deletions only, 30% of reused modules require changes in up to 20% of KSLOC, 30% of reused modules require changes in more than 20% of KSLOC.

      This classification can be calculated with the configuration management tool. Therefore 2 metrics must be added to determine the versions of the original and the released modules.

      M.21.2 For each SW module where code was reused: name and version of the original reused module.

      M.21.3 For each SW module where code was reused: name and version of the released reusing module.

      M.21.4 For each SW module where code was reused: name of subsystem the module belongs to.

Q.22   What is the relationship between module reuse and reliability?
  M.22.1 For all modules: what is the level of reuse?
  M.22.2 For top faulty modules: what is the level of reuse?
  M.22.3 For top non-faulty modules: what is the level of reuse?
  M.22.4 For all modules: what is the fault density?
  M.22.5 For reused modules: what is the fault density?
  M.22.6 For non-reused modules: what is the fault density?

9.6.2   Project A feedback session report

In this section project A's final feedback session report is given.

FEEDBACK SESSION REPORT			
Project Name: Project A	Project No: QAxxxxxx	Date:	Rev: 00.02
Meeting Date:		Present: xxxxx	
Authors: xxxxx		Absent: xxxxx	
Subject: Final feedback session of the GQM based measurement results for project A			

Introduction

In February year 1 a measurement programme was started at the R&D department. The goals of the measurement programme were defined as:

Analyse: the delivered product and development process
for the purpose of :   understanding
with respect to: reliability and its causes
from the viewpoint of: the software management team
in the context of: project A

Analyse: the delivered products
for the purpose of :   understanding
with respect to: effectiveness of reuse
from the viewpoint of: the software management team
in the context of: project A

This is a report of the final meeting during which the results of the measurement programme were presented by the GQM team and the results were interpreted by the project team and GQM team according to the questions and goals as stated in the GQM plan.

It appeared that the GQM plan as available is a design document of the measurement programme, and difficult to apply as a basis for interpretation. The GQM team has therefore interpreted the questions in the GQM plan in a way that the feedback material supports reaching the Goals.

Results of feedback session on 'reliability'

The meeting started with an overview of the project A software product:

- 52 modules;
- 60 KSLOC;
- system fault density: 1.9 Faults/KSLOC;
- average repair time: 2.7 Hours/Fault.

The average time needed for repairs is not used to schedule repairs. Instead, about 70% of time is scheduled for normal tasks and 30% is reserved for other work like fault finding and fixing.

The distribution of trouble reports was 81% failure reports and 19% change requests. The hypothesis made was that this distribution would be 50-50%. The reason for this deviation of results from hypothesis was explained by the fact that change requests are handled in a different way than originally expected. Change requests with a high priority and/or a short time to implement were included in Trouble Log (TLOG) whereas other change requests were sent to the Marketing Department to be planned as additional functionality. Previously, all change requests were reported in TLOG. The criteria for including a change request into TLOG are:

- Is the specification of the CR clear enough to be directly implemented?
- Is the effort required for implementing the CR relatively low?
- Is the risk that the CR will not succeed within this time low?

The measurement programme created a better understanding of failure detection by engineers. The amount of failures found by engineers was much higher than originally expected. Causes for this were:

- The installation tests found less failures than expected. This was very important: if failures are not found within R&D, it is more likely that those failures will be found in a pilot than in an Installation test.
- Another reason is that no test group exists anymore (unfortunately).
- Before a release all new or changed modules are tested by the engineers.
- By reusing modules, faults in existing code are detected by the engineers.

With respect to the original goals of understanding product reliability and the influence of the development process, it can be stated that:

- The goal is reached, it is understood how to identify product reliability.
- A measurement programme is a source of information that gives some visibility to the reliability of the product.
- The most important identification of product reliability is that no failures are reported from the field. Keeping good contact with pilots in the field is therefore very important.
- Combining field information with a measurement programme gives better insight to the reliability of the product.
- The measurement programme would give more information on product reliability if it would include testing effort and system use.

Without information on how much effort is put into failure detection, the number of failures found doesn't give enough information. Not finding failures gives less visibility on the reliability, than finding failures. The fact is that when many failures are detected, it means that the product is not reliable. The opposite, not finding failures, however, does not mean the product is reliable.

Results of feedback session on 'reuse'

Few modules in the Driver functionality have been reused. The reason for this is that no reusable modules were available. It is expected that those modules will be reused in the future.

Module X has been developed by reusing Module Y. The decision for reusing has been based on the measurement data, because it has been identified that reuse results in lower fault density. From the 8 largest modules, only one has been developed from scratch.

With respect to the reuse goal it was stated that:

- The goal is reached, it is understood what the effects of reuse are.
- It would be interesting also to look at the influence of reusing modules on development effort.
- It is not possible to draw general conclusions whether new development or reuse is absolutely better, since only one of the options is completed. Developing a module both from scratch and with reuse would create the possibility to compare, but this is not done.
- Reusing large parts of a module that is already fixed, results in significantly lower faults than developed from scratch
- Faults in reused modules are detected more before delivery, because reused modules are reviewed and tested more intensively than new developed modules.
- The results on the effects of reuse must be shown to other parts of the organisation, in order to show the benefits of reuse.

Conclusions

The project A measurement programme was successfully completed, all goals were attained. The project did not only create more insight to the product and the development process, but also supported the project team in particular decisions. Another benefit was the increase of experience in how to set up a measurement programme.

Project A will get continuous support of measurement by defining a new measurement programme on testing, and similar measurements on module X.

Action list

The following action list was established in the final feedback session:

- Define measurement programme on test goal.
- Define measurement programme on module X.
- Post mortal analysis on project A measurement programme.
- Present some major results of project A over the organisation.

It was concluded that subsequent meetings needed to be organised for defining a new measurement programme on a test goal. It was expected that a large amount of such a new measurement programme could be based on the measurement programmes project A and RITME. Also module X should be supported by some measurements similar to the project A measurement programme.

9.7   Questions and assignments

9.7.1   Questions

1.   Which aspect of reuse, would you consider most apparently missing in the reuse measurement goal of this chapter?
2.   What do you consider the main purpose of Figure 9-3?
3.   Explain why a chart such as Figure 9-5 should only be interpreted by a project team?
4.   What are the main differences between *fatal*, *major* and *minor* failures?
5.   Should failure severity classification (of fatal, major, minor), be interpreted from the perspective of a developer, or from the viewpoint of an end-user?
6.   Give examples of interpretations derived from Figure 9-7 that are contradictory, but would, however, be supported by Figure 9-7.
7.   What does Figure 9-5 imply about the effects of reuse on product reliability?
8.   Is cyclomatic complexity an adequate metric for measuring software complexity according to the data of Figure 9-14?
9.   Which two main topics do you consider missing in the feedback session report of project A in Section 9.6.2?

9.7.2   Assignments

The GQM plan of the case study presented in this chapter was the first GQM plan developed by that particular organisation. Therefore, it does not comply to the criteria set in Chapter 6. Review the GQM plan and identify the mistakes in this plan. Use the validation mechanisms introduced in Chapter 6 as a reference.

10   Case B: review and inspection measurement

10.1   Description of project B

This chapter describes the results of the RITME measurement programme. RITME was the acronym for 'Reviews and Inspections: The Measurement of their Effects'. The RITME measurement programme investigated the aspects of fault detecting and learning effects of reviewing. A review was defined as a *cross reading of a document by another person than the writer of the document*. Reviewed were deliverables such as designs and programming code of project B.

A review involves two people: the developer of the designs or programming code, and a reviewer. The developer decided whether a document requires a review and assigns it to a reviewer. The reviewer read the document and made notes upon detected faults or obscurities. Following, the reviewer and developer discussed the reviewer's notes. Finally, the developer removed the detected faults from the document.

Reviews were measured for two purposes. The first purpose was finding faults, '... *a brief inspection by competent co-workers invariably turns up mistakes the programmers would not have found by themselves*' (Humphrey, 1989). The second purpose was to train new people: reading documents not only teaches about the contents of the document, but also about what lay-out or coding standards were used.

In the RITME project a high-end cashing and fuel station management system was developed. Software code was primarily written in the C^{++} programming language, with additional application of component libraries. The total duration of the project was approximately 6 years of which 3 years was spent on the first increment of the product. In total 20 software engineers worked on this product. Also, several customised versions for specific countries or customers were developed.

The results presented in this chapter are based on the complete measurement programme. Results are not only the measurement data, but also conclusions drawn by the project team, or action taken based on the measurements. The RITME measurement programme will be described by the four phases of the GQM method: planning, definition, data collection and interpretation.

This chapter also includes a lot of documentation of this measurement programme, such as the GQM plan, data collection forms, and feedback charts. Documentation that one can copy for similar measurement programmes.

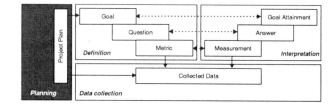

10.2 Planning

An independent GQM team already existed in the department. This team discussed with the project team what the role could be of the measurement programme in the context of the organisation's improvement programme. Due to successful application of goal-oriented measurement in foregoing projects, it was decided to apply the GQM method towards an operational improvement goal relevant to the project. The necessary training for the project team was given by the GQM team, which had experience of the practical application of the GQM method. The planning phase delivered the RITME Project plan.

Based on the current status of the project and the changes in the department it was decided to consider reviews and inspections as the measurement topic. The two reasons for this were:

- The main development work was shifting from initial development to changes and expansion of functionality. Testing therefore became less efficient, because minor changes would need large testing efforts. Reviewing those changes or additional developments was expected to be more effective and efficient. System testing was still performed, but only in the process of a new version release, and by a separate test group.

- The department was recently expanded with five new engineers, who were educated by 'training-on-the-job'. Reviews were considered a powerful tool during this training process in two ways. Firstly, new engineers could review deliverables of senior engineers to reach understanding of the system. Secondly, senior engineers could review deliverables of the new engineers, to check conformance to the departments coding and quality standards.

So, the purpose of reviews was not just the detection of faults or failures, but also a major tool for teaching (new) team members on parts of the product. This educational function of reviews was also included in the measurement programme. Measurements were also conducted to identify the effects of reviews on learning capability.

The effort of the project team for reviewing was limited to 4 hours maximum per week per project member. This effort was already planned to be spent on reviews for training new engineers. The overhead of the measurement programme for the project team needed to be extremely low due to time constraints of the project. The GQM team gave as much support as possible, and executed most of the operational tasks of the measurement programme.

The general expectation was that the time spent on reviewing and the supporting measurement programme, would result in better quality of the product. Therefore, less time was expected to be spent on repairing faults in later stages of the project.

The project supported during RITME, was Project B. The Project B team consists of 9 engineers and a project manager.

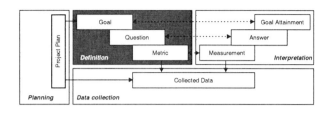

10.3   Definition

The improvement goal defined in this project was already quite operational. Reviews would be introduced in the department and held structurally. Because of the two main purposes of these reviews: fault detection and training, the measurement goal could be formulated directly from the improvement goal.

Reviews:
Analyse the:	effectiveness of structured reviews
for the purpose of:	understanding
with respect to:	- the detection of faults
	- the learning ability of the technique
from the viewpoint of:	the project team
in the following context:	project B

Achieving this measurement goal would yield a better understanding of reviews, focused on the fault detection capabilities and training effectiveness. The project team supported this measurement goal, even though the project manager initially identified it.

The definition steps used in the RITME measurement programme were similar to those presented in Chapter 6. The main difference of the definition process of RITME compared to that in project A (Chapter 9), was that the complete GQM method was used as described in this book, instead of the QIP-based approach. The main reason for this was that experiences from project A had provided knowledge as to the importance of the several steps. Because of the efficiency requirements of RITME it was decided to perform only the critical steps of the GQM approach. Furthermore, process modelling was done for the review process, which was a learning point from earlier GQM application.

Knowledge acquisition was supported by structured interviews. The main purpose of the structured interviews was to make implicit knowledge of the Project members explicit. Developing a documented description of the review process was executed during structured interviews with two representatives of the project team and the project manager. The ETXM model that was developed based on the interviews is included in Figure 10-1.

The definition of questions and metrics was also provided by structured interviews. Documenting the question, metrics, and hypotheses in abstraction sheets, checking completeness and consistency between abstraction sheet and the process model and writing the GQM and Measurement plan was executed by the GQM team. The GQM plan of RITME is attached in Section 10.6.

Review
Entrance criteria: Product to be reviewed is available Reviewer(s) has been assigned Exit criteria: Review report is available and approved Tasks: Review the product Fill in review report Transfer the review report to the author Correct the product based on the faults noted in the review report Approve the review report if all faults have been addressed Measurements: Number of faults detected during review Size of reviewed product Complexity of reviewed product Estimated resource time for review Resource time for review Schedule time from start to finish for review Severity of faults detected during review

Figure 10-1: ETXM model of a review.

The questions to be answered by the RITME measurement programme were:

- Question 1: What are the baselines (rules of thumb) for executing reviews?
- Question 2: What are the characteristics of a document, to get optimal effects of a review?
- Question 3: What are the acceptance criteria for the quality of the document, after a review?
- Question 4: Are reviews a useful and efficient method for training new engineers?

Additionally, an analysis plan was produced to present the interpretation phase beforehand. The analysis plan was created on a number of virtual data and contained graphs and tables, based on these data, that were related to the stated questions and goals. In this way, a starting point was created for the creation of future feedback material.

Reviews of the GQM plan, measurement plan and analysis plan was conducted in a meeting. During this meeting, the GQM team repeated the concept of the GQM method to the project team. The GQM team also presented some results from previous measurement programmes to motivate the project team for measurement. Finally, the GQM team presented the RITME measurement programme: the goal template of the measurement programme was introduced along with the refinement into questions and metrics. All material was discussed by all attendants of the meeting, ambiguities were solved, and a number of remarks were noted for improvement of the plans.

10.4   Data collection

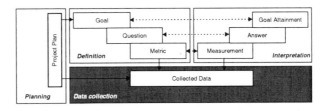

Data collection started with a 'kick-off session' in which the data collection forms were explained. The metrics defined in the measurement plan were collected by one manual paper form. A number of metrics that had to be filled in on the 'Review Form' (size, cyclomatic complexity and number of comment lines) were calculated using an automated tool, provided to the project team via the network.

Data correctness was checked when importing the data into the metrics base and during reviews of the feedback material.

10.4.1   The RITME measurement support systems (MSS)

The goal of the measurement programme was twofold: the fault finding effects and the learning effects of reviewing were investigated. As these aspects were heavily intertwined, only one analysis sheet was created. To improve the possibility of analysing historic data, a new implementation was created. The links between metrics base and analysis sheet were not implemented. Instead, the data from the metrics base, that were to be analysed, had to be copied into the analysis sheet. Automatic updating was implemented within the analysis sheet as far as supported by the spreadsheet tool (Figure 10-2).

Another change included the exclusion of hard-copy transparent slides for the presentation of measurement results. Instead, the graphs and tables that were to be presented, were linked to an on-line presentation tool and directly projected by means of an LCD display, connected to a computer. This implementation supports automatic updating of graphs and tables and gives additional support for selecting and editing presentation material (useful for highlighting interesting results). Furthermore, it provides a better appearance of the slides. The main advantage of a LCD display is that the original data can be accessed on-line. Once specific questions occur during the feedback session, the underlying data can be consulted immediately.

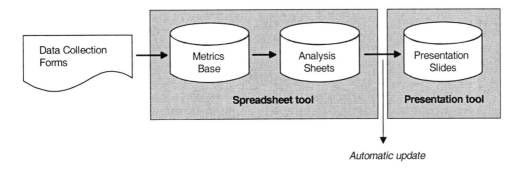

Figure 10-2: MSS of RITME, included with linking analysis sheets to analysis slides.

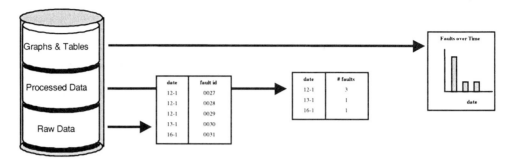

Figure 10-3: Three layers within an analysis sheet.

The MSS was set-up with the concepts presented in Section 7.4. Each analysis sheet consisted of particular worksheets for the questions that relate to a goal of the analysis sheet (question worksheets). Each analysis sheet was built up from three layers (Figure 10-3):

• raw data layer;
• processed data layer;
• graphs & tables layer.

The raw data layer contains the links to the metrics base and, therefore, like the metrics base itself, contains raw data only. The results of processing the raw data are kept in the processed data layer. Finally, the graphs & tables data layer contained the questions from the GQM plan, which they intended to answer, added to the relevant charts or tables.

10.5   Interpretation

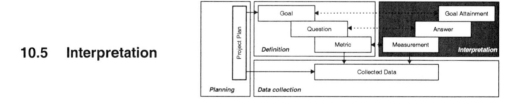

This section presents interpretation results of the RITME project. Due to a relative slow delivery of data points (around 3 reviews were conducted per week), feedback sessions were held every four months. During the RITME measurement programme three feedback sessions were held. However, reviewing was not expected to end when the measurement goal was achieved. Therefore reviews were included in the normal process after the measurement programme had ended.

The results of the measurements are not only presentations of empirical data on the different subjects, but also conclusions drawn or actions taken based on the measurements. A selection of conclusions drawn and actions taken by the project members based on the measurement results is presented:

- Reviews are an efficient aid to detect faults.
- Reviews improve uniformity and maintainability of code.
- Reviews increase communication, synergy and understanding within a development team.
- Reviews detect more than 1 Fatal/Major per hour.
- Reviews detect 7.5 faults per hour.
- Reviews should be done on documents smaller than 50 pages.
- Reviews are more effective on documents of maximum 20 pages.
- Reviews are at least four times more efficient than testing.
- Reviews should be done for at least one hour a week per engineer.
- New engineers learn most from reviewing code from experienced engineers
- Training of new engineers should subsequently consist of:
  - courses to provide relevant theory and general overview;
  - reviews to learn system details;
  - on-the-job training to provide practical experience.

Feedback was provided to the project team in feedback sessions. All project B members were involved in the interpretation phase. However, compared to the project A measurement programme, improvements were made in the way feedback was given.

- Firstly, in theory, feedback sessions should be held often and the quantity of material presented should be low to achieve learning in many small steps. This implementation of feedback in a business environment would, however, create a number of practical problems: first, feedback sessions would present few new data points, and second, it is already hard to get an entire project team to attend a meeting every eight weeks. Therefore, it was decided to provide some feedback on posters every two to three weeks. In this way, feedback would be provided more frequently. However, these posters had little effect compared to feedback sessions.
- Secondly, to improve data correctness, the presentation material was reviewed internally before the feedback session: one GQM team member prepared the material and another would review the material. Simultaneously, the reviewing GQM team member could evaluate whether the created graphs and tables were understandable and whether any other related metrics should be included in the graphs (or tables).
- Thirdly, it was decided to conclude every feedback session with an evaluation of the results accomplished in the session, in relation to the stated goal.
- Finally, to create a framework for the interpretation, it was decided to relate measurement results to the questions they were intended to answer by presenting the questions along with the measurement results. Therefore, each session followed the questions in the GQM plan: each time, a slide with GQM questions was presented preceding the graphs and/or tables that contributed to answers to these questions (Figure 10-4).

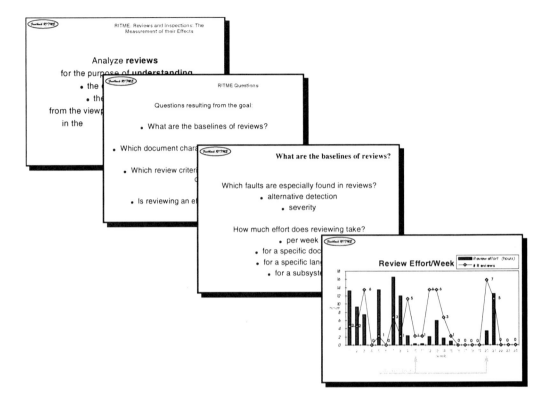

Figure 10-4: Presentation of results in relation to goals and questions.

Another aspect that was learned through the experience in providing feedback for RITME concerns scales. Intuitively, all graphs should have scales. Just as important as having scales in graphs, is using equal scales in different graphs to make it easier to compare different graphs.

In RITME, problems occurred through the definition of classes: faults found were to be classified according to their expected alternative detection (ie how they would have been detected if not by reviewing). During the definition of the measurement programme, it was decided to include both a class 'never' and a class 'unknown'. In practice, it appeared that these classes were used too easily: many faults were rated to belong to these classes, and none to the 'field test' and 'installation' classes (Figure 10-5), whereas in reality faults were also detected in field tests and by installation's (remark of the project manager). During the feedback sessions, it was recognised by the project team that the 'unknown' and 'never' faults were probably better rated as 'field test' or 'installation'. Therefore it was decided to delete the 'unknown' and 'never' classes from the Review Form.

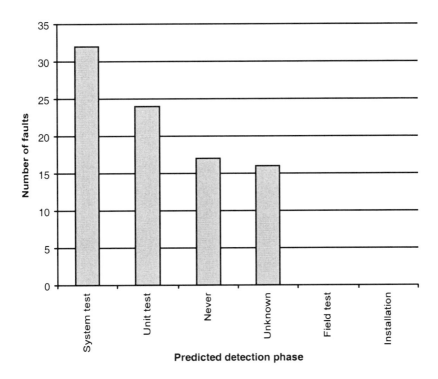

Figure 10-5: Fault classification according to alternative means of detection: bad use of classes.

The second feedback session started with a thorough evaluation of the actions defined in the first session. In the first session (week 15), it was for instance decided to limit the maximum length of a document for a review, initiated to find faults, to 50 pages (Figure 10-6). During the second feedback session it was evaluated whether this 50 pages limit was held. Only one review exceeded the 50 pages.

In providing feedback for RITME, a background was introduced to the slides. The background was introduced to create a recognisable look for the RITME feedback slides and posters. When doing so, the background should not be too fancy: the first background for the RITME feedback material was experienced as being too disturbing.

The results of the measurements will be presented for both the faultfinding capabilities and the learning capabilities.

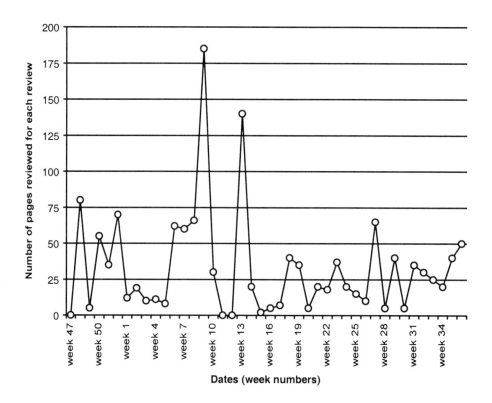

Figure 10-6: Evaluation of action points.

10.5.1 Fault finding capabilities of reviews

The faultfinding results of reviews are summarised in Figure 10-7. Considering the number of detected faults per page, the number of faults detected by reviewing Project B was 0.4 faults per page equalling 24 SLOC[3](Figure 10-7). Grady reports that inspections[4] resulted in 0.3 faults per page (Grady, 1992).

---

[3] The number of 24 SLOC per page was based on a sample of documents containing programming code of the Project B systems.

[4] Grady does not define inspections beyond them being reviews of requirements models, designs, code and other work products.

Faults found by reviewing documents							
Total effort for reviewing:				43 hours			
Total effort including meetings and repair:				74 hours			
Total number of pages:				998 pages			
Total number of lines:				24 KSLOC			
		Distribution		Faults/hour		Faults/page	
	# Faults	hypothesis	real	hypothesis	real	hypothesis	real
minor	292	70%	77%		6,8		0,3
major	57	25%	15%		1,3		0,1
fatal	29	5%	8%		0,7		-
TOTAL	378			20-65	8,7	3-7	0,4

Figure 10-7: Overall results of RITME.

	Review	Acceptance test	Novice user test
Number of faults	378	111	49
Hours spent	43	322	32
Faults per hour			
minor	6,76	0,09	1,2
major	1,32	0,15	0,3
fatal	0,67	0,11	0,1
TOTAL	8,75	0,34	1,5

Figure 10-8: Comparing faults found by reviews, an acceptance test and a novice user test.

Comparing reviews to tests showed large differences in fault-detecting performance (# detected faults per hour). During the execution of RITME, two tests were executed: an acceptance test and a monkey test (novice user test). In the acceptance test, 0.34 faults were found per hour testing, in the monkey test 1.5, while reviews produced a number of 8.7 faults per hour reviewing (Figure 10-8): an important indication for the effectiveness of reviewing. The effectiveness of reviewing over the acceptance test differs a factor 25; over the monkey test it differs a factor 5. AT&T reported inspections[5] to be a factor 20 more effective (Humphrey, 1989). No subsystem was identified in which significantly more faults were found than in other subsystems[6] (Figure 10-9).

---

[5] Reviews as performed in Project B comply more to Humphrey's definition of walkthroughs than inspections.

[6] The high faults/page value of the Sybsys 1 subsystem is caused by the very low number of reviewed pages.

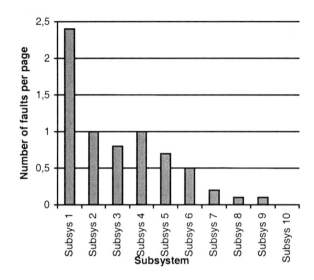

Subsystem	Number of faults	Number of pages	Faults/page
Subsys 1	12	5	2,4
Subsys 2	41	42	1,0
Subsys 3	130	158	0,8
Subsys 4	1	1	1,0
Subsys 5	4	6	0,7
Subsys 6	80	152	0,5
Subsys 7	71	302	0,2
Subsys 8	37	255	0,1
Subsys 9	3	38	0,1
Subsys 10	0	455	-

Figure 10-9: Detected faults/page by reviewing per subsystem.

Under the assumption that the major and fatal faults found by reviewing, would have been detected during the monkey test if no reviewing was performed, reviewing resulted in 86 prevented test defects: twice the number of actual test defects of the monkey test. A prevented test defect is a defect that would have been detected through testing if not through another means of fault detection (Rooijmans et al, 1996). In their study of inspections[7], Rooijmans et al found the numbers of test defects prevented through inspections ranged from 1.4 to 3.9 in comparison to actual test defects (Rooijmans et al, 1996).

---

[7] Note that the investigated inspections concerned inspections of requirements and design documents, not programming code as in the investigated reviews.

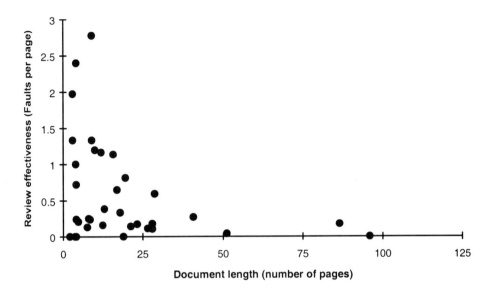

Figure 10-10: Decreasing number of detected faults/page with increasing document length.

In RITME, it appeared that the number of detected faults per page decreased with increasing length of the document under review (Figure 10-10). The cause of this phenomenon might be identified by a decreased effort spent per page (Figure 10-11). Wenneson found that inspections of FORTRAN code took 3 to 10 hours per KLOC (Humphrey, 1989). Reading KLOC as KSLOC[8], this translates to 4.3 to 14 minutes per page. These numbers are significantly higher than the numbers found in RITME. No clear cause for this deviation could be identified. Possible causes include the difference between an informal review and a formal inspection, differences in code complexity, and difference in programming language.

---

[8] KLOC - kilo lines of code (1000 lines of code), KSLOC - kilo source lines of code (1000 source lines of code, excluding comment).

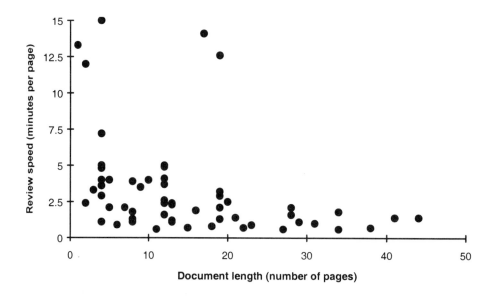

Figure 10-11: Decreasing effort per reviewed page with increasing document length

Resulting from both results, a maximum number of pages for a review was defined: the maximum number of pages for a review was not to exceed 50. This result was tracked throughout the measurement programme. The result of this tracking is depicted in Figure 10-6; the maximum was defined in the first feedback session, held March 8. Thereafter, no reviews exceeded the 50-pages limit.

Besides a maximum document length for reviews, RITME has caused a standardisation of reviews: before the measurement programme started, reviews were carried out in an unstructured, informal manner. As a result of RITME, existing review checklists were updated and re-introduced for the execution of reviews directly after goal attainment and formal 'end' of the measurement programme.

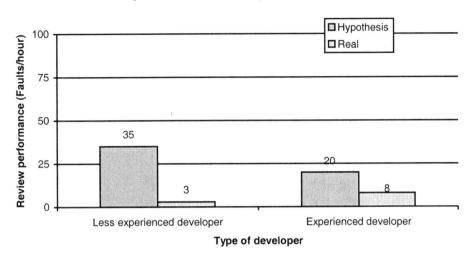

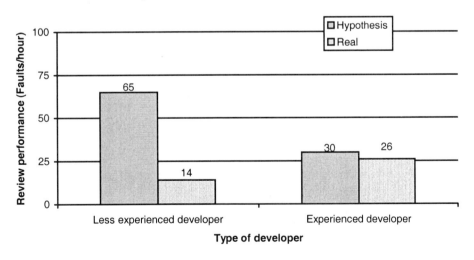

Figure 10-12: Review performance and experience of engineers.

Other results of RITME include (Figure 10-12):

- Experienced reviewers detect over three times more faults per hour than less experienced reviewers.
- Experienced reviewers detect two times more faults per page than less experienced reviewers.
- More faults are detected per hour in code developed by experienced engineers compared to code developed by less experienced engineers.
- Less faults are detected per page in code developed by experienced engineers compared to code developed by less experienced engineers.

10.5.2 Learning capabilities of reviews

In project B, reviewing is not only performed to detect faults, but also to train new people. This method of training was also measured by RITME as the learning effect of performing a review. The main result from this aspect of RITME is a good insight into how new people can be trained optimally. RITME indicated that reviewing is an important element in training new people, but should be part of a larger training programme. Besides reviews to learn system details, training should include courses to provide relevant theory and general overview and on-the-job training to provide practical experience.

The change in learning effect over time was remarkable. Figure 10-18 shows the results on learning effects during the first half year of the measurement programme. Most learning effects occur when a less experienced engineer reviews the material of an experienced one. During the second half year of the measurement programme this picture changed totally.

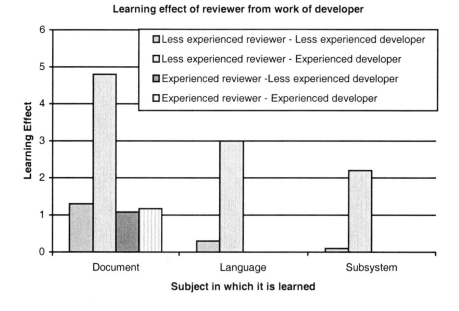

Figure 10-13: Learning effect of reviewing.

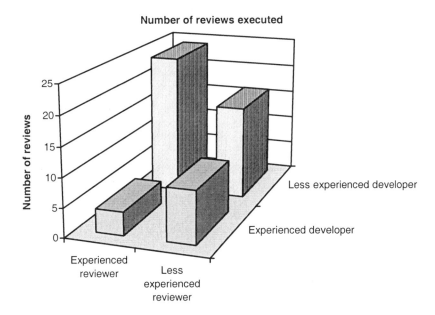

Figure 10-14: Executed reviews, divided according to experience level of developer or reviewer.

The less experienced became much more experienced and started to learn much more from each other than from experienced engineers. This lead to the conclusion by the project team that six months is about the time needed to train people to work in their development group.

Considering these results, the distribution of reviews among (in)experienced reviewers is remarkable (Figure 10-14): while the learning effect of a review is the largest when an less experienced reviewer reviews a document of an experienced developer, the number of reviews executed in this category is relatively small. A possible explanation could be that the emphasis of reviews is on fault finding.

10.6   Documentation of RITME project

This section contains:

- RITME GQM plan and measurement plan;
- applied review form;
- example of a feedback session report.

These documents will subsequently be described.

10.6.1 RITME GQM and measurement plan

Introduction

Software measurement programmes are started in the R&D department. The methodology used for introducing and defining a software measurement plan is the GQM method. This method emphasises specific use of measurement data. Cooperation from, and feedback to, the project team is therefore considered to be the main success factor of this approach. Due to the success of current experiences, management has decided that such project support by a measurement programme must be introduced in all development projects.

This is the GQM plan for the RITME measurement programme. Measurement will be introduced for a better understanding of current processes, to provide information on the performance and in that way identify areas of improvement. This document will be used for three purposes:

1. Feedback to the project B team members by the GQM-team.
2. Definition of data collection, since all direct measurements are defined in this document.
3. Analyses and feedback of collected data, because the GQM plan identifies which questions need to be addressed.

RITME stands for: Reviews & Inspections: The Measurement of their Effects. The Project B team will start investigating the effects of reviews. In a meeting with the group leader and two team members this goal has been identified. Since then interviews have been held with the same people and, based on these interviews, questions have been formulated and metrics have been defined with associated hypotheses.

In this document a representation is given of the information that has been gathered during those sessions. For each goal the following aspects are described:

- goal description and the refinement to questions;
- refinement from questions to metrics and direct measurements;
- abstracted direct measurements that have to be collected for the goal;
- hypotheses to the direct measurements given by the project team members.

The GQM plan will be subject to changes during the measurement period due to new information and experience gained in the feedback sessions.

Reviews

A review is an activity that will cause improvements in a document, by:

1. detecting and fixing of faults;
2. defining (quality) improvement areas in the document;
3. increased understanding of the product by engineers (learning).

A review is organised by the following steps:

1. Preparation phase, in which the document is identified, assigned to a reviewer, and the necessary relevant documentation is studied and understood.
2. Review phase, in which the actual cross-reading of the document is done, and detected faults and questions found are reported.

3. Review meeting, in which the review is discussed, open questions from the reviewer are answered, and after which the final review report can be finished.
4. Follow-up phase, in which actions are taken based on the review. It will be examined, to which extent faults found in a review are also really corrected.

The follow-up phase is included in this process in order to identify what the real result of a review was. This is also a check for identifying whether required changes are really implemented.

From goal to questions

The goal that will be addressed is:

Analyse:	the effectiveness of structured reviews
for the purpose of:	understanding
with respect to:	- the detection of faults
	- the learning ability of the technique
from the viewpoint of:	the project team
in the following context:	project B

This Goal will be attained when answers can be given to the following questions:

- Q.1 What are the baselines (rules of thumb) for the execution and results of reviews? This question focuses on identifying objective, quantifiable numbers that are related to the review and is answered when the relation between all factors involved in a review are clear and values are available that visualise the baselines and rules of thumb, that are related to reviews, objectively.
- Q.2 What are the characteristics of a document, in order to obtain optimal effect of a review? This question focuses on the definition of criteria that define whether a review will obtain the required effects and will give an answer to which characteristics a certain document should posses in order to result in a specified result of a review.
- Q.3 What are the acceptance criteria for the quality of the document, after a review? This question focuses on the possibility to identify if a reviewed document has an acceptable quality level. Therefore it should be investigated whether criteria can be defined to which the performance of a review must be met in order to identify an acceptable quality level. This question is answered when the possibilities for such criteria are understood, and when possible values to those criteria are known.
- Q.4 Are reviews a useful and efficient method for training new engineers? This question is answered when all learning abilities have been identified, and their effects can be quantified.

From questions to metrics

Question 1 was 'what are the baselines (rules of thumb) for the execution and results of reviews'? This question focuses on identifying objective, quantifiable numbers that are related to reviews. This question is answered when the relation between all factors involved in a review are clear and values are available that visualise the baselines and rules of thumb, that are related to reviews, objectively.

Detailed questions focusing on practical experience by the project team are:

- Q.1.1 Which kind of faults are likely to be found in reviews?
- Q.1.2 How much effort is spent on reviews per week?
- Q.1.3 What is the average time required to review a document of a specified size?
- Q.1.4 What is the average time required to review a document in a specific language?
- Q.1.5 What is the average time required to review a document of a specified complexity?
- Q.1.6 What is the average fault detection performance of reviewing documents?
- Q.1.7 Does the average performance of reviews change over time?
- Q.1.8 How effective is it to review a certain document for the second time?
- Q.1.9 What is the effort I can estimate for a review on a document of which the characteristics are known?
- Q.1.10 What is the difference in review performance between subsystems of the product?

The following metrics have been associated to these questions:

- subsystem of the document;
- document size;
- document specification language;
- document complexity;
- effort for a review;
- effort per page for a document;
- number of faults found for a review;
- other ways in which the faults could have been detected for a review;
- distribution of faults over severity for a review;
- number of faults per page for a document;
- date on which the review was held.

The above metrics resulted in the following direct measurements:

- M.01 Document name for each review.
- M.02 Document subsystem for each review.
- M.03 Document length for each review.
- M.04 Document cyclomatic complexity for each review.
- M.05 Number of necessary related documents for each review.
- M.06 Document (programming) language for each review.
- M.07 Effort spent on each review.
- M.08 Date for each review.
- M.10 Severity for each fault for each review.
- M.11 Other detection mechanism for each fault for each review.
- M.12 Name of the reviewer.

Question 2 was 'what are the characteristics of a document, in order to obtain optimal effect of a review'? This question focuses on the definition of criteria that define whether a review will obtain the required effects. The question will give an answer to which characteristics a certain document should posses in order to result in a specified result of a review.

Detailed questions focusing on practical experience by project team:

- Q.2.1 What is the influence of document size on the review performance and effectiveness?
- Q.2.2 What is the influence of document complexity on the review performance and effectiveness?
- Q.2.3 What is the influence of a number of related documents on the review performance and effectiveness?
- Q.2.4 What is the influence of specification language on the review performance and effectiveness?
- Q.2.5 What is the influence of product subsystem on the review performance and effectiveness?

The following metrics have been associated to these questions:

- document name;
- subsystem to which the document belongs;
- document size;
- document specification language;
- document complexity;
- effort for a review;
- average number of faults found;
- average distribution of faults over severity;
- number of faults per page for a document;
- number of faults detected in the document after the review.

The above metrics resulted in the following direct measurements:

- M.01 Document name for each review.
- M.02 Document subsystem for each review.
- M.03 Document length for each review.
- M.04 Document cyclomatic complexity for each review.
- M.05 Number of necessary related documents for each review.
- M.06 Document (programming) language for each review.
- M.07 Effort spent on each review.
- M.10 Severity for each fault for each review.
- M.99 Document name for each fault found later on in the process (this metric will be very important to answer the question, however, at this stage it is not clear how this will be measured).

Question 3 was 'what are the acceptance criteria for the quality of the document, after a review'? This question focuses on the possibility to identify if a reviewed document has an acceptable quality level. Therefore it should be investigated whether criteria can be defined to which the performance of a review must be met in order to identify an acceptable quality level.

This question is answered when the possibilities for such criteria are understood, and when possible values to those criteria are known.

Detailed questions focusing on practical experience by project team:

- Q.3.1 Is the number of faults a usable criteria for identifying whether a second review is necessary or not?
- Q.3.2 What is the amount of failures to be found on average, in order to claim that a document is of high quality?
- Q.3.3 What is the effect of a review on the improvement of a document?
- Q.3.4 Is the effort spent on repairing failures a usable indicator of product quality?

Metrics:

- document name;
- subsystem to which the document belongs;
- document size;
- document specification language;
- document complexity;
- effort for a review;
- average number of faults found;
- average number of faults repaired;
- effort for repairing faults found;
- average balance between faults found and faults repaired;
- average distribution of faults over severity;
- number of faults per page for the document;
- number of open questions per page for the document;
- another review necessary for the document;
- quality improvement due to the review;
- number of faults detected in the document after the review.

Direct measurements:

- M.01 Document name for each review.
- M.02 Document subsystem for each review.
- M.03 Document length for each review.
- M.04 Document cyclomatic complexity for each review.
- M.05 Number of necessary related documents for each review.
- M.06 Document (programming) language for each review.
- M.13 Number of faults transported to TLOG.
- M.14 Another review of the document required (Yes/No) for each review.
- M.07 Effort spent on each review.
- M.15 Effort spent on repairing failures.
- M.10 Severity for each fault for each review.
- M.16 Repaired/Not Repaired for each fault found in the review.
- M.17 Number of open questions for each review.
- M.99 Document name for each fault found later on in the process (this metric will be very important to answer the question, however, at this stage it is not clear how this will be measured).

Question 4 was 'are reviews a useful and efficient method for training new engineers'? This question is answered when all learning abilities have been identified, and their effects can be quantified. What is the difference in review performance between new and experienced engineers?

- Q.4.1 Detailed questions focusing on practical experience by project team
- Q.4.2 Does a new engineer learn much from reviewing?
- Q.4.3 What is the learning effect of asking questions based on a review?
- Q.4.4 Does knowledge on a document improve quickly, by reviewing it?

Metrics:

- knowledge of reviewer on the document before the review;
- knowledge of reviewer on the specification language before the review;
- knowledge of reviewer on the subsystem before the review;
- knowledge of reviewer on the document after the review;
- knowledge of reviewer on the specification language after the review;
- knowledge of reviewer on the subsystem after the review;
- amount learned from the review;
- experience in software engineering for the reviewer;
- experience of the reviewer;
- number of open questions for the review;
- number of necessary questions during the review;
- number of questions resolved after the review meeting;
- subsystem to which the document belongs;
- document specification language;
- effort for a review;
- effort for review meeting;
- another review necessary for the document.

Direct measurements:

- M.18 Knowledge of reviewer on the document before the review.
- M.20 Knowledge of reviewer on the specification language before the review.
- M.22 Knowledge of reviewer on the subsystem before the review.
- M.19 Knowledge of reviewer on the document after the review.
- M.21 Knowledge of reviewer on the specification language after the review.
- M.23 Knowledge of reviewer on the subsystem after the review.
- M.24 Amount learned for each review.
- M.17 Number of open questions for each review.
- M.25 Number of questions resolved after the review meeting for each review meeting.
- M.02 Document subsystem for each review.
- M.06 Document (programming) language for each review.
- M.07 Effort spent on each review.
- M.26 Effort spent on each review meeting.
- M.14 Another review of the document required (Yes/No) for each review.

Hypotheses regarding direct measurements

During the interviews hypotheses have been collected regarding the expected outcome of the measurements. The expectations were combined, and when their hypothesis did not differ too much, an average was calculated. The following hypotheses are defined:

- The balance between minor, major and fatal faults respectively is about 70%, 25%, 5%.
- If a document is created by an inexperienced engineer, an experienced engineer will find 65 faults per hour in that document, if reviewed by an inexperienced engineer, 35 faults per hour will be found.
- If a document is created by an experienced engineer, an experienced engineer will find 30 faults per hour in that document, if reviewed by an inexperienced engineer, 20 faults per hour will be found.
- An experienced reviewer will have 2.5 open questions after reviewing a page.
- An inexperienced reviewer will have 5 open questions after reviewing a page.
- If a document is created by an experienced engineer, 3 faults will be found per page.
- If a document is created by an inexperienced engineer, 7 faults will be found per page.

Distribution of faults among the categories in which the faults would have been detected if not reviewed is given in the table below.

A number of other, more detailed, hypotheses were defined as well. These will be described in the forthcoming analysis phase.

Measurement plan

The measurement plan included the following measurements:

- M.01 Document name for each review. This metric gives the name of the document that will be reviewed.
- M.02 Document subsystem for each review. This metric gives the name of the subsystem of the product to which the document belongs.
- M.03 Document length for each review. This metric describes the length of the document in lines of code. The scale will be KSLOC, which are all lines minus blank lines and comment lines.
- M.04 Document cyclomatic complexity for each review. This metric describes

	Experienced engineer	Inexperienced engineer
unit test	40%	12%
system test	10%	3%
Installation test	20%	6%
field test (pilot release), customer use	10%	3%
never because is exceptional situation	10%	3%
never because is lay-out fault (coding standard)	10%	73%

Figure 10-15: Executed reviews, divided according to experience level of developer or reviewer.

McCabes cyclomatic complexity which gives the number of possible programme paths in the code.

- M.05 Number of necessary related documents for each review. This metric describes the number of documents that is referred to in the document for the review. In the case of programming code this means the number of other files that are necessary to review that specific part of the code.
- M.06 Document (programming) language for each review. This metric describes the language in which the document is written. Possible values are natural language, specification language, assembler, plain C, C^{++}, Sycero, etc.
- M.07 Effort spent on each review. This metric gives the amount of time that is spent on reviewing the document. This effort can be given in minutes or hours.
- M.08 Date for each review. This metric gives the date on which the review is executed.
- M.09 Effort estimated for each review. This metric gives the amount of time that is estimated in advance, for the effort that will be spent on reviewing the document.
- M.10 Severity for each fault for each review. This metric describes the level to which the fault may influence future performance of the product. The categories are minor, major and fatal.
- M.11 Other detection mechanism for each fault for each review. This metric describes in which fault detection event a fault would be found, if it was not found during the review. Possible values are: unit test, system test, field test, installation test, never and unknown.
- M.12 Name of the reviewer. This metric defines the name of the person who has reviewed the document.
- M.13 Number of faults transported to TLOG. This metric describes the number of faults found that could not be solved during the repair phase, but which were serious enough to be solved at a later stage.
- M.14 Another review of the document required (Yes/No) for each review. This metric gives advice as to whether it is necessary to review the document again, after the faults have been repaired. This metric defines a kind of trust (reliability) in the document. Possible values are Yes or No.
- M.15 Effort spent on repairing failures. This metric describes the amount of time that is used for repairing the faults that were found in the review.
- M.16 Repaired/Not Repaired for each fault found in the review. This metric describes each fault found in the review whether it has been repaired or not. If a fault is not fixed, it is possible to enter a reason for that on the form.
- M.17 Number of open questions for each review. This metric defines the number of open questions that are raised, by reviewing the document.
- M.18 Reviewer's knowledge of the document before the review. This metric describes the reviewer's knowledge of the document before the review is started. This level of knowledge is given on a scale from 0 to 10.
- M.19 Reviewer's knowledge of the document after the review. This metric describes the reviewer's knowledge of the document after the review has been done. This level of knowledge is given on a scale from 0 to 10.
- M.20 Reviewer's knowledge of the specification language before the review. This metric describes the reviewer's knowledge of the specification language before the review is started. This level of knowledge is given on a scale from 0 to10.

- M.21 Reviewer's knowledge of the specification language after the review. This metric describes the reviewer's knowledge of the specification language after the review has been done. This level of knowledge is given on a scale from 0 to 10.
- M.22 Reviewer's knowledge of the subsystem before the review. This metric describes the reviewer's knowledge of the subsystem before the review is started. This level of knowledge is given on a scale from 0 to 10.
- M.23 Reviewer's knowledge of the subsystem after the review. This metric describes the reviewer's knowledge of the subsystem after the review has been done. This level of knowledge is given on a scale from 0 to 10.
- M.24 Amount learned for each review. This metric scales the amount that has been learnt by reviewing the document. This level of learning is given on a scale from 0 to 10.
- M.25 Number of questions resolved after each review meeting. This metric describes the number of open questions of the reviewer that were resolved after a review meeting.
- M.26 Effort spent on each review meeting. This metric identifies the amount of time spent on a review meeting.
- M.99 Document name for each fault found later on in the process (this metric will be very important to answer the stated question, however, at this stage it is not clear how this will be measured).

10.6.2 Review form of the RITME project

Explanation of the review form

The review form of the RIME project is illustrated on the next two pages. General guidelines for filling in the form:

- The form is divided according to phases and/or persons.
- Wherever input is expected, a line is depicted: ....
- When a selection is required, characters are typed using italic, underlined capitals: *YES / NO.*

1. Defining the review:

Document name:	....
Subsystem:	....
Current release.:	.....
(Progr.) Language:	.....

Date: ...../...../.....

Estimated effort for the Review: *MINUTES/HOURS*

Developer: ....
Reviewer: ....

Primary review focus: *fault finding/learning*

2. Review preparation:

	None	Low		Medium		High		Super
Knowledge of the reviewer of the document:	0	1	2	3	4	5	6	7	8	9	10
Knowledge of the reviewer of the subsystem:	0	1	2	3	4	5	6	7	8	9	10
Experience of the reviewer of the progr. language:	0	1	2	3	4	5	6	7	8	9	10

Document Length: ....LOC   Cycl.Compl.(VG2):   ....   # Comm. lines: ....

These values can be calculated by executing the COUNT program. If a path is available to U:\UTIL\ it is OK to run it from the source directory. Syntax: **TELMET filename.ext ext** (So CPP or C has to be typed again)

3. Executing the review:

Review Date: ...../...../.....

Number of questions asked during the review: ......questions
Number of Faults:
Minors: ....   Majors: ....   Fatals: ....

Where would the **major** and **fatal** faults be found if this document was not reviewed?:
Unit test:.....   Acceptance test:.....   Integration test:.....   Installation:....   Field(test):.....

Effort spent on the review: _____   *MINUTES / HOURS*
Number of questions to ask in the review meeting: ..... questions

4. Review meeting:

Review meeting held with: ....

Effort spent on review meeting: _____   *MINUTES / HOURS*
Number of questions solved: ....questions

If all faults found are repaired, is a second review then necessary?   *YES / NO*

	None	Low		Medium		High		Super
Knowledge of the reviewer of the document:	0	1	2	3	4	5	6	7	8	9	10
Knowledge of the reviewer of the subsystem:	0	1	2	3	4	5	6	7	8	9	10
Experience of the reviewer of the (progr.) language:	0	1	2	3	4	5	6	7	8	9	10
How much did you learn from this review?:	0	1	2	3	4	5	6	7	8	9	10

5. Review fault repair:

Number of faults repaired:
Minors: ....   Majors: ....   Fatals: ....

Number of faults reported in TLOG: ....
Effort spent on repair: _____   *MINUTES / HOURS*

6. Comments:

No.	Page	Line	m	M	F	Description	Repaired
1							
2							
3							
4							
5							
6							
7							
8							
9							
10							
11							
12							
13							
14							
15							
16							
17							
18							
19							
20							
21							
22							
23							
24							
25							
26							
27							
28							
29							
30							
31							
32							
33							
34							

Guidelines for specific elements:

- 2. Review preparation:
  Document length: the length of the reviewed part of the document.
- 3. Executing the review:
  - *Number of questions during the review*: the number of questions asked during execution of the review in order to be able to continue reviewing.
  - *Number of faults*: all faults found during the review; when the same fault is found more than once, every occurrence should be counted.
  - *Number of questions to ask in the review meeting*: the number of questions the reviewer has on the reviewed document after reviewing the document.
- 4. Review meeting:
  Number of questions solved: those questions resulting from the review (as recorded as 'Number of questions to ask in the review meeting' in point 3) that were sufficiently answered in the meeting.
- 6. Comment:
  If desirable, the reviewer or developer can add comment to the items on the form.

Definition tables:

- For fault severity the following table was used.

Minor	Major	Fatal
Faults that would affect only the non-functional aspects of the software element	*Faults that would result in failure of the software element(s) or an observable departure from specification*	*Fault that results in the complete inability of a system or component to function*
Aesthetic problems such as: • misspelling • output formatting problem	• system refuses legitimate transactions • system produces redundant outputs with small impact on performance	• system fails • system executes wrong transactions • system loses transactions

- For alternative detection the following table was used.

Unit test	Separate testing of a (separately testable) component
Acceptance test	testing to determine whether a system satisfies its acceptance criteria
Integration test	testing of which components are combined and tested to evaluate the interaction between them
Installation	customisation and installation of the system
Field (test)	operational use of the system

CODE REVIEW CHECKLIST

1. Are the comments added to the modules and procedures sufficient?	
2. Are the comments useful? Do they agree with the code?	
3. Does the product match the coding standard?	
4. Is the code clear and easy to understand?	
5. Are meaningful names used that won't get confused?	
6. Are there redundant code segments?	
7. Are all variables and parameters being used?	
8. Was 'Check programme' used to check the code?	
9. Does the code use local rather than global variables whenever possible?	
10. Is all memory allocated (via 'new') freed again (via 'delete')?	
11. Is all memory allocated(via 'malloc') freed again (via 'free')?	
12. Does each CASE statement contain a 'default' switch?	
13. Are all variables initialised before use?	
14. Are constants used whenever possible?	
15. Is the branch taken the correct way on logical tests?	
16. Will the code work correctly under the loop boundary conditions?	
17. Were any EXIT commands used?	

What other items should be included in this checklist? Which should be eliminated?

_____

_____

_____

_____

_____

_____

_____

_____

_____

_____

_____

10.6.3 Example feedback session report of the RITME project

This section contains the final feedback session report of RITME.

FEEDBACK SESSION REPORT		
Project Name: Project B	Project No: QAxxxxxx	Date:
Meeting Date:	Present: xxxxxxx	
Author: xxxxx	Absent: xxxxxxx	
Subject: Final feedback session for the RITME measurement programme		

Introduction

This is the report of the final feedback session of the RITME measurement programme. It was the objective of this session to try to answer all original GQM questions and by it reach the goal. A clear learning process had been visible within the group on reviews and their effects. This report had two purposes:

1. report on the final feedback session;
2. capture the learning points of the reviewing programme, to be spread to other engineering groups whenever they are interested in the results.

The structure of this report equals the structure of the original GQM plan. First the goal of the measurement programme is presented again:

Analyse:	the effectiveness of structured reviews
for the purpose of:	understanding
with respect to:	- the detection of faults
	- the learning ability of the technique
from the viewpoint of:	the project team
in the following context:	project B

To give some more explanation to this goal, what the characteristics of reviews are related to their detection capability is studied. At the same time the way in which reviewing contributes to group-learning and individual learning is also studied. Finally, it is added that a feedback process as implemented within this programme also contributed to establishing a team-spirit. It also created self-critique within the team, which resulted in a self-evaluation of the team during a feedback session.

General conclusions on measuring reviews

The reviews during the development process turned out to:

- be an efficient aid to detect faults;
- improve the uniformity and maintainability of code;
- increase communication and understanding within a development team;
- require five minutes per page;
- detect more than one fatal/major fault per hour;
- detect 7.5 faults per hour;
- should be done on documents smaller than 50 pages;
- are more effective on documents of a maximum of 20 pages;

- are four times more efficient compared to testing;
- should be done for one hour a week per engineer;
- should be supported by measurement to maintain continuation.

Conclusions regarding Q.1: What are the baselines (rules of thumb) for executing reviews?

The associated effort of executing reviews was stated as follows:

- Reviewing detects faults with a speed of 7.5 faults per hour.
- Divided over severity this is:
  - fatal and major: 1.25 faults per hour;
  - minors: 6.25 faults per hour.
- Many minors are detected in a review, which improve readability, maintainability, and create a generic coding style.
- Several types of minors are detected. Classification of those could be helpful to show detailed effectiveness of reviews.
- Reviews are useful to make sure that coding standards are applied, and maintained.
- When reviewing speed is faster than two minutes per page, results get reasonably lower.

Alternative detection:

- Comparing reviewing to testing, the technique appears to be four times more efficient, considering fatals and majors.
- Comparing reviewing to testing, the technique is over six times more efficient for minor faults.
- Alternative detections for faults found in reviewing are mainly 'unit test' and 'system test'. Although these findings were concluded to be incorrect during feedback sessions, since installation and field-test *do* find faults. It was noted that a 'never' category should be added.

Planning reviews:

- Reviewing takes on average 20 minutes per week per engineer.
- This depends on development phase. During weeks with intensive reviewing each engineer spends 1.5 hours on reviewing.
- Each hour of reviewing needs 15 minutes to repair the faults found.
- On average, reviewing takes three minutes per page.
- Cyclomatic complexity did not give a better indication for estimating review length, but this was also caused by problems with the calculation tool.

Document characteristics:

- Reviewing design documents in text processor format takes twice as long: six minutes per page.
- But also twice as much faults are found per page. For code 0.2 faults are found per page, for designs 0.4 faults are found per page. (Note: literature describes a rule of thumb of 10 faults per page, when 15 minutes per page are spent on reviewing).

Influences from subsystems:

- Subsystems appear to give differences in reviewing effort. It is expected that this is caused by characteristics of that sub-system. Also, object orientation requires more time than sequential code. More detailed analyses have not been performed.
- The subsystem characteristics should be examined, as should their relation to review effort.

Conclusions regarding Q.2: What are the characteristics of a document, to get optimal effect from a review?

Size:

- Documents with more than 50 pages are unsuitable for reviews.
- Results show a drop in review performance for documents larger than 20 pages.

Language:

- Both text processor and CPP documents find 4.0 faults per hour.
- However, text processor documents require twice as much effort per page, and twice as many faults per page are detected for text processor documents.

Subsystem:

- Results of subsystems differ, but underlying causes are not clear yet.
- Further analyses should be done, based on more detailed subsystem characteristics.

Complexity:

- Results of comparing cyclomatic complexity were disappointing, mainly caused by trouble with the calculation tool.

Conclusions regarding Q.3: What are the acceptance criteria for the quality of the document, after a review?

This question appeared to be a little over-ambitious. During this project we learned that statistical acceptance criteria for documents after reviewing seem unrealistic. Both reviewer and developer have enough insight to accept or reject a document based on a subjective quality assessment.

Conclusions regarding Q.4: Are reviews a useful and efficient method for training new engineers?

Regarding the learning curve of new engineers:

- New engineers learn most from reviewing code from experienced engineers.
- Level of understanding after a review is sufficient (score: 6), not depending on whether the reviewer or developer is experienced or not.
- During the first six months most reviews were carried out by experienced engineers that reviewed documents from new engineers. After six months this changed, then the new engineers were reviewing each others documents.
- New engineers learn more from other new engineers after six months of reviewing.

- Training should subsequently consist of:
  - courses to provide relevant theory and general overview;
  - reviews to learn system details;
  - on-the-job training providing practical experience.

Learning effect of holding review meeting:

- No data was available on this subject, however, review meetings were experienced as an important means for learning and communication.

Difference between new and experienced engineers:

- Experienced engineers review two times faster than new engineers.
- Experienced engineers find twice the number of faults as new engineers.

Action points resulting from the measurement programme

The following action points were formulated during the measurement programme:

1. Define a new measurement programme focused on project management, including time spent and fault management. This measurement programme should also cover reviews.
2. Study subsystems in more detail, to clarify the various relations stipulated in this document.
3. Promote (this kind of) reviewing to other engineering departments, preferably in department '...'.

10.7   Questions and assignments

10.7.1   Questions

1. What are the two most important purposes of reviews in the RITME measurement programme?
2. Which metrics of the GQM plan, are not included in Figure 10-1, however, could well have been included?
3. What is the main difference between the measurement support system of Chapter 9 and of Chapter 10?
4. How many defects are detected per hour on average in software reviews?
5. Figure 10-8 contains a comparison between reviewing of software and two tests of software. Which mistake can be made in comparing these data regarding defects found, considering that reviews and tests were performed on the same product?
6. What can be concluded regarding review effectiveness and document size, considering Figure 10-10 and Figure 10-11?
7. Figure 10-13 illustrates learning effects. What was concluded from this figure and how does this conflict with what happened six months later?

10.7.2 Assignments

The GQM plan of RITME also contained more detailed questions raised by project team members.

1. Do you consider that the abstraction to higher level questions was done appropriately? Do the questions, for example, meet the criteria given in Chapter 6.
2. Take the final feedback session report and identify which questions in the GQM plan can be considered over-ambitious, also explain why?

11   Case C: interrupt measurement

11.1   Description of project C

This chapter describes the results of an interrupt measurement programme. This measurement programme investigated the causes and effects of interrupts during software development work. An interrupt is defined as a: *distortion that makes a developer stop his actual activity to respond to the initiator.* Even though many of the interrupts were necessary, they still caused problems for the interrupted engineer. An interrupt does not only stop an engineer from working, but also implies additional (often not planned) work. Eventually, this may cause project planning problems, stress, quality problems, or delay of delivery dates.

The project team of this measurement programme was dedicated to develop and maintain the central control unit in a fuel dispenser of a petrol station. This control unit was termed a 'calculator' and controls all fuel transactions, from activating the fuel pump and valves, to authorisation requesting and transaction processing to the cashing or payment device. Such calculators consist of about 50,000 lines of source code, about equally divided over the programming languages C and assembler. The project team developed and maintained both hardware and software in parallel and consisted of two hardware engineers, two software engineers and their manager. At the time of the interrupt measurement programme the team was maintaining a new (lower cost) increment of a calculator, which was developed in a period of six months.

This measurement programme was started because the development group experienced problems with interrupts, mainly reflected by planning problems and project delays. The aim of the programme was to achieve basic understanding of the frequency of interrupt occurrence and interrupt causes. Based on that level of understanding it was expected that interrupts could be planned, causal analysis could be performed, and corrective actions could be taken.

Most software measurement literature warns against, or even forbids, measuring people (Goodman, 1993). Although one should always consider the delicate nature of measuring people factors, in this case it is not possible to avoid measuring individuals. Perry reports

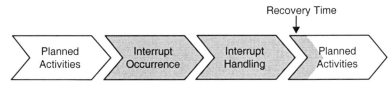

Figure 11-1: Model of an 'interrupt'.

Aspects of Interrupts	
Positive Aspects	**Negative Aspects**
• Part of developer's task	• Not a part of developer's task
• Supports problem solving	• Does not prevent problems
• Stimulates social interaction	• Requires extra 'interrupt' effort
• Random communication essential for development work	• Causes projects to delay
• Provides overview of current status development work	• Disturbs concentration of developers
Aspects of Measuring Interrupts	
Positive Aspects	**Negative Aspects**
• Creation of interrupt awareness	• Discourages 'appropriate' interrupts
• Establishment of 'improvement' culture	• Requires additional effort (but profits can be gained)
• Visualisation of interrupt causes and effects	• Measuring human aspects is 'not allowed'

Figure 11-2: Example of positive and negative aspects of interrupt measurement

from his research in development organisations that *'people are willing to be observed and measured if you take proper precautions'* (Perry et al, 1994).

Some positive and negative aspects of interrupts learned from this measurement programme are described in Figure 11-2.

No consensus exists on whether interrupts are in the end positive or negative. Although many developers consider interrupts part of development work, interrupts are not always positive. One of the strengths of interrupts is their ability to solve development problems. However, this is also a weakness since problems must be prevented, which is not done when an organisation relies on the interrupt mechanism. Measuring interrupts results in awareness of the negative aspects of interrupts. Negative aspects appear to decrease when this interrupt awareness increases, because initiators of interrupts start considering the importance of each interrupt.

The results presented in this chapter are based on the complete measurement programme. Results are not only the measurement data, but also conclusions drawn by the project team, or action taken based on the measurements. The Interrupt measurement programme will be described by the four phases of the GQM method: planning, definition, data collection, and interpretation.

This chapter also includes the practical deliverables of this programme, such as the GQM plan, data collection forms and feedback charts. Deliverables that might be reused in similar measurement programmes are included in the last section of this chapter. More information on interrupt measurement can be found in the article 'Interrupts: just a minute never is' (Solingen et al, 1998).

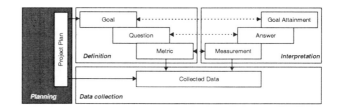

11.2   Planning

An independent GQM team already existed in the department. This team discussed with the project team what the role could be of the measurement programme in the context of the organisation's improvement programme. By means of a refinement method from business goals into operational improvement goals, the measurement goal was selected. It was decided to focus on a problem that the project team struggled with: Interrupts. The necessary training for the project team was given by the GQM team, which already had experience with the practical application of GQM. The planning phase delivered a project plan.

Before measurement goals could be specified, it was identified which improvement areas, problems, or organisational (business) goals were relevant. We used a structured brainstorming session to identify the improvement areas. In this brainstorming session all the people involved in the measurement programme were present. It was started at a company wide level and concentrated on what the purpose of the organisation is, focused towards the specific team, and finalised by ending on a level of specific problems or improvements. We applied the 'seven questions' approach for Goal-oriented measurement (based on Parker et al, 1988) that proved to be applicable for such sessions:

1. What are the strategic goals of your organisation?
2. What forces have impact on our strategic goals?
3. What are your strategies to reach the strategic goals of your organisation?
4. A. How can you improve your performance?
   B. What are your major concerns (problems)?
5. What are your improvement goals?
6. How will you reach your improvement goals?
7. A. What are possible measurement goals
   B. Which measurement goals will you take?

We customised these 'seven questions' to the situation of this particular project team. An improvement goal definition session was held to identify the need for a measurement programme, to instruct on the application of the software measurement programme, and to define the improvement goals. The (summarised) answers that were formulated by the project team are:

1. What is the objective of the project team?
   - The group is responsible for all functionality that is available between the dispenser and the shop.
   - Development, maintenance, knowledge acquisition, training and support.
   - The group must anticipate the market (customer) and technology.
   - The group has a central position between all departments.

2. What is the function of (software/hardware) development in the project team?
   - The realisation and implementation of required functionality.

- Optimisation in terms of reliability (serviceability), efficiency (manufacturability) and extendibility (maintainability).
- The realisation of significant cost reduction

3. What are the strategic goals of the project team?
    - Visibility in the development process.
    - To guarantee the reliability (quality) of products
    - Cost reduction.
    - Analyse and optimise the distribution of functionality in products.
    - To implement connectivity to the different devices

4. What are possible performance improvements?
    - Improve effectiveness of testing (eg more testing time, external testing and end user testing).
    - Reduction of failures in products after release.
    - Improvement of specifications.
    - Improvement of communication and information.
    - Management of time and in particular of interrupts.
    - Management of responsibilities.
    - Reduce the impact of organisational changes.

5. What are the major concerns (problems)?
    - The project members identified that the major problems were already defined in question 4.

6. What are possible measurement goals?
    - Effect of interrupts on work and planning, types of interrupts.
    - Classifying interrupts and their effects.
    - Origin of failures after release and the reasons for not detecting failures before release.
    - Cost reduction as a cause for faults.

7. Which measurement goals will be chosen?
    - Understanding interrupts.

The project was characterised by filling out a characterisation questionnaire. This questionnaire included both quantitative and qualitative questions. The results of the characterisation were used to create the project plan for this specific measurement programme. The characterisation was carried out prior to the session in which the improvement areas and measurement goals were selected.

This measurement programme did not support a specific project, but supported a department. The people in this department are, however, referred to as 'the project team'. This project team develops components consisting of hardware (electronics) and software. However, the project team also gives support to the national representatives on new and old products.

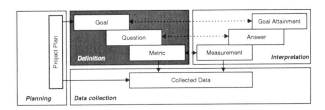

11.3   Definition

During the meeting on defining the improvement goal, the measurement goal was defined as well. Restated in a goal template the measurement goal was:

Analyse:	interrupts and their effects
for the purpose of:	understanding
with respect to:	- impact on schedule
	- the cost/benefit of interrupts
from the viewpoint of:	project team
in the following context:	project C

The refinement of the measurement goal into question and metrics was done using the knowledge acquisition techniques described in Chapter 4. However, in this case no individual interviews were held, but the project team was divided in groups of two to three persons for the definition of questions, metrics and hypotheses. Since the project team consisted of hardware and software engineers, the groups were so organised that at least one hardware engineer and one software engineer were in each session. The question session with the project manager was held separately since he might have a different viewpoint than the engineers.

As described in Section 6.2.4, questions should be described on an intermediate level between the goal, and the metrics. The questions that were formulated during these question sessions appeared to be of a practical but too detailed level. It was found difficult to define questions on a more abstract level. The GQM team decided to perform this abstraction, and let the project team define the practical questions they found relevant. Each session was started by repeating the concepts of GQM, summarising the activities that were already performed, and explaining the activities that are planned. Also the purpose and structure of each session was explained. After each question session two documents were made:

1. Preliminary GQM plan. Describing the goal to question refinement, and already abstracting some of the questions to a more abstract level. An initial abstraction sheet was also included.
2. Report on the session. This report was distributed to each project team member that was present during a session. Abstracting some of the questions to a more general level, was already done in these reports, creating the possibility for the project team to respond to these changes.

Abstracting all the questions to a general level was necessary because the questions were formulated as metrics (for example: 'How many interrupts are caused by documentation issues?'). The part of the GQM plan that describes the goals, and the refinement to question for this measurement programme is included in Section 11.6.1. The question definition sessions were effective for defining the measurement questions. Following the question definition sessions, the preliminary GQM plan was developed, that described all questions and their relation to the measurement goal. These questions are:

- What is the distribution of interrupts over particular factors, related with the occurrence of an interrupt?
- What factors influence treatment and effort for handling an interrupt?
- Is prevention of interrupts possible?
- Should we change our reserved effort for interrupts?
- What is the influence of interrupts on the work that was interrupted?
- What are the total costs of interrupts?

The next step could now be performed: defining metrics that should provide answers to these questions.

Metrics had to be defined that provide the information that is needed to answer each question. Also hypotheses were needed from the project team on expected measurement results. During the sessions, the project team supported the definition of the metrics and in according classifications, and stated their hypotheses. These sessions were also supported by on-line display on the overhead projector, creating an interactive group-working environment that was suitable to formulate definitions by a group. The hypotheses were given by the project team members on a numerical scale (eg 0 to 10, 1 to 5 or 1 to 100) and those numbers were recalculated to percentages. This was done to give all project members the possibility to define hypotheses in their personally preferred way. Recalculating these hypotheses to percentages gave the possibility to compare them between the group members.

Refining the questions to metrics was not very difficult, because the questions were abstracted from 'metric-like' questions, so the process of defining metrics was already carried out implicitly. The definition of influencing factors and hypotheses regarding the metrics was done in these sessions as well. After the goal formulating sessions, question sessions and metric sessions, the GQM plan was completed, describing the refinement from goals to questions to metrics. For every question it was defined which metrics had to be collected in order to answer the particular question. Both direct metrics (measuring only one attribute), and indirect metrics were defined. An additional layer was added to the GQM plan defining all direct metrics that had to be collected to construct all indirect metrics. For the direct measurements, the following issues had to be identified:

- When they should be measured?
- What possible values their outcomes could have?
- What they would actually measure (textual description)?
- What medium would be used for data collection?

These issues were addressed in the measurement plan. The measurement plan also presented the data collection media (forms, procedures and tools). When the measurement plan and GQM plan were constructed and approved, measurement started.

As described in Section 6.3, the GQM approach applies software development process and product models for checking the GQM metric definitions. The availability and development of these models in parallel with the definition of goals, questions and metrics appeared to be very useful. Through a model on interrupts it became clear, how interrupts could occur and how they could be handled. It was also assumed that the availability of the models prevented many problems, because the data collection forms and procedures could be cross-checked. The availability of these models on software development offer the possibility to apply a second source of relevant information. The first sources are the participating project members. However, when the project members were focusing on a certain problem (or goal), it was difficult to extract all their knowledge, and at the same time maintain a global overview. By applying formal models of software development processes and products, this missing overview was compensated for. The models should be suitable for defining metrics, and should, therefore, focus on both processes and products.

Checking the GQM plan against the software development process models was continuously done during the definition of the measurement programme. This provided the possibility to discuss possible inconsistencies immediately with the project team during each session. The models also provided a framework to the GQM team when they were preparing the various sessions.

During the definition of the GQM plan there was a continuous focus on possible problems with the analyses of the data. The GQM plan should describe how to analyse measurement data, in order to answer questions of the project team, and/or to conclude on a measurement goal.

11.4   Data collection

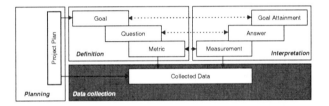

The data collection forms were developed in parallel with the development of the measurement plan, and iteratively enhanced by the GQM team. After some adjustments to the forms, they were agreed upon, and a measurement kick-off-meeting was held. During this meeting the GQM plan, the defined models, and the data collection forms and procedures were explained and presented to the project team. It was decided to start interrupt measurement the week after.

The data collection resulted in a significant amount of data (more than 1000 data points were collected in the first week).

The MSS for handling the data was developed using a spreadsheet tool. Manual data collection forms were used by the project team, which were manually entered into the metrics base by a member of the GQM team. The data collection form was designed in such a way that the registration of an interrupt by a project member would only take a couple of seconds, already in the perspective that many interrupts were expected.

While entering the data into the metrics base, data correctness and completeness was checked manually. The MSS was developed in parallel with the first measurement period. Once the MSS was completed, the first feedback session could be held. No linking features were included in this MSS, because no knowledge or experience existed at that time.

11.5 Interpretation

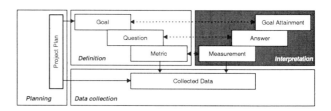

This section describes the results of the measurement programme as discussed in the feedback sessions. The measurement programme was started to identify the influence of interrupts on schedules, the cost of interrupts, and the causes for interrupts. The possibilities to manage, decrease and plan interrupts were also investigated.

After six weeks of measurement it already became clear that the number of interrupts doubled the expected amount, and a large percentage of them were caused by personal visits (55%). Personal visits require more effort compared to telephone or e-mail. The average effort per interrupt for personal visits were 13 minutes, for telephone 10 minutes, and for e-mail 8 minutes. The project team defined three action points:

- Reduce the number of personal visits.
- Promote applying e-mail, at least for less urgent interrupts.
- Create interrupt awareness among the initiators in order to make clear to initiators that interrupts are sometimes a burden.

The department spent approximately 20% of its total time on handling interrupts. Measurement results identified that 25% of all interrupts were about products or tasks that the department was not responsible for.

It appeared that due to the measurement activities, project members and initiators of interrupts became more aware of the impact of interrupts. This already caused some improvements in the occurrence of interrupts in the department. Initiators started to balance the importance and urgency of an interrupt before disturbing a project member.

The first feedback session was a bit disappointing since no real conclusions were drawn, or discussions were started. The project team appeared to be a bit passive in interpreting the analysis material. In the second feedback session the project team was challenged significantly. A list of observations and statements on the data analysis slides were created and handed over to the team members a week before the feedback session. Together with the statement and observation list each team member received:

- a set of personal data graphics;
- a one page overview of his personal interrupt data;
- a set of personal interrupt data overviews (one page each) of the other team members;
- a set of data graphics and a one page interrupt data overview of the whole group.

Instead of showing a lot of data graphics, the list of observations and statements was discussed to structure the feedback session. In this meeting there was much more discussion, and several clear action (improvement) points were defined. The general impression of all attendees about the meeting and the delivered data was positive. Remarks on the observations and statements in the feedback sessions were:

- Interrupts were perceived as being useful and not negative. Interrupts provided the possibility to remain informed about other activities and were necessary to run the business. Also interrupts on products or tasks the dispenser electronics group were not responsible for, were often regarded as useful.
- It was stated that the measurement programme influences the behaviour of people. Several examples were given of people that became cautious about interrupting team members. Therefore, informing the rest of the organisation about the results of the measurement programme and explaining the effects of the interrupts, would be a clear action point for the next period.
- Persons visiting caused a majority of the interrupts (55%). The idea was to reduce this number by using other ways of interrupting such as electronic mail. Other ideas would be gathered during the next period. The fact that 55% of all interrupts were visits, did not imply that those interrupts could have been done by e-mail or phone, however, the project team estimated that a certain part of the interrupts could be made in a less disturbing way.
- The rule of thumb used in the department is that 20% of the total available time is spent on miscellaneous issues (including interrupts). Due to the measurements it was identified that already 20% of the total time was spent on interrupts. The idea of the project team was that an additional 10% is spent on other miscellaneous issues than interrupts. When 20% is included in the planning this implies that 10% of the project teams work must be done in spare time (1 hour per day additional effort would be required).
- The maximum level of interrupts is expected to be 10 per day. At higher rates the time between interrupts cannot be used efficiently anymore. Proposals for handling this were for instance: use a 'do not disturb' sign, closing the door of the office, or promoting making appointments.
- Level of detail of information contained in the interrupt appeared to have no influence on the handling of the interrupt. This was derived from the measurement data, and the project team confirmed this observation.
- A new, more simplified interrupt registration form was suggested and it was agreed to also use the form to add ideas for corrective actions on specific interrupts.

Three practical conclusions from the interrupt measurements are listed:

1. If more than ten interrupts occur during a day, the time between the interrupts is too short for development work. This is in line with the results from Perry, which show that developers perform work in blocks of two hours (Perry et al, 1994).
2. Project plans used to include 20% slack for unexpected activities. It appeared that more than 15% is already spent on interrupts, which could be an explanation for planning delays. One possible solution is to increase slack in planning, or to reduce the number of interrupts.
3. Interrupts during meetings should be reduced to zero. Such interrupts turned out to be very expensive because discussions are blocked for so many people.

Improvements were achieved regarding interrupts. For example, the number of interrupts during meetings decreased to almost zero. For the remaining interrupts during meetings, the effort was reduced by 50%. Also, the number of interrupts on documentation issues was reduced by 80%, mainly by updating and distributing documentation.

To influence the initiators of interrupts, a focus was created to establish a company-wide 'interrupt awareness'. For this purpose, the measurement results were distributed over the organisation, through presentations, posters and on-line availability of relevant information. This interrupt-awareness should contribute to a more efficient delivering and handling of interrupts, from the point of view of both initiator and developer.

The hypotheses showed that the project team expected that a lack of information details would cause an interrupt to take longer. They assumed that 50% of all interrupts had insufficient details. However, measurement showed that 90% of all interrupts were formulated with sufficient details.

The feedback session material will be discussed here according to the following questions on interrupts:

- What is the workload of interrupts?
- Through which medium do interrupts occur?
- Who causes interrupts?
- What is the recovery time after interrupts?
- How are interrupts handled?
- What are the underlying reasons for interrupts?
- Which actions can be taken to solve the interrupt problem?
- To which products are interrupts related?

What is the workload of interrupts?

Looking into the effort spent on interrupts, we found that interrupts require an average effort of 15 minutes for the initiator to sufficiently handle an interrupt. Developers spent around 1.5 hours per day on interrupt handling, consuming 20% of total time available for development work. This was similar to the percentage found in other empirical work (Perry et al, 1994).

The project manager always included 20% slack in the planning for unexpected activities, including organisational communication, training, social talks and interrupts. However, the measurements showed that this slack was already fully consumed by the interrupts. This indicated a possible cause for planning delays. Action was taken to increase interrupt awareness, and to try to decrease the number of interrupts in the department.

Through which medium do interrupts occur?

Figure 11-3 shows the distribution of interrupts over the three possible media: personal visits, telephone, or e-mail. Of all interrupts, 95% were delivered by personal visits or telephone calls, whereas the rest of the interrupts are delivered by e-mail. Please note that interrupts delivered by personal visits or telephone calls occur to the developer in random order with 'number 1' priority (whereas only 25% of all interrupts are classified as urgent)! This meant that the initiator of the interrupt determines the moment of interruption, and that the developer has to respond immediately to satisfy the initiator. However, e-mails could be handled at a later moment suitable to the developer. Furthermore, personal visits and telephone calls needed more handling effort from the developer than e-mails. We found the reason for this to be that interrupts delivered by e-mail are usually well formulated by the initiator.

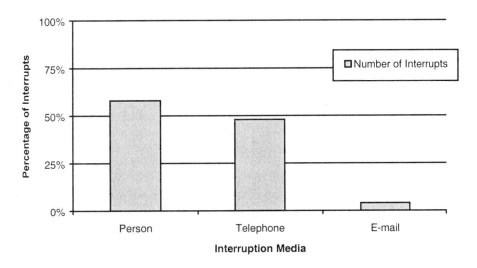

Figure 11-3: Interrupt occurrence by medium.

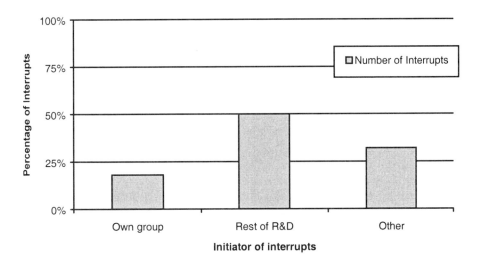

Figure 11-4: Initiators of interrupts.

Who causes interrupts?

Figure 11-4 shows the distribution of interrupts over the types of initiators: own group, other R&D groups and other groups outside R&D. The measurements showed that the R&D department (including their own group) were the 'number one' initiator, contributing to 70% of the total amount of interrupts. The developers found this quite remarkable, as they expected that other departments would be the main source of interrupts. This indicated that interrupts were a inherent R&D problem, and that solutions for this problem should primarily be found within the R&D departments.

What is the recovery time after interrupts?

In the measurement programmes we initially included a metric on the *'recovery time'* after an interrupt. Unfortunately, it appeared to be too difficult to measure this and after the first measurement period we omitted this measurement from the programme. However, we could observe that the recovery time was primarily a problem when an interrupt occurred during actual programming work, and less when it occurred, for instance, during documenting or meetings. It was assumed that the level of concentration that was required for programming caused this.

Other sources in literature reported that the recovery time after a phone call is at least 15 minutes (DeMarco and Lister, 1987). Even though we could not measure this exactly, we had the same impression. One of the conclusions from the measurements was that when more than ten interrupts occur during a day, the remaining time for planned work became insufficient. Taking these ten interrupts a day, and the measurement that an interrupt required approximately 20 minutes to handle, it then seemed reasonable that the recovery time from an interrupt was roughly 15 minutes, explaining why the time left was useless for development work.

How are interrupts handled?

Figure 11-3, on interrupt media, indicated that interrupts occurred for 95% in such a way that it was difficult for developers to avoid the interrupt *occurrence*. However, it would have been possible to postpone the *handling* of an interrupt. Of course this depended on the type of interrupt. Most interrupts were minor questions or requests which developers preferred to handle immediately. Also, some interrupts could not be postponed because of the urgency of the initiator.

During the measurement programme it was measured whether interrupts were handled immediately, or whether handling was postponed. It appeared that 90% of the interrupts were handled immediately and that only 10% were postponed. The interrupts that were postponed needed three times more effort to handle. This might also very well be the reason why they were postponed in the first place.

It was expected that interrupts were also postponed because of a lack of information details. Both organisations assumed at the beginning of the measurement programme that 50% of all interrupts would have insufficient details. However, the measurements showed that 90% of all interrupts were formulated with sufficient information.

What are the underlying reasons for interrupts?

Figure 11-5 illustrates the reasons of interrupts over a number of classes. Discerned were: knowledge or experience exchange, social issues, documentation, organisational issues and other.

Issues related to knowledge or experience caused approximately 30% of all interrupts. Furthermore, 20% were caused by what was called documentation issues, such as inadequate documentation, non-existing documentation, and review of documentation. About 10% of all interrupts were caused by organisational shortcomings, as initiators were unaware of the exact responsibilities of the particular developers.

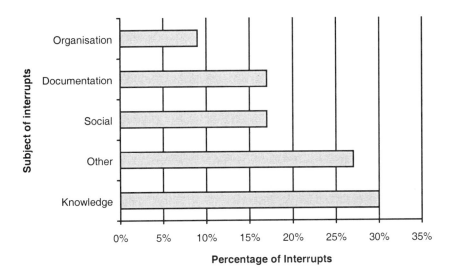

Figure 11-5: Underlying reasons for interrupts.

Which actions can be taken to solve the interrupt problem?

The developers considered interrupts to be 'inappropriate', if an interrupt was delivered to the wrong person, or if the initiator himself could have handled the interrupt. It appeared that approximately 30% of all interrupts were experienced as 'inappropriate'. To improve 'interrupt-efficiency' it was first tried to minimise these 'inappropriate interrupts'. It appeared that many inappropriate interrupts were caused by unclear organisational responsibilities. Therefore, more effort was spent on communicating responsibilities of employees throughout the organisation.

To influence initiators of interrupts, a company-wide 'interrupt awareness programme' was established. For this purpose, the measurement results were spread throughout the organisation, by presentations, posters and on-line availability of relevant information.

Based on the notion that developers handled interrupts delivered by e-mail more efficiently than interrupts delivered by personal visits or telephone calls, an e-mail policy was established, especially for less urgent interrupts within the department. Urgent interrupts could be delivered to the developer by telephone, however, preferably not by personal visits, because such visits proved to be quite inefficient and would also distract other people besides the developer.

To which products are interrupts related?

Figure 11-6 shows the relation between the products that the dispenser electronics department is responsible for and the number of interrupts. The actual number of interrupts was the total number in the first six weeks of measurement. Because the measurements were done for a relatively short period of time the total number of interrupts could be shown in this chart. When larger periods of time are considered, it is probably better to present the total number per time unit (for example, total number of interrupts per week). The number of interrupts concerning old products (released to the field and in maintenance phase) appeared to be quite high. The average effort per interrupt for the two calculators (central control unit in a dispenser) appeared to be twice as high as average.

11.6   Documentation of interrupt measurement programme

In this last section of Chapter 11, the GQM plan and the data collection form are described. This section contains no new information on the case of the interrupt measurement programme.

11.6.1   GQM plan

Introduction

In this subsection the GQM plan for the interrupt measurement programme is described. The measurement programme was executed within the department of Project C. Measurement was introduced for a better understanding of current processes, to provide information on the performance and to identify areas of improvement. Subsequently, the measurement goal, questions, metrics and hypotheses will be described. This GQM plan would be used for three purposes:

1.   Feedback to the project team members by the GQM team.
2.   Definition of data collection, since all direct measurements were defined in the GQM plan.
3.   Analyses and feedback of collected data, because the GQM plan identified which questions should be answered.

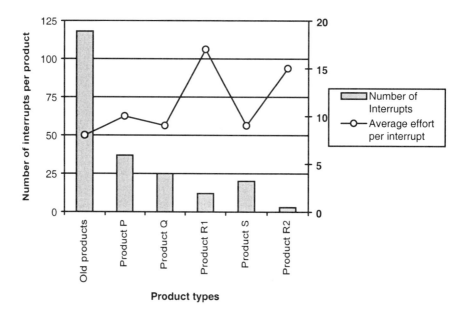

Figure 11-6: Relation between products and interrupts.

Interrupts

An interrupt is an event that disturbs a person during the activity that person is working on. An interrupt exist of three phases:

1. Occurrence of interrupt including a quick decision on whether the interrupt must be handled at that certain moment, or can be postponed/planned.
2. Handling of the interrupt, where the initiator of the interrupt is helped onto a satisfactory level. After handling the interrupt, the interrupt is officially finished.
3. Follow-up of interrupt where the activities are executed that are necessarily involved with the interrupt, but that are not related to the initiator of the interrupt. For example update in a document.

From goal to questions

The goal of the measurement programme was as follows:

Analyse:	interrupts and their effects
for the purpose of:	understanding
with respect to:	- impact on schedule
	- the cost/benefit of interrupts
from the viewpoint of:	project team
in the following context:	project C

This Goal will be reached when answers can be given to the following six questions.

Q.1 What is the distribution of interrupts over factors, related to the occurrence of an interrupt?

This question focuses on the occurrence of an interrupt. The question will give an answer to the event of the interrupt and the factors that relate to that event. Therefore the question will investigate the relation between the initiator of the interrupt, the subject the interrupt is about, the cause of the interrupt, the treatment of the interrupt and the interruption medium. This question is answered when the relation between all factors involved with the occurrence of an interrupt are clear and values are available that visualise the distribution of interrupts over these factors.

Q.2 What factors influence treatment and effort for handling an interrupt?

This question focuses on the reasons why an interrupt is handled right away or included in a planning (postponed), and the reasons why an interrupt requires more effort. The question will give an answer to the amount of time that is related to the types of influencing factors and the treatment of these specific interrupts. This question is answered when the relations between all these factors and the treatment/effort for the interrupt are known and values are available that visualise these relations

Q.3 Is prevention of interrupts possible?

This question focuses on the possibility to eliminate interrupts that are unnecessary. It should therefore be investigated whether such interrupts exist and, if so, how their occurrence can be prevented. This question is answered when the possibilities for interruption prevention are known and when the amount and effort of interrupts that should not have occurred is visualised by values.

Q.4 Should we change our reserved effort for interrupts?

This question is answered when the amount of time estimated for handling interrupts can be compared to the actual effort spent on handling interrupts.

Q.5 What is the influence of interrupts on the work that was interrupted?

This question focuses on the work that is being interrupted. This question is primarily answered when the overall effort spent on interrupts is known. Values need to be available regarding the occurrences of interrupts and the associated decrease in concentration.

Q.6 What are the total costs of interrupts?

This question investigates the costs of interrupts in relation to the 'normal' work of the project team. This question is answered when the effort spent on different types of interrupts is known, together with other costs that are related to these interrupts.

From questions to metrics

The six questions of the measurement programme are restated below, together with their associated metrics.

Q.1 What is the distribution of interrupts over factors, related with the occurrence of an interrupt?

Detailed questions focusing on practical experience by project team:

- What is the number of interrupts that are not related to the current project (or current work)?
- What is the number of interrupts that have informal contacts as initiator?
- How many interrupts can be scheduled or must be treated immediately?
- How is the occurrence of interrupts distributed over time (during the day and week)?
- What is the relation between interrupts and their initiator?
- What is the number of interrupts that are caused by (unclear or uncompleted) documentation?
- What is the object (product) that the interrupt is about?
- What is the nature of an interrupt?

Metrics:

- number of interrupts for current work;
- number of interrupts for not current work;
- number of interrupts that are treated immediately;
- number of interrupts that are planned;
- number of interrupts per day;
- number of interrupts per initiator;
- number of interrupts per subject of interrupt;
- number of interrupts per interruption medium;
- number of interrupts due to documentation;
- number of interrupts per product;

- number of interrupts per subject;
- number of interrupts due to unclearness of organisation;
- number of interrupts per cause.

Direct Measurements:

- initiator of each interrupt;
- subject of each interrupt;
- cause of each interrupt;
- object (product) of each product related interrupt;
- effort spent on each interrupt;
- interruption medium for each interrupt;
- treatment for each interrupt (immediately/planned);
- number of interrupts for each day of the week.

Q.2 What factors influence treatment and effort for handling an interrupt?

Detailed questions focusing on practical experience by project team:

- What is the impact of (status of) initiator on the way the interrupt is treated?
- What is the effort spent on interrupts per initiator?
- What is the impact of the communication medium (eg fax, letter, e-mail, personal visit or other) on the way the interrupt is handled and the required effort?
- What is the relation between communication medium and the effort needed for collecting the interrupt information?
- What is the impact of the level of detail in which the interrupt is described on the effort spent on the interrupt?
- What is the efficiency gain, when interrupts are presented with more details?
- What is the impact of the associated object's characteristics (eg age of the product, complexity, documentation) on the way the interrupt is treated and the effort required?

Metrics:

- effort spent on interrupts per initiator;
- effort spent on interrupts per interruption medium;
- effort spent on interrupts by level of detail of interrupt description;
- effort spent on interrupts per subject of interrupt;
- effort spent on interrupts per cause of interrupt;
- treatment of interrupts per initiator;
- treatment of interrupts per interruption medium;
- treatment of interrupts by level of detail of interrupt description;
- treatment of interrupts per subject of interrupt;
- treatment of interrupts per cause of interrupt;
- level of detail of interrupt description per interruption medium;
- level of detail of interrupt description per interrupt initiator.

Direct Measurements:

- initiator of each interrupt;
- interruption medium for each interrupt;

- level of detail of each interrupt description;
- subject of each interrupt;
- cause of each interrupt;
- effort spent on each interrupt;
- treatment for each interrupt (imediately/panned).

Q.3 Is prevention of interrupts possible?

Detailed questions focusing on practical experience by project team:

- What is the amount of (and effort on) interrupts that are caused by (un)clearness of organisation by the initiator?
- How could interrupts have been prevented?
- How many interrupts could have been prevented?

Metrics:

- number of interrupts due to unclearness of organisation;
- effort spent on interrupts due to unclearness of organisation;
- number of interrupts due to unclearness of organisation per initiator;
- number of interrupts due to non existing documentation;
- effort spent on interrupts due to non existing documentation;
- number of interrupts due to incomplete/unclear documentation;
- effort spent on interrupts due to incomplete/unclear documentation;
- number of interrupts due to badly executed follow-up;
- effort spent on interrupts due to badly executed follow-up;
- number of repetitive interrupts;
- effort spent on repetitive interrupts.

Direct measurements:

- Subject of each interrupt
- Cause of each interrupt
- Effort spent on each interrupt

Q.4 Should we change our reserved effort for interrupts?

Detailed questions focusing on practical experience by project team:

- What is the difference between total reserved effort and actual effort for handling interrupts?
- What is the difference between planned and actual time for activities due to interrupts?

Metrics:

- total number of interrupts;
- total effort spent on interrupts;
- average effort per interrupt;
- estimated number of interrupts;
- estimated effort spent on interrupts;
- estimated effort per interrupt;

- planned effort for interrupts;
- actual delay due to interrupts.

Direct measurements:

- effort spent on each interrupt;
- estimated effort for each interrupt;
- date for each interrupt;
- treatment of each interrupt (immediately or planned);
- planned effort for handling interrupts.

Q.5 What is the influence of interrupts on the work that was interrupted?

Detailed questions focusing on practical experience by project team:

- What is the additional effort needed for planned activities due to the fact that these activities have been interrupted?
- What is the level of concentration for the activities that are interrupted?
- How many times are activities interrupted?
- How many interrupts are really inconvenient?

Metrics:

- number of interrupts per activity;
- number of interrupts and associated level of concentration of present activity;
- number of interrupts classified as inconvenient.

Direct measurements:

- work per interrupt;
- level of concentration per activity.

It should be mentioned here that a number of members of the project team proposed to omit this question due to the expectation that measurement would be too complicated.

Q.6 What are the total costs of interrupts?

Detailed questions focusing on practical experience by project team:

- What is the effort spent on handling interrupts?
- What is the cost of interrupts that could have been prevented?
- What is the cost of repetitive interrupts?
- What is the cost of interrupts that should have been handled by people outside the project team?
- What is the cost/impact of not following up and completing an interrupt?

Metrics:

- effort spent on interrupts that could have been prevented:
    - effort spent on interrupts due to unclearness of organisation;
    - effort spent on interrupts due to not existing documentation;

- effort spent on interrupts due to incomplete/unclear documentation;
- effort spent on repetitive interrupts;
- total effort spent on interrupts;
- estimated effort spent on follow-up;
- effort spent on follow-up;
- interrupt(s) causing follow-up;
- effort spent on interrupts per treatment.

Direct measurements:

- subject of each interrupt;
- cause of each interrupt;
- effort spent on each interrupt;
- treatment for each interrupt (immediately/planned);
- estimated effort for each follow-up;
- effort spent on each follow-up;
- interrupt(s) causing each follow-up.

Direct measurements

The direct measurements that have been defined for the stated goal, and that will provide enough information to answer the questions are:

- Interrupts:
  - initiator of each interrupt;
  - subject of each interrupt;
  - cause of each interrupt;
  - effort spent on each interrupt;
  - interruption medium for each interrupt;
  - treatment for each interrupt (immediately/planned);
  - estimated effort for each interrupt;
  - date for each interrupt;
  - activity working on per interrupt;
  - level of detail of each interrupt description;
  - object (product) of each product related interrupt.
- Follow-up:
  - estimated effort for each follow-up;
  - effort spent on each follow-up;
  - interrupt(s) causing each follow-up.
- Level of concentration per activity.
- Planned effort for handling interrupts.

Hypotheses regarding the direct measurements

The project leader and project team members suggested different hypotheses for particular measurements. The hypotheses of the hardware project team and the software project team, were roughly the same. When the hypotheses of the project team are combined, the following hypotheses are formulated:

- Production and the project team are the largest initiators of interrupts, together responsible for 30% of the interrupts.
- Students (trainees) are expected to cause 10% of the interrupts.
- Most interrupts refer to operational problems of the product that is currently being worked on (19%), failures (14%), consultancy (13%) and old products (12%).
- The reason that somebody is interrupted (member of project team) are problems with documentation (31%), and his/her knowledge and experience (25%).
- More than 50% of the interrupts require an effort of less than 5 minutes to handle.
- 75% of the interrupts require less than 30 minutes to handle.
- The largest numbers of interrupts are caused by telephone calls (43%) and persons visiting (27%), these two sources together cause 70% of the interrupts.

11.6.2   Measurement plan of interrupts

In this subsection the measurement plan is described. Subsequently, the metrics will be defined regarding:

- occurrence of an interrupt;
- handling of an interrupt;
- follow-up of an interrupt.

All 16 metrics have already been identified in the previous subsection on direct measurements and are only formally defined in this subsection.

Occurrence of an interrupt

A number of metrics were identified regarding the occurrence of an interrupt, including a quick decision whether the interrupt should be handled immediately, or should be postponed/planned.

M.1   Initiator of each interrupt
Classification of persons initiating interrupts.

Values:
MT: Management
OW: Own project team
PE: Product engineering (all mechanical and hydraulic engineers)
MK: Marketing (marketing people)
IN: Installation engineering and service
MA: Manufacturing
QA: Quality
RD: R&D
SA: Sales
ST: Students
GV: Governmental institutes
EX: External (persons outside the company)

Data collection medium:
Interrupt registration form

M.2   Interruption medium for each interrupt
Classification of media that interrupts are done with

Values:

Telephone	Telephone
Person	Direct visit by initiator
E-mail	Computer electronic mail
Fax/letter	Written material

Data collection medium:
Interrupt registration form

M.3   Treatment for each interrupt (immediately/planned)
Classification of the way in which the interrupt is treated

Values:

Immediately	The interrupt is handled at the moment that it occurred
Planned	Handling the interrupt is postponed/planned to another moment

Data collection medium:
Interrupt registration form

M.4   Date for each interrupt
Day, Month, Year, day of the week at which the interrupt occurred

Values:
DD/MM/YY
Day of the week (Mon, Tue, Wed, Thu, Fri, Sat, Sun)

Data collection medium:
Interrupt registration form

M.5   Estimated effort for each interrupt
Effort estimated to be spent on handling the interrupt. Collected only when an interrupt is planned/postponed.

Values:
Estimated effort in minutes

Data collection medium:
Interrupt registration form, estimated time is filled in the planned/postponed cell of that interrupt

M.6   Level of detail of each interrupt description
Classification of levels of detail of the description of interrupts.

Values:
Sufficient information available
Not sufficient information available

Data collection medium:
Interrupt registration form

M.7   Level of concentration per activity
Level of concentration per activity defines if an activity can be interrupted or not.

Values:
Strictly related to the interrupted activity:

Meeting:	High concentration and very inconvenient to be interrupted.
Development:	High concentration
Documentation:	Low concentration

Others: Rest, low concentration

Data collection medium:
Interrupt registration form

M.8   Activity working on per interrupt
Activity that was interrupted

Values:
Name of the activity
Meeting: High concentration and very inconvenient to be
                  interrupted in
Development: High concentration development activity
Documentation: Low concentration writing activity
Others: Rest, low concentration

Data collection medium:
Interrupt registration form

Handling of an interrupt

Handling of an interrupt, where the initiator of an interrupt is helped onto a satisfactory level. After handling an interrupt, it is officially completed.

M.9   Subject of each interrupt
Classification of subjects the interrupt is about

Values:
Existing functionality
New functionality
Products
Consultancy
Organisational subjects
Social

Data collection medium:
Interrupt registration form
Product abbreviations must be entered, when interrupt is about a product

M.10   Cause of each interrupt
Classification of causes that the interrupt is done by the interrupted person

Values:
Documentation
System failures
Wrong system usage
Knowledge and experience
Organisational shortcomings
Job (function) related
Social
Repetitive

Data collection medium:
Interrupt Registration Form

M.11   Effort spent on each interrupt
Effort spent on handling the interrupt, so that the initiator is helped

Values:
Effort in minutes/hours

Data collection medium:
Interrupt registration form

M.12   Object (product) of each product related interrupt
Product relation of interrupt

Values:
Name of the product

Data collection medium:
Interrupt Registration From
Product abbreviation is entered at the subject category (M.9)

M.13   Interrupt(s) causing each follow-up
Each follow-up is caused by (one or more) interrupts

Values:
Interrupt numbers: Date, number

Data collection medium:
To do list
Follow-up must be entered on To do list.

M.14   Estimated effort for follow-up on interrupt
Estimated effort required for executing follow-up if necessary

Values:
Effort in minutes/hours

Data collection medium:
To Do List

Follow-up of the interrupt

Follow-up of an interrupt where activities are executed that are necessarily involved with the interrupt, but that are not related to the initiator of the interrupt. An example is an update of the product documentation.

M.15   Effort spent on each follow-up
Effort spent on executing the follow-up

Values:
Actual effort: Minutes, hours

Data collection medium:
To do list

M.16   Planned effort for handling interrupts
Total effort planned for handling interrupts during the project

Values:
Planned effort: Hours, days

Data collection medium:
Project plan

11.6.3   Interrupt data collection form

The form below illustrates the interrupt data collection form which was used in the interrupt measurement programme. This form is not exactly in line with the GQM plan included before, because it is a second version and some measurements were already omitted from the programme for various reasons.

Name : _____   Date: _____ / _____

	1	2	3	4	5	6	7	8	9	10	11	12	13	14
Interruption Medium	Enter "1" for urgent interrupts (should this interrupt have occured now?)													
Telephone														
Person														
E-mail														
Fax/Letter														
Initiator of the Interrupt														
Effort for Interrupt														
Immediately handled effort														
Planned: Estimated effort for handling														
Actual effort for handling														
Interrupted Activity														
Meeting (enter number of people present)														
Development High concentration														
Others														
Subject of the Interrupt														
Maintenance Team														
Development Team														
Documentation problems														
Products (enter: abbreviation of product)														
Organizational subjects														
Others														

Initiator of interrupts:

MK: Marketing   **PE**: Product Engineering   **RD**: R & D

O : Own project team   **ST**: Students   **IN** : Installation

EX: External   **QA**: Quality   **MA**: Manufacturing

                         OT: Others

Figure 11-7: Relation between products and interrupts.

11.7   Questions and assignments

11.7.1   Questions

1. What is the definition of an interrupt?
2. Which effects in Figure 11-2, are experienced as positive and negative at the same time? Explain why.
3. What do you consider the most important property of a data collection form for interrupt measurement?
4. What is the most apparent difference between phone and visits as interrupt medium, and e-mail?
5. What are the advantages and disadvantages of an 'e-mail only' policy for interrupts?
6. How much effort did the developers spend on interruptions per day? How many hours is that per week?
7. Who was the initiator of the majority of the interruptions?
8. How many minutes is the recovery time from an interruption?
9. Compare the measurement plan of this case with the one of case B in Chapter 10. Which one is better, and why?

11.7.2   Assignments

1. Take the GQM plan of this chapter and make a new chart or table that you could include in the analysis plan for each question.
2. Compare the charts and tables of the previous assignment with those provided in this chapter and analyse the completeness and validity of the results presented in this chapter.
3. The GQM plan of this case contains no abstraction sheet on the interrupt goal. Create this abstraction sheet based on the information in the GQM plan.

'The goal of software engineering is to build something that will last at least until we have
finished building it'
Source unknown

12   Case D: effort measurement

12.1   Description of project D

This chapter describes the results of a measurement programme to support a project team during a reorganisation. This project team had to change from development to maintenance work. To support a project team in its learning process from development to maintenance work, we applied GQM to measure how the change impacted on the workload of the team. This measurement programme was called the SUPSYS project.

The project team that worked on the SUPSYS project contained the same members as in Chapter 10. The project team had already released several versions and increments of the product, and was facing a phase in which support on local customisation should be provided instead of development.

The SUPSYS measurement programme will be described again following the four phases of the GQM method: planning, definition, data collection and interpretation. This chapter also includes the practical deliverables of SUPSYS, such as the GQM plan, data collection forms and feedback charts. These documents can be useful as example for similar measurement programmes.

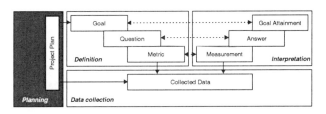

12.2   Planning

An independent GQM team already existed in the targeted department. This team discussed with the project team what the role could be of the measurement programme in the context of the project team's improvement programme.

The project team used to develop a system for a global market. However, this product is also customised to national requirements in separate distributed teams. Those teams integrated, for example, company logos, languages, national currencies, etc into the system. Major customisations were also done by the national teams, for example, integration with other systems, or connections of the system to national bank cards, air-miles or governmental standards.

After developing the basic product it was released to those national customisation teams. However, those customisation teams needed support from the original developers. Relevant customisation projects in one country might also be relevant to another country. After the second release of the product, management decided to change the objectives of the team that originally developed the product. Their focus on development was changed to maintenance, which included giving support to the customisation teams and integrating customisation functionality into the basic product.

This organisational change implied that the team could no longer plan their activities as they used to do. They also became dependent on questions and demands from the customisation teams. In order to support this project team in their learning process from development to maintenance, we applied the GQM method to measure effort spent to learn how the change impacted on the teamwork.

It was not necessary to train this project team on the GQM method, because it was the same team that worked on the RITME measurement programme, which we described in Chapter 10. For efficiency reasons, the project plan was not documented separately, but immediately integrated into the GQM plan.

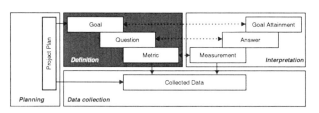

12.3 Definition

This measurement programme was again defined according to the steps described in Chapter 6. Measurement goals were defined in a session with the project team. Two goals were identified for this measurement programme, these two goals are depicted below.

Analyse the:	time spent on support activities
for the purpose of:	understanding
with respect to:	- the ongoing projects in the national customisation teams
	- the support given by the team
from the viewpoint of:	the project team
in the following context:	project D

Analyse the:	quality of support
for the purpose of:	understanding
with respect to:	support given by the central department
from the viewpoint of:	national customisation team-engineering
in the following context:	project D

It was decided to focus the attention of the measurement programme on the first goal. The second goal was put on hold and would be addressed later, because the support role was new, so some time had to be spent on support before national customisation teams could be asked for their opinion.

During the first measurement period we intended to focus only on support the activities of the project team. However, it became clear that the team could not make a clear distinction between 'support' activities and 'normal' activities. Therefore the team decided to broaden the initial measurement goal to effort spent on all activities. This was experienced as a strong point of a GQM measurement programme: as the project team learned from their activities and the measurement programme could be enhanced.

This measurement programme differed from the ones described in the previous three chapters, because the shift in the department also caused the developers not to know what would happen. As the GQM definition phase is particularly based on 'knowledge acquisition', we had to adjust this approach. We did hold the interviews to find out the most important questions of the engineers and to identify which metrics were necessary. The questions that were defined are:

- What are the main characteristics of the support activities?
- Which projects are ongoing to be executed by the national customisation teams from the viewpoint of the central department?

However, problems arose regarding the identification of influencing factors and especially regarding the definition of hypotheses and process modelling. We realised that this specific measurement programme was started to find out new knowledge, and that we could expect some rigorous changes on the way. Therefore, we did not make a process model for support, nor did we ask for hypotheses, because these would become available during the measurement programme itself.

The definition phase was documented in a GQM and measurement plan, which is detailed under Section 12.6.1.

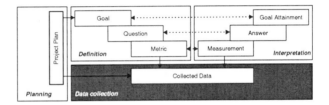

12.4   Data collection

The data collection and analysis and the different programmes that were used have been illustrated in the figure of the measurement support system (Figure 12-1). A paper data collection form was used to quickly register some notes when the support was requested. At the end of the day the support-requests were entered in the database. Based on this database several queries were defined based on the GQM plan. Those queries were expressed in charts, that were automatically updated by the MSS. Only the final link to the presentation tool could, unfortunately, not be updated automatically. This had to be done by copying the charts to the presentation tool manually.

The database tool was used to gather the data of the support activities. It was possible for members of the project team to enter the data directly into the database. It was also easy to link the data in the database with other applications such as a spreadsheet tool or presentation tool.

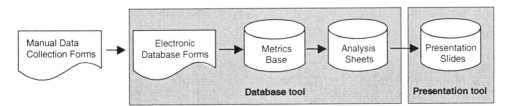

Figure 12-1: Data collection procedures

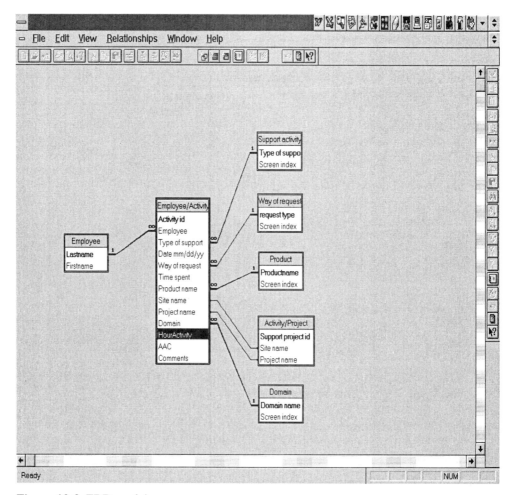

Figure 12-2: ERD model.

An ERD model was designed from the measurements. This ERD model is presented in Figure 12-2. The electronic form that was used to enter data should be easy and quick. It was developed with these two things in mind. The form was just big enough to be displayed on a full-screen. So no scrolling was needed to enter the data. The database and form was improved several times. The electronic data entry form is displayed in Figure 12-3.

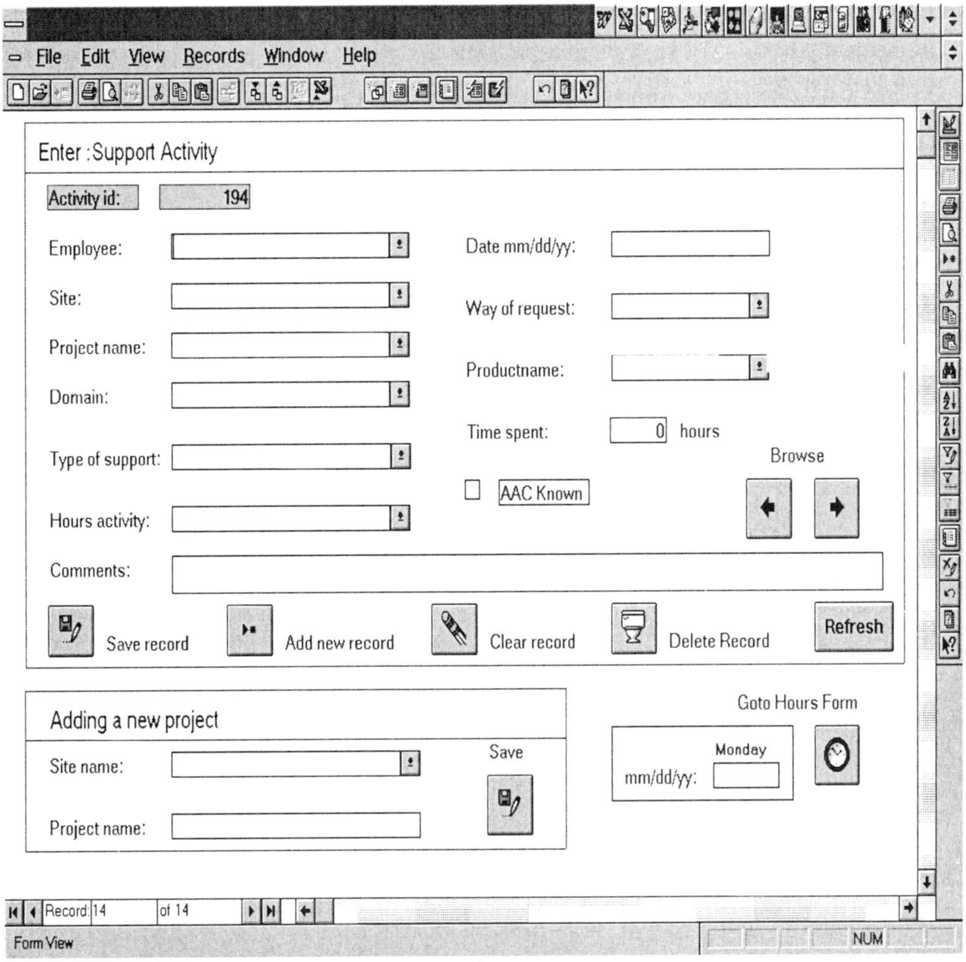

Figure 12-3: Electronic data entry form.

It was attempted to establish a link between the new support database and the database of the existing hour registration system, so the employees would not have to enter their data twice. This link was, however, not established. Therefore, it was decided that a report would be retrieved from the MSS, which would then be manually imported into the existing hour registration system by the GQM team.

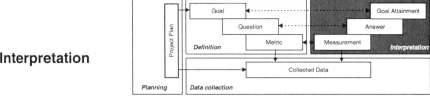

12.5   Interpretation

This section describes the results of the measurement programme. The results are based on two measurement periods of two months each. This section contains the four main topics which were analysed during the feedback sessions:

- support requests to the team members;
- effort spent on the different maintenance activities;
- effort spent on product subsystems;
- effort spent for national customisation teams.

What were the baselines of support requests to the team members?

This section describes the nature of the support requests that occurred to the team members during the measurement period. The project team concluded that most numbers of requests came by telephone. Although these calls took on average only half an hour, they could still be very inconvenient when they quickly followed each other or exceeded a particular number per day (see also Chapter 11). The project team concluded that the number of requests per engineer differed and that the number of telephone calls were according to the expectations. The other media differed from their expectations (see Figure 12-4).

According to the data, a request by the project manager needed, on average, most effort, followed by meetings/visits by other persons. Some engineers expected newsgroups would be used to request support, however, the data showed no requests at all by this medium.

We also studied the total number of request per week. A representation of the data is shown in Figure 12-5. The low amount of requests in the second week is caused by a holiday period, so only a few engineers were available. From the data it was concluded that roughly 80 support requests a week could be expected.

Medium of Request	Actual	Hypothesis	Number	Time per request (hours)
Telephone	34%	33%	119	0.5
Meetings/Visits	27%	21%	95	2
E-mail	22%	33%	79	1.4
Project Manager	17%	6%	58	2.2
Newsgroup	0%	7%	0	0

Figure 12-4: Effort expenditure by medium.

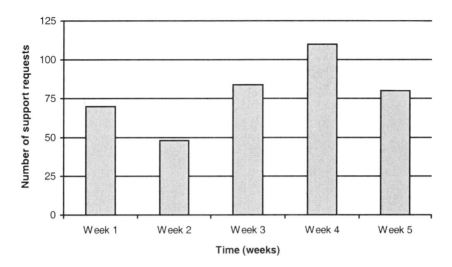

Figure 12-5: Total number of support requests per week.

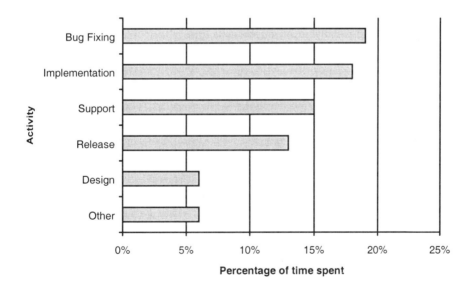

Figure 12-6: Percentage of time spent per type of activity

What is the effort spent on maintenance activities?

Figure 12-6 illustrates the distribution of effort over the top six activities. The project team concluded that they were still spending 20% of their time on implementation, even though the organisational change intended that they should be fully available for support activities. Design and review should be done in cooperation with the project team and the national customisation teams should implement. The project team could now conclude that this was not the case.

The 'review' category that was not in the top six of Figure 12-6 required 4% of the overall effort. However, the recent quality assurance audit resulted in a 'non-compliance' because no review reports were available. The project team defined an action point to make a review report for each review.

What is the effort spent on sub-systems?

Figure 12-7 shows the average daily time spent on support for each subsystem. From this figure the project team concluded that for the I/O functions subsystem one engineer should be available. Two other engineers should always be available to manage the support requests for the other subsystems. The project team explained that the high percentage of 'other' was caused by the fact that it was difficult to identify for which subsystem several activities were executed. In other words, sometimes activities were performed for more subsystems or for no subsystem at all.

One of the reasons that so much effort was spent on the I/O functions, was that many versions of this subsystem were available. Action was taken by the project team to reduce this amount of versions.

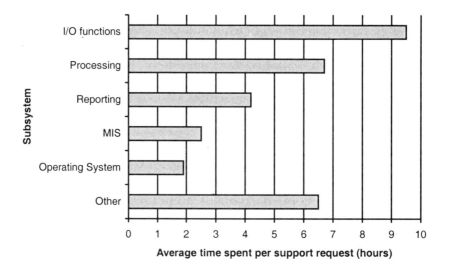

Figure 12-7: Average time spent daily per subsystem.

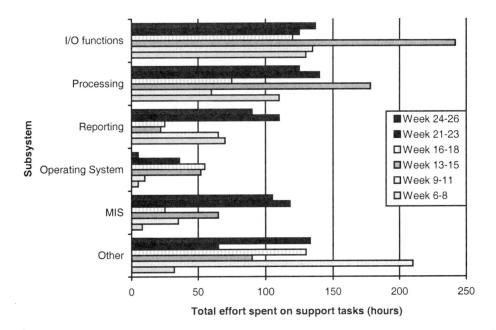

Figure 12-8: Total time spent per period per subsystem.

Figure 12-8 shows the trend in total amount of time that is spent on the subsystems per period of three weeks. The 'other' category was again high because the activities could be for more subsystems at once, or it was not clear for what subsystem the activity was performed. The project team concluded that the peak in the third period for the I/O subsystem was caused by the release of a new version of that subsystem. The peak in the third period for the subsystem 'cashing functions', was caused by a project that had high implementation priority according to the project team.

What is the effort spending for national customisation teams?

Figure 12-9 shows the percentage of time that was spent per national customisation team. The miscellaneous category was high, because often it was not clear for which site the activities were performed. An improvement action was defined to improve communication with the national project teams.

Within the category of requests of the own group a part could also be for other sites although a member of their own team requested them. The percentage for site 1 is high because there was urgency to performing these activities. For the other areas only a limited amount of effort was spent.

Which actions were taken based on the measurements?

Goal-oriented measurement implies that measurement results in interpretations, conclusions or actions. Interpretations and conclusions were described before, together with the feedback charts. In this section we list some of the actions taken by the team during this measurement programme.

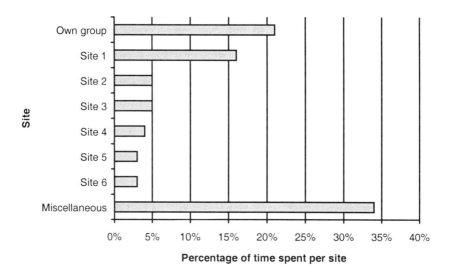

Figure 12-9: Percentage of time spent per site.

- *Show support performance to management.*
  The project manager sent parts of the measurement data to management, to show the support tasks performed by the department.
- *Communicate national projects to the project team.*
  Based on the measurements it became clear that the project team lacked information on projects going on in the national sites. Action was taken to keep all project team members informed by the project manager.
- *Report reviews to quality department.*
  The measurements showed that quite some effort was spent on reviewing deliverables. However, the recent project audit had signalled that no review reports were available. It appeared that the team members did review, but neglected reporting this. Action was defined to improve review reporting which was successfully done.
- *Plan support effort.*
  Measurement showed that the effort spent on direct support to the national sites consumed about 25% of the total effort of the team. Based on this number, the planning of the team included this amount of space for support.
- *Integrate measurement classes with new hour reporting system.*
  A new hour reporting system was set up for the whole business unit. The experiences of the measurement programme were used as input to define the necessary classes, such as activities, sites, projects and domains. By the time this new hour reporting system got fully operational, the measurement programme attained its goal.

12.6   Documentation of SUPSYS measurement programme

In this final section the GQM and measurement plan, and the data collection forms are described. This section contains no new information on the case of the SUPSYS project and is added only to illustrate both documents.

12.6.1 GQM plan

In this section the GQM plan is described. The GQM plan was subject to changes during the measurement period due to new information and experience gained in the feedback sessions.

The GQM plan consisted of three parts. The first part contained the goal that were formulated for this GQM plan. The second section described the questions that were derived from the goals. The third section described the metrics derived from the questions. For each question the necessary measurements were also given.

Goals of the GQM plan

Two goals were identified for the measurement programme, these two goals are depicted below. The attention was focused on the first goal of the measurement programme. The second goal was put on hold.

First goal:
Analyse: time spent on support activities
for the purpose of: understanding
with respect to: - the ongoing projects in the national customisation teams
                               - the support given by the team
from the viewpoint of: the project team
in the following context: project D

Second goal:
Analyse: the quality of support
for the purpose of: understanding
with respect to: national customisation team-support given by the project team
from the viewpoint of: national customisation team-engineering
in the following context: project D

Below the associated questions are formulated.

From goal to questions

Two questions were formulated to reach the first goal described in the section above. The first question focused on the baseline characteristics of the support activities being performed at the central department.

- Q.1: What are the main characteristics of the support activities? This question focused on identifying objective and quantifiable aspects that were related to support activities. The question would give an answer of the properties of support activities.
  The second question was focused on the visibility of the project that were currently going on at the national customisation teams from the viewpoint of the central department.
- Q.2: Which projects are ongoing in the national customisation teams from the viewpoint of the central department? This question focused on identifying the projects

that were ongoing in the national customisation teams from the viewpoint of the central department. This question could be used to answer questions about the visibility of running projects at the national customisation teams in the central department.

From questions to metrics

This section describes the metrics that were formulated to answer the questions. The two questions were worked out into sub-questions that were formulated based on the practical experience of the project team. This experience was captured during interviews with the members of the project team. The sub-questions were worked out in metrics and these metrics were again reformulated in direct measurements.

Sub-questions for Q.1: 'What are the main characteristics of the support activities?':

- Q.1.1 In which way is the support requested (phone, e-mail, etc)?
- Q.1.2 On which date is the support requested?
- Q.1.3 For which project is the support requested?
- Q.1.4 By which national customisation team is the support requested?
- Q.1.5 For which domain is the support requested?
- Q.1.6 Which employee is going to give support?
- Q.1.7 How long is the support going to take?
- Q.1.8 How long did the support take?
- Q.1.9 What kind of support activity was it?
- Q.1.10 Is the project authorisation number for the support known by the department?
- Q.1.11 How is the difference between support for old and new products?

Metrics:

- How are the support activities distributed over the national customisation teams?
- How are the support activities distributed over the domains?
- How is the distribution of the way the request are made?
- What is the average time of a support activity?
- What is the average time of a specific support activity?
- What is the percentage of support activities of which a project authorisation number is known at the central department?

Direct measurements:

- M.01 Type of support activity.
- M.02 Domain of the support activity.
- M.03 Date of the support request.
- M.04 Way the request reached the domain manager.
- M.05 National customisation team that requested the support.
- M.06 Project the support is requested for.
- M.07 Project authorisation number known (yes/no).
- M.08 Name employee.
- M.09 Product.
- M.10 Time spent.

Sub-questions for Q.2: 'Which projects are ongoing in the national customisation teams from the viewpoint of the central department?'

- Q.2.1 Which national customisation team is the project running?
- Q.2.2 How is the project indicated?
- Q.2.4 Which domain manager is assigned?

Metrics:

- How many of the projects are known at the central department?
- What is the distribution of the activities for which a project is known?

Direct measurements:

- M.01 Project the support is requested for?
- M.02 National customisation team the support is requested by?
- M.03 Name domain manager?

Hypotheses on the direct measurements

During the interviews hypotheses had to be established. However, these appeared to be difficult to define, because the project team was unfamiliar with their new role. Some 'educated guesses' were formulated:

- The numbers of support requests expected per day are between 7 and 12.
- Average time spent on a support request is expected to be 0.25 to 1.0 hours.

Other hypotheses could not be agreed upon.

12.6.2 Measurement plan

In this section the measurement plan that was used to collect the data is described. The following metrics were defined:

- M.01 Type of support activity. This measurement described the kind of activity that was performed by the employee (reviewing, coding, etc).
- M.02 Domain of the support activity. This measurement gave the name of the domain for which the support activity was requested.
- M.03 Date of the support request. This measurement gave the date at which the support activity was requested.
- M.04 Way the request reached the domain manager. This measurement gave the medium that was used to reach the domain manager or the domain specialist.
- M.05 Site which requested the support. This measurement gave the name of the site that requested support.
- M.06 Project the support is requested for. This measurement gave the name of the project for which the support activity was requested.
- M.07 ACC known (yes/no). This measurement indicated if at the moment of the request the central department knew about a project authorisation number for the project, that the support was requested for.
- M.08 Name employee. This measurement gave the name of the employee of the central department that received the request for the support activity.

- M.09 Product. This measurement gave the name of the product the support activity was requested for.
- M.10 Time spent. This measurement gave the time that was spent to complete the support request.
- M.12 Project the support was requested for. This measurement gave the name of the project the support is requested for.
- M.13 National customisation team the support was requested by. This measurement gave the name of the site at which the project is running.
- M.14 Name domain manager. This measurement gave the name of the domain manager the support is about.

12.6.3 Data collection form

The applied data collection form is given in Figure 12-10. For the activities stated in this form, only the begin and end time had to be filled in. Furthermore, the following data needed to be filled in:

Activity Registration Form

Name:

No.	Date	Start	End	Activity Description				
				Medium	Domain	Site	PAN	Activity
1								
2								
3								
4								
5								
6								
7								
8								
9								
10								
11								
12								
13								
14								
15								
16								
17								
18								
19								
20								
21								
22								
23								
24								
25								
26								
27								
28								
29								
30								

Figure 12-10: Data collection form project D.

- medium of request;
- domain for which the activity was executed;
- site for which the activity was executed;
- Yes/no if the project was known or a project authorisation number was known;
- type of activity that was performed.

The GQM team collected the forms and put the data in a database. It was preferred to use one of the terms in the table below, but it was not compulsory. Improvements could also be made.

Activity description
1. Activity
Medium of request
Telephone E-mail Visit/Person Newsgroup None
Domain
Domain 1 Domain 2 Domain 3 ………
Site
Central department-site 1 Central department-site 2 Central department-site 3 National customisation team 1 National customisation team 2 National customisation team 3 National customisation team …. Test group
Type of activity
Advice/Assistance Design Implementation Meeting Merging/Integration Release Requirements analysis Reviewing Testing Training Trouble log solution
2. Other activity
Network supervision Travel Legal absence Training Assist marketing Assist service Assist manufacturing Technology watch Hardware platform development

Figure 12-11: Data collection form project D.

12.7 Questions and assignments

12.7.1 Questions

1.   What kind of tasks does 'support' include?
2.   What was the reason to start the SUPSYS measurement programme?
3.   What is wrong with the second measurement goal of this measurement programme?
4.   What is new in the way the measurement support system was set up for this measurement programme compared to the previous cases?
5.   Which problems occurred during definition of the measurement programme regarding the formulation of hypotheses? What were the reasons for this problem and what could be possible solutions?
6.   Figure 12-4 contains data that is similar to data used in the previous Chapter. Given this similarity, what is, however, the main difference between the support measurement programme and the interrupt measurement programme?
7.   What is remarkable in Figure 12-6, considering the new objectives of the project team?
8.   What are the advantages and disadvantages with the inclusion of an 'other' category (see for example, Figure 12-7 or Figure 12-9)?
9.   What were the actions taken by the project team based on the measurement data?
10.   Which way of documenting a measurement plan is better: the measurement plan of Chapter 11 or the one in Chapter 12?

12.7.2 Assignments

Design your own GQM tree for your personal interrupts, looking at the questions in both Chapter 11and Chapter 12.

1.   Refine your questions (maximum of six) into metrics and design a data collection form you can use.
2.   Use this form to collect your personal interrupt measurement data during a period of 1 to 4 weeks.
3.   Store your data in a spreadsheet and perform data analysis in order to answer your questions stated in the GQM tree. And remember: analysing these data is the most important part of measurement. Without analysing your measurement data, you could have spent your effort and energy better!

References

Basili, V.R., D.M. Weiss, 'A methodology for collecting valid software engineering data', *IEEE Transactions on Software Engineering*, Vol. SE-10, No. 6, 1984.

Basili, V.R., C. Caldiera, H.D. Rombach, 'Goal Question Metric Paradigm', *Encyclopedia of Software Engineering* (Marciniak, J.J., editor), Volume 1, John Wiley & Sons, 1994a, pp. 528-532.

Basili, V.R., C. Caldiera, H.D. Rombach, 'Experience Factory', *Encyclopedia of Software Engineering* (Marciniak, J.J., editor), Volume 1, John Wiley & Sons, 1994b, pp. 469-476.

Bemelmans T.M.A., *Bestuurlijke Informatiesystemen en Automatisering* (Management Information Systems and Automation), Stenfert Kroese, The Netherlands, 1991.

Berghout, E.W., D.S.J. Remenyi (editors), *Evaluation of information technology*, Proceedings of the fourth European Conference on the Evaluation of IT, Delft, Delft University Press, 1997.

Birk, A., R. van Solingen, J. Järvinen, 'Business impact, benefit and cost of applying GQM in industry: an in-depth, long-term investigation at Schlumberger RPS', *Proceedings of the 5th International Symposium on Software Metrics (Metrics'98)*, Bethesda Maryland, November 19-21, 1998.

Boehm B.W., *Characteristics of software quality*, New York, 1978.

Cavano J.P., J.A. McCall, 'A framework for the measurement of software quality', *Proceedings of the software quality and assurance workshop*, 1978.

Curtis, B., W.E. Hefley, S. Miller, *People capability maturity model (P-CMM)*, CMU/SEI-95-MM-02, Software Engineering Institute, 1995.

DeMarco, T., T. Lister, *Peopleware: productive projects and teams*, Dorset House Publishing, 1987.

Fenton, N.E., S.L. Pfleeger, *Software Metrics, a rigorous and practical approach*, Thomson Computer Press, 1996.

Gibbs, W.W., 'Software's chronic crisis', *Scientific American*, September 1994, pp. 86-95.

Glass, R.L., *Software creativity*, Prentice Hall, 1995.

Goodman, P., *Practical implementation of software metrics*, London, McGraw-Hill, 1993.

Grady, R.B., *Practical software metrics for project management and process improvement*, Prentice-Hall, Englewood Cliffs, 1992.

Heemstra, F.J., R.J.Kusters, R.Nijhuis, Th.M.J. van Rijn, *Dealing with risk: beyond gut feeling: an approach to risk management in software engineering*, Maastricht, Shaker Publishing, The Netherlands, 1998.

Humphrey, W.S., *Managing the software process*, SEI Series in Software Engineering, Addison-Wesley, 1989.

Humphrey, W.S., *A discipline for software engineering*, SEI Series in Software Engineering, Addison-Wesley, 1995.

IEEE, *Software Engineering*, IEEE Standards Collection, Institute of Electrical and Electronic Engineers, 1994.

ISO9000-3, *Guidelines for the application of ISO9001 to the development, supply and maintenance of software*, International Standard: Quality Management and Quality Assurance Standards - Part 3:, International Organization for Standardization, 1991.

ISO9001, *Quality Systems - Model for quality assurance in design/development, production, installation and servicing*, International Organisation for Standardisation, 1994.

ISO/IES 9126, *Information Technology - Software Product Evaluation - Quality Characteristics and guidelines for their use*, International Organisation for Standardisation, 1991.

ISO12207, 'Software life cycle process standard 12207', *Online presentation at: http://home.sc7.ctisinc.com/sc7/ustag/12207/ sld001.htm.*, Issaquah (WA), Software Engineering Process Technology, February, 1995.

Karjalainen, J., M. Makarainen, S. Komi-Sirvio, V. Seppanen, 'Practical process improvement for embedded real-time software', *Quality Engineering*, Vol. 8, No. 4, 1996, pp. 565-573.

Kooiman, E., *Towards a feedback theory*, Masters Thesis, Delft, Delft University of Technology, August 1996.

Kuvaja, P., et al, *Software process assessment and improvement: The BOOTSTRAP approach*, Oxford, Blackwell Publishers, 1994.

Latum, F. van, R. van Solingen, M. Oivo, B. Hoisl, D. Rombach, G. Ruhe, 'Adopting GQM-based measurement in an industrial environment', *IEEE Software*, January/February, 1998, pp 78-86.

Looijen, M., *Information systems: management, control and maintenance*, Kluwer Bedrijfsinformatie, 1998.

McCall, J.A., P.K. Richards, G.F. Walters, *Factors in software quality*, Vol. I, II, III, US Rome Air Development Center Reports, 1977.

Möller, K.H., D.J. Paulisch, *Software Metrics: A practitioner's guide to improved product development*, London, Chapman & Hall, 1993.

Parker, M.M., R.J. Benson, H.E. Trainor, *Information Economics: linking business performance to information technology*, Englewood Cliffs, Prentice-Hall, 1988.

Paulk, M.C., B. Curtiss, M.B. Chrissis, C.V. Weber, *Capability Maturity Model for software*, Version 1.1, Pittsburgh, Software Engineering Institute, 1993.

Perry, D.E., N.A. Staudenmayer, L.G. Votta, 'People, organizations, and process improvement', *IEEE Software*, July 1994, pp. 36-45.

Pfleeger, S.L., *Software engineering: the production of quality software*, New York, Macmillan Publishing Company, 1991.

Pulford, J., *AMI: A quantitative approach to software management*, ESPRIT Report 5494, 1992.

Radice, R.A., N.K. Roth, A.C. O'Hara Jr, W.A. Ciarfella, 'A programming process architecture', *IBM Systems Journal*, Vol. 24, No. 2, 1985, pp. 79-90.

Rooijmans, J., H. Aerts, M. van Genuchten, 'Software quality in consumer electronic products', *IEEE Software*, January, 1996.

Senge, P.M., *The fifth discipline: the art and practice of the learning organisation*, New York, Doubleday, 1990.

Solingen, R. van, *Goal-oriented software measurement in practice*, Master thesis, Delft, Schlumberger RPS and Delft University of Technology, 1995.

Solingen, R. van, F. van Latum, M. Oivo, E.W. Berghout, 'Application of software measurement at Schlumberger RPS: towards enhancing GQM', *Proceedings of the 6th*

European Software Control and Metrics (ESCOM) conference, The Netherlands, May 17-19, 1995.

Solingen, R. van, E.W. Berghout, E. Kooiman, 'Assessing feedback of measurement data: Schlumberger practices with reflection to theory', *Proceedings of the 4th International Symposium on Software Metrics (Metrics'97)*, Albuquerque, New Mexico, USA, IEEE Computer Society Press, pp 152-164, November, 1997.

Solingen, R. van, E. Berghout, F. van Latum, 'Interrupts: just a minute never is', *IEEE Software*, September/October, 1998.

SPICE 1997, *Introduction to SPICE*, Software Engineering Institute, Online documentation at http://www-sqi.cit.gu.edu.au/spice/, July, 1997.

Index